The Murder Of The Holly King

Caeser Pink

TIO Publishing

New York, New York

The god of Celtic mythology has two dimensions, the Oak King and the Holly King. Twice a year these two deities battle for control of the world. According to tradition, on the day of the summer solstice the Holly King wins the battle and ushers in a period of darkness. On the winter solstice the two battle again. This time the Oak King slays the Holly King and the world is reborn for a period of light and warmth. This cycle of death and rebirth repeats itself forever more, as long as the Earth exists.

#1 - Elvis & America

A lone cowboy rides the rugged terrain of the big country as a Marlboro cigarette dangles from the side of his mouth. A proud Marine storms the beach of some faraway land as he risks life and limb to free an oppressed people from their mortal enemy. James Dean, dressed in blue jeans and white T-shirt, leans against a brick wall with an attitude of cool disdain. A voluptuous Marilyn Monroe giggles and coos, her white dress billows above her benevolent hips as cameras flash and crowds cheer.

America is a dream. A myth in the grandest sense. America lives in our minds like a shining beacon of all that is good and true. But what is America? What is that dream? Who are these lofty beings who are bold enough to call themselves Americans?

If we go to its border and stand with one foot on American soil and the other on that of facile Canada or heathen Mexico, this random invisible line drawn in the soil that makes us American or not, seems like some kind of joke. A flight of madness.

Yet for it great wars are fought. The poor die trying to cross that line and join the dream of America. Within our own borders we fight for its future, we fight to define its meaning, we fight to find that dream of America that so often even alludes the children born of its own soil.

Jack Kerouac, Henry Miller, the pioneers of the wild frontier. We never cease in sending out search parties in our quest to discover America, and yet it seems we never truly find it...

Two weeks before the events of 9/11 I was leaving my home in Greenpoint, Brooklyn and driving over the Williamsburg Bridge heading towards Manhattan. It was bumper-to-bumper traffic and we were crawling at about five miles per hour, allowing plenty of time for my mind to wander as I gazed off into the distance. As I overlooked the Manhattan skyline I had an odd vision. In my mind's eye I saw jet planes flying head-on into the skyscrapers with explosive results.

I didn't take the vision as an omen, but I did think long and hard about how America would change once we were hit by our first big terrorist attack. And it seemed inevitable that this day would eventually arrive.

I hadn't taken a vacation outside New York City for many years, and I always wanted to drive across the country, so a few days before September 11th I left Gotham to begin my own journey to discover America. I had no game plan. I just wanted to wander across the United States until I hit the big ocean rumored to be on the other side.

I began my journey by heading south, down through Pennsylvania and Virginia where I picked up the Blue Ridge Mountain Highway. I didn't have money for hotels so I slept in the back of my car and ate as cheaply as possible.

In the beginning I had a hard time finding places to sleep where I felt safe. The first night I slept in a gravel parking lot by an old railway station. The next I slept in the parking lot of a doughnut shop that was closed for the night. Neither seemed quite right. The railway station was too isolated and creepy. The doughnut shop was too public and I feared I might attract the attention of either the police or the criminals. Either way, bad news.

The Blue Ridge Mountain Highway winds across the top of the Appalachian Mountains heading south through the Carolinas and into Georgia. It is a beautiful drive filled with majestic scenic overlooks, mountain streams, and grand rock formations. Nothing but green trees and blue skies for days on end.

When I got too hot I would pull over and bathe in the cool waters of a babbling brook. With a little searching you could find some old-fashioned bluegrass music being broadcast from a low wattage radio station that is too insignificant to be eaten up by Clear Channel or one of the other corporate behemoths.

The important thing was that I was free. Freedom is something we experience all too rarely in life. It is something many people never know at all. No clocks to punch. No appointments to keep. Nobody looking over your shoulder. If I was tired I slept. If I was hungry, I ate. If I saw a highway that aroused my curiosity, I took it. If I drove too far in either direction I would eventually hit an ocean, so I couldn't get too far off course. If you have nowhere to be, you can't get lost.

I did have a half-hearted goal of reaching Memphis before Sunday morning so I could get some religion courtesy of one of Al Green's legendary revival meetings. Meandering as I was, even that goal soon had to be abandoned.

Those first days on the road were filled with bright sunshine and mild breezes. My CD holder was well stocked with all of my favorites. As I entered Tennessee I put P.J. Harvey's "Stories From The City, Stories From The Sea" into the player and turned the volume up to 11. As the miles rolled past, the wind blew through my unkempt hair. All the while P.J's voice, brittle and desperate, shared tales of love, loss, and independence. At the CD's end, the last song finds strength by rising above life's passion plays. "We float...take life as it comes," the mournful refrain repeats like a sigh with no tears left to shed.

Although I had heard the song many times before, this was the first time I really heard its message, and it seemed to suit my mood perfectly. When I stand back with room to breathe, with space to view the whole picture, what does my life amount to? So many people have come and gone. Sometimes I suspect my legacy is little more than a trail of wounded souls. My chaotic lifestyle has seemed to wear women out, to slowly break them down, to covertly steal away the confidence of even the most emotionally stable woman.

And what I am left with? My life is itself a journey filled with people, wonderful and colorful people, yet each day I find myself feeling more of a social outcast, more alone, ever in search of something I cannot name.

As the people of my past run through my mind, memories of Sasha take hold. A few days before I was scheduled to leave I called her. It had been almost ten years since we last spoke, and those final conversations were strained with anger and frustration. In order to get her number I had to pay an Internet service ten dollars for the information.

A few years previous I had tried to get contact information from one of her girlfriends named Amira. She told me that Sasha didn't want to hear from me. But my recollection was that Amira never liked the idea that Sasha and I were together. She always seemed a bit jealous of our romance, and like many women in Sasha's life, Amira seemed to want to hold some sort of control over her. In her eyes I was a threat to that control.

Sasha was like an exotic butterfly that seemed slightly blinded by the sunlight and was flying on a chaotic course without direction. She seemed desperately in need of protection. But the one who protects also controls, and this butterfly could never be controlled by anyone, though many had certainly tried.

It was late in the evening when I took a deep breath and made the call. Since Sasha now lived in San Francisco the hour was a bit earlier for her.

"Hello," a voiced answered the phone with a tone of skepticism. The voice was solid with confidence, nothing like the soft girlish voice I remembered.

"I'm trying to reach Sasha," I explained.

"This is her," the unfamiliar voice replied.

"Hi Sasha, this is your old friend Caeser. How are you? I just wanted to say a quick hello and see how you're doing."

She replied with civility, but after a few moments of small talk she fell silent.

"Are you OK?" I asked.

"I'm just trying to take in what's happening here. I don't quite know how to handle this," she explained.

"Yes, it's strange," I tried to agree.

We managed to get through another ten minutes of catching up. Throughout our little chat I sensed that she was straining to speak to me in a friendly manner. Before I brought the conversation to a close I said, "Sasha, I know the past doesn't matter, but I am sorry for everything that happened."

"Well," she replied, adopting the tone of voice of a wise teacher, "Sometimes we look back on our actions and see that they were wrong and we wish we could undo them."

The response was disappointing to me. I suppose I had hoped that she might respond in kind with an apology of her own. A truce of admittance that it was a complicated situation and we both bore responsibility for the emotional bloodletting that our breakup unleashed. Instead it was clear she took no credit for any of the chaos we caused in each other's lives. I was the villain. I was the guilty party.

Her response suggested that despite her talk of self-knowledge and spiritual growth, she was unable to look into the dark mirror of the self and take a clear account of her own actions. But I also imagined that her friends and mother helped to paint me as the villain. As a regular Snidley Whiplash endangering, ensnarling, entrapping the innocent little butterfly that they all longed to control as their own.

Summoning an end to the conversation I said, "Well girl, it was nice talking to you. I'm glad to hear you're doing well."

The casual tone of my voice seemed to unleash the repressed anger in her. Her voice was calm, but seemed to have a slightly desperate quality to it.

"I just want you to know that in all these years I've never wanted to see you or talk to you," she insisted. "I've been just fine. I have no feelings about the past at all. I feel nothing. I'm over it all."

I congratulated her, but couldn't help feeling that there was rage hidden beneath her calm assurances.

As I hung up the phone I felt like it was a breakthrough for me. Our relationship and the painful events of the breakup had cast a shadow over my life for many years. I wanted to put the past in its place, but to do so I needed to feel a sense of peace between us. We were hardly there, but perhaps it was a step in the right direction.

During the conversation I didn't mention my trip across the country, or that I expected to be visiting the city of her abode. But I figured we could cross that golden bridge when and if the time came.

When I finally did roll into Memphis it was Monday morning on a balmy southern day. Memphis, the home of Elvis, Sun Records, and rock n' roll. Its dilapidated streets and poverty stricken population seemed a fitting backdrop for the birth of rock 'n' roll. A place where white-trash peasants and downtrodden blacks could commune in the knowledge that they have more in common with each other than they do with those who hold wealth and power and are the real oppressors of the poor of all colors.

Every great American art form has been birthed from the mixing of cultures. Blues, jazz, rock 'n' roll; those who say whites steal from blacks are correct, but they also miss the point completely. Musicians steal of out love. Every great musician understands that love of music trumps racial division any day of the week. All artists steal, it's just the way it's done. It's those who imitate that should be avoided!

Elvis, James Brown, Bob Dylan, The Beatles, Jimi Hendrix; the great ones are great because they are great. Those who love them for their talent and artistry couldn't give a fuck what color their skin is.

As a white-boy who worships the godfather of soul, don't try to tell me I can't play the funk because of my skin color. It is in me. Funneled into the core of my being through the ecstasy I feel when listening to those entrancing grooves and primal yelps. Many times I have been the one to tell a young black rapper that he needs to study James Brown or Grandmaster Flash & The Furious Five so that he knows his roots. Not his racial roots, his musical roots.

Where would rock 'n' roll be if some racist had told Jimi Hendrix that a black man can't play hard rock guitar? But let the racists divide, musicians know better. The great music created from the mixing of cultures is something that should be celebrated.

The entire history of rock 'n' roll seems to be mapped out in the life of Elvis Presley. The purity, the gospel, the downtrodden kid who rises to fame and fortune through music, the controversy, the repressed sexuality, the taming of the primal fire in order to appease the authorities, the Hollywood sell-out, the Las Vegas parody, and the premature end brought on by hedonistic excess.

There was cosmic perfection in the fact that Elvis died in the same year that the Sex Pistols released their first and only cataclysmic album. The excess of the past died to allow the rebirth of the original spirit of rock 'n' roll.

All these things flowed through my mind as I walked aimlessly past crumbling buildings, rusted cars, and half-abandoned strip malls. I got a bad haircut from a Dolly Parton look-alike named Winona and ate stale tamales in an empty blues bar with a giant plastic crawfish hanging from the ceiling. I was a stranger in an all-too-familiar land of urban decay.

Throughout most of my life I never cared much for Elvis. He was just an overweight cheeseball who made embarrassing movies. That is until I heard the Sun Session recordings. Suddenly I heard the spark that the New York record execs and Hollywood film producers had trampled into the ground. The raw brilliance that made teenage girls scream with a hysteria that made the devil smile and Eisenhower's America tremble.

"This rock 'n' roll music is designed to pull white children down to the level of the nigger," they said. "Amen and halleluiah," I reply. Bring it on.

But never underestimate corporate America's ability to take a flash of light and life, and mould it into something so safe and squeaky-clean that even the church elders soon patted his head with approval. Nothing seems to be too cheesy for the American public. Not Clam Bake. Not the whores of Las Vegas. If you want to wrench every cent of profit from an artist he must appeal to the lowest common denominator.

The next morning I drove to Graceland. I expected the tour to serve as little more than a funny gawk at bad tastes in tacky furnishings. Instead the experience turned out to be something much more complex.

Outside we were all lined up waiting for the shuttle to take us into Graceland. The usual Graceland crowd is made up of aging tourists dressed in khaki shorts and pastel flavored polyester tops. On this day we were joined by a busload of down syndrome patients who took their place directly behind me in line.

Before you enter Graceland everyone has a picture taken in front of a white screen. The photo is magically doctored to make it look like you are standing in front of the hallowed gates of Graceland. (As I recall, my ex-klu klux klan member grandmother had one of these keepsakes on the mantle in her house trailer.)

The photos are then placed all together on a wall. As the line moves past you are able to buy your photo for the nice price of $19.99. When I arrived at the wall I beheld a truly beautiful sight. My photo was placed dead center in the middle of the wall, surrounded by a mosaic of downs syndrome patients.

At the moment when the flash went off I managed to look to the west with my left eye, and to squint my right eye, giving my face a distorted look that made me fit right in with my new friends. I had about four days of stubble on my face and my hair hadn't seen a comb in weeks. All together we were a cockeyed looking bunch from head to toe. And we had all come together to worship the great white-trash Adonis.

Give Mecca to the Muslims, the Wailing Wall to the Jews, and send the Christians… well, wherever wealthy Christians go, but we children of a lesser God, who were birthed in trailer parks and backwoods shanties, in row houses and newly-built prefab-family-units, we come to Graceland to commune with He, who was all that we might hope to be in our wildest imaginings.

Once inside Graceland we were herded past zebra-skin living room suits and leopard skinned bedspreads, through hallways lined with gold records, past gold-lamay jackets and white-leather jumpsuits, all enclosed in glass cases like museum pieces. Video clips of TV appearances on Ed Sullivan and Steve Allen flickered in grainy black and white. Throughout it all the king's music played softly, seeming to come from everywhere, yet nowhere. His reverb-laden falsetto quivered as he sang "Blue Moon," providing an eerie ambiance that haunted the lower levels of the shrine.

When we exited through the back door we found ourselves standing at his gravesite in the back yard. Laugh as we may at his gaudy excesses, one couldn't help but to feel sadness, and even a bit of reverence after witnessing this hollow spectacle that is the sum legacy of an artist's life.

In a way he is America. America whose dreams are as pathetic as its sorrows, whose joys are as childlike as its tears, whose achievements are as empty as its failures once life's vitality is drained from its shell. The go-kart races, the banana, bacon and peanut butter sandwiches, the karate heroics, the guns, the drugs, the madness, they are all America.

Inside Graceland a video of Elvis singing Hound Dog to a confused basset hound loops endlessly. Outside those hallowed gates we dream of a country-boy who became a king.

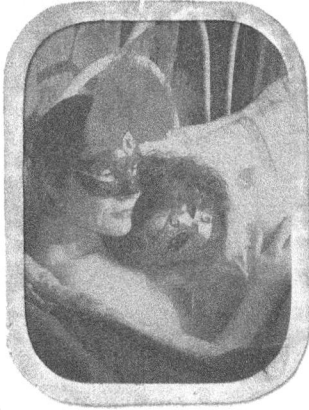

#2 – Where Have All The Celebrities Gone?

Every town should have one street that is dedicated to nothing but fun and partying. Like Bourbon Street in New Orleans, Beale Street is just such a street. It is one block where live music can be heard coming from every direction. Bands play right out on the sidewalks. From beginning to end it is nothing but gin joints, blues bars, outdoor cafes, tacky tourist museums, and cheesy gift shops.

Like Bourbon Street in New Orleans, if you walk to the left or right in either direction the scene quickly dissolves into urban squalor. Poverty lurks all around. But on Beale Street the good times never stop. It is a little slice of gay illusion designed to separate tourists from their hard earned dollars.

Walking Beale Street by myself was like going to a party where you don't know a soul. I ate Cajun chicken at an outdoor café where the waitress thought it was very strange that I would put milk in my tea. I watched a cute young couple jitterbug like-no-tomorrow to a 20-piece swing band that was crammed inside a small booze hall. At night's end the alcohol began to steal my energy away. I sat on the curb and watched a blues band play on the sidewalk in front of a taffy store on the opposite side of the street.

Feeling the first pangs of the loneliness that is to be expected on a long journey alone, I began to watch the thinning crowd pass by. The late hour began to weed out the tourists, leaving only the small-time tough-guys dressed in black dungarees and sleeveless Levi jackets. The necks of their wife-beater T-shirts revealing the mysterious blue lines of jailhouse tattoos and the soft white ripples of pool hall scars. The lucky ones accompanied by margarita-soaked sex-kittens whose clown-make-up failed to disguise the weatherworn-texture of their well-lived-in faces. These details of little concern to the gentleman of the street whose attentions are easily distracted by half-opened discount-store-sequined-blouses, chipped high heels, and too-short skirts that might have turned the heads of more selective men in days long gone by.

As the nightlife wound down I ventured off of Beale Street into the seedy neighborhoods surrounding it. The windows of run-down row houses glowed with warmth. Some folks sat on their porch steps looking bored. Teenage thugs stood on street corners dreaming of ways to get a buck in their pockets.

A little further from the center of town old men could be seen sleeping in cardboard boxes, some simply curled up in doorways with just their balled-up fists for pillows, their ragged clothes dirty and stained. One man sat on the sidewalk with a cardboard sign claiming that he was a Vietnam vet, as I walked by he held up a paper cup. The look in his eyes so hopeless that he seemed to barely care whether I slipped a few coins in or not.

America's homeless are a class unto themselves. One of the most eye opening things I ever experienced was the making of a documentary film on poverty. To make the film I traveled down the East Coast, from New York to New Orleans, visiting with the beggars, prostitutes, and con men that live in the crevices of urban affluence. I was a director of the film that was produced by Samantha D. At the time Samantha and I were in the early stages of a romantic relationship. We left State College, PA to begin our project on August 16, 1992.

On our first morning we went to a shelter called The Samaritan Inn in Roanoke, Virginia. At first we were intimidated. After walking by the building a few times we gathered our courage and began interviewing the people who were streaming in for free plates of hot dogs and beans. In the next hour we interviewed fourteen people. Among them a young man who tried to commit suicide on his first night in the streets, a red faced wino who cursed President George Bush for sending aid to the Russians, and an elderly veteran who after fighting for his country in two wars could not afford to pay for a roof over his head. As tears welled up in his eyes he stated simply "This ain't no life, this ain't no life."

In the following days we traveled to Cherokee, North Carolina, Atlanta, Georgia, and on to New Orleans. Our first day in New Orleans was spent talking to street beggars and filming under bridges where the cardboard box communities tend to thrive.

That night, because our budget was getting increasingly slim we rented a room at a $20 dive on the Chef Montour Highway. Once inside we found it to be far worse than we could have imagined. Besides general dilapidation, we found stained and dirty sheets, unbearable stench, and a polluted bathroom.

Our complaints to the manager turned into a heated argument and we ended up without a room and with no money refunded.

With nothing left in our budget for another room we drove for hours wondering what we could do. At the time the irony of the situation never crossed my mind. Of course we would never have considered joining our subjects in their shelters or cardboard boxes, so we broke into a campground, pitched tent and slept, then left before the owners found us out. It's surprising how quickly one will resort to illegal activity when you are down on your luck.

After a second day of shooting in a New Orleans shelter we returned to Atlanta to film fifteen hundred people standing in the rain waiting for a free meal dished out by a Catholic church. Inside the kitchen we watched as a nun spoke to the crowd over an antiquated P.A. system. As she spoke they ignored her and went about eating their food and talking among themselves. To my surprise I heard the sister speak my name then she placed the microphone into my hand. Almost instantly the room went silent. As the faces of hundreds of downtrodden human beings gazed at me questioningly I found myself searching for a way to explain our intentions and account for our motives in this project.

As filmmakers we would like to believe that our work would help these people, but the more likely truth is that as individuals they would never see a noticeable benefit. On the other hand with every story of poverty and degradation we captured on tape we would personally gain. I stammered through a declaration of our altruism and the potential film subjects abruptly turned away and resumed their conversations.

Assuming we had struck out we waited outside the kitchen exit with our camera. After about an hour of waiting they began to pour out of the building, many eager to speak their peace. It was as if we had unstopped the gap for an endless flow of bottled up emotions. People stood in line and we couldn't move the camera fast enough.

I felt overwhelmed by a flood of pathos, wrath, and resigned consternation. We heard stories of every kind. From rich college kids who threw their lives away to drugs, to middle class workers whose plants closed down leaving them without a future. We heard street corner preachers who warned of the end of times. We heard of an old woman turned away at a church gate in the freezing cold. One man told us of his method of robbing at knifepoint those who would ignore his request for donations.

We heard from the mentally ill, shunned by their families and cast out of psychiatric hospitals. Of men and women who gave up, too discouraged to care or try, and of a man who claimed he had equal opportunity but drank it away. And one particularly eloquent black man described the homeless situation in terms of a system of social/economic exploitation where the rich earn profits from tax write-offs on the homeless shelters and soup kitchens.

The stories went on and on. We no longer had to ask questions. The voices went on of their own impetus. And all this from one shelter in one city. And there were more stories in every city in the United States. Beyond that we may only imagine what horrors exist elsewhere in the world.

As the voices continued I felt numb. My eyes began to wander from the unending parade of faces up to the horizon of the Atlanta skyline. Up to the top of the skyscrapers where men of power went about the business of making the decisions that create our economy and define our society. My eyes were filled with the images of humanity's power and success, and my ears were filled with the stories of humanity's sorrow and disgrace.

I thought, "With all the wealth and power of our nation, can't we do better than this?"

It reminded me of an interview with anti-big government economist Milton Friedman that I had recently seen on television. He waived off the poor be saying that every economic system has poor people and there will always be people living in poverty. He was implying that they should not be helped because in a dog-eat-dog world there will always be casualties and it should just be accepted. We are all animals so let natural selection take its course.

It is a view that is increasingly popular in America. If we can condemn the poor as simply being bums who are too lazy to help themselves, then we can give ourselves permission to write them off and still feel morally righteous. The facts that I found from my investigation are that there is no simple answer to why the homeless are where they are. Some are lazy and some our self-destructive. Some are drug addicts and alcoholics. Others are people who ended up where they are due to outside forces beyond their control. Many are mentally ill or physically disabled and have nowhere to turn for help. In an age when companies are downsizing, merging, mechanizing, and sending jobs overseas, anyone can find themselves in dire straights. As one homeless man expressed it, "Believe it or not you're just one paycheck away from being where we are."

Perhaps the main thing I learned is that regardless of how one becomes homeless, once you are down, it's very hard to get back up. If you did not drink or use drugs before, once you are homeless you need to in order to get through the days. If you were not depressed, stressed, or mentally ill before, once you are homeless you are all of the above. The spiritual effect of homelessness, the shame and degradation, cripples one's ability to fight their way out of the situation.

And many felt there are forces that want to keep the homeless where they are. As one man explained, "If I'm doing nothing for myself all these churches and agencies are willing to help, but if I get one foot out of that grave, they do everything they can to suck you back in…so they can make money off of you.

People are getting rich off of the homeless. We are just dollar bills to these rich people."

When asked if he tries to find a job one man explained to me, "I go and fill out applications, and they say we'll call you. But who is gonna call a man on the streets. No one wants to hire a homeless man."

Before this experience homeless people were an abstraction, a theoretical 'they' without name or face. Now that is not the case. The strongest image I hold from the journey is of a woman in Nashville who simply said, "We're people too. We just don't have the things you all do." Another elderly man looked deep into my eyes as he slowly pronounced without emotion, "A homeless man is the loneliest man in the world."

But one man expressed his frustration another way, "We're out here surviving on the streets. If you give a homeless man half-a-chance he'll take it to the bank. If you give the homeless a chance he'll probably do better than you!"

That night I drove in circles through the streets of Memphis trying to find a location where I could sleep safely. Eventually I realized there is no location in Memphis where one can sleep safely, so I drove over the border to Arkansas and quickly found a friendly looking highway welcome station and pulled in.

Throughout the trip I was fighting a losing battle to keep my cell phone charged. I found an outdoor outlet hidden behind a hedge on the welcome center wall and plugged in the charger.

As I waited for the phone to charge I sat on a dark picnic table under a pine tree and played guitar. It was a warm night, stroked lightly by a cool breeze. As I sang songs I have sung a thousand times before, travelers straggled in and out of the welcome center bathrooms then drove off into the night. On the highway cars buzzed by in the distance. Everyone was on their way. Everyone had somewhere to go. It seemed I was the only one who sat alone and with no direction, and without purpose, except to play guitar and wait for the next cool breeze to caress my tired muscles.

My trip had just begun and already it was a wonderful adventure. When you step outside of your work-a-day routine, almost immediately your perspective on life's priorities begins to change.

When you travel on your own you begin to transform. Shyness melts away. The invisible social shield that separates us from our fellow man begins to dissolve. There is an openness that is born on the highway.

Lonely travelers seem to be able to pick each other out. Long distance truck drivers think nothing of shouting across a crowded diner in order to share a few minutes of casual conversation with another traveler. Truck stop waitresses understand the good deed they provide by speaking to road-weary strangers as if they were old friends.

You instinctively begin to look people in the eye, always open to make a new friend. Or perhaps just engage in banter about the weather or the sights and sounds of the highway with a stranger who has a few minutes to kill. Humanity itself seems to take on a friendlier hue.

Contrast this with New York City where we swarm through the streets like a colony of insects. Yet despite the forced intimacy we are a million miles apart. Jammed into subway trains like cattle we never look each other in the eyes. We rarely speak to strangers even when we are crammed tight up against them.

There is little that makes one feel lonelier than to spend every day of your life isolated in a crowd. I believe New Yorkers would like to break out. I think they are just waiting for a chance to do something nice for one another.

I have seen a woman's shoe heel break off on a crowded street and hands reach out from every direction as people tried to catch her before she hit the ground. On the rare occasion when I have a chance to open a door for woman, I almost feel like thanking her for giving me an opportunity to feel like a gentleman.

I believe we dwellers of Gotham maintain our invisible shield, not because we have cold hearts, but because we fear intruding on another's space.

Simply commuting and surviving a day of New York City life is such a challenge that we mentally shut down. There is too much stimulus, too much stress, just too much of everything.

I often walk so deeply entrenched in my thoughts that people have spoken to me and I walked on by without even realizing it.

I once watched a documentary film where scientists placed a group of monkeys in a small room and videotaped their behavior. The usually rambunctious simians suddenly became very quiet and still. Crammed into close quarters, like their human counterparts in subway cars, the monkeys became very careful not to disturb their neighbors.

It takes a lot of work to be polite in the hustle and bustle of frenzied city streets. The subways always seemed like an odd conundrum. If you bring a bunch of strangers together it would often be called a party. Yet subways riders are usually as morose as funeral mourners.

Anyone who breaks the sanctity of the subway quiet by speaking too loudly is usually looked at as a bit daffy. Whether it is a religious fanatic calling people to the Lord, or beggars singing do-wop tunes for pocket change, we tend to avert our eyes lest we find ourselves in the line of fire. Rarely does anyone speak up to complain, but we try to avoid the disturbance so we do not become entangled in an uncomfortable situation.

On one occasion I was on an uptown train heading to some day job when I heard a man's loud voice rambling at the other end of the train car. The train was crowded, but I had managed to get a seat. The man with the loud voice came down and forced himself into a too-small space beside a pretty blonde girl who sat directly across from me.

As soon as he sat down he began a tirade in a booming voice. He was a tall, strong looking fellow who arched his back forward with his hand above his kneecap and his elbow arched out with a demeanor that suggested he had some particularly vexing problem on his mind.

"Where have all the celebrities gone?" he asked the crowd.

Everyone looked away from him, trying not to make eye contact. The poor girl beside him crossed her arms and tried to make herself smaller in a futile attempt to gain a little bit of personal space. She was young and fresh-faced and appeared to be dressed for a day in the office.

"Where have all the great ones gone?" he repeated his query. "I'm around every day and I don't see them anywhere!"

We were trapped on an express train giving him ample time to complete his soliloquy without annoying interruptions from stops at every point on the line. Or with any opportunities for his trapped audience to escape.

"Where is Perry Como?" he asked, gesticulating with his hand held open as if waiting to receive the answer from God himself. "Where is Andy Williams?"

The sincerity of his inquiry, and the fact that his list of celebs was so far out of left field, struck me as absolutely ridiculous. I peeked at him, then quickly looked away so I wouldn't give in to the urge to laugh at his surreal performance.

"Where is Guy Lombardo? Where is Engelbert Humperdink?"

He had obviously been walking the vacant streets of some easy listening netherworld.

"Where is Desi Arnez Jr?" he demanded indignantly.

When he pleaded as to the whereabouts of Annette Funichello the pretty girl beside him made eye contact with me. Our exchange of glances lasted just long enough to communicate the sense of absurdity we both felt. Immediately the laughter we were trying to suppress burst out. And not just a little laughter, we both had a complete meltdown while the subway funeral mourners looked on, their steely expressions making it clear they did not find the situation nearly so humorous.

Unconcerned by our laughter, his litany of has-beens continued unabated, "Where is Frankie Avalon? I never see Bobby Vinton anywhere any more. Where the hell did Art Linkletter get to?" he shouted.

By the time the train pulled into the station we were both holding our stomachs, crippled by uncontrollable laughter. Due to our outburst, in the eyes of our fellow passengers we had been demoted to the unsavory ranks of those who break the sanctity of subway silence. When the train doors opened we both dashed out, gasping for air.

As we exited the subway on opposite stairways, she looked back and smiled sweetly. I nodded and winked in response. Once the shield had been broken it was suddenly ok to make a warm gesture to a stranger.

Sometimes in the morning when walking over the Pulaski Bridge that connects Brooklyn and Queens, I say a big smiling hello to people walking in the opposite direction, just to gauge how uneasy it makes them. People seemed to be completely flummoxed by such behavior.

Yet now as I sat at an Arkansas rest stop, peacefully playing guitar and turning these thoughts over in my mind, little did I know that events would soon befall us that would break the invisible shield for all New Yorkers for many months to come.

But tonight was a beautiful night under a star-filled Southern sky. America lay before me. The future was an open highway filled with potential, and ripe for fun and adventure. As I retrieved my newly charged cell phone I peeked at the time and date. The time was 11:59PM and the date was September 10, 2001.

#3 – A House Divided

I was awakened by a warm beam of sunlight coming in through the car window. It was a perfect day. Clear blue skies as far as the eye could see. I always awoke eager to feel the road beneath my wheels. As soon as I woke up I jumped into the driver's seat, started the car, and began backing out of the parking lot of the welcome center.

When the car started the radio automatically came on and was tuned to the local NPR station that I was listening to the previous evening. The female voice of the news reporter was filled with tension as she described some events that I couldn't quite make sense out of in my half-awake state. It seemed some planes had flown into buildings, the north Tower of the World Trade Center had collapsed.

I groggily assumed it must be some kind of War Of The Worlds type radio drama. Public radio was full of odd things like that. Within a few seconds though, it began to dawn on me that this was all real. Still my mind could not grasp the events being described. How could a Trade Tower fall? It was impossible.

I got on my cell phone and tried to call Jeanie and Samantha to ask what the hell was going on, but the phones would not connect. Not comprehending that there was a national emergency and the phones lines were overwhelmed, I cursed Sprint for their half-assed service. I jumped out of the car and tried again from a phone booth. The pay phone seemed to be broken as well. Angry at modern technology I slammed the receiver down and raced back to the car and sat listening to NPR, trying to comprehend what was taking place.

I tried to think clearly and put together the pieces; we were under terrorist attack, two planes hit the Trade Towers, another hit a government building in Washington, the north Tower had collapsed, it was feared as many as ten thousand were dead. No one knew what might happen next.

When a witness began describing people jumping to their deaths from the upper floors of the Towers I was overcome with nausea. That image finally made it sink into my thick skull what a nightmare this really was.

I staggered into the welcome center in a daze. A group of people sat watching a TV. I sat down and watched the horrible images. The North Tower crumbled, floor after floor dissolving into a puff of ash as the top of the building fell downward crushing everything below.

Everyone in the room was quiet and frightened, but I was aghast, stunned, still unbelieving. At the time I worked as a web designer a half a block from the Towers. On most days over lunch I would spend a few minutes reading magazines in the Border's Bookstore that was on the ground floor of the Trade Center. I looked at those Towers every day. It was like telling me a mountain had crumbled. It just seemed impossible.

"I work right there," I said to the silent room with a slow, shaken voice.

The Towers were not great looking buildings aesthetically. Their 1970's minimalist design was gray and boring to the eye. The only hints of elegance were the pinstriped bars that ran up the façade of the lower levels before merging into a pitchfork design and then fading away.

The most impressive thing about the Towers was just how

damned big the things were. If you arched your neck up to look at them, you really couldn't even take them in. They were like some kind of mirage. Their mere existence as a feat of human architecture was both humbling and inspirational. To destroy them with an act of terrorism was truly the height of anti-social behavior.

As we watched the carnage on the TV, I kept thinking of a little church that was snuggled in beside the Towers. It was an old church with an ancient graveyard hidden underneath a grove of bushy trees. It was so old that one of the founding fathers used to attend the church.

Over my lunch hour the graveyard provided a perfect escape from the chaos of the financial district. Only a few people seemed to know about it, even though it was there for all to see and you could walk right in and find a quiet bench among the weathered tombstones. Once inside, the lush greenery shielded one from the noise that roared from all directions, transforming it into a distant purr.

The churchyard was a little haven of peace and solitude where the mind could wander away to think of greater thoughts, far from numbers, dollar signs, and in my case, creating new ways to hock VCRs and microwave ovens over the Internet. I could only assume that sitting right beside the Towers as it did, that the church had been destroyed.

"I'm sorry, but everyone has to leave," the little old lady who managed the welcome center explained apologetically. "The governor's office just called and said we have to close down."

Apparently every public building in the state was closing down, just in case the terrorist's next target might be a welcome center in Arkansas. You can't be too careful.

I stumbled out to the Blazer and drove off. For some reason I assumed the Palestinians were behind the attack. Although I always supported their cause, now I cursed them.

"Fuck them! Fuck them!" I shouted out loud.

Before 9/11 few of us had ever heard of Osama Bin Laden or Al Queda. Most people are still unaware of The Muslim Brotherhood, the organization funded by the Saudis and Ronald Reagan, and who were the roots of Al Queda and worldwide terrorism.

I hated the terrorists for making me hate. It wasn't my way. But now I was full of hate. To that extent they had won already.

I had no illusions about America. We have been sowing the seeds of bad karma around the world since the first Puritans stepped foot on Plymouth Rock. God knows there were days when I hated America myself. I can only imagine how people in other countries see us.

Although I could see both sides of the picture, killing thousands of innocent people was going far too far. Plus they brought it right to my neighborhood. I had no way of knowing if my friends had been killed, or if I would still have a job. Once you bring it to my block it's no longer political anymore, it is the law of the jungle, it is survival, it is personal.

As I drove I stayed on the speed dial trying to reach friends who might have been in danger. After dozens of unsuccessful calls I got through to Samantha. She was safe in her eighth-floor apartment on Fourteenth Street. She and her roommate were watching the historic events unfold from her bedroom window. In her excitement she almost sounded gleeful.

"I was taking a picture of Traci in front of the window with the Tower burning in back, and we turned around and suddenly it was gone!" she said breathlessly. "All you can hear are sirens everywhere. It's crazy."

Throughout the remainder of my journey I felt as if I should be in New York with my friends and neighbors.

"Do you think I should come back," I asked.

"No. Keep going with your trip," she said sympathetically. "Even if you wanted to come back you couldn't. All the bridges and tunnels are closed. You couldn't get into the city."

Grateful that at least one of my loved ones was safe, I drove listening to the radio until the nausea overwhelmed me so much that I flicked it off, only to turn it back on again a few minutes later once I had regained my strength.

I called my father who wasn't aware that I was traveling across the country.

"Oh Caeser, it's you. How ya doing?" he asked happily.

"I just wanted to let you know I'm OK," I said.

"What," he replied somewhat confused.

"I just wanted to let you know I'm OK," I repeated

"Oh, OK," he said cheerfully, "Talk to you later."

At the time I didn't realize he was blissfully unaware of the events in New York City. When he finally caught on he panicked. Meanwhile I carried on with my journey assuming his mind was at ease.

I drove on, heading west. My mind was in a fog, my heart deep in mourning.

I stopped in Little Rock, the home of Bill Clinton. What a sordid place it was. To look at this urban swamp one is not surprised that it is infested with the snakes and rats that teamed up with the Republicans to create the dramas of the Clinton scandals.

For good measure I cursed Kenneth Starr, the national media, and the Republican Party for wasting years of the country's time and resources for their own political gain. The Clinton scandals were an ugly case of politicians placing their own self-interests above the needs of the country they were elected to serve. And they managed to bring the work of the U.S. government to a dead halt, all over a couple of secretarial blowjobs.

Seething with anger I recalled the parade of Republican senators screaming bloody murder on the evening news when Clinton bombed one of the terrorist training camps in Afghanistan. Soon these very same hypocrites would be waving the flag and accusing Democrats of being soft on national security.

With no desire to explore Little Rock further I got back on the highway and drove towards the Oklahoma border. Within a few hours it was clear that the America I had set out to see was gone. On this expedition I would be exploring a brave new America that was just beginning to emerge.

Everywhere I looked flags were being hung mournfully over porch railings and at half-mast on flagpoles. Every restaurant marquee, from Kentucky Fried Chicken to the finest steakhouses, took down their weekly specials and put up "God bless America."

Normally patriotism makes me feel uncomfortable. Usually flag-waving means some politician is trying to brainwash the simpler folks until supporting some hair-brained scheme to take over a third world country or cut taxes for the rich. But given the day's events I couldn't help but to be moved by these sentimental displays of national unity.

These events made me consider what I loved about America; the freedom to believe or not believe in religion, the freedom to speak out against corruption perpetrated by those in power, the fact that in New York City I can live among people of every race, every color, every creed, and we all get along pretty well most of the time.

I thought back to my vision of planes flying into skyscrapers a few weeks earlier. Because of the pondering I did in the wake of that vision I was not as surprised as most Americans by the changes that the country would soon undergo.

But what I did not foresee was how the politicians would exploit this wave of patriotism for their own benefit. I should have, but I didn't foresee how it would unleash a new era of McCarthyism, or how the public would be manipulated by fear, or how the corporations and their political stooges would use this opportunity to undo some of those pesky civil rights that stood in the way of complete social control. I didn't foresee how they would exploit the good will of small town Christians in order to undertake the greatest grab of wealth and power ever seen in American history. And all of this perpetrated on behalf of those same millionaires and billionaires who already had so much wealth and power that it was unimaginable to the common man.

In the end the public was caught in a crossfire between the police and the thieves. And the public, as usual, was getting screwed on both ends.

History has taught us that the right-wing hawks and the military-industrial complex they represent always prosper when they have a bogeyman to scare the public with. Whether it's the communists or the terrorists, they thrive on scaring the hell out of people, then convincing them that only they can protect them.

But communists and terrorists will come and go. Of late they have found an even greater bogeyman. One that will not go away until they assume complete and total control. Of course I am referring to liberals. Thanks to a highly coordinated media effort over many years, they have created a giant rift within American culture.

Thanks to their work they have managed to make many Americans hate their fellow countrymen. Right wing commentator Anne Coulter would soon go on Fox News and declare that residents of New York City are not Americans, and later that the widows of the police and firemen who died in the Towers on 9/11 are media whores who are happy about their husband's deaths.

The hate propaganda brought the stew to a boil, and in it you find all of our worst instincts. In it you find racism, sexism, religious intolerance, and prejudice of every kind. They direct their hate at liberals, Democrats, Californians, New Yorkers, New Englanders, intellectuals, Hollywood celebrities, environmentalists, feminists, college graduates, you-name-it, they-hate-it. Their ability to hate seems a bottomless pit that pulls the country apart. And to what end?

The only answer I can come up with is that its only purpose is to allow those in power to consolidate their dominance. Was it Hitler who said, "You have to give the people someone to hate"? In those dark days after 9/11 the right wing instigators were certainly putting that dictum into practice.

On June 16, 1858 Lincoln said, "A house divided against itself cannot stand." Soon a country that was more unified than ever-before by the events of 9/11, would be divided more than it had been since the 1960's social revolution or the great civil war. But that was all still in the future. On this day as I drove through Alabama we were still united in grief and fear.

As I crossed the border into Oklahoma the radio was explaining that all air traffic had been suspended, and the President was hidden away in some unknown location. The estimates of the dead had fallen to the six thousand-range.

It was getting well into the afternoon and I still hadn't been able to reach Jeanie. I thought she was safe, but it was hard to say. Only a few weeks before, she was working at American Express whose office was next to the Towers. Recently she was sent to another office in New Jersey. The only catch was that her subway to Jersey went right under the Trade Center.

As I drove I tried to think of other things, but it was hopeless. Driving the highways of Oklahoma I looked out on the great expanse of the flatlands. In that open space my mind raced. My thoughts were filled with violence. I had always believed in peace. But in a flash I had been turned into a man who could only think of war and vengeance.

When I arrived in Oklahoma City, afternoon was beginning to wane. Being that Oklahoma City is the only other American city to have experienced a major terrorist attack, they weren't messin' around. They had shut down the whole place. The entire downtown area was blocked off.

I found a small park on the outskirts of the city that had a nice little gazebo in the middle with a few wooden benches inside. I laid down on one and was able to get a short nap.

When I awoke I was finally able to get Jeanie on the phone. She was stranded in Manhattan, sitting on the doorstep of one of her many suitors. The subways lines were all down so she couldn't get back to Brooklyn. Jeanie was at a vocal lesson that morning when it all came down. She no longer had a job. The effects of the attack were spreading far and wide. By evening it was snowing white ash all over the city as the charred remnants of the Towers fell back to Earth like poisoned manna from heaven.

That night I drove to the edge of the Texas panhandle before pulling over for the night. I got a five-dollar shower at a travel center. The hot water helped wash away the day's stress. I laid down to sleep in the travel center parking lot. The sounds of travelers closing their car doors and walking past my car stayed with me through the night. My windows were tinted so that even when someone passed by my car a few inches away, I remained hidden.

This part of the country is barren, harsh. It affects one's spirit. My mind was so exhausted that I could no longer think about the day's events. As I faded off to sleep I surveyed my friends trying to take account of who was safe and who was in question.

The day of September 11, 2001 had come and gone.

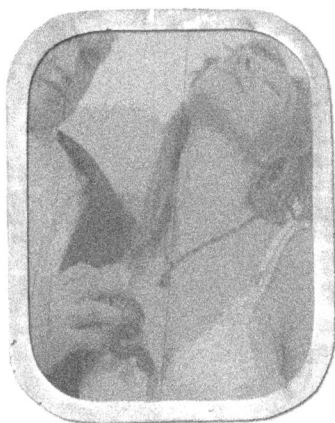

#4 – The Big Cross & The Hairy Hand

The morning finds me driving through the endless Texas flatlands. Through miles and miles of straight-arrow highways that are lined on each side by tall stalks of corn.

In Texas they don't go for any of that commie-public radio nonsense. The only things I can find on the dial are hellfire and brimstone preachers screaming that Armageddon is nigh upon us. "God hates America," they enthusiastically proclaim. The previous day's horrors are all due to homosexuals, abortions, and other assorted perversions that the city of sin revels in.

I had to admit that I've done a bit of reveling in some of those same sins, but boy-oh-boy, Allah was out to get us, Christ had us in his crosshairs, one could only assume that Moses, Buddha and Krishna must be a little pissed off at us as well. America was in deep shit according to the holier–than–thou mindset.

I suppose that given the cataclysmic events that had befallen us we could only expect such behavior from backwoods evangelists, but I felt exhausted by their venom. I tried to be amused by their over-the-top diatribes, but soon flicked off the radio.

I felt so sick of hate and prejudice and intolerance. The dreams the flower children of the 60's once proclaimed of a world that lived in peace and harmony only brings a bitter taste to my mouth.

As we began the new millennium hate ruled the day in America. And sadly, much of it was all brought into being by flag-waving politicians and religious fanatics pointing fingers of accusation. Meanwhile the whole lousy bunch-of-them are busy lining their pockets with silver and gold. And of course, with petro-dollars gleaned from the profits of Texas oil wells and kickbacks from corrupt Saudi princes.

When I was a small child I witnessed a race riot in our nation's capital. We were at the zoo and my father was eager to leave, but I wanted to see the giant sea turtles. As I peered through the chain link fence and dreamed of riding heroically on top of one of the poor creatures, the sirens began to wail. My father seemed to panic.

"I told you we have to get the hell out of here. Now get to the car."

By the time we got out of the parking lot it was utter chaos. The only white people to be seen were the police and firemen. Entire blocks seemed to be burning. I saw a black man walking with his face covered with a blood-soaked towel. A woman chased another man down the street screaming as she tried to beat him with a mop handle.

"Don't look at anyone," my father warned.

I sat frozen with fear underneath my mother's arm, staring straight ahead. As we searched for the shortest route out of the city, on every block someone seemed to yell at us, "Hey white face!" I had never known this kind of fear before.

"Fuckin' niggers, they're just a bunch of animals," my father cursed.

"Oh Dad, don't use that word," my much older at 16, big sister pleaded.

In my child's mind I thought that things like this didn't happen in America. It was a shock and an awakening. I didn't really understand what it was all about, but even at that tender age I knew that whatever the hate was that these people expressed by calling us "white face," and my father expressed by using that 'N' word, I wasn't apart of it. It didn't make any sense to me and I wanted nothing to do with any of it.

About this time I noticed a sign on a Texan telephone pole that read "The biggest cross in America. Turn right 2.3 miles."

The biggest cross in America? How could I say no to that? Soon the cornfields gave way to a clearing and with a quick right turn the cross came into view. I pulled off and got out of the Blazer. It was a perfect morning. The skies were crystal clear.

I walked up to the gargantuan crucifix and looked straight up. "Damn, that is one big cross," I thought to myself. I sat on one of the railroad ties that marked the parking spaces and meditated on the beautiful weather and why there were so many big things in America. Already I had seen a big cross, a big peach, a big shoe, and more than one big hot dog. And what was more perplexing was why I couldn't resist pulling off the highway to look at them. That is, look at them for about 30 seconds before I lost all interest.

A red van pulled up and a bald, round faced priest got out and began doing his morning absolutions. He nodded to me with a warm smile. His face radiated kindness, not a hint of judgment. He was picking up bits of litter left by yesterday's tourists with a peaceful smile on his face. He reminds me that sometimes you meet Christians who actually embody the best ideals of that philosophy. People who live with peace in their hearts and have good will towards all they meet. People who would never be the one to cast the first stone.

When I have had the good fortune to meet one of these rare pure-spirited Christians, I have always made a fast friend. What they responded to above all else was mutual respect and goodwill towards others. I could be Satan in black jeans, but if you showed yourself to possess these basic virtues they would never speak a word against you.

One such friend of mine did away with religious intolerance with a single thought; "Well it only makes sense that God would reveal himself to other cultures with a face that looks like their own," she casually explained her view to me.

It was such a simple thought, but hidden within it is an esoteric truth held sacred by the mystics of every religion since the first human asked himself, "Who am I." A truth that allows the Buddhist and the Hindu to see the face of God in every living thing, both plant and animal, as well as in every object on Earth and in the universe. A truth that if recognized by the religious leaders who preach hate and prejudice, would suddenly melt their hearts and inspire them to bring a message of unity to the world.

Unfortunately too many men of the cloth only see God bleeding from crosses or sealed up safely behind church doors. The material world is the devil's playground and holds nothing sacred. All else is heresy and all who don't believe as they do are heretics.

Back on the highway Texas merged into New Mexico without much notice. It was hours of nameless towns filled with chain stores and strip malls. Each one looking just like the other. Each one with its own McDonalds, Wendys, Lowes, Barnes and Nobles, Staples, KFC, Wal-Mart and the list goes on.

Between these nondescript hamlets I passed the occasional oil rig churning in the distance, or fields of cattle who always looked much angrier than the good natured Holsteins that provide milk and butter to the folks of rural Pennsylvania.

Back in territory where I could get civilized radio, all of NPR's normal programming was cancelled to focus solely on the events of 9/11, as it was now being called. The entire country was in mourning. The newswoman explained that all through the previous day New York City's hospitals were at full staff expecting to be overwhelmed with patients. By evening it became clear that none were coming. Throughout the day rescue workers were searching for survivors, but were finding very few. In the pit underneath the debris a hot fire continued to burn. In time this fire would have a profound effect on my life.

Between newsbreaks callers told their stories of loss and heartbreak. They vented their anger and tried to make sense of the senseless. One woman from Arizona told a story of her sister who was working in the Tower. She got a last call from her on her cell phone. She was walking down the stairs trying to escape from the burning building. Despite the danger she was lighthearted and joked that she was going to die for America. A few seconds later she screamed as the sound of the building collapsing was followed by the phone line going dead. Call after call, it was a nationwide therapy session that would continue for months to come.

For me, it was the trip of a lifetime and I was trying to enjoy it as much as possible, but my mind was in a thick fog. I felt as if a wet blanket had been placed over my body making it hard to move my limbs. It was the deepest mourning I had ever experienced.

It was a strange time to see America. It was America at half-mast. America frightened, wounded, angry. An America whose citizens often imagine that we are all-good, and therefore beloved by the world. An America suddenly realizing we had mortal enemies, and an America being forced to ask "Why?"

It could have been a time of national introspection. A time to reconsider the tangled web of Middle Eastern policy that brought us to this place. A policy filled with deals made with devils whom we deceived ourselves into calling friends. The entire mess leading to oil, founded on oil, awash in oil, polluted by oil.

If it wasn't for oil we wouldn't pay any more attention to the Mid-East than we do to Africa. Unfortunately our entire economy and our nation's very survival are dependent on Saudi oil. And a wise statesman knows that any friend that you are dependent on is a potential enemy. Until we deal with the fundamental problem of our dependence on Middle Eastern oil, America will never be safe and secure.

It could have been a time to look at the big picture and fix this problem that underlies so much of our foreign policy. It could have been a time to make a major shift in our nation's priorities and focus our resources and technical prowess on finding new sources of energy so we can finally stand on our own two feet and end our dependence on dubious allies.

Those that were listening closely would soon learn that the Saudis were dictators nearly as bad as Saddam Hussein, and were a hundred times more involved with the terrorists who carried out the attacks than Iraq was. On the very night of 9/12/2001 the Saudi ambassador, often called "Bandar Bush" by the Bush family because of his close ties with the clan, stood on the balcony of the white house smoking cigars with the president. It would soon be discovered that even the ambassador's wife had unknowingly donated money to Saudi charities that ended up in the hands of the terrorists who brought down the Towers.

This could have been a time of hope and new direction for America, but too quickly it became evident that instead of looking at the big picture we would focus on the small. While it was only right that we would go after the terrorists, it was the ultimate failure of vision and leadership that it became our only focus. Meanwhile our leaders would continue to ignore the big issues that kept us entangled in the worsening Mid-East quagmire.

As I drove I kept a notebook and pen on the seat near my right hand. Years before I had written a verse to a song, and then was never able to get any further with it. It went:

Send in the raven, call out the lark

Everybody's got a job to do

Everybody's got to find their way home

Destiny is a crossword puzzle written on a chain-link fence

Compassion is a parable spoken by a tongueless monk

Devotion is a paper train burning in the railroad yard

So hosanna, heysanna, what do we do now?

When I speak in gestures and you call out at night.

Now driving through the cornfields I turned over the plight of America in my mind, trying to understand the new spirit that had taken the country. Suddenly a second verse came to me for this as yet untitled song.

I heard a noise out in the cornfield, heard a scream out in the dark

Everybody's got a cross to bear

Everybody's got a skeleton somewhere

Sisyphus is the paperboy, Atlas is the morning sun
There's a fire in the lighthouse
There's white shark in the bay
There's a tempest in a teapot
There's another child gone astray
So hosanna, heysanna, what do we do now?
Should we huddle in the corner?
Live with fear in our hearts?

I didn't make any effort, they just flowed out. I scribbled them into the notebook with one hand as I drove.

It was a long stretch of driving at one go. When I finally arrived in Albuquerque it was well into the afternoon. As soon as I got there I liked the place. It had the youthful energy of a college town. The main drag was filled with bookstores and poetry soaked coffee houses. For the first time on the trip I thought, "This is a place I could live for awhile."

I drove around a bit looking for something to explore. I was looking for something a little off the edge. Something to make me forget the newscasts of death and destruction. There were no signs of nightclubs or bars in the area. No small time drug dealers or prostitutes to mingle with. Not even any homeless vagabonds or afternoon alcoholics to converse with.

Finally I settled for an adult "gift shop." Inside, a few shoppers milled around looking at DVDs and girlie mags. On the back wall was a row of video booths from which could be heard the moans and groans of cheap porn movies.

I walked into one of the booths and slipped a few quarters into the slot. The 12-inch screen flashed on and I pushed a big red button switching through the video selection.

I have always found porn movies pretty boring. Actually I find them pretty distasteful. I'm not sure why, but most men's idea of erotic material usually strikes me as ugly. Most of the porn movies I've seen feature big mustached guidos pummeling a worn out stripper who has so many man-made body parts that she's only one or two operations away from being categorized as a bionic woman. I like the idea of erotic films, but porn movies don't really do it for me.

Despite this I was committed to going through with the experience. I chose a lesbian scene that wasn't too gruesome and unzipped my pants and began masturbating in the privacy of the small booth. My half-interest in the video was reflected in my half-erect response to it.

As I went about my project, I failed to notice that there was a small round hole in the right wall of the booth that served as a peephole into next booth. But a few moments later I was *very* surprised to see a large hairy hand reaching through the hole into my booth. Startled by the intrusion I instinctively jumped backwards against the door of the booth, which swung wide open, throwing me further off balance. I fell three steps backwards before catching myself. By the time I came to a stop I was standing in the middle of the shopping area with my pants unzipped and my penis bouncing around like a deranged jack in the box clown.

I think everyone in the room was as shocked to see me suddenly standing there, as I was to find myself standing there. The shoppers glared at me with furrowed brows. The large man behind the counter yelled out, "Whoa, there cowboy, ya got that thing under control?"

Without answering I zipped my pants, held my chin up, and tried to make a dignified beeline for the door. The fake moans and groans of the lesbian sex scene still echoing from the booth. Out in the fresh air I thought, "I guess there's another side to these jerk-off booths that I wasn't aware off."

I left the car behind in the parking lot and began walking alongside the highway. After the unseemly events at the adult gift shop, I decided that perhaps a slightly more conventional form of entertainment might be what I need. A few blocks up the road I found something that fit the bill perfectly. It was a large country fair on the other side of the highway.

I walked around the fair trying to get a sense of the place and the people. Of all the places I've seen in America, New Mexico seems to have the highest ratio of Native American people. Of course with the mixing of whites, Latinos, and Indians, it is pretty hard to tell exactly who is what.

I walked through the animal exhibitions to view the "best of the barnyard" competition. I saw prize-winning goats, rabbits, sheep, chickens, ducks, and a few local rodents I couldn't really identify.

I watched a troupe of Chinese acrobats who were so impressive that I assumed they must have fallen on hard times to be performing in such a place. I watched the mayor hand out good citizen awards to local boy scouts. I ate carnival food at picnic tables with overweight couples and noisy teens.

Overall it was a grand old time. If you want to see the people of America, here they were, in folk costumes of blue jeans and faded T-shirts, without pretension and in their natural habitat. Walking around one heard carnival barkers calling out from every direction, amusement park rides whizzed up and down and around and around, children gorged themselves on funnel cakes and cotton candy, teenage girls displayed their newly discovered sexuality with jittery giggles.

Peering at the sights I thought; this is America. And although I might be immersed in it, surrounded by it, although I might love it or hate it, I would never really feel a part of it. Somehow I would always feel like an alien, like a voyeur studying a strange culture from which I was born, yet which I could never fully understand.

The biggest shock of the county fair was the art show. I have attended a lot of art openings. New York City is supposed to be the capital of great art and avant-garde ideas. Yet the art I see there usually bores me to tears.

New conceptual ideas are a thing of the glorious past. Worse yet, many artists don't seem to have anything they want to express personally or politically. They put about as much effort into their art as they did the kindergarten finger paintings that their mothers proudly displayed on their refrigerator doors. And with a confidence in their own genius bestowed by these same mothers, they expect that fame and fortune should be handed to them in exchange for their modicum of effort.

Over time I have learned to approach art with low expectations. To my surprise the art at the county fair was astounding. The best of it seemed to come from pure childlike inspiration. No thought of celebrity, just art created for the joy of creation.

Among the works were religious sculptures made from worn out wooden fence posts and barbed wire that had an eerie voodoo feeling about them. There were paintings on windows and pottery in regional American Indian patterns.

It is hard to articulate what separates great art from mediocre art, but when you see it, you can feel it in your bones. I was so excited I went and found the curator of the exhibition.

"This is great," I said enthusiastically. "You've got to show this in New York City. People would love it."

She responded with a friendly response, but seemed to think I was a little nutty.

I left inspired and hopeful. It is purifying to experience artistic inspiration. It is to glimpse the primal source. It is like discovering the simple insights sometimes found when speaking with small children. Or like the moment when a person who will soon become a lover, first opens up their soul to you during a long night of conversation.

The world is full of bullshit. Truth and passion are such rare commodities that just a little taste can restore one's vigor for life and belief in the world.

#5 – A Mormon Girl In La Trapeze

By the time I left the county fair the heart of the afternoon was beginning to wane. My plan was to change course and head north toward Utah to visit some friends.

As soon as I left Albuquerque the scenery began to change. Flatlands gave way to magnificently sculptured rock formations that stood in solitude under skies painted with streaks of blue and white, while a deep pink seeped in from the edges as if the horizon was a sheet of wheat paper dipped in red wine.

It appeared I had entered the land of the coyote and the roadrunner. It was part Salvador Dali and part spaghetti western. The rocks were the color of dried blood and the earth was scorched a sallow yellow. Here and there a few heroic sheaths of green managed to break through the dry land and reach for the sky.

It is a magical place that looks more like the moon than America. It was completely empty of people except for one or two house trailers that sat alone, miles and miles from human contact.

As the hours passed and I crossed the border into Utah the landscape returned to more familiar looking terrain. Soon the flatlands began to be disrupted by the first hints of the Rocky Mountains.

By nightfall the road became treacherous. Except for the beam of my headlights it was pitch black in all directions. The highway began to twist and turn and the four lanes were reduced to two, one going in each direction.

The driving was made more dangerous by the abundance of wildlife that didn't seem to know its proper place in the world. Every mile or two a deer or antelope would suddenly appear in my headlights as if they were spooks in a haunted house carnival ride. When I came upon them they looked into my headlights as if to say, 'What are you doing here? This part of town belongs to my gang." Between sightings of the larger creatures, small furry ones scurried back and forth across the highway.

I was so far into the depths of nowhere that cell phone service had gone extinct hours ago. The radio selection had dwindled to a few high megawatt stations programmed by men in grey flannel suits. The road went on mile after mile without as much as a one-horse town for respite, and my gas gauge was sagging alarmingly close to E.

As the hours rolled by, my eyes turned red and my vision bleary. I suppose the smart thing to do would have been to pull over and sleep till sunrise. Perhaps it was cowardly, but I just didn't feel safe sleeping in the middle of nowhere. A dark car parked along an isolated highway is just too tempting for a gang of teenagers out on a drunken late night joy ride. Given the high status accorded to carrying guns in both rap and country music, God knows what America's youth might call a good time in the wilderness of Utah. Some friends during my teenage years were known to spend Friday evenings taking LSD and shooting out the windows of parked cars. It's a miracle that no one was ever killed.

The situation dissolved to a point where I was so exhausted I feared falling asleep behind the wheel. The gas gauge was now drooping well below E. Just when it looked like I would be traveling on foot, a quaint little village came into sight. Although I never thought my lips would utter these words, thank halleluiah there was a Mini-Mart with overpriced gas that was open into the late hours of the night. I filled my tank and then pulled into the parking lot of a dentist's office to get some sleep.

With morning the world was a friendlier place. It was another day of clear blue skies and mild temperatures. The high elevation gave the air a different quality, making one feel a bit woozy.

On the radio the drums of war were beating. Pakistan was given an ultimatum. Afghanistan was doomed. It was learned that in a strategic coup, the day before 9/11 the Taliban had assassinated Ahmad Shah Massoud, the leader of the Afghani rebel movement that would soon partner with the U.S. government. I was aware of Massoud because he was portrayed heroically on a 60 Minutes profile a few months earlier.

Around the world our allies stood behind us. The French people said, "We are all Americans." In Russia shrines to 9/11 were piled high with heartbreaking sentiments of condolence.

Around noon the sky began to darken and I began to search for a meal and a bathroom. By the time I found one of those modern truck stops that are now called "travel centers," the heavens had burst open with a torrential rain that came down so hard it was impossible to drive. As I walked into the travel center a flash of lightning filled the sky, followed by a violent boom. The lights in the travel center flickered briefly then went dark. The country music that filled the air went silent. I used the men's room and then learned that no food was being served because of the power outage.

With the electricity off everyone seemed a little jittery. I was having some problems with my cell phone so I went to a pay phone to call Sprint. I found a row of pay phones with stools in front of them. When I sat down to make my call I noticed that sitting beside me was a large Middle Eastern man in a black trench coat with a large duffle bag at his feet. He wasn't making any calls. He just appeared to be waiting for something.

It sounds ridiculous now, but a surge of adrenaline raced through my body at the sight of him. I couldn't control my behavior. I looked deep into his eyes, searching for a sign that he might have some evil intention with that big duffle bag of his.

Looking back I'm sure he must have guessed what I was thinking. I can't imagine what he must have felt when I looked at him with fear and suspicion written all over my face.

It certainly was a new world we lived in. If I could be taken by such paranoia, I shudder to think what might have been going on in the minds of less open-minded Americans. Already news reports told of a confused racist in Utah who burned down an Indian restaurant in retaliation for 9/11. In Chicago a young man felt such rage that he drove his Toyota truck head-on into the doorway of a Mosque. It seemed evident that dark times lay ahead for the land of the free, home of the brave.

Realizing I was losing my composure I ran through the rain and jumped into the Blazer. I crawled into the back for an afternoon nap. The super-sized raindrops battered the Blazer with a chaotic rhythm that soon transformed in my mind to become a calming oceanic hum. Between crashes of lightning the fierce gusts of wind rocked the truck back and forth like a cradle. I quickly dozed off into a deep sleep.

After the nap, as I headed towards Salt Lake City I began to think about the friends I would be meeting there. I use the term "friends" loosely, considering that two of the people, Christopher and Jeff, I only knew through Internet chat rooms.

The only one I really knew is Jodi, and even she was something of a mystery. When I first met Jodi she was taking a break from being a nurse at a children's hospital. Later I found out that she was working as an Internet cam girl under the name Miss Modesty. You never knew quite what to expect from her. One day she would casually mention that a publisher just released a book she had written, even though I didn't know she was a serious writer. During our next conversation she might mention she is doing medical research and having papers on her work published.

In her spare time she might be taking belly-dancing classes, or perhaps donating her time to draw blood from sick children, saving them from a distressing and expensive trip to a hospital. On another given day she might be teaching classes on etiquette, hosting a party for the local S&M scene, or giving lectures on cunninligus or felatio.

I met Jodi after she visited The Imperial Orgy website and began sending me seductive photos of herself wearing cheerleading outfits or lying in a tub of green Jello. Even then it was all kind of mysterious. Although she was a woman with a city full of suitors, all there for her choosing, she seemed to choose me to offer herself to, sight unseen.

Eventually she made a trip to New York City so we could meet. I thought it was quite brave of her. She had never been to New York City, now she came to the big city alone to meet a stranger involved with an organization called The Imperial Orgy.

When I knocked on her hotel room door the first time, she opened it and we stood staring for a second, quickly trying to size each other up.

"You look just like your photos," she said with a smile.

She had a country girl's good looks. Long reddish hair that streamed over a pretty face. Her body was full and voluptuous. I felt like it was Christmas in a schoolboy's fantasy world.

We went to Indian row and ate Chicken Korma while sitar and tabla players caressed our ears with exotic music. The room seemed to glow with dim candlelight and the crowd filled the room with the soft murmur of hushed conversations.

I sat watching her eat. She chattered nervously, her composure that of a demure schoolgirl. I reached across the table and stroked her face with my fingertips.

"You're really beautiful," I whispered.

This comment silencing her chatter and bringing a lovely blush to her round cheeks.

It seems a bit strange, but she wanted to experience an adult party club. So with only having met a few hours earlier we headed for Le Trapeze. After paying the $115 cover charge we went into the front room that was tackily decorated with wagon wheel ceiling lamps and a small disco ball. It looked like something out of a bad episode of the old TV show Love American Style.

We sat on the couch taking in the scene. I leaned close and kissed her for the first time. As I kissed her neck and shoulders she seemed to lose herself completely. She gasped and moaned so loudly I was both startled and aroused. Her reaction seemed that of a Victorian lady on the edge of hysteria at a molester's touch.

Not wanting things to go too far too fast, I leaned back and sat staring at her, taking in this odd and beautiful woman that seemed to fall into my life. My eyes studied her from head to toe like a fine work of art.

To enter the other parts of the club the rules dictated that we must first disrobe. Only towels were allowed to cover one's nakedness. We went to the locker rooms and I told her that if she wanted she could change in the woman's bathroom. She returned a few minutes later wrapped in a white towel. I had a similar towel tied around my waist.

La Trapeze is a bizarre place to say the least. One's first experience there can be quite shocking. I'm not sure why nudity is such a taboo in America, but it certainly does freak out the good children of our puritan forefathers. So to see a room full of people that are not only nude, but also having sex in public, tends to set you on your heels at first glance.

Jodi and I chose a large public room with a low ceiling and a soft mat covering the floor like one might see at a high school wrestling match. (And there did appear to be a bit of wrestling going on.) The room's only light came from a few corny star-shaped lights in the ceiling that gave the room a bluish haze.

Jodi and I lay alone in a quiet corner. We sat silently watching the unusual sight of copulating couples. One of the first things you feel is that there is something natural about it all. It's as if you've lived your entire life in a madhouse and suddenly you've walked out into the land of the sane. As if you've been forced to keep up the pretense that a lie is truth, and suddenly the burden of the fallacy is lifted. There is nothing as liberating as truth.

There is something primitive, something church-like about the experience. Afterwards I feel as if I have bathed in purified waters and the stresses of modern life have been temporarily washed away.

Mainly the couples stay with their partners. If there is any interaction with other couples it is usually the women who initiate it. Woman on woman play is the most common type of interaction outside of the couples. Very little sharing of women between men seems to occur.

Usually interactions begin timidly, a slight caress of a stranger's hand or arms to see if they react in kind. Things progress slowly as people try to be respectful of each other's boundaries. Trust is very important in such an environment. If someone is too bold or aggressive, it can make everyone freeze up.

Jodi seemed mesmerized.

"Are you OK?" I asked her with a voice usually reserved for libraries and funeral homes.

She nodded yes. We kissed and I peeled down her towel just far enough to expose her breasts. I sucked on her nipple with the peace of an infant lost in a mother's all-encompassing embrace. The whole environment made one feel soft and weak. My mind filled with white light and white noise as she pulled my head against her bosom.

Throughout the evening we never took it too far. Even though we were essentially at an orgy, I guess you could say that I still followed some sense of first date etiquette. We never had intercourse, and we never interacted with any other couples. Somehow it all seemed very innocent and beautiful.

On the second day of her visit we did the traditional romantic tourist routine, the Empire State Building and a walk through Central Park. The kinds of things New Yorkers never do until guests arrive.

Although Jodi and Jeanie had never met, Jeanie offered to put Jodi up at her Brooklyn apartment to save the hotel expense. That evening the three of us went to a party at an art gallery hosted by a friend of Jeanie's. The event was a poetry reading and art show. Most of the performers were Harlem poets who read with the peculiar rhythms of the slam poetry scene. I believe Jeanie was the only light-skinned poet to read at the event.

By midnight the party was beginning to drag on. Jodi and I were ready to exit, but we were having difficulty gathering up Jeanie. This was her scene and her crowd. Jeanie was known to frequent the New York nightlife with a harem of Harlem boys at her side and was having too much fun to want to leave.

When we finally got back to my apartment in Brooklyn I lit a soft candle and sat on the couch beside Jodi. We began to prod

Jeanie into dancing for us. It was a moment that seemed innocent on the surface, but was filled with expectant tension.

Jeanie put on a CD of club mixes of Cure songs and began to dance in the middle of the living room while Jodi and I sat on the couch watching her. As we watched, Jodi stroked my inner thigh outside my jeans.

Sometimes there are moments that are turning points, and you watch them as they happen as if outside yourself. Sexual exploration is a delicate thing. It can enflame insecurities, fears, and passions of all sorts. In order to explore territory few are willing to travel, we needed to be three people with open hearts and uninhibited spirits. On previous occasions I had seen situations that appeared ripe with potential, dissolve into embarrassing disasters, so I was pensive as I watched events unfold.

Jeanie was dressed in knee-high boots and a jean skirt as her thin frame shimmied in the darkness. She seemed scared as Jodi and I began to stroke her legs. She became the object of our affections as we tried to calm and seduce her. We pulled her on top of us on the couch and smothered her in kisses and soft caresses. Once it was clear we were all open to sharing this experience I pulled the foldaway bed out from the big couch we were sitting on.

If approached with sensuality, sex with multiple partners can deliver heights of pleasure almost beyond imagination. The feeling of four hands lightly caressing your body brings waves of pleasure that are almost more than the mind can comprehend. It is as if the brain cracks open like an egg, hatching a new being that is all corpuscles and nerve endings throbbing with expectation. A kiss shared by three, opens your consciousness to a new way of seeing that most basic show of affection.

We explored each other's bodies with childlike wonder. The excitement heightened by the knowledge that we were breaking taboos that most of proper-society would condemn us for. Even as their own fantasies of such experiences haunt their secret thoughts.

Often you hear people claim that women have lesbian experiences only in order to please men. My experience has been that women use men as an excuse to allow themselves to explore their lesbian desires. In this instance Jeanie and Jodi left me a mere voyeur as they focused on each other.

I'm not sure why guys are so obsessed with seeing two women together, but it is undoubtedly a sight so erotic that it puts a man on the edge of madness. Perhaps it is because women tend to approach each other with a level of tenderness that men usually overlook. There is also something about seeing your sexual partner express her libido in a way that doesn't require you, that seems downright lascivious. It is an affront to all of men's traditional beliefs about what a woman is, that is both frightening and erotic.

Jeanie seemed in ecstasy as she kissed and sucked Jodi's abundant breasts. With a sure understanding of each other's bodies the women brought each other to waves of orgasm.

Afterwards I squeezed in between them and lay on my back with Jodi on my right and Jeanie on my left. As each woman lay cradled in my arms, although I hadn't came, I felt an unfamiliar sense of satisfaction. A sense of fulfillment more spiritual than physical.

This serenity was soon disturbed by a phone call. It was Christopher, interrupting us with perfect timing. Christopher was madly in love with Jodi, and was having trouble dealing with her trip to New York City. He would call every hour or two and panic if he couldn't reach her. She went to the kitchen to talk in private. As the conversation dragged on we could hear her crying.

When she came back to bed she explained that Christopher had gotten it into his head that The Imperial Orgy was a cult that was going to "sacrifice her with big knives." As Jodi was still upset, it was decided I would take the girls back to Jeanie's apartment to get some sleep.

As we drove I realized that the intense sexual excitement without release had given me an award-winning case of blue balls. We stopped at a gas station and as I began to walk inside to pay, a bolt of pain twisted my knees inward and sent my feet pigeon-toed. I stood outside the gas station door holding myself with my legs squeezed together like a schoolboy trying to make it to boy's room. It must have been a ridiculous sight to anyone who was passing by. Nature has a cruel way of demanding that the rules of procreation are respected. I was experiencing the punishment for not respecting those rules.

It is interesting how such an experience can change you. Once a fantasy is fulfilled it no longer has a hold on you. In the weird house of mirrors that make up our egos, the experience gave me an extra boost of confidence. It even redefined my self-image somehow.

Sometimes we walk through doors we can never re-enter. Each passageway brings both loss and gain. My life has been a series of such passageways. Each one of which alienates me more from the society I live in. Each one makes me feel more of an outcast, and a threat to the traditions and mores of mainstream America.

With these memories making my mouth wet with expectation, and softening my heart with nostalgia, I ascended the city of the great Salt Lake.

#6 – A Slap Of Reality

I met Jodi the next morning at a busy outdoor mall area. She was conservatively dressed because we were attending a Mormon church-service that would include a sermon on 9/11.

Inside the large temple we took seats in the very back. Although the wounds of 9/11 were still fresh, and I was more susceptible to sentimentality than at any other time in my life, the sermon was an absolute bore. The preacher droned on with a voice drained of any sign of passion. Soon I found myself wishing for just a little speaking-in-tongues, or maybe some snake handling to liven up the proceedings, but unfortunately there wasn't even a soulful gospel choir to raise the spirits.

At the end we drank a thimbleful of water in a ritual so devoid of visceral meaning that I might as well have been drinking tap water from the men's room sink. I guess this is the kind of squeaky-clean religion that we can blame for unleashing Donnie & Marie Osmond on the world. Perhaps this is what happens to the heirs of white Europeans when alcohol content is reduced to 3.2 per cent and you need a photo ID to purchase soda with caffeine in it. Take away our stimulants and sedatives and we become as vibrant as Wonder Bread.

That evening we went to Christopher's apartment. I must say that considering that I was his rival for Jodi's attention, both he and Jeff were as hospitable as could be. Christopher's bachelor pad was decked out with Halloween decoration spider webs, medieval weaponry, and assorted sci-fi toys.

By way of entertainment Christopher treated us to a show and tell of his BDSM toy-box. People into S&M play are usually *really into* having a variety of odd devices and colorful gadgets with which to spank, bind, tickle or torture. As he demonstrated each device he often made spanking motions in the air, and seemed to be imagining using them on Jodi. At one point he took a few playful swats at her, an act that was greeted with a mild reprimand.

At night's end he graciously offered to let me stay at his place, but I felt more at home in my usual bed in the back of the Blazer.

I awoke with the morning light, hungry and in need of a men's room. I had slept along the street of a residential neighborhood lined with pretty white houses. I decided to take a walk and explore Salt Lake City. The city seemed to be set upon the slope of a mountain ridge. As I walked toward the heart of the city I traveled downhill, which provided a panoramic view of the place.

The city was sparkling clean. Not a shrub was out of place. No garbage, no littered streets. Everything was healthy. Everything was good. The city didn't even appear to be pockmarked with the porn shops and strip clubs like good ole' Gotham was. Only private clubs serve alcohol, and even those looked respectfully clean.

The place was also oddly devoid of blacks, Latinos, or any of those other pesky minorities. But I must confess that being around nothing but white people always gives me a bit of the creeps.

Despite the squeaky clean appearance something seemed askew. Nature is made of light and darkness. If you upset that balance the results can be ugly. Repress one side of the balance and it can transform into something evil.

As I walked past picture-perfect homes, immaculately groomed lawns, and sterile looking business fronts, I had the odd feeling that the sidewalks were about to break open and all the pent-up darkness would burst out into the open air.

I have noticed that puritanism often gives birth to alcoholism, drug addictions, unsafe sexual practices, and criminal behavior of all sorts. There is a Hindu saying that goes, "each extreme creates its opposite." Nature demands balance. When Puritans tell people that they are evil for having natural human instincts, people will begin to believe it, and then play that negative self-image out with self-destructive behavior. The hometown of my youth has been scourged by this dynamic.

Psychiatrist Carl Jung expressed a theory that the visions in the book of Revelations were brought on by a psychic eruption caused by living in a community of Christians, who in the process of trying to live up to the high ideals of love, chastity, and goodness that Christ offered, had created a repressed psychic imbalance. The repressed impulses finally broke through with a hallucinogenic vision of death and destruction.

I believe a similar principle might be at work across America. America is a country founded by Puritans and criminals. The Puritans were trying to escape religious persecution, the criminals were trying escape criminal prosecution. This dynamic of extremes still polarizes our culture. In recent years America has been gripped by a wave of religious fundamentalism. Few are aware that during that same time there has been a parallel explosion of sexual exploration. Communities of people interested in alternative lifestyles seem to be crawling out of the woodwork in every city across the country.

Walking the streets of Salt Lake City one could feel that things were out of balance. The questions I kept asking myself was, "How does all the repressed energy reveal itself?"

Down in the shopping district I went inside a mall where there was a food court with tables and chairs. There were a few large-screen TVs sitting around the court and all were tuned to CNN. I had not seen a newscast in a few days so I took a seat close to one of the screens.

It seemed the horrible images of the Towers collapsing were repeated endlessly. For the first time I saw the images of the dust cloud that rolled through the streets when the buildings fell. I kept wondering what I would have done if I had been there.

I always arrived to work early so I definitely would have been in the office. Maybe I would have cowered under my desk? Or perhaps I would have just stayed with my co-workers and followed the herd? On the other hand maybe I would have run to the Towers to see if I could be of any help. If so, I might be dead right now. The images on the screen made that much clear.

Although days had passed since 9/11, my mind was still enveloped in a haze. Each moment in the day was weighed down by a heavy undercurrent of mourning, regardless of how light things might appear on the surface.

That afternoon Jodi, Jeff, Christopher and I went to a German festival at a park high in the mountains. We ate sausage and sauerkraut while a rollicking polka band played. The musicians were decked out in Robin Hood hats and green shorts held up by suspenders.

The four of us were a strange crew. Given the messy details of the tangled social web, one might have expected it to be far less congenial than it actually was. Perhaps it is a tribute to Mormon goodwill that I was treated, or perhaps tolerated, with such hospitality.

In the center of it all was Jodi, the apple of everyone's eye, and the reason we were all here together cheerily eating sausage and bouncing our heads to lively polka rhythms. Then there was Christopher, who seemed to have devoted his life to Jodi, body and soul. And there was Jeff, the long suffering, or maybe not suffering at all, husband of a marriage of convenience. And I, of course, was just here for the sausage and polka tunes.

Jodi and I left the boys behind and rode to the mountaintop on a sky car suspended on cables. Unfortunately I have an irrational fear of heights. I can control it intellectually, but my body still reacts. Even when I watch TV, high camera angles overlooking drop offs make my stomach turn. As we soared through the air, even though I tried to play it cool, my body tensed up. Jodi put her hand on my arm and whispered, "It's OK," in a soothing tone of voice.

At the top of the mountain the air was cold. I stood behind Jodi and put my arms around her as we looked out over the mountains and valleys. The air was crisp and clear. Neither of us was dressed for the cold, making it even more pleasurable to feel the warmth of her body against me. The thin air of the high altitude made my mind go woozy, and the beauty of the majestic landscape before my eyes as I held her made my heart go soft.

I was well past the halfway mark on my journey to the far ocean. Someday I would return to a home that was wounded and mourning, but that was still far in the future. Standing there with her in my arms was a moment onto itself. It was one of those rare moments when you awaken to life as you live it and realize no events elsewhere in the world, nothing in the future or the past, could take away the beauty of the moment.

On the way back to town Jodi was driving and I sat in the passenger seat. Christopher and Jeff sat in the back. The highway wound down the mountain, snaking through sharp turns and running along steep cliffs. Jodi drove like a wildcat, pushing the speed limits and following close behind slower drivers.

"Don't follow so close," Jeff growled from the back seat.

She pulled back for a while, then began to push it again. It had been a few years since I had ridden with another driver and the whole thing had me sitting tensely in my seat. Even though I was visibly bracing myself on each turn, I tried not to let on how on edge I was.

I always thought it said something about a person's personality when they drive aggressively, and I was surprised to find that she did so. Although it certainly wasn't the first time that I met a seemingly demur young lady who pushes everything to the limit when behind the wheel.

Having survived our ride down the mountain, we pulled over to get gas. Christopher got out to pump the gas and Jodi went inside to pay. When she came back out she was carrying a small white bag.

"He gave me doughnuts," she said with thinly disguised satisfaction.

"What?" Jeff asked.

"That guy, I went up to pay for the gas and he gave me doughnuts."

"Here we go," Christopher said, shaking his head with a weary laugh. "Jodi lives in a free McNugget world. Everywhere we go people give her free stuff."

"The guy at McDonalds always gives me a couple extra nuggets," She explained as if it were nothing out of the ordinary.

Later that evening Jodi, Christopher and I went to an apartment owned by Jodi's mother. Her mother was away for a few days and offered to let me stay there while she was gone. It was a large apartment decorated with tastes appropriate to an elderly Mormon lady. It was immaculately clean and even had a silver Christmas tree in the living room that apparently stood all year long.

Jodi and I sat on the couch and Christopher rested on a lounge chair on the opposite side of the room. We chatted and joked lazily. The evening had an air of boredom that I rarely experience in New York where there is always some frenetic activity filling one's time.

Jodi got out a book of family photos and took me on a tour of her past. They looked like an average American family in the 1970's. She had two sisters and one brother. Her father owned or managed a restaurant, I believe.

"They treated us like little princesses," she said warmly.

The color in the photos had faded into hazy sepia tones, giving them a slightly haunting appearance. The males wore polyester pants and shiny silk shirts, the little girls wore Sunday school dresses. As I paged through her past I searched for answers to the mystery of this woman who was both so extraordinary and odd.

Although the photos presented the appearance of a happy middle class family, it seemed something must have gone off course. Her father was now out of the picture and estranged from his wife and children. Her brother was a junkie who was hiding out from the law. Her sisters seemed to have strings of failed marriages, and one had ruined Jodi's credit rating by running up piles of debt in her name without her knowledge or permission.

They were a good Mormon family. How could things have turned out as they did? I thought back to the dark undercurrent I felt when walking those pristine streets of Salt Lake, wondering how the repressed energies reveal themselves.

There was a soft warm feeling in the room. Jodi sat beside me, her hand resting gently on my arm as she explained the stories behind each photo. When someone opens up and shares their past with you it is always a moment of vulnerability.

I pulled back a few inches to look at her. She was like a picture I couldn't quite get into focus. A jigsaw puzzle whose center pieces had been carefully hidden beneath the cushions of the couch. She was intelligent, but acted with naiveté. She was good, kind, pure of heart, but chaos and confusion swirled around her. She was chaste with husband and suitors, yet drawn to salaciousness.

I tried to make sense of the bizarre stories that trickled out from time to time. There was the boy who attempted suicide after she broke up with him. When she went to visit him afterwards his mother threw her out of the house.

It seemed every man she came in contact with became obsessive; husbands abandoned wives, gentlemen became madmen in her presence. One suitor so completely lost control of his senses that during a quiet conversation he unexpectedly jumped her, penetrated her, and came the instant he touched her skin, and all in a few seconds time.

Saudi princes offered her the lavish life of a millionaire's concubine. Suitors showered her with gifts with no expectation of winning her favors. Even women were not immune to her enchantments. One frustrated girl grabbed a knife and cut a gash into Jodi's forearm in order to "give her something to remember her by." A few days later the poor girl attempted suicide. Although I never met the woman, somehow I ended up being her suicide counselor over the Yahoo instant messenger.

In casual conversation these stories would slip out. Even in Utah she managed to catch the eye of celebrities. As a teen, a member of the heavy metal band The Scorpions became her frustrated suitor. Artists wanted to draw her. Photographers wanted her as a model. Everyone wanted to possess her. All would fail.

You never knew what was coming next. At any moment she might be torturing herself while studying the disciplines of the geisha. On one visit her skin was slightly burned. It turned out she had taken part in a religious ritual where her skin was coated with a flammable substance and she was lit aflame.

She was kaleidoscopic. A shape-shifter who performed the dance of Kali on the sterile streets of Middle America. She was a shattered house of mirrors that sparkled in the void, hypnotizing all who beheld the spectacle, while concealing a non-existent point of ultimate weight and gravity.

As we paged through the photo album and I pondered the mystery of her, my mind wandered back to her second trip to New York City. On this trip it was preplanned that she would stay with Jeanie. Among the fun times on this visit was a disastrous night at Webster Hall, a four-story dance club in the East Village. Although I'm not a big fan of the club scene, I started out the evening with a positive attitude.

As we entered the club I was feeling proud to have two lovely women at my side. We got some overpriced drinks and headed for a side room on the fourth floor. It was around midnight, which is early in the evening for a New York City club, so the place was pretty empty. The room was dark except for a few black lights and some lamps with red shades. The club music echoed in from the main hall that was right outside the door.

The girls were dancing and flirting with each other and I was taking it all in when four club boys came over to our area and made a show of being loud and obnoxious. Immediately I began to feel aggressive. I'm not a tough guy, but when I am angry I become fearless to the point of stupidity. I suppose it's that nasty mix of Irish, Polish, and Apache blood handed down from my father and which made him such a wild man when in one of his endless barroom brawls.

I just wanted to have a nice evening with my lovely companions without any trouble, so we moved out onto the balcony of the Grand Ballroom. The three of us stood at the balcony's edge looking down onto the dance-floor. From that lofty vantage point it looked like some kind of hedonistic pagan festival as hundreds of scantily clad bodies twisted and twirled and writhed and rocked underneath the flashing lights. Puffs of fog filled the room with a multicolored haze. At the end of the gigantic ballroom two large pedestals were arranged symmetrically on either side of a giant video screen. On each pedestal a G-string attired goddess did the nasty bump and grind.

I became so taken in with the spectacle that when I turned around I hadn't noticed that Jodi had left my side. Through the shadows I could see that she was talking to a man in the corner. As long as I could keep an eye on her I wasn't too concerned.

In a place like Webster Hall, if you get separated from someone you might never see them again. In a scene like this, nice young ladies have been known to disappear in a flash, only to turn up years later as crack whores spotted on the TV show Cops, or as junkie sidekicks on America's Most Wanted.

In public Jodi could be a challenge. She had an innocence about her that made me feel like I had to protect her. (I once put her on the wrong subway train that left her lost in a bad neighborhood, and about went out of my mind till I found her.) On the other hand, that innocent demeanor seems to bring out the lecher in men. She would naively insist that the world was simply full of very friendly people. (All of who just happened to have erections, I might add.) It was a deadly dynamic to get tangled up in.

But this wasn't Salt Lake City. In Webster Hall men are aggressive and they will push the boundaries until a woman stops them forcefully. Some women know how to limit such behavior without much effort. Jodi didn't seem to possess those skills.

I went to the bar to get a drink and when I returned she was nowhere to be found. Jeanie and I hung out for a bit, assuming she would return. Once some time passed I decided I better go look for her.

Webster Hall is a huge place with multiple dance-floors and endless side rooms and hallways. Trying to find someone in this maze was almost impossible. As I wandered from room to room, trying to see through the darkness and colored lights, I became increasingly annoyed to be spending the evening this way. After lapping the place a couple times I returned to the balcony to find that Jeanie had gotten sick of waiting and went off on her own.

The place was beginning to get crowded. I stood watching the people all around me. This was definitely not my scene. Club culture always seemed shallow to me. Perhaps the dull look in everyone's eyes came from too much time spent listening to the soulless music that blasted through the place. With inhuman precision a giant electronic bass drum thumped flat on every quarter note. It was the same mind-numbing beat in every song, and so oversimplified that even the stiffest white folks could find it. None of those confusing syncopated rhythms found in funk music that requires you to actually feel the groove before you can move your body to the music.

To look at the men it seemed that John Travolta's turn as king of the guidos in Saturday Night Fever still echoed through their fashion sense. The men were all about easy pussy and the women were all about men with money. It was the human mating ritual distilled to its basest elements. The men were trying to get it for free and then flee the scene, the women were hoping the product was so good that it would seal the deal on a long-term partnership.

As I stood alone in the midst of the growing crowd, I wondered how I allowed myself to get stuck in this place. With my temperature starting to rise I decided to take another tour of the place looking for the girls. Jeanie had been through this scene and knew how to take care of herself, but I still wanted to find her since the plan was to spend an evening with my friends. As I strode through dark hallways, up and down endless flights of stairs, past crowded bars, and weaved in and out of dancing couples, I became increasingly angry to be wasting my time with such nonsense.

In one room a man walked through the crowd perched on ten-foot high stilts. Couples made out on couches and go-go dancers shimmied on every bar. On an average night this place made Fellini's Satyricon look like an Avon party.

Finally I found Jodi in the basement rap room with a large black guy whose body was pressed tight against her from behind as they danced. The rap room was a small room with red walls that was always packed tight with wall-to-wall people. I'd been in that room many times and it was always thick with sex and violence. The men were there to fight or fuck. The line between a club dance and a lap dance did not exist there.

I grabbed Jodi by the hand and lead her out of the room to a lobby outside the women's bathroom.

"I'm not one of your boys, treat me with some respect," I

yelled angrily.

As I grabbed Jodi's arm to lead her out of the basement, she responded with a hearty slap across the face. And it wasn't just a little slap. She delivered a full force whack that left me stupefied. Stars swirled around my head, and people stood staring at the spectacle with bemused looks on their faces.

"You don't even know me!" she replied, her eyes filling with tears.

I have to confess that the shock of the slap pacified me a bit. Somehow we made our way up the stairs just as Jeanie was passing by. I lead them out the back door into the fresh air. The three of us stood leaning against the velvet ropes while I tried to get my wits about me. After some conciliatory conversation we decided to go back in and try to have a good time.

Jodi smooth-talked the bouncer into letting us slip in the back door. This time we chose a smaller disco room and settled into a soft couch in a quiet corner. As I nursed my vodka the girls decided they wanted to dance. Jodi ask if I would hold her purse while she danced.

Once you find yourself holding a woman's purse, somehow you immediately feel like a eunuch. So here I was sitting alone on the couch as the girl's danced to some long-forgotten 70's disco hit. Usually I am not a jealous guy, and I am definitely not a violent person, just the opposite. Unfortunately this night seemed to bring out the worst in me.

Many times during my youth I watched in horror as dear old Dad exploded into a violent rage over some slight from a drunken lout in one of the beer joints he frequented. Barely over five foot in height, he was a barroom-brawler who could go from calm to ballistic at the drop of a bottle cap. Because of this it has been a lifelong project to control such impulses within myself.

In my younger days I had a tendency to let people walk all over me without a word of complaint. As I became older and supposedly wiser, I have been careful not to allow myself to be in situations where I felt disrespected or became entangled in people's dramas. Despite this I seemed to be regressing into behavior I thought I'd outgrown long ago.

On the disco floor a large muscular man began to dance with the girls. He focused on Jodi as the dancing became increasingly dirty. What was pissing me off was that he was completely ignoring Jeanie. It seemed to me that the etiquette of dirty dancing should prescribe that it is rude to ignore one woman when invading a pair of dancers.

As the dancing steadily became more erotic between Jodi and this Adonis, my blood began to boil. Completely losing my composure, I walked over to him and although he stood a good six inches taller than me, I grabbed him by the back of his neck and pulled his ear down to my mouth.

"Dance with her, don't fuck her," I shouted, "and give the other one some attention!"

I must say he took it all with a mild temperament. I strode back to mind Jodi's purse while things cooled off with the dancers. I felt like a fool. An image came to my mind of a nature documentary I once watched where an alpha male mountain goat was running around in a frenzy trying to protect his harem of nannies when another male goat wandered into his territory.

Back in Salt Lake City Jodi turned the page in the photo album and laid her head on my shoulder. On the page I looked at the photo of a smiling little girl. With my index finger I traced the line of her face through the thin sheet of plastic that covered the photos. Wondering who this person truly is, her words after she slapped my face in the basement of Webster Hall, echoed in the recesses of my mind, "You don't even know me."

In my youth I had the arrogance to imagine I knew a lot about women. I theorized that being an artist opened me up to my own feminine side and allowed me to have more insight into their souls. Plus I had two older sisters, and growing up, I was always surrounded by female friends, making the ways of women familiar to my mind.

But the older I get the more I realize I know nothing of women. And perhaps it is this unfathomable mystery that enchants me so.

The Goddess Kali is the creator and destroyer, she is nature itself, she is the dark moist earth from which all of creation grows. Further she is the wheel of life around which man's ceaseless activity swirls. Need we mention that man, born from the womb, spends his life trying to conquer that from which he came?

There was a time when I believed there was one woman and life without that one woman seemed unimaginable to me. I lost my self within her. I died and was reborn while mired in her chaos. The flavor of her womb was still on my tongue as I shed the tears of separation.

It was she who asked me to reveal my wounds. She opened those wounds with the intent to apply a soothing ointment, but upon seeing how deep they went, drew her own dagger, concluding it was better to just complete the job. And I testify that she succeeded where all others had failed.

But as I look back over life, what I see is that people come and people go. The knowledge of love's impermanence helps me to savor every moment, every smile, every act of kindness or beauty, every sweat soaked kiss or impassioned moan. The acceptance of that impermanence allows me to savor every drop of life's essence and yet approach it with a sense of detachment. Possession is a fragile illusion, and people desire that which they cannot possess.

But also I cannot forget that through women I have traveled to foreign lands, eaten exotic foods, lived among strange cultures, and yet never left the shores of America. Through women I have danced to music in foreign tongues, bowed my head to strange gods, and breathed-in the odors of incense and spices unknown in the house of my humble beginnings. Every lover has been a teacher who taught new words, new ideas, and new customs with which to live day-to-day life.

In my secret mind I believe every one of them are with me at all times, that no matter what twisted paths their lives may take, we are wedded in spirit and will remain so until we settle into dust and our atoms mingle in the invisible electric dance that underlies the material world and upholds all of existence.

#7 – Who The Fuck Is Caeser Pink?

As Jodi turned through the final pages of the photo album the timeline changed to her teen years, revealing the first hints of the woman she was now. She looked thin and delicate, less confident but poised. Her parents had definite ideas about how a young lady should act, even going so far as to send her to finishing school.

In the final picture the father stands with his brood. The brother has a precocious smile on his face, but one might imagine there is a hint of anger concealed therein. The girls are lined up like summer daisies, dreaming of sunshine, but knowing they need rain. Everything looks perfect.

Part of the mystery about Jodi is where do I come in? Why did she seek me out? I look into her eyes searching for an answer. She looks back at me with doe-eyed innocence. But if I look deeper, I see the wisdom of Eve in the moments before she offered Adam the apple.

To the woman who would soon be the mother of all of humanity the garden must have seemed an awfully boring place, and Adam a never-ending lout. Sure, he could be counted on to always be there, but as each day faded into another, without direction, without change, without a crease ever crossing his brow, or a new idea ever lighting up his face, perhaps she thought it better to live in struggle and savor each meal procured in toil, then to enjoy an abundance of food with no flavor.

Jodi found me over the Internet. She found The Imperial Orgy in a search engine. One can only guess what word she must have been searching for.

But why seek out a stranger named Caeser Pink? The image that is projected of Caeser Pink on the Internet and through the media is…well, I really don't know what to say. Perhaps a few press clippings would explain it best:

"Caeser Pink easily seduces everyone in the audience with his animalistic stage presence...pink is a little bit more than just hypnotizing...he's a new rock and roll icon for the millennium, and most definitely ahead of his time." -Dig This Real Magazine

"I have never seen anything like it! I was truly blown away. Caeser was a snarling, predatory beast-like man, venturing out onto the dance floor and enticing women to take a bite of his apple and writhe around with him. His persona was pure sexual confidence. The stage was his and the man was drawing out the crowd's sexuality almost beyond their control. At one point the stage was covered in bodies gyrating to the music, falling over each other and Caesar was in the middle of it all, a sinister smile playing around the corner of his lips. This was the magic man." -Bully Mag

"Looking sort of like an English cousin of Leonardo DiCaprio, Caeser Pink and his crew takes their mission to have a blast very seriously. Their pop-fun songs keeps fans dancing while giving them brain nourishment in the form of serious lyrical themes mouthed by the confident lounge singer cool of Caeser. " -The Bronx Times

"The Imperial Orgy is a creative feast. Lead vocalist Caeser Pink exudes an air of self-assurance and sex appeal reminiscent of John Travolta's character in Grease. Their music embodies a free spirit that infects everyone in the audience. The Imperial Orgy is an experience that broadens the mind and the senses." -Good Times Magazine

"Caeser Pink is the enigmatic leader of a troupe of entertainers called The Imperial Orgy. Take yourself higher with this great show, these great artists and let your mind move to new and higher highs. There's no let up in the rush...takes you places you've never been. The best stadium show in the nation!"
-Online TV

"The Imperial Orgy is a multimedia onslaught of music, video, artwork, and performance. Mr. Pink is the tall, dark, and devilishly handsome frontman. The Imperial Orgy follows his lead and tries their hardest to break down the boundaries that keep you and me from partaking in the feast of life. The Imperial Orgy's sound has a striking diversity with no limitations. Caeser Pink and the Imperial Orgy want to blow your mind, but they will be content to make you stop and think for a second." -Ampcast.com

This image is something I grapple with on a daily basis. It is a never-ending tug-of-war between the peasant boy reared in the trailer park, and whatever this other being is. Although I created it, and live it, I don't really understand it.

The first time I stepped onstage with The Imperial Orgy I knew I was possessed. Possessed, yet I felt more truly myself than ever before.

In the months before The Imperial Orgy's first full performance I began falling into deep trances. Sometimes while in these trances I visualized things that would be used in the music or staging, other times I saw events that would soon come to pass, yet seemed too outrageous to be true.

Our first full performance was at a little bar near the Penn State University called Stoney's Posthouse Tavern. Usually the entertainment consisted of top 40 cover bands that were ignored by the audiences who came to drink with friends. That was about to change. Due to a series of provocative flyers and radio ads the room was filled to capacity.

Along the back wall of the empty stage a dark, surreal, sometimes violent video collage created by the multimedia artist Jon Mertz began to flicker. Fog, soaked a deep pink by the red lights began to seep in from the corners, blurring the disturbing images on the video screen. I walked out onto the empty stage dressed in black jeans and a shiny 1970's style leather jacket. As I looked at the faces of the silent crowd I could see the skepticism in their eyes. To make matters worse, instead of singing a familiar cover song I began shouting an apocalyptic poem.

As I move through the days I experience nature's duality

As I enter the physical realm

I see all men striving blindly to fulfill their desires

Creating a mad, frenzied, insectile order

My delivery challenged the audience. I hurled the words at them like insults. Meanwhile our guitar player Michael Mordes wandered out onto the stage dressed in a red pair of coveralls and with a brown beer-ball over his head, giving him the appearance of a spaceman from a 1950's sci-fi movie. Underneath my tirade he began playing abstract guitar improvisations that had nothing to do with the words I was shouting.

The Poor live lives of desperation

Their dignity stolen by poverty's cunning

The rich search for ever more subtle means

To carry out their genteel acts of self destruction

As I read the words I paced back and forth in the red haze, reading the poetry from a black notebook like a caricature of a beat poet. One by one the musicians wandered onstage and began playing random atonal noise. As the cacophony grew the audience became increasingly agitated.

"Sing it! Sing it!" people began to shout. The sound beneath me evolved into a horrendous barrage of chaotic noise. Overtop I screamed the final lines of the poem.

Down on my knees

Worshipping, eating, fucking, sucking the beast

The flames enter my stomach

Burn my lungs

Singe my senses

I tried to maintain eye contact with the audience, challenging and taunting them. Their faces registered anger and confusion. Just when I thought they were about to get up and walk out the door, with a flick of my wrist the entire ruckus came to a dead stop with razor's edge precision.

I stood silent for a moment, allowing it to register with the crowd that the cacophony was actually a purposeful assault completely under our control. Slowly I walked over the invisible line that separates audience and performer, by doing so announcing that I would not hesitate to enter their territory. Staring into their collective eyes I read the poem's final lines.

With my eyes finally opened

I see all things are on fire

With another flick of my wrist the band broke into a punk rock version of Brave New Hymn. As the song went through verse, chorus, and back again, although it was not a safe and familiar cover tune by the latest grunge band, at least we seemed to be behaving like a nice little rock band should. I could see that the audience was becoming comfortable with the idea that the first assault was just an aberration and they could now settle into a night of drinking without further annoyance from the living jukebox.

Just when they thought it was safe I disappeared from the stage and the band switched into a minimalist new wave funk groove. I returned a few second later with the background singers on each side of me. They were dressed in matching skin-tight black lycra skirts. We walked in unison to center stage. On the first beat of the verse I hit the microphone and the girls froze into a pose with their arms crossed and their chins held high, each in half profile aimed away from me, looking like sexy sentry guards.

Again the lyrics and presentation challenged the audience, asking them to take part in an evening of carefree partying while children starved in Africa and racists raped in Sarajevo.

> *Now I'm looking out among you*
> *Now I'm speaking right to you*
> *This is my condemnation*
> *Can you look me in the eye?*
> *Murder, famine, rape, and poison*
> *We unleash upon the world*
> *But weekend is the time to party*
> *We will drink and dance tonight*

Between verses the girls broke into angular dance routines. During the chorus I again went into the audience, imploring them with outstretched hands, "Can you even call me human?"

The girls responded with silky voices, "Don't say yes, don't say yes."

"I just close my eyes again," I finished then turned my back on the crowd and returned to my space between the women.

Near the song's end a young man who had obviously had enough of this nonsense ran up onto the stage and demanded that we stop the music. We continued on as if he wasn't there. He took an angry stance behind me with his arms folded over his chest as if to say, "I'm not leaving until you stop this shit." A few of my backwoods friends stood up, ready to provide assistance if any trouble broke out. I stood directly in front of the angry fellow and let myself fall backwards unto him. I'm not sure what happened to him after that. He disappeared and was not seen again.

By this time it was beginning to dawn on the audience that we weren't going to provide an evening of safe entertainment, and they would have to go with it or get out. By the fourth song a few of the more confident women had begun to dance in front of the stage area. Throughout the first set we took them on a musical journey. We sat down for an unplugged-style acoustic ballad, I wore a large dunce cap for an industrial rocker called Idiot Love. With each song the group of people dancing in front of the stage grew larger.

By the set's end the audience had grown to trust us. Although we stepped far outside the boundaries they were used to, they began to feel like they understood the parameters of where we might go. Now it was time to break through even those parameters and see how far we could actually take them.

As the keyboard player began to fill the room with sounds of church organ music, I introduced "The Imperial Orgy's spiritual advisor and pharmacist…the Reverend Blue Blotter."

Guitarist Michael Mordes stepped up to the mic and began preaching with the voice of a Southern Baptist evangelist. Between lines I lead the audience in shouts of "Amen" and "Halleluiah."

Good evening my people out there. I am here with a message from the Lord. I am here to tell you that we're all going to heaven. Yes, everyone that's here tonight. And I know you may be looking for meaning in your life and I'm here to tell you that you'll find it! You'll find it in heaven! Because many don't know this, but God is a woman. Yes, that's right. A beautiful, sexy, big-breasted woman."

*"Now God wants me to tell you that while we're on this earth we need to love each other. Wait a minute people, God is speaking to me right now…and God wants me to spread the word of love right here to you. So children right this very moment turn to that person beside you, be they stranger or friend, and extend your hand. Extend your hand and touch them…in a very intimate place. That's right my friends, feel the spirit of God's creative powers. Cause while you're here God wants you to practice for Her. So please people do God's work, and while you're here… F**k like Bunnies! "*

At that moment a pair of copulating rabbits filled the video screen, followed by a Noah's Ark parade of mating animals both large and small. As he completed his sermon I walked to the microphone and yelled, "Let the orgy begin!" The band broke into a funky Prince-esque groove, and I pulled a large red apple from my pocket and began blowing my breath on it and shining it on my jacket lapel.

I walked slowly out onto the dance floor, my face aimed downward, but my eyes peering upwards at the faces in the crowd, providing an expression of lechery as in the old movie posters for A Clockwork Orange. I bit into the apple as if taunting the crowd, chewing nonchalantly as the guitarist took a solo. When the chorus came I held the apple out to an innocent looking college girl. She hesitated for a moment than grabbed my hand, pulling the apple close to her mouth and took a large bite as the crowd cheered in approval.

I wanna show you sex salvation

I wanna give you a sensual revelation

I wanna show you sex salvation

I'll lead you to erotic devastation

Now that they understood the game, the women were not only willing to bite the apple, they seemed to be jumping out of their skin in hopes of being next to take part in the new ritual. By the middle bridge three apples had been chewed to the core.

Finally the musicians broke down to a simmering groove. I walked through the crowd of dancers searching for an appropriate consort. I chose a woman whose dark eyes suggested she was more acquainted with the ways of love than the average schoolgirl. As I whispered into the microphone I circled around her.

"Woman you look so fine.

What I wanna know is do you read the Bible?

Cause I wanna know you."

She looked into my eyes as she danced. Feeling the heat, she pulled her outer shirt off over her head, leaving only a thin white undershirt covering her medium sized breasts. Bringing my mouth close to her right ear from behind I continued...

"Can I kiss the back of your neck three times?

Maybe even seven?

And then move down and down and down..."

Circling around her I fell on my knees in front of her. Taking her hand in mine, I slid down flat on my back. She straddled me, placing her behind on my crotch as she sat upright atop me. She began grinding her hips against me in rhythm to the music. Looking up at her I asked,

"Baby can you thrust?"

On cue the band responded with a loud James Brown style horn blast. With the blast I thrust against her, raising her into the air with my pelvis. I repeated the question.

"Baby can you thrust?"

Again the band responded with a blast and I raised her into the air with my hips.

"Gimmie two," I begged and the band obliged

"Make it faster, faster, faster, faster!"

In quick succession the music hits responded and with each hit I lifted her skyward as she gyrated atop me. The audience seemed stunned. The women seemed in a frenzy of sexual excitement. With that we ended our first set and ran towards the basement storage area that we were using as a dressing room. The audience had never seen anything like The Imperial Orgy, but in all my years as a musician I had never seen a crowd reaction like what we had just experienced.

During the second set we took them on a new journey. The first third of the set focused on political rock and reggae. During Dancing Now I dressed like a third world guerrilla with a ski mask and toy machine gun. The girls dressed like corporate executives. With strings attached to the shoulders of my jacket they controlled me like a puppet, slipping money into my pockets and pointing at people in the audience, who I would then pretend I was shooting with the toy gun.

The middle section of the set was all deep funk and trip hop. During Exhibition I carried a video camera as I sang. The plan was to film people in the audience as they danced and project it onto the video screen behind the band. The first woman I put the video camera on immediately ripped her shirt open, her naked breasts filling the video screen and bringing cheers from the crowd.

For the set's end we went into dark gothic music. The set finished with Struggle The Void. As the song came to a close I stared into the horizon screaming at God like a madman. Behind me the music de-evolved into a barrage of noise.

"Standing on life's edge

Looking out into the darkness

How can one live in the face of death

Knowing all is nothingness?

I call out to you from the darkness

But you remain silent

Hiding in a mist of unspoken promises

Is there anyone out there?

Speak to me

Reach out your hand

Reveal yourself

I want answers not faith

In our fear we make an image

A myth

A babble of insanity

I will tear you from my heart

And if in the final hour you are there

I will spit in your face

I am alive!

I search and I find nothing"

With the din still echoing in their ears we ran offstage. As we changed our costumes in the kitchen's basement, using cardboard boxes for dressing tables, a writer for the local paper yelled down the stairs with an excited voice, "You guys are fucking awesome!"

For the third set I dressed in a shiny turquoise suit and the girls dressed in evening dresses. As we walked single file out onto the stage the audience gave us a standing ovation. Another first for the bar band scene. Throughout the evening the sexual tension continued to rise. Twice women dropped to their knees and imitated performing felatio on me as I sang. Later I reached out for a woman's hand and she responded by bending down and kissing mine.

During Sleepwalk Heaven I was tearing the strings off my guitar, each making a menacing twang as they popped, when suddenly a young man ran out of the audience holding his middle finger in the air and yelling "Fuck you, Fuck you!" angrily into my face. He then ran into the crowd and disappeared.

For the encore we performed a ragged version of Iggy Pop's "I Wanna Be Your Dog." During the third verse we brought down the volume to a sexy grind. On my hands and knees I crawled onto the dance floor and collapsed on my back. One of a set of Armenian twins crawled on top of me and gave me a long slow kiss as the crowd danced around us.

As I moaned the chorus refrain, "Now I wanna be your dog..." I pulled the dancers into a pile on the floor. The crowd writhed in a slithering pile of bodies that became an impromptu petting orgy. Video of the performance shows our guitarist looking down at the scene on the dance floor with a comically confused look on his face. By the night's end I felt we had earned the right to carry the audacious name "The Imperial Orgy."

Upon awakening the next morning, the previous night's events seemed unreal. Usually on the morning after a performance I am in a contemplative mood, but on this morning I felt like I had undergone a transformation and was unsure how to grasp what had taken place. I felt as if a long hidden part of myself had suddenly emerged and briefly took control.

It was a gray autumn Sunday morning. I walked the empty streets of State College, PA trying to make sense of it all. As I walked an unknown voice shouted "Caeser Pink," from a passing car as if my name was some kind of football cheer.

I wandered into the Ye Ole' College Diner, a worn-out hangout for college kids and visiting parents. The place was almost empty.

"Seating for one?" a fresh-faced hostess asked me.

I nodded through my haze. As I followed her to the booth my eyes traced the soft lines of her form. Her hair was a dirty blonde and fell in curls around her shoulders. Without thinking I reached my hand out to touch her, catching myself only inches away running my fingers across the curve of her back.

As I sat down it dawned on me that last night so many social taboos had been broken with such ease that my mind believed such freedom is natural. From now on I would have to live day-to-day life censoring every action so that I didn't get myself in trouble. As I thought about the behavior of the women at the performance, I felt as if I had peeked behind a curtain to catch a glimpse of the truth behind women's often-repressed sexuality.

I looked down at the thick wooden table that my arms rested heavily upon. Although it shone with a glossy coat of shellac, the wood was etched with a jumble of twenty-plus year's worth of graffiti. "Jenny is a bitch, Delta House bar tour 87, AC/DC, Billy Z died here," on and on it went. A history of college-town names, rude comments, and insults to lost loves, carved one upon another to create a mosaic babble of meaningless words and symbols. It felt like it buzzed with an electric energy that was frozen into the grain of the wood. I felt exhausted by looking at it. I laid my head upon the table, feeling like I could sink down into its depths, never to be seen again.

My sense of self was both found and lost by the transformation that was taking me. Sometimes you just have no idea who the fuck you are. The Rolling Stones once sang, "What's a poor boy to do except play in a rock and roll band." I respond, "Hail, hail, rock and roll." These gifts of life given to me by rock and roll had blown this poor boy's mind.

In the months that followed the events of the performance became a template for a ritualized ceremony that was repeated in a variety of venues and to a growing number of fans. We seemed to be especially popular with Catholic and Indian girls. Both come from some sort of sexually repressed background I suppose.

At the same time The Imperial Orgy was surrounded by controversy. A performance was canceled due to threats from Christian groups who warned of terrorist acts against a frightened bar owner, claiming that they would riot if the performance was allowed to take place. The Penn State University banned our flyers from public display because they were "distressing to some students." When the local newspaper took up our cause as a first amendment issue, lawyers were called in and the University officials backtracked, even claiming the flyers were never banned in the first place.

On any given day the local paper would print a letter to the editor either for or against The Imperial Orgy. Women's Studies classes argued about the group's presentations of sexuality. Eventually they sent an emissary to invite me to speak before the class, giving me an opportunity to defend our behavior I assume. Ironically, although I was willing to meet the class, after the emissary offered herself to me for an afternoon of fun, the event never materialized.

During one concert chaos broke out when a bouncer became offended by the performance and threatened to turn off the electricity. When I responded by getting the audience to chant "Turn off the power, turn off the power," he upgraded his threat to

"Giving me a beating I wouldn't forget." Eventually the police were called in and a couple of fans whisk me away to avoid arrest on an outstanding warrant.

During this time, the community of people who were following the group were using us as a catalyst to explore their own sexuality. First time lesbianism was rampant.

Some women became confused by it all. A kiss shared on the dance floor during a performance lead to delusions that affairs were taking place that never existed. It seemed everyone was questioning their sexual identity, expanding their boundaries, and trying to overcome the repression hard-wired into the brains by family and society.

Most of the women who followed us were brilliant, but bordering on lunacy. There was Sasha, a neurotic Indian lotus who would one day earn a doctorate, despite her never-ending emotional turmoil. Sasha was a new age hippie type and when she was nervous would say things like, "What color are you feeling right now?" She would ply me with homemade baked goods and her dreams of sexual abandon. After one show she handed me a copy of her apartment key and said, "Just come in and take me during the night."

There was also Ornelia, a tall Catholic Goddess with a mane of flaming locks surrounding her ivory-white face. Her icy demeanor struck fear into the hearts of the other girls. I kissed her before I ever spoke a word to her. We were playing in a large industrial club with a set of high balconies. She was standing against the railing on one of the balconies when I spotted her. I crawled up onto a barstool and then onto the bar, then crawled up onto the balcony. As I hung over the crowd while clinging to the outside of the railing, with Ornelia facing me on the inside of the railing, she greeted me with a warm wet kiss.

And there was Sneha, another Indian princess and future doctor of psychology. Her dark beauty and sensual playfulness hid the fact that she was fighting her family to avoid honoring a prearranged marriage to an Indian man who she only met once during the marriage ceremony on a trip to the homeland.

There was Jen, one of the Armenian twins who was

spreading her wings and her love for the first time. Her guileless innocence was like a leaf that had broken free from the tree and was willing to float on a breeze, going whichever way life would take her, as long as she could experience life to its fullest.

And there was also Amala, another wounded Indian princess who carried her virginity with her like Atlas with the globe on his back. Every word that came out of her mouth was sex. Sex swirled around her like an impenetrable fog.

The first time I went to her apartment I noticed tampons were hung from the lampshades as decoration. In every corner penis shaped candles burned and melted into soft mush, I suppose as did her suitors at the gates of her blessed virginity. She wore a thin gauze dress that barely covered her bulging caramel colored breasts. She tuned the TV to a soft-core porn cable channel and sat down beside me on the couch.

Then in an environment swollen with sexuality, she began to sing the praises of her virginity. She bore its burden like an albatross. With words dripping with sex, she told stories of every man who tried to seduce her, the lurid details of every blocked advance, and every frustrated suitor. How far they went, the debaucheries they wanted to assault her with, and how she ached for the one love who would one day receive her bounty. She was a bear's trap waiting to maim, so I kept a safe distance no matter how much I was tempted.

There was also Chrisanne, a well-read intellectual and local legend as a free-love hippie-chick gone-cynical. She was thin as a rail and almost six feet tall. She had a model's fashion sense and used her provocative attire like a whipping post. I once took her to see a movie. With an elderly couple sitting just two seats away, she nonchalant took my hand, lifted her long flowing skirt and placed my hand directly on her silken snatch before calmly smoothing her skirt and settling down to enjoy the flick.

Beyond this menagerie of half-insane, over-sexed fallen-angels, was a parade of faces that came and went. I know there must have been some men mixed in with them, but I can't seem to remember much about them. What I do recall is that our fan-base transcended social and musical cliques. We had Dead-Heads, metal dudes, aging prog-rockers, goth kids, funk fans, and the random folkie who hid safely in the back of the room. The only group we didn't connect with was the grunge crowd, whose shoe-gazer aesthetics found our unseemly displays of fun and passion far too uncouth to suit their "misunderstood and always suffering" middle class pretensions.

This chaotic period went on for about six months. During these days I seemed to have boundless energy and health. I think it was the only winter in my life that I didn't come down with at least one cold. It was a snowy winter and it seemed every other day I was digging the band's van out of the snow so we could do a gig.

As a way of dealing with the changes in my life and in my self, I began to think of my stage persona as a separate identity from my true self. I was a child of the 70's feminist age and my ideas of manhood were shaped by those values. I was taught that a good man was expected to be sensitive and non-aggressive, and definitely not a chauvinist pig, as they were once called.

Because of this I felt that my new persona as Caeser Pink was somewhat embarrassing and offensive. Plus this was the age when political correctness was rampant on college campuses and women's studies classes were teaching young women that if a man makes sexual advances of any kind it is bordering on rape.

To the women who knew my stage persona before they knew me personally, I often found myself exclaiming, "That's not me, I'm really not like that." This approach to self-identity soon created an unworkable psychic schism. Events were soon to make this problem worse.

I convinced the group to move to New York City to be at the center of the music business. In late summer the band members made the move, but due to a run of bad luck I was unable to follow. When I finally came up with a little money and was ready to join my friends in the big apple it was late October. For months I had not played or written music. To get myself back into the frame of mind I gathered my lyrics together and bound them into a little book at Kinkos. As I proofread the lyrics I noticed that some of the songs seemed to be written with a voice that was clearly not my own. Among them was "Circus Circus."

Caligula was a friend of mine
The Marquis De Sade used to drink my wine
I was with Krishna when the gopi danced
Now I'm here won't you take a chance?

I'm the author of the Kama Sutra
I'm the singer of Solomon's song
Embrace the sinner, liberate the saint
Lust for life baby that's the way

Often I don't remember writing my lyrics and this strange voice seemed very alien to me. I thought back to the performances and my stage persona. It all seemed very far away. It seemed that to inhabit that persona and bring about those reactions was now an unattainable dream. It was always hard for me to reconcile the trailer-trash peasant that I saw myself as, and the persona of Caeser Pink. Now it seemed incomprehensible.

In some ways the fracture in my identity was related to issues of how manhood is defined in America. Although men always receive messages in the media that we should be sensitive guys who defer to their partners on all things, it seemed that within relationships this behavior did not make women happy. The women I knew would have preferred a strong man who took control of situations and provided direction. It seemed that the women who mouthed feminist ideology, were the ones who most wanted a stronger man.

Around this time I saw Camille Paglia in a debate on Larry King's TV show. She was brash and aggressive, obnoxious even. She was attacking the current state of feminist thought on gender issues. She argued that masculine aggressiveness was good for society and should not be something to be ashamed of.

For my birthday a few days later Samantha bought me a copy of Paglia's book Vamps & Tramps. Her iconoclastic ideas seemed new to the world, but rang true in my heart. Her words helped me to embrace the masculine feelings that seemed natural to me, yet which I had always rejected. It made me feel less ashamed of the part of my persona that women seemed to respond to, but which I disavowed out of fear of being a sexist jerk.

There was something else in her book that captured my attention. She kept referring to rock and roll as "pagan." She compared rock stars to modern incarnations of ancient gods and goddesses. She argued that despite our lip service to Christianity, America was a wholly pagan society.

The idea seemed mysterious to me. I had made an effort to study all the major religions and most of the minor ones in my never ending search for meaning. But one area that I had neglected was pre-Christian European earth religions. I went out and got a few books on the subject in order to learn more.

In the books they described an ancient ceremony where a man personifies a deity who represents masculinity as a universal principle. He was a god of hunting, war, and fertility. In the ceremony the man wore animal skins and deer antlers on his head. As Christianity was trying to give the old religions a bad reputation this is where the image of Satan as a horned demon came from.

The job of this horned spirit was to evoke the spirit of the Goddess in a woman at the ceremony. The modern Wiccans call it "drawing down the moon." The goal is to fill a woman with the universal spirit of femininity and female fertility, the counterpart to the masculine deity that the horned man represents.

When I read this a light of recognition went off in my head. This seemed very similar to the ritual that played out at Imperial Orgy performances. If one believes that universal images reside in our collective unconscious, I may have tapped into something both in myself and in the audience members, something that none of us were conscious of, but that had a powerful effect when triggered.

I always felt that to some extent the women in the audience were reacting to something more than myself as an individual. And that reaction seemed to cause them to act, almost against their will, as if taken by a spirit of feminine sexuality that caused them to behave in ways that they normally never would have.

In this light the strange voice that wrote the lyrics in some of my songs suddenly seemed to be revealed.

I'm the Satan here to possess your soul
I need your body, I'll take control
Have mercy baby, I want you on top
Forgive my passion, it never stops

Further, this verse from Sex Salvation seemed to describe this pagan ceremony outright.

Life is sacred, don't let it pass
Take my desire, break from your past
You're the Goddess, I'm the beast
Join me in life's wanton feast

I knew nothing of these things when I wrote those lyrics so it came from somewhere in the unconscious. For the first time the conflict in my identity made sense. I once heard shock-jock Howard Stern say that when he is on the radio he is more truly himself than at any other time because he can be more honest and uninhibited than in his day-to-day life. I have also heard actors say that playing a role has made them discover a part of themselves that they didn't know existed. I could relate to both of these ideas because when I inhabited the persona of Caeser Pink I was discovering parts of myself that had always been buried, and I definitely felt freer to be myself in that state.

With this revelation I was able to integrate my fractured psyche. I embraced "Caeser Pink" and allowed the more dominant persona to absorb the weaker. For the first time, perhaps in my entire life, I began to feel whole.

Now that I understood my self and had more control of my identity and how it related to my creative work, I decided to write a new song that would make use of this knowledge. I titled it Oak King Blues, named after a Celtic god who dies and is reborn each year.

Spear to cauldron, lance to grail
Death and resurrection, surrender to love

Good evening children, without horns or fur I rise tonight
Our golden father sleeps in the West and the moon hangs heavy with seed
In the forest deep, the odor of musk rides the warm summer breeze
The fecund fields give birth to green and the peach is swollen with sweet nectar

Here I am
And I've come for you tonight

I possess this man so I may find you
I am the mirror, I'm the flame that burns inside you
Look into these eyes
Do you see something you recognize?
Look deep into these eyes
Without beginning, without end, your deepest secrets lie within

On summer's eve I'll ask you to dance with me again
After the autumn feast I'll invite you to sacrifice yourself at my hands
Close your eyes, I'll pierce your soft flesh and slice your middle through
Blood will flow and your mother's tears with spill on the fallen body of her innocent child

Girl you must die
And I've come to take your life

Your corpse is my possession, but from dust a woman will arise

I call to the virgin within you, I call out to the whore

My soul needs yours

Let my desire awaken you from your child's sleep

I evoke the Goddess

Know your beauty, feel your power, can you recognize yourself?

Because life is calling and I've been waiting since time began

My eternal bride

Mystery of the waters, desire in the hearts of man

You are the alter that awakens life

He has died for love of earth

Kiss of lips, harvest of womb

Bewildered mind but heart adores

Love crystallizes into blood

Communion of polarities

His wounds to heal

From that time on the name given to me at birth was an empty shell that had no meaning to me. Out of courtesy I let my oldest friends call me whatever they want. Although I might respond when they call me that name from my past, in my heart that person is a ghost. A soul consumed by a greater soul.

And in the end, perhaps that is what death is? And the often-repeated ritual meant to prepare us for that mysterious transformation, whether the ritual is the Christian being born again, the Buddhist reaching enlightenment, or the Freudian becoming self-actualized.

It was this image of Caeser Pink that is projected in the media and through our websites that brought Jodi to me. Of all the men in the world, of all the lost souls on the Internet, the millions searching for women in chat rooms and dating sights, and the millions of web sites of every kind imaginable, it is this image that sparked her imagination and brought her to me.

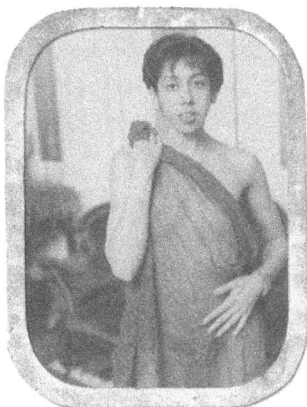

#8 – God Smiles As Precocious Children Play

The hour was getting late. Jodi and I sat on the couch and Christopher sat sideways on a plush chair, his legs dangling over the arm. Even though I was on his territory, the tables had somehow turned and he was the third cog in the wheel. Although I was the actual guest, he became the guest who wouldn't leave.

It seemed to be a battle of wills between he and Jodi. His will was to chaperone us in hopes that she would tire and leave with him. Her will was to allow us a few minutes alone, something we have rarely experienced.

I tried to stay removed from the situation. "Whatever happens will happen," I thought. The conversation in the room began to be punctuated by increasingly long periods of silence. Christopher seemed to mope, but Jodi remained firm. In a battle of wills, she was destined to win.

Eventually Christopher sulked out to the kitchen with his head hanging with resignation. Jodi followed him for a few moments of quiet conversation.

"Use a condom," he implored in a hushed voice.

She hugged him and said goodnight.

"Oh how civilized we all are," I thought. Perhaps he would

have been better off to grab me by the scruff of the neck and toss me out the door. Better to fight for his beloved or die trying.

But like it or not, she was a Goddess whose light mesmerized the minds of mortal men. A man cannot even dream of conquering She who is unknowable, She who he worships, She who he prostrates himself before.

And the true value of a Goddess is that she allows us to surrender ourselves like helpless children before her grace. Although it is to become drunk on a poisoned wine, it is a glorious and liberating feeling. It is like free-falling over a cliff while believing you can fly.

But to worship without reserve, to give oneself with utter and complete surrender, is certain death. It is to lose the soul. In fact, it is to give one's very self to that greater soul.

I have knelt before that alter and died that certain death. But a man can only die so many times before he begins to inhabit a netherworld, to eat the fruits of life's abundance like the kings of Olympus, to greet life's folly with a wry smile, and to carry a serene secret behind his brow.

To be banished to those lofty heights is to share a laugh with God, as we too, stumble our way through life. And our curse and our salvation is that we perceive that in each tear of sorrow there hides the sweetness of life, and that within each moment of joy and laughter there is the bitter reminder of the absurdity of life's cruel game.

But along with the glory, the burden of being a Goddess must be exhausting. To bear the burden of men's desires, and to hold the weight of their hopes and dreams, must be a responsibility that terribly limits one's freedom. On occasion even a Goddess must long for something outside her life to surrender to. Like the Beatles seeking the Maharishi, or Jesus assigning his fate to Judas. Dominatrix' in New York tell me that most of their clients are powerful businessmen. It seems that after a week of controlling others and being in control, all they want is to submit completely to another.

It is strange, the writing process can give one self-knowledge, it can reveal the meaning of past events, and it can help one to understand those around us. As I write this it occurs to me that I may have answered my own question, and perhaps herein lies the answer to why Jodi sought me out.

As Christopher took his leave, my mind wandered back to that evening on Jodi's second New York visit when we made the disastrous trip to Webster Hall. Afterwards the three of us went to Jeanie's apartment in Park Slope, Brooklyn. We pulled out the sofabed that Jodi was to sleep on and all three of us undressed for sleep and fell into it.

I squeezed in between the two girls, thinking, "This is my favorite place in the world." After the events at Webster Hall we were emotionally raw and a bit drunk. I slid my fingertips slowly up the inside of Jodi's forearm, moving cautiously to see how she would react, and to see how Jeanie would react. Jodi laid her head back with her eyes half open and her lips parted slightly.

Jeanie sat up and gently ran her fingers down Jodi's thigh. Her face registered ecstasy under our caresses. To allow Jeanie to be closer to Jodi, I moved to her other side. She gasped and bit her lip as Jeanie and I ran our fingertips across her belly and ribcage.

As I began placing light kisses on her neck, Jeanie began to kiss her belly and abdomen. Jodi moaned a weak, "aah," as I ran my tongue across her breast before gripping her nipple between my lips. Her moans became a stuttered, "ah, ah , ah.." as Jeanie bowed between her legs and began to lap at her swollen lips.

I lifted myself up upon my knees and Jodi took my deliriously erect penis into her mouth. Her moans delivered a vibrating massage as I shook with pleasure. My body was enraptured by her ability to give oral pleasures, and my mind was maddened by the delicious sight of the two lovely bodies spread out before me.

I withdrew from Jodi's lips as she shrieked with orgasmic pleasure thanks to Jeanie's work between her thighs. She was so loud I placed by fingers on her lips and whispered "shhh," so she wouldn't alert the entire neighborhood.

Soon we fell into each other with blissful abandon, a writhing mass of caressing hands, kissing lips, and thrusting pelvises. In our delirium we lost track of where one began and the other ended. We dissolved into each other.

As the girls locked into a long kiss I pulled back, sitting on the bottom of the bed watching them from below. Jodi was atop Jeanie and their bodies were molded into a unifying embrace. Their thighs and behinds each created a V shape that came together to form a soft white diamond. I stared in awe of the rare vision before me, as if their flesh formed the arches of a great cathedral. Both were shaved clean and the lips of the cunts stared at me like two little prayer books, each open to page 69, beckoning all to sing a hymn that begins, "Oh dear Lord, for the gift of life we thank thee."

The sight made me feel a little insane. It was shocking to the eyes and jolted my central nervous system. My mind was swimming with lust. It seemed to trigger impulses from the most primitive recesses of the brain. My blood surged with violence and greed. My breathing became quick and shallow.

I believe it was the only time in my life that I completely lost my mind to sexual frenzy. I crawled atop them, with both of them encircled by my arms. My erection was bucking up and down with a will of its own. With no help needed from guiding hands, I inserted myself inside Jeanie's dripping womb and glided in and out with slow, deliberate thrusts.

After about 30 seconds I withdrew and raised myself up about six inches and touched the tip of my penis to Jodi's lips. They seemed to pull me inside with magnificent ease. Her grip was enthralling. My mind went white with ecstasy. After another minute or so I withdrew and returned to Jeanie, then back and forth, and back and forth, with a madman's delirium.

Eventually the girls parted below me and I collapsed between them, my chest heaving with long deep breaths as I tried to regain my strength. In unison they moved down me, twenty fingers tickled their way down my body, further enhancing my delirium. Their lips kissing their way down my torso, which was flushed pink with passion.

Once they reached my exhausted erection Jeanie took my balls into her mouth and tugged at them as she sucked. Jodi took my erection fully into her mouth, caressing it with blood filled lips. The pleasure they delivered was more than the mind can digest. I looked down at them and their faces looked positively angelic. The expressions they wore were of serene beneficence. The expression of a kindly nurse as she cares for her favorite patient. With purity of heart they bestowed blessings too few men are lucky enough to ever know. They sucked, caressed, coddled, pulled and plied me into a mindless mass of throbbing nerve endings.

When I could summon the strength to lift my head far enough to look down at them, the juxtaposition of their innocent faces and their lurid behavior was glorious to the eyes. Call us sinners, call us perverted, but in my heart I know that if there is a God, that this God was smiling, as his or her or its, precocious children played, reveling in the gift bestowed upon them.

As my penis became increasingly engorged my scrotum pulled upwards towards my body, but Jeanie pulled in the opposite direction constricting the erection tighter and tighter. Finally it began to spasm, jerking wildly like a psychopath in a straightjacket. Jeanie pulled and sucked with more force, causing my semen to shoot out with inhuman propulsion. To guess from the expression on Jodi's face she savored the flavor as she drank, only a single glistening drop rolling out over the curve of her lower lip.

I screamed like a murder victim, my face went numb, and my arms and legs quivered uncontrollably. Trying to regain my composure I laughed, embarrassed by my own loss of control.

I don't remember much after that, except the warmth and security of their bodies beside me. I slept with the peace of mind of a child on a summer's morning as the far away sound of lawn mowers purred through the bedroom window.

By now Christopher had made his exit. As Jodi took my hand I reluctantly returned from my reverie, my face flushed by the heat of those memories. She led me towards the bedroom of her mother's apartment for our first real time alone. We closed the door for a rare moment of privacy.

In the morning Jodi left early to go see Christopher to make sure he got through the night without too much distress. Surely he must have spent the night haunted by visions of what debaucheries went on behind that closed door with his beloved Goddess.

In the afternoon Jodi and I went to the great Salt Lake from which Salt Lake City derived its name. As we walked along the muddy beach we were greeted by a stench so overwhelming it made one want to gag. Jodi explained that millions of brine shrimp would die in the waters and their rotting bodies would fill the air with the smell of death. She said that on hot summer days the smell would permeate the entire city.

We went into a large public building that sat on the beach. The cavernous building was empty except for a few stragglers who wandered about. The place was a bit creepy, reminding me of the abandoned carnival houses on Asbury Park's dilapidated boardwalk.

To look at the photos on the wall the building must have been a relic of a bygone era. The photos appeared to be from the 1930's or 1940's. In those days the building was filled with happy people creating a carnival-like atmosphere. In those days the beach seemed to be filled with families dressed in modest swimsuits and rubber-scalloped bathing caps. The lake seemed to have a glorious past. Given the stench that emanated from it, it was hard to imagine.

We sat on a bench holding hands, trying to have a romantic moment in these strange surroundings and amid the foul odor.

As evening approached I prepared to take my leave. Jodi was dressed in some kind of pink Indian or Middle Eastern outfit that reminded me of I Dream Of Jeannie. She seemed to inhabit the archetypes of masculine fantasies as a way of life. But I must admit she looked lovelier than ever.

In order to show me how to get to the highway out of town she drove in her car and I followed in the Blazer. She drove fast and I had to abandon my usual conservative driving habits in order to keep up with her. As we neared the highway she waved energetically. I imagined she must have been exhausted by the burden of having a guest to entertain.

Seeing her through the window of her car reminded me of another story I once heard her tell. She said that sitting at a red light she slowly unbuttoned her blouse until her breasts were exposed. She did it as an experiment to see how much traffic confusion it would cause.

As I drove away the highway passed by the Salt Lake and that horrid odor again filled my lungs. The strange pit of death that the lake had become seemed an odd contrast to the pristine streets of the city. Perhaps it is the price one pays for the sin of perfection. Perhaps the lake is the living embodiment of the darkness that I felt was so repressed in Salt Lake City.

I thought back to my second grade history book. I recall it with an unlikely clarity. It had an orange cover and was filled with black and white drawings to illustrate the stories for young readers. The section on the Mormons described how they were driven westward because of the practice of polygamy. The associated drawing showed three frightened men being chased by a group of men carrying torches as they ran through the dark forest. The section seemed designed to create prejudice in the young minds that would be reading the book.

Another section of the book described the gold miners who went to San Francisco. It said that when they had dances there weren't enough women, so the men had to dance with other men. The drawing showed two scruffy gold miners dancing arm and arm around a campfire. It went over my head that this was a warning that the city was inhabited by homosexuals.

Of course Utah officially banned polygamy in order to gain statehood, but some sects are rumored to still continue the practice. In a note of self-aware humor, there is a brand of beer in Utah called Polygamy Porter.

As the city receded into the background I thought about Jodi. Although she lived so far away and I have only seen her on a few short visits, she had become an important person in my life. Yet it seemed the more I knew her the more she remained a mystery. Perhaps she would always be so.

Then a troubling memory came to me. She once told me that when she was a teen her father used to watch porn movies with her in the room. She said he felt that if he was going to do it, he should be open with his family about it. She explained that because of these movies for a long time she believed that sex was something just for men to enjoy. It was a breakthrough when she learned to take pleasure for herself. Although I found this a little unusual, she spoke of it as if it were nothing out of the ordinary.

At a later time she mentioned that her sister accused her father of molesting her, but she and her mother knew it couldn't be true because her father would never do such a thing. Still, it was never clear to me why the father was now out of the picture.

With the smell of the lake receding behind me, the lush landscape begin to give way to a barren desert, leaving me alone with nothing except these uneasy thoughts to fill my mind.

#9 – A Horse With No Name

Before this trip I had never seen a desert. I kept hoping it would look like they do in cartoons with three-pronged cacti and tumbleweeds rolling by, but in reality the desert is simply more desolate.

After a few miles I began to see piles of white on the side of the road that looked like snow. Of course it couldn't be snow, so I was confused by what it was. Soon the white stuff began to cover the entire desert. I called Jodi to ask her what I was looking at. She said it must be the Salt Flats. I guess even in a desert you can discover things you've never heard of.

An hour in, the cell phone service went dead and radio dried up except for the big corporate stations. At two hours loneliness began to set it.

The radio announcer was reading a sound-byte version of the news at a rapid-fire pace and with steroid-laden intensity. His voice was compressed into a loud bass-heavy boom that menaced the eardrums.

Once you hit the Midwest, classic rock rules radio. It's hard to find anything except tired Zeppelin riffs and worn-out rock anthems with long-winded guitar solos. Start at one end of the dial and scroll down to the other end, I'll lay 50/50 odds that you'll run into Free Bird somewhere along the way.

It's a never-ending irony how Hendrix, The Who, and other revolutionary artists of the 1960's became the easy listening fodder of trailer-trash chicks and good ole' boys all across the U.S. of A. I turned off the dial and opted for silence.

With the radio off and the phone line dead, I was alone with my thoughts. It was really nothing new to me. I was always a loner and always felt lonely, regardless of how many people I was surrounded by, or even if I was in an intimate relationship.

It reminded me of a TV show I once saw where a group of teenagers were each left alone in the woods without anything except a notebook for company for three days. Without televisions, cell phones, computers, or video games to fill their time, each and every one of them had a complete meltdown. To be alone with their own thoughts was shattering to them. Internal dialogue was not only alien to them, but also frightening. The quieted mind is like a mirror. For many the first sight of themselves reflected in that mirror is a truly horrifying thing.

The desert is the Earth in minimalism and parched of life. The dry curves of the sand dunes affect one's mind like the waves of the ocean. To drive among them for hours on end is like chanting a thousand 'Ohms.' The chaos of the modern world begins to fade and the disruptions of the mind begin to settle.

In meditation one tries to clear the mind, but as I drove I was searching for anything to fill my thoughts. I tried to think of music I wanted to write, women I dreamed of seducing, anything to fill the void. Too often my thoughts fell back to the pain and anger of 9/11. Eventually though there just weren't enough thoughts to ground out the energy of my brain and I was left empty, except for the road and the sand.

Driving across America to "find yourself" has become a cliché of laughable proportions. I have known many friends who drove across country or backpacked over Europe in search of that great spiritual adventure. When they returned from their trips and I would ask them about the journey they usually ticked off a few tourist destinations and left it at that. The trips never seem to have inspired any passion or imbued any meaning for them.

As I grew tired and increasingly lonely I began to question the whole thing. The city of my home is in crisis, the entire country is in crisis, what the fuck am I doing so far from home, wandering aimlessly through this desert?' Like so much else that I do, it seemed a flight of narcissistic madness.

If I were to fall asleep at 70 MPH and die behind the wheel, what would I have to show for my life? For the sake of being an artist I have sacrificed all the things that a normal man desires: wife and children, home and material wealth, even leaving friends behind to pursue the egoistic dreams of the artist. In dark moments it all seemed a huge mistake from the day I drew my first breath. Perhaps my life would have been more fulfilling if I had become an accountant, married that girl I knew from Stepford, Connecticut, and had 2.3 children and a house with a white picket fence....But then, maybe not.

From day one I seemed the odd man out, poisoned in the womb. In grade school the parents of my boyhood friends referred to me as a freak. Why, I can't rightly say. Maybe they were just wise enough to see the truth before I did. But I wasn't a criminal. I wasn't violent or getting into trouble. When I think back I really can't fathom why they reacted that way to a third grade kid.

By high school I was earning the title of "freak." By then I was disgusted by the willful conformity I saw all around me. To me they were all cowards. Afraid to stand out. Afraid to do anything except follow the herd.

In my high school years the archetype of the cool outsider did not yet exist. A freak was just a freak. Yet I chose to accept that role because the last thing I wanted was to be like my classmates. To this end I wore crazy rock and roll clothing and my hair in an oversized white-boy afro. It stood so high that my eighth grade science teacher came up to me after class one day and said, "I'd like to study your hair, it just seems to defy gravity."

Despite all this, except for a few backwoods cretins, most of my classmates were friendly enough. I generally got more harassment from the faculty than the students. I do recall one instance while waiting in line to enter shop class. A jock with a chip on his shoulder came up to me while his friends watched from a few yards away and asked me, "Why are you so weird?"

I replied matter-of-factly, "I'm not weird, you guys are the one's that are weird."

He seemed completely flummoxed by this response. The audacity of even considering such an idea seemed to completely baffle him. As his friends giggled he returned to them and said with astonishment in his voice, "Did you hear that? He said we're the ones that are weird!"

But perhaps the seeds of my corruption go further back. My paternal great, great grandmother was said to be a niece of Sitting Bull. She was purchased from the Apaches for eighty-five cents by my Scottish great, great grandfather who wore the name McCartle. Stories are told of how he would awaken during the night of the full moon to see her performing ritualistic dances in a ray of moonlight that spilled in through the bedroom window.

My own father was said to see 'omens.' When he was a young man he once turned on the kitchen faucet at the very moment it was struck by lightning. Instead of water, flames shot out of the faucet. An hour later, in the same room, his sister accidentally spilled boiling water on her infant child, killing the baby and emotionally scarring her for life.

I recall a time during my own childhood when my father woke my mother during the night to tell her he had seen a bouquet of roses floating down the hall towards him. My mother told him to go back to sleep and that he was dreaming. A bit later he woke her again and said he saw two bouquets of roses floating down the hall. The next morning we found that the woman who lived on the other side of our double house had died during the night of a sudden heart attack. Often he would smell roses and say that he thought a sick friend or relative would be dying soon.

Once when my parents walked out the door their house trailer my father was greeted with the aroma of flowers. He began to asked my mother where the smell was coming from, then he caught himself. They were on the way to the hospital for my mother to have a heart operation from which she never recovered.

In his later years my maternal grandfather would hold long conversations with Jesus Christ. It seems he saw the deity walk right into the living room and take a seat on the couch.

His wife, my maternal grandmother, was known as 'Lottie The Healer.' It is said people came from miles around to engage her services.

Even my oldest sister is a medium, reiki healer, animal communicator, and ghost chaser.

We can never really know what it looks like in another person's head so we may judge what is the norm, but my own head buzzes with manic energy. That energy can too easily transform into poison that floods the bloodstream.

As I child I would often hallucinate. We lived in a spooky old house and the daughter of the previous tenants had died in my bedroom. I found her initials carved into the wood behind the closet door. I'm not one to believe in wandering spirits or that sort of thing. When people tell me they saw a ghost in the basement or in a field on Halloween night, I find it a little irritating. Whether coming from myself or from another it all sounds like nonsense to me. So it is with some embarrassment that I must admit that as a child I would often imagine I saw strange people walking through the house. An overactive imagination, I suppose. Many years later after we moved out of that house, I overheard my father tell my sister that when he would walk past my bedroom door the hair on his arms would stand on end.

After my father died for many months the hallucinations returned. Each morning I would awake with the sunlight to see a figure standing at the foot of the bed. One morning it transformed into a fox that ran towards my head, dissolving into air a few inches from my face. I never got too distressed about this, just a minor annoyance to contend with. In time it passed.

Despite so much evidence to the contrary, I have always felt grounded in reality. Often looking existence straight in the eye when others preferred to cling to fairy tales and happy illusions.

Suddenly as I drove I noticed a rest stop. It is the first man-made object I have seen in hours. I pulled off into the deserted parking lot. Instead of using the men's room I urinated standing in front of the car looking out over the expanse of desert sand. My heels firmly on the parking lot macadam and my toes resting in the edge of the soft sand. All around were signs forbidding people to enter the desert. "Why would authorities forbid people to enter this vast emptiness?" I wondered. I thought of the opening page of The Imperial Orgy website that begins:

"The Buddha Gautama sat silently under the bo tree. Jesus Christ wandered in the desert for 40 days and nights. Prometheus ascended the heavens, Aeneas dove into the underworld, and Virgil traveled through the inferno. For hero and heroine, the journey is within and without, and to look into the dark mirror will transform or defeat."

Those in power, those who want to preserve the status quo and protect their place in the social structure, never want the masses to look inward. Because when one looks inward the entire edifice of the modern world begins to appear as a colossal nightmare, a house of cards held up by a fragile web of mass delusions. One moment of satori, even one single word of truth, creates a mortal danger that could bring the whole thing tumbling down.

It always appeared to me that we are all involved in a grand conspiracy to perpetuate the delusion. Certainly politicians, religious leaders, and corporate executives don't want us to question the nature of reality or the meaning of life, they have far too much to lose. Advertising agency chiefs are cynically aware that their job is to brainwash the public into embracing materialism and conformity. The first advertising agency was founded by a nephew of Sigmund Freud, specifically for the purpose of using psychology to manipulate the public.

But what is perhaps even more disturbing is the role that entertainment plays in our social conditioning. Movies, music, magazines, and television; all are mediums of artistic expression that could be used to inspire and enlighten, yet all we see and hear is mindless nonsense that plays to our basest instincts, and all seemingly designed to divert our attention from introspection and meaningful thought. To question ones self, to question the values of our society, is to threaten all in authority.

In the early days of television live broadcasts of stage plays were a favorite among viewers. Plays written by French existentialists were surprisingly popular. Soon the advertising sponsors put a stop to the heavy subject matter being presented in the broadcasts. If people are thinking about the meaning of life it made it too hard to hock vacuum cleaners and refrigerators. And so the path was set. The people with the money decided that the media must be used to keep us dumb. And they do keep us dumb.

Even the great Greek philosopher Socrates was condemned to death for corrupting the youth of Greece. It seems he would cause young people to question every word those in authority spoke. A crime punishable by death.

Zipping my pants I walked past the warning signposts and wandered about thirty yards into the desert, stopping on the other side of a dune that blocked the rest area and parking lot from my field of vision. I slowly turned around, taking in the horizon, first north, then east, then south and west.

It was a vast nothingness, almost devoid of life. For some reason the sight brought feelings of despair into my chest. My limbs felt heavy and a dreamlike malaise overtook my mind.

I reached down and picked up a handful of dry sand. As I opened my fingers to try to look at it, the tiny grains seeped out between my fingers like water, leaving me with an empty grasp except for a few grains that clung to my skin. With a closer look the granules seemed to glitter and shine like tiny diamonds.

"What is this stuff?" I wondered. We take what is before us for granted. We give things names and believe we understand them. But look deeper and we must admit we know nothing of the world around us. We live in a world of mystery. A tree, a rock, the Earth, the stars and the galaxies of the universe, everything is in motion, nothing is in stasis. Everything is becoming or decaying, and we know nothing of what these things truly are, nothing of their relationships to each other, or what their place is within the workings of the universe.

But stand back and look at it from a wider perspective and it surely looks like something is going on. It may have no goal and no purpose, it may be a crazy clock that keeps no time, but *something* appears to be going on.

We focus on what we know, because to admit that we live in a world we don't understand is too frightening. I wonder, "What is alive, what is dead?" For all of our scientific discoveries, for all the words in all the textbooks in the world, we are still lost in an unknowable phantasm of objects and actions. The Hindus call it "Maya," the delusion of the material world, the dream to which we cling in desperation.

Everyday we build a tower of steps reaching towards the heavens, but each day the heavens appear further away. And it is our endless toil as builders, the blueprints and construction details, that blind us to the truth that is right before our eyes and buried within our own chests, yet which we look for somewhere out there.

One thing I perceive is that the universe echoes itself. All the phenomenon of reality can be reduced to a few simple patterns from which infinite complexity emerges; the golden mean, the sacred circle, the waves of the oceans, the angle, the slot and the rod. During my life I have been blessed to catch a glimpse behind the curtain just long enough to glean a few secrets. Yet I find that the more truth I behold, the more that I realize how little I know. Each pearl of wisdom only makes me understand my fundamental state of ignorance.

Plato tells of story of a sage who was teaching the young men of Athens. The students asked the sage, "Who is the wisest man in all of Greece?"

"Socrates," the sage replied.

The student ran to Socrates and told him what the sage had said. Socrates explained that he could not possibly be the wisest man in Greece because he didn't know anything at all, and he spent his life searching for answers. Socrates went to the sage and asked him why he made this false statement to the students. The sage explained to Socrates that most men think they have wisdom, but really know nothing. While Socrates may know nothing, since he doesn't believe that he knows anything, he is in fact wiser than all the others.

It is a story I keep close to my heart. As a younger man my desire to seek truth was a fire that burned with white heat. Today it is a cool blue flame that simmers beneath the skin and within the ribcage.

But at this moment, standing in the desert heat, I felt weak and alone, and even somewhat frightened by the mystery surrounding me. I long for the comfort of my own bed, or the warm embrace of a familiar lover. I begin to scan the four directions once again, searching for an answer to why a wave of anxiety has taken me.

As I turn to the west a gust of wind rises up and lashes my face with sand, like a bully challenging me to defy his superior power. My eyes are filled with dirt. "The Gods must be happy," I think. "They are having a bit of fun at my expense." Or perhaps it is just my comeuppance for having the audacity to attempt to peep through the keyhole into their secret world.

Blinking my eyes, which are being scratched by the sharp crystals of sand, I staggered back towards the car. My pace a little too-hurried, as if I suspect a pack of wolves might be lurking behind the next sand dune. The job of walking made harder because with each step the sand melts beneath my feet, pulling me into the soft embrace of Mother Earth. The harder I try to push myself, the further I sink into the dry sand.

I reach the car out of breath. Unsure of why I am on the verge of panic. To calm myself I sing the first song that comes into my head.

"Jesus, he's my friend," it is the bridge of a lousy song sung by the Doobie Brothers with white-boy soulfulness.

"He took me by the hand. Led me all across this land."

I sometimes sing this song at inopportune moments in order to annoy my friends.

"Jesus, oh yeah, he's my friend."

I start the car, and before pulling out onto the highway, I take one more look out onto the desert. As vivid as the material world is to the eyes, close our eyes and it seems all too willing to dissolve into static and white noise.

As I head onto the highway I press the 'play' button of the CD player and the last disc played begins to blare from the speakers. It is a minute or so into a Public Image Limited song called Fodderstomp. A stuttered electronic disco beat rolls repetitively, the song's disco authenticity undermined by a rubbery bass guitar line that can't quite find a melody. Atop the rhythm two singers whine with voices that sound like Mickey Mouse chewing off a limb that is caught in the teeth of a mousetrap.

"Only wanted to be loved. Only wanted to be loved," they whine.

"Love makes the world go 'round." The second voice answers sarcastically.

This song is from what might be considered the first post-punk album, and wasn't created to be an easy listen.

"Only wanted to be loved. We really, really need it, like all the mountains and the flowers and the trees," they continue.

There always seemed to be something empowering about mocking our most basic needs and insecurities. After my moment in the sand a healthy dose of cynicism is just what the doctor ordered.

"We only wanted to be accepted by society," they intone with mock sincerity.

'We only wanted to be looooovvvedd," the other screams as if falling over a cliff.

Within a day I should be standing on the beach of the Pacific Ocean and have achieved my stated goal. But in the back of my mind there is another goal, a goal that I can't quite admit to myself. When I hit that ocean the goal will be just within my grasp and demons of the past might be confronted and possibly released.

"Only wanted to be loved. I'm going to release my frustrations at society by spraying off that fire extinguisher, right over there," the singer continues. After a few seconds of silence a loud wooshing sound fills the speaker and the singers guffaw like schoolboys.

The song is a funny joke, but goes on far too long.

"Only wanted to be…" with a flick of the dial I cut them off mid-sentence. Again it is just the road, the desert, and my thoughts.

#10 - The Dreams They Allow Us To Dream

Hours passed on the empty highway. Occasionally a car passed by going the opposite direction, or a group of teenagers in a hot rod blew by me at suicide velocity. But overall this was a land that belonged to nature. The environs are so harsh that they are not worth exploiting. There was not a man-made object to be seen as far as the eye could see.

Man-made objects are full of sharp angles, parallel lines and bold geometric repetitions. Nature is soothing chaos, smooth random curves and irregular jagged edges. Manmade objects suggest order and lull the mind into unconsciously working to analyze and embrace a false sense of security.

The chaos and randomness of nature offers no sense of order and forces the mind to surrender. The curves of the sand massage the mind like a Japanese shiatsu, urging you to relax and expand your thoughts. Or urging confession to an unseen priest whose curtain is the Earth and skies.

It seems that much of my personality has been shaped by poverty. In America a man is judged by his material wealth. I have heard women in New York say they look at a man's shoes, if his shoes don't look expensive enough they don't bother to speak to him.

To be an artist in America is not an honorable profession. Of course if you've made a lot of money at it then it's respectable, otherwise it is a joke. The act of creation for its own sake has no value in modern culture. The artist is often advised to grow up and get serious about life. To take the left hand path, to devote your life to gaining spiritual wealth is to be seen as a pauper, if not a bit cuckoo to boot.

The house I was born in was a little cement block building in a tiny village called Alfarata. More often than not the house had no running water and my mother and sister would trudge out into the field to bring water back from an old metal hand pump.

My parents were peasants. Both were forced to drop out of high school during the eighth grade to help support their families during the great depression. When they married and had children they lived from paycheck to paycheck. They had neither the education nor foresight to escape their lot.

As a child I couldn't have cared less about my family's lower class status. The only time it bothered me was when my parents were upset by it. In those days the bill collectors would come right to the door and just about pound the thing off its hinges. Often we would hide until they left. I believe it was a ritual played out in working class homes across America in those days.

To me this all seemed a big game, but I could sense the sorrow it caused my mother, and my young mind eventually took on her sense of shame. My sister would have her friends drop her off a few blocks from our street because she was embarrassed by our ramshackle old house. I can recall many times when the TV, telephone, or electricity were shut off as utility bills piled up.

By my teen years these class issues became more important. In high school, class became apparent at first glance. Besides the obvious things like clothing, the rich kids walked and spoke with more confidence, and they had a sense of entitlement that seemed to magically pave their way through life. It was a confidence that we denizens of trailer parks and run-down row-houses sorely lacked.

This lack of confidence naturally created a social order. We on the lower levels automatically took our place at the back of the bus. We knew we were not winners in life's game, and we protected

ourselves by not reaching for the brass ring, and in fact, by mocking
the entire system in which others naturally succeeded and we
naturally failed.

Although I am no longer one who takes a seat at the back
of the bus, this outlook on life shades my approach to the world
even today. The system seems to me to be a rigged game, so I am
always looking for an outside angle, a novel approach with which to
beat that rigged game. If the herd is moving in one direction, I
assume there must be something wrong with that direction and go
in the opposite. I mistrust the masses at every turn. I instinctively
place myself as an outsider at odds with the status quo.

I suppose this outlook was enhanced by the fact that during
my childhood there was still a dying whiff of 1960's spirit in the air.
Although my parents were of another generation, somehow those
anti-establishment values seeped in from the media and from the
music my older sisters played on their stereos. These values lodged
themselves in my heart before I was old enough to develop a critical
mind. Or perhaps they just seemed logical to me, because certainly
the value system that embraced racism, conformity, blind
patriotism, and sexism were just as, if not more prevalent in society
than the ideals promoted by the hippies, but my child's instinct was
to reject the mainstream view in favor of a more progressive belief
system.

In the fifth grade an older neighbor girl gave my best friend
a fistful of old rock albums; Grand Funk Railroad, Black Sabbath,
Jimi Hendrix, The Rolling Stones. At that time my friend was
learning to play the bass guitar and I was learning to play the drums.

The music on those crickly slabs of wax were an elixir of
life which poisoned our souls to the world of the nuclear family, the
Protestant work ethic, and blind allegiance to authority. But it also
made our spirits swell with a sense of purpose, an alternative
system of values, and a belief that the man on the street could
change the world.

Suddenly, freaks that we may have been in our own
hometown, we were connected to something larger. We were
initiates into a cult that existed right under the noses of parents and
teachers, yet which they failed to see or understand. And even more,
they failed to understand that their sweet innocent children were

gone forever. We were little lost heathens who were likely cursed to be trampled underfoot by the realities of survival that we would soon encounter as adults. Many like us would find themselves never quite able to join the straight world, but completely unable to make it as an outsider.

The old rock and roll albums we listened to often carried a political message that resonated with me. It's hard to imagine today, but there was a time when rock and roll was taken seriously as an art form. The best of those artists were seen as spokespeople for their fans, and leaders for a generation of social revolutionaries. But oh how times have changed.

The political idealism of the music fit right in with the anger and frustration I felt because of poverty. Beyond my own poverty I saw injustice all around me. Most of the people I knew lived a hand-to-mouth existence. Unless they won the lottery there was little hope for a better life. And when people lack hope, problems of all sorts soon follow.

In my hometown there was a spirit of nihilism that permeated the culture and lead to drug and alcohol addictions, criminal behavior, self-destructive sexual practices, a high suicide rate, and random violence of all sorts.

As a young man and a struggling artist I vowed that I would never forget where I came from, and that I would try to find a way to create a better world for my hometown and the thousands of towns like it all across America. This is what underlies my drive towards political expression and social activism. As I look back on that vow, although I have never forgotten my roots, when it comes to affecting social or political change I must admit I am complete failure.

During my high school years my family's economic problems reached the level of high farce. By the eighth grade we were bouncing from house to house as fast as the back rent would pile up. I could always tell when things were getting bad because we would find ourselves dining on homemade potato soup. Often flavored only with stale bullion cubes or garlic powder.

At one point we lived in a double house and our electricity had been shut off. My father crawled over the attic wall and ran an extension cord from the neighbor's outlet so that we might have a few hours of electric light each evening.

When I graduated from high school, college wasn't even an option that could be considered. By then I was playing drums in a punk rock band called Friction and drinking and using drugs. One evening I was out partying and at night's end returned to the trailer that I lived in with my parents. The electricity was shut off again and my mother was asleep in a chair in the living room. She had lit a candle for a little light and it had melted onto the coffee table and then down onto the carpet on the floor.

I sat down on a chair on the other side of the room and watched her sleep. The sight filled me with deep despair. My father was out on the road trying to make a buck and she looked so lonely in that dark room. She could have easily burned the place down with the melted candle. I hated that she had to go through such things, but felt powerless to change the situation.

Not long after my eighteenth birthday I spent an evening tripping with my girlfriend Leilani. Many people say that using drugs such as LSD makes them lose touch with reality. I found that LSD often made me painfully aware of reality's harsh truths.

At the time I was living with my parents in a rented apartment. As always they were struggling financially. I remember being overtaken by an overwhelming sense of guilt for being a burden on them. I took what little money I had in my wallet and insisted that my mother put it towards one of their many outstanding bills. I was so distressed by my guilt that I stayed out all night so I wouldn't have to face them. Nine days later Leilani and I moved into our first apartment.

At the time Ronald Reagan's trickle-down economy was sinking fast. For nearly two years I could not find a job, regardless of how hard I searched, or how many potential employers I tried to impress with my enthusiasm. With no job I was quickly swallowed into a spiral of downward mobility. One of Reagan's first actions was to end welfare assistance for all able-bodied males.

There is one moment from that period in my life that has remained clear in my memory. I was in a local grocery store and I had five dollars with which to feed Leilani and I for four days. It was as I stood in front of the neatly stacked boxes of Kraft Macaroni and Cheese that my feelings of hopelessness and desperation transformed me.

I watched the happy shoppers piling their carts high, enjoying abundance that far exceeds any human need. Suddenly the entire structure of our civilization's moral codes began to fall into absurdity. My mind raced; "Every society, whether democratic or communist, is based on the ideal that each individual is part of the whole. It is expected by the whole that the individual will obey laws and follow social norms for the good of the whole. In exchange for this the individual will share in the bounty that the whole creates and enjoys. The problem is, if an individual has fallen out of the whole, and is excluded from the bounty that the whole enjoys, even to the point where not only the individual's dignity, but his entire existence is in peril, does the society still have the right to expect the individual to obey the laws that benefit the whole?"

In that moment a criminal was born. Although I was raised not to steal, and I had never stolen anything in my life, not even a candy bar from a convenience store, poverty had now reduced me to thievery. As a homeless man once said to me, "A man does what a man has to do in order to survive." My self-image would never be the same. A minute later I lifted a five-pound package of ground beef off the shelf and stuffed it into my pants.

On another occasion someone saw me committing the very same crime, a manager chased me out the door and ordered me to stop. He looked me over from about ten feet away. He must have seen the desperation on my face because he walked up to me and half-heartedly tapped my jacket pockets then whispered, "Just get out of here."

My girlfriend Leilani was a much better thief than me. She was cool as a cucumber. I think she must have been a criminal at heart.

One day my shoes were falling off my feet so we went to the Jamesway department store and Leilani slipped a pair of sneakers under her jacket. On the way out the door she met a friend and the two calmly chatted in the doorway of the store. The friend told her that she knew of a waitress job at a local truck stop. We drove right to the truck stop and they hired her on the spot. The only problem was that now she needed shoes to start work. So off we went. Right back to the Jamesway and stole a pair of work shoes for her.

When you are poor many people deride you for any meager help that the government might offer. And believe me if the government provides help, it *is* meager. In my frustration I reasoned that if these people's well paying jobs were reduced to four instead of five days a week there would be enough work for everyone and they would not have to worry about their tax dollars going to feed those who could not find work. But my 'pinko' suggestions would never be considered as a viable option by such kind-hearted Americans.

Those who oppose social welfare programs believe that every person should stand on their own two feet and earn their own way in life. It sounds good in theory, but in order for that theory to work there has to be opportunity. If there is no opportunity to do an honest day's work and earn a livable wage, and there is no social safety net, then a man *does* have to do what he has to do in order to survive. Every day of the week in America poverty makes beggars, prostitutes, and criminals out of honest men and women.

Poverty made me an insolent example of the proverbial "angry young man." Age may have tempered my disposition, but I hold fast to the memories of my struggles. I look to them to help me appreciate any blessing that life bestows. I look to them so I am never blind to the injustice that is an inextricable part of our world. Every nation in every age has had its forgotten poor. And while I condemn the rich for their lack of charity, I feel guilt because compared to so many in the world I live in unimaginable wealth.

During those days I recall sitting in the back seat of a car smoking dope with a group of my loser friends when the Sex Pistols punk anthem, "God Save The Queen," came on the stereo. Although it was a few years after the fact, the lyrics spoke to me.

"We're the flowers in the dustbin
We're the poison in the human machine
There's no future for you

There's no future for me"

"Yep, that's me, that's us," I thought. "No future."

At age 20 I wrote my first song to try to express the frustration and confusion I was feeling. It is called Dancing Now and was the title track of Friction's first E.P. In those days people thought punk rock might become a social/political movement like in the 60's, but when we played in clubs all that I saw was a bunch of kids drinking and partying. I found it hard to imagine that these people would ever be the base for a grass roots political movement.

We're angry now, but sedated still

We've been drugged, and too much time to kill

The media can always pacify

It's just another propaganda lie

Preaching the American way

Society has gone astray

Violence has filled the streets

Soon they'll be turning up the heat

*We're dancing now

But we could be shooting

We borrow now

Soon we may be looting

And it's so damned hard to appreciate

The things you've always had

Sit in your comfort so secure

Believe your future is so bright and pure

The way I feel these days you can't be sure

Anarchy may be outside your door

Say that it can't happen here
The USA has nothing to fear
Iran screams and the Irish burn
But narrow minds will never learn*

They will call the gunman mad
Talk about the wealth they had
There's revolution in minds and hearts
But chaos ends where frustration starts
If you're brave turn on the news
Or try to hide if you choose
But when your children start to turn
You may wish you'd been concerned*

After years of not being able to find a job a small miracle happened. Leilani and I bought a scratch off instant lottery ticket. It was called the "Baker's Double." When we scratched it off we won $5,000, and that was doubled to $10,000 thanks to another slot that contained an image of a loaf of bread.

Ten thousand dollars doesn't seem like much, but to me it could've been a million. I had never been around any money before this, so I didn't really have a clear idea of what it meant. Given my lack of experience with money I didn't do too badly with it.

I had never had a checking account or a credit card, so banking and interest rates were all a mystery to me. The problem you have when you're from the lower class is that you can't get access to credit. In order to build up a credit rating I put the money into a money market CD and borrowed against it. This way I still had the original money, but I was building a credit rating as I paid off the loan.

After I won the lottery money I bought a decent used car and was able to go to the next town and find a job at the Kentucky Fried Chicken. I believe I made $3.15 an hour, hardly a living wage.

In my lifetime I've spent more years wearing a paper hat and polyester uniform than I care to remember.

Around that time I made another investment that changed my fortunes. A dope-dealer friend convinced me to take an ounce of weed and sell nickel bags to my pothead buddies. By that time I had lost interest in using drugs myself, but it is amazing how much money you can make selling small amounts of pot.

Soon between the lottery money and the pot money I owned an eight-room house, a rental property, a fifty-per cent share in a recording studio, and a rather extravagant collection of Asian and African artwork.

During these years I studied art, music, performance, and film, as best I could in the backwoods of Pennsylvania. It was during this time that I developed the concept that would one day become The Imperial Orgy.

But at the same time my political and spiritual interests receded into the background. Being stuck in a small town makes one feel irrelevant. It seems egotistical to think one can affect the world.

At very least I tried to express my political frustrations through music and performance. Friction often had political lyrics and the group had a general anti-establishment attitude, but more often than not our words fell on deaf ears. People wanted cute pop stars singing loves songs and party anthems, not angry punks bitching about the state of the world.

I was the most radical of the band members, often taping photos of Ronald Reagan to my drum kit or draping half-burned flags over the bass drum. Overall though, I felt like we were running into a brick wall as far as using music to express political messages. In the age of MTV people no longer thought of rock music as anything more than nice non-challenging entertainment. The days when music was seen as a force for social change were long gone, drowned in the rising tide of conservatism that was sweeping the culture.

I generally had a sinking feeling about it all. Friction was having no success commercially within the music industry, and therefore we had no access to a wider audience to get our message heard. Behind the scenes the Reagan and first Bush administrations were rumored to be pressuring the record labels not to support artists who promoted social activism. Distraction and complacency were the dictates from above. The storyline was that the government felt threatened by the Live Aid concerts, if you can imagine that.

Meanwhile the more comfortable I got financially, the more lost I felt spiritually, politically, and artistically. Security and contentment are the artist's greatest enemy. There are always forces urging you to grow up, settle down, and conform. Just as it looked like I would follow that path and surrender, I took a sharp left hand turn and threw it all away.

Thanks to the pot money I was able to attend college at the Penn State University where I studied filmmaking. In the university film department I found a lot of support from the left-leaning faculty for my non-conventional film work, although behind my back the surprisingly conservative students whispered that I shouldn't be allowed to attend classes because of the raw images and ideas I confronted them with.

Although my reputation caused most of the students to avoid me, a few bolder sorts sought me out. Mhina Dada, a Jamaican fellow who would one day help found The Imperial Orgy, became my partner in film crimes that shook the little film department.

Another fellow named Donn Garton, the handsome son of a New Jersey preacher came to me after class one day and said, "I'll do anything, I'll get down on my knees, I just want to work with you."

Although we never managed to actually work together, I soon became his unspoken mentor as he struggled with coming of age issues of sexuality, religion, and politics.

My first project with Mhina was a short documentary on the issue of Flag Burning. For a bang-up ending we burned a flag in the middle of town and filmed the resulting chaos. As the flag burned two young marines ran out of nowhere and put it out, then proceeded to threaten to kill me. As the filmmaker I felt like I couldn't take sides, so I stood nonchalantly as the angry jarhead screamed into my face from two inches away, "Why don't you get out of MY country homeboy! The next time I see you burn one I'm gonna hunt you down and I'm gonna fucking kill you!"

Oddly a couple of brave hippies that I never met before suddenly ran up and one shouted, "I helped him burn it!"

Quickly an angry debate ensued that verged on the edge of violence. Each side expressed the traditional arguments on the issue, sometimes with hilarious clarity. I couldn't have written it better myself.

"The flag is a symbol. We need to protect the freedom, not the symbol," the hippie explained.

"Yeah, then you're a traitor. Do you know what traitors do? They get fucking killed, assassinated…by death!" the marine replied.

"Why is he a traitor for burning a piece of cloth?" the second hippie replied.

"Why don't you go try to say that shit in fuckin' Russia and see what happens? Why don't you go wipe your ass on some fucking toilet paper," was the marine's well-reasoned response.

Thinking I was well outside the camera's frame, I turned to Mhina, who was behind the camera and gave him a knowing nod and a broad smile, as if to say, "Look what we created!"

Little did I know that the camera was in a wide angle and my gesture was caught on the edge of the frame as the melee ensued in the foreground. To viewers it appeared as if I was looking right at them and inviting them in on a naughty joke. When the film was eventually viewed by film classes the students burst out laughing at my gesture. It perpetuated the image they held of me as an agitator who manipulated people to create havoc and disorder.

The irony of the project was that we got a zero grade on it. Most of the students were complaining that they had to spend four or five hours editing their documentaries. Mhina and I got the keys to the film building and locked ourselves in the deserted editing room for a week straight over the Christmas vacation.

When we asked the faculty to look at the film they said we were past deadline and would get a zero grade. The next semester we convinced the professors to show the film to the students just to share our work. As the film came to a close our professors stood up and left the room. Soon they returned and asked us to come with them. They took us to the next classroom and immediately screened the film there. Later the film was screened for the dean of the communications department.

I don't think it was really that the film was that great, as much as it was that we were working at a different level than the rest of the students. And although we got a zero grade on the project, tor years the film was used as a teaching tool by film theory professors at the university as an example of documentary filmmaking.

The Flag burning scene caused controversy among the students even before we filmed it. Senior level students were wisely counseling us that it was immoral for us to carry out our plan. They felt that we were crossing a line by creating an event that could lead to violence. I didn't give a fuck about their line. What I saw when it was over was that people were excited, they were thinking, they were talking about issues. I had achieved my goal as a filmmaker, let the timid tow the line.

During my college days my old life began to unravel. Friction came to an end without a bat of the eye, my relationship with Leilani came apart in an ugly feud, I lost my recording studio business thanks to some shady dealings by my business partner, I was chased out of town by corrupt elements in the police force and sheriff's department, and soon after I lost my home.

I lived through crisis after crisis, dazed by the events that had taken my life. When I look back I realize that I was at war with myself. My conscious mind fought to be loyal and true to the people and things of my past, but in my heart I felt that the past was a prison that limited my horizons. My unconscious mind led me kicking and screaming down a path of self-destruction. If I had been a little smarter I could have broken with my past with much less pain and financial loss, but I clung to the past even as I destroyed it.

Malcolm McClaren once said of the punk band the Sex Pistols, "Sometimes you have to destroy in order to create." I can testify that this is a cruel truth, a truth that I lived and experienced the horrifying results.

When it was all over I found myself living in a basement apartment near an airport by the Penn State University. Mhina and I were plotting a new documentary on the "Trail Of Tears." A horrible chapter in American history when the Cherokee people, after being repeatedly betrayed by the U.S. government, were forced to walk from North Carolina to a reservation in Oklahoma. Along the way a third of the population died. A few remnants hid in the mountains and later formed a new community hidden in a valley in North Carolina. These people are now known as the Eastern Tribe.

I am part Cherokee on my mother's side and I felt passionate about telling their story. In order to get permission to do the documentary we had to appear before the council of tribal elders to appeal our case.

On a cold December day Mhina and I began the drive to Cherokee, North Carolina to meet the elders. I was sick as a dog with a nasty cold and we only had a few bucks between the two of us. The air was freezing and snow littered the sides of the roads. For supper we found a convenience store that had large bags of popcorn for 59 cents, and we bought a box of week-old doughnuts. Most of our cash was spent on a cheap motel room that was discounted during the winter months when no tourists come to the reservation.

In the morning we split the last of the stale doughnuts and scarfed down the rest of the popcorn. By this time I was so sick and feverish that I could barely speak. I wrote out my presentation and told Mhina he would likely have to speak for me.

When the moment came we walked into the council room to find a tall desk like a judge sits at, except it made a long U shape around three sides of the room. The council elders sat around the table high above us. Mhina and I stood on the floor inside the U looking up at them. After a middle aged man gave the council an overview of why we were there he asked that a letter I had written many months before be read. A fragile old woman at the center of the table began to read the letter with a shaky voice.

I no longer recall exactly what I said in that letter. I know I spoke of having pride in my Cherokee ancestry, and of believing that film was a medium for social change. Listening to this elderly Native American woman read my words moved me nearly to tears.

The oration must have affected the others as well because as soon as she finished they took a quick vote and unanimously gave our film project the green light, then they came down to the floor and showered us with handshakes and warm embraces. I left feeling proud, although I'm not quite sure of exactly what I was feeling proud of.

Mhina and I got on the highway right away. We drove late into the freezing night. During the drive we fell into one of those soul-mining conversations that one sometimes shares with friends late in the night.

Although I was excited about the new film project, something was turning within me. As soon as I left college I landed a job as an audio editor at an industrial film company. I bypassed the intern process and went straight into a pretty good position. At the time I thought, "I made it, I'll never have to wear another paper hat and serve up greasy chicken again." Of course the company was only paying me $6.50 and hour, even though they sometimes charged clients $120 an hour for my services, but it was still more than I'd ever earned before.

When you work in the creative arts, you have to be careful about earning your pay in the same medium where you work as an artist. It can spoil your love of the art form. This was happening to me with film. My company sent me on shoots on endless boring subjects. I made films on pharmacies, on cancer treatments, college recruiting films, and on rehab clinics. I knew more than you'd ever want to know about potatoes, fertilizer, and hip replacements.

I was beginning to feel the need to return to the immediacy of live performance. There is nothing like looking your audience straight in the eye. To this end I spoke to Mhina about the concept that would soon become The Imperial Orgy. Mhina was learning to play the drums. A few days later we met with another film student, Michael Mordes, who played guitar and was obsessed with James Brown and Parliament Funkadelic. He was a perfect fit.

It was late December and by spring we were doing test runs as a four-piece band, by the next fall our little reign of musical terror had begun.

I thought my life as a fast food peasant had come to an end, but another hard lesson was on my heels. The world was changing. The Berlin wall had fallen and the Soviet Union disintegrated. As the first Bush administration came to an end the economy was sinking. Business at the film company dried up and I was out looking for work again. To my surprise there were no jobs. And I wasn't being snooty, I was filling out applications for furniture stores, factories, any damn thing that paid the bills. Eventually, when I was even turned down by McDonalds I knew I was in trouble.

By this time the rest of The Imperial Orgy had moved to New York City and soon I was homeless and living in the back of my car. By the time I got to New York my health was a wreck from months without proper food or sleep. It was November and I walked the cold city streets with resume in hand. One day I walked the West side in a cold rain. Although I had an umbrella, by day's end I was soaked from head to toe.

The next morning my shoes were still too soggy to wear so I borrowed a pair of black work shoes from Samantha that could have passed for men's. They were a few sizes too small so I had to walk all day with my toes curled up. It was another rainy day and by evening my toes had turned purple and red from the abuse.

After a few months of this nonsense I found some part time work in the office of a multimillion-dollar children's theatre company called TheatreworksUSA. We lived in Staten Island and to get to the job I had to take a bus, then the ferry, then a train. On the first day of work I didn't have a buck in my pocket, but I had one subway token to get on the train.

As I got off the ferry I held the subway token between my thumb and index finger. Just then someone bumped into me and the token flew out of my fingers and rolled off into the crowd. It was lost in the sea of feet that streamed past me.

I felt like God wanted to slap me down one more time. With no money for another token I had to call my new boss and explain the humiliating details of why I would be late my first day. I had to walk about thirty blocks to get to the job. During that walk I felt about as low as you can go.

At first it felt good to be in a 9-5 job, even if it was a poverty wage. Once your sense of self-worth has been trampled down for so long, you're proud to have the crumbs from the table, to even get near the table. This state of mind is a curse that turns many a young man yellow, makes them walk with their heads bowed down for a lifetime to come.

In time I bounced around from one shitty job to the next, but always seemed to land back at Theatreworks. I didn't stay grateful for the crumbs too long. I was too angry for that. I had seen, had lived with too much injustice.

After a couple years I began to get very angry at Theatreworks. Most of the people there made good pay and had good benefits. The boss in the office across from me was bringing in $200,000.00 a year. The place was a non-profit organization and the money for his salary was coming from public donations and government NEA funds, so it burned me up all the more. Other people in the place were making ninety, eighty, and sixty thousand a year. It was only the five or six peons in my department that got less the fifteen thousand a year and zero benefits. The lack of medical benefits was the thing that really pissed me off.

All the people in the place were snooty liberal types who saw themselves as always on the right side of every issue and morally superior to everyone else. But when it came to their own back yards they were just as greedy and heartless as the biggest fat cats.

I started bitching about it to the top dogs. They would twist themselves up like contortionists trying to find a way to justify their behavior. One of my favorites was that it was an honor to work there, a stepping-stone into the elite world of theater. I knew none of those people were trying to break into anything but a hot meal. One guy was a single father working two jobs to raise his kid.

As is usually the case in the corporate world, those who get paid the least, do the hardest work. Our job was to schedule field trips with teachers all across the country. Most days the phones were ringing off the hook until you wanted to go mad. I used to hear the things ringing in my sleep.

If you want to cure what's ailing our education system a good place to start is with the teachers. Many of them couldn't do basic math or speak coherent English. Lots of 'em were liars and thieves to boot. The worst ones were from the ghettos of Chicago and New York City.

Anyway, I kept stirring the pot until I had the whole group so riled up they were planning to walk off the job the next Monday if we didn't get a raise. I wrote a letter to the boss demanding a three dollar an hour raise and medical benefits. But the bosses were just smart enough to know how to play the suckers, just how to keep the rabble quiet.

Come Monday they took us all into an office and announced a fifty cent an hour raise. It was just enough to keep the mules in the harness, but not enough to make a damn bit of difference. As far as I was concerned they could have taken their fifty cents an hour and shoved it up their highbrow do-gooder asses.

But the others were happy as clams. I was the hero of the day for getting everyone a raise. But I wasn't buying it. This wasn't success, it was a sucker-pop with barely a lick of value in real terms. I quit soon after that and when the tech boom hit, I landed a job designing websites for a porn company. Then after that I went to the electronics company at ground zero.

Back on the highway in Nevada I snapped out of my reverie to find that I was grinding my teeth and my fingers were white from gripping the steering wheel. A hundred miles of desert had passed without my noticing. The world had faded away and I drove on autopilot.

I switched on the radio and scrolled through the dial. Judging from the number of stations I must have been getting close to civilization again. Scanning the dial was like viewing a mosaic of the world's troubles. The stock exchange was now open, but the president still had not spoken to the nation after 9/11. Reporters described lower Manhattan as a place where armed militiamen patrolled with machine guns in tow. I wondered just what kind of nightmare I would one day find when I returned to New York.

We lived in a new world. A dark new era. To be an activist had a different meaning now. To be anti-establishment would be a dangerous game. People like me usually believe in America as an ideal, and believe we can work to perfect that ideal, but now everyone would be focused on protecting America from outsiders who were clearly worse. My place in this world was not clear.

It reminded me of another political action I once carried out. One that would never be tolerated in this new era. It was a street theater piece called 'Our Daily Bread.'

I had bread in the back of my mind for years, ever since I read Salvador Dali's account of how he came to America with a loaf of bread strapped to his head.

For Our Daily Bread I rounded up a group of people from The Imperial Orgy circle and dressed them in peasant outfits. Everyone made a mask that had some kind of money theme to it. Isabelle, the Orgy's keyboard player talked the people at Wonder Bread into donating a hundred loaves of bread to use in the project. Then we went down to Wall Street and placed a loaf of bread every five feet along the sidewalk around the stock exchange. Attached to each loaf of bread was an advertisement from Satan offering to buy people's soul in exchange for materialistic prizes. The letter read:

Good evening ladies and gentlemen. I have an exciting new offer for you! An offer that's so very exciting that I know you cannot say no!!!

Now don't get frightened until you've heard the details of this fabulous new offer -I'm paying top prices! And if you act now, in exchange for your soul, just look at all the beautiful prizes you'll receive.

You'll get a new Hi-Fi stereo system! A clock radio! A 25-inch color television set!! An entire new wardrobe with all the latest fashions! A new Toyota minivan with a full tank of gas!!! (seats 8!), A shower massage with rotating head! A new credit card featuring the classic rock superstars 'Kiss'!, A VCR! A new high speed computer system! The complete Bon Jovi compact disc collection!!! A beautiful microwave oven with a spinning rotisserie! The Popeil Pocket Fisherman! Great Sex with beautiful partners of your choice!! Free movie tix! Night club adventures! Attractive friends! More sex!!! Instant popularity! More sex!!! Fun! Fun! Fun!!! Sex! Sex! Sex!

Plus if you act now! For a limited time you'll also receive - A pocket calculator, 20 Ginsu Knives, a personally autographed picture of Darius Rucker, A wireless telephone, Free phone sex, a pinball machine, 324 channels of cable TV, A snow white shit-zu named 'Koko,' plus Sex! Sex! Sex! and much, much, more...

And here's the best part! All you have to do is this - look in the help wanted ads, or hurry out to your local employment office, and get a 40-hour a week job in a factory or office. It must be work doing something that is totally meaningless to you. Preferably making money for a corporate fat cat.

Then with your paycheck, buy all the things listed above! Yes, it's as easy as that! Then after you've settled in, I'll come and take your soul. I'll do it slowly, bit by bit, so you'll never even notice it's gone. You'll be too busy to even care.

It's true that at times you might wonder if your life is passing before your eyes as the best part of your time and energy are sucked away for economic slavery. Perhaps, in quiet moments, your life might seem meaningless. But what the hey, it's a small price to pay for all the great stuff you'll receive from this generous offer. Besides, spirituality is a greatly overrated thing in my book. Absolutely passe! So just don't even think about it. You'll have a million mindless diversions to keep yourself from looking inward. Just enjoy your goodies and do your work with a vacant, obedient smile.

See you in hell.

The performance was great fun. At one point I looked around Wall Street and as far as the eye could see there were businessmen and women reading the letters with confused looks on their faces. Soon the cops came zooming in, bomb-sniffing dogs were brought in to inspect the bread for explosives, it was a regular circus. In a video of the event Samantha D. can be seen hugging the bomb-dog as he wagged his tail happily.

One man came up and yelled at me, "Pick this up, you can't leave bread on the streets!"

"Why not?" I asked.

He got a confused look on his face as if he'd never thought about it before, then he caught hold of himself and bellowed, "You just can't!"

The performance created an open debate on the streets with a bunch of passing students. By the time it was over we were taking pictures with European tourist in front of George Washington's statue, and even the cops seemed to be smiling and laughing.

In an ominous note, given the close proximity to the Trade Towers, a middle eastern man came up to me and passionately explained that you can't create change by doing art stunts, you have to use violence, guns and bombs to create change. I guess there is some pragmatic logic to what he said, but all through his speech I kept thinking, "There is a higher principle that he just doesn't get."

When we look back on history we see that Gandhi led his people to freedom without ever firing a shot, yet the Palestinians and the Israelis use violence and only dig themselves into a deeper and deeper hole.

That night we all went to celebrate at a club called Naked Lunch in honor of the book by William Burroughs. By chance they were filming a scene for one of the TV police dramas in front of the club. The club was playing an Imperial Orgy song over the sound system that happened to be written for a girl that was a casting director for the TV show.

The show's main actor, a large black man with a suave demeanor, came in and joined our group. Scanning the scene he said, "What is this? Andy Warhol holding court with his retinue?"

In that moment I think we all felt like we were alive and doing something. Even if it didn't amount to a hill of beans politically, at least we were out there expressing ourselves, making waves, waking people up for a moment.

To paraphrase Henry Miller, "We can never change the world until we change the hearts of men." And it is easier to move a mountain than change people's hearts and minds.

I created the Daily Bread performance because I was feeling numb and losing my own soul within the mechanical grind of the corporate world. Every day I seem to lose myself a little bit more. The mundane existence of day-to-day survival pulls me into a fog where I can only see myself as a regular working stiff.

But a working stiff has limited horizons, limited abilities. In order to achieve anything extraordinary, to affect any real change in the world or in my own life, I must see myself as something more, as someone capable of more. And for this reason I find myself wandering across the United States, through deserts and between cornfields, across prairies and through forests, just trying to taste a little freedom and clear that fog from my head.

Sometimes when I feel lost I watch videos of my past work or read things people have written about me. I view my reflection as a stranger. "Who is this person?" I wonder. How could I ever inhabit this myth? So many extraordinary things have happened to me. So many times I have led friends and fans into lovely flights of madness.

Looking at my image reflected back at me I shake inside. Perhaps like the Incredible Hulk in his moment of transformation into monster. Or like a voodoo priestess when the spirits capture her soul.

I know the things I see and read are true, I can vaguely recall living them, yet they are alien to me. I try to find this being hidden in the soul of the commonest of common men. Over the years I have had a pretty rough go of it from time to time. But I've also been handed some gifts without ever having asked for them, handed to me gratis by an unknown force.

The truth is that every day I feel like a failure. A failure for not having used those gifts to their fullest potential. Every time I plop down in front of the idiot box to watch some prime-time drama, I feel like I have betrayed whatever force imbued me with potential.

So many times in my life people have handed over their lives to me. Whether for the length of a pop song or for years on end, they put their destinies in my hands, dreamed my dreams, and saw the world through the visions I painted. How can I feel any way other than that I failed each and every one of them?

I grew up believing that art and music would be my voice, my medium to communicate. But these days the corporations control everything, all that is spoken and all that is heard. The last thing they want is a piper calling their obedient children to awaken from the dream they have so laboriously created, and so painstakingly perpetuated.

Because in the end, the greatest work of art is the illusion that this is the way life is, and the only way it could ever be. This myth of materialism and drudgery, this nightmare of obedient automatons, and this dance of soulless livestock whose only dreams are of new electronic gadgets, flashy cars, and empty mansions, this swarm of humanity that only dares to dream the dreams that they allow us to dream.

But I can't help believing there is something more. I have glimpsed it on a few occasions. I have seen it reflected in a young woman's eyes, heard it in music of bygone days, seen the echoes of disappointment of that promise in the faces of junkies and alcoholics, felt the frustrations of that promise in bar fights and war cries, in crimes of passions and suicide notes.

But this something more alludes us with such perfection that few dare even speak of it, few dare to even admit its possibility, even in their secret thoughts, because compared with this dream the reality of life is too heartbreaking to face.

#11 – Love, After The Fall

The next morning I awoke and got back on the road. The desert finally began to give way to green. After about an hour I pulled over by a riverbank and stripped down naked.

One pleasant surprise I have found on my trip is that there are decent showers available at truck stops all across the country. Usually for five or six bucks you can get a hot shower and most are surprisingly clean.

During the desert drive there were no truck stops and no travel centers. My body felt grimy with highway dust and with the sweat of my troubled thoughts. I used a paper cup from McDonalds and dipped it into the stream and poured the cool water over my head and back. The cold water was a revitalizing shock to my body that was warm in the hot sun.

By the end of the day I would be in San Francisco. It was a long journey, the joy of it undercut by the shock of 9/11. But I didn't feel road-weary. I felt strong. I could have kept on going for months to come if time and money would have allowed it.

I stood naked on the riverbank washing my body with a bar of Dove soap and a blue washcloth. The highway was just behind me. A little too close for comfort really, but beggars can't be choosers. A few yards away a yellow steamroller sat nestled among the trees. This little sanctuary was already threatened by the proximity of concrete and combustion engines, perhaps soon they would be plowing the whole place under.

It's funny how boys are attracted to construction equipment. I never quite got it, although I suppose it might be cool to drive that big thing and maybe run over a few things for fun. Maybe flatten over all of America and make a fresh start of it? When David Letterman's show was young and irreverent he used to run over stuff with a steamroller; six packs of beer, TVs, packs of hot dogs… It seemed hilarious at the time, but perhaps it is the kind of humor that only guys find funny. Like the Three Stooges poking each other in the eye.

Despite my tales of struggle and woe, humor has always been a big part of my life. I think my childhood was a golden era for comedy. Richard Pryor could make you angry, laugh and cry, and in the end leave you enlightened and hopeful. He spoke of racism and poverty, yet brought people together in the process.

George Carlin was brilliant in his prime. These comedians seemed to be reaching for something more than just delivering one-liners. They were philosophers and social commentators who helped bring self-awareness to a society struggling with change and upheaval.

In its early days Saturday Night Live seemed revolutionary. It was a national catharsis that spoke the unspeakable. They were really letting the cat out of the bag. Every one of the original cast members seemed to have a major chip on their shoulders. The truth they expressed with their humor, as often as not, made you want to holler out "Amen" and "Halleluiah." They wielded comedy like an axe, cutting away at hypocrisy, commercialism, and rampant materialism. On that show the drug culture walked right out of the closet and the moral majority just about had a hemorrhage.

I suppose my love of absurdist comedy comes from my father who had a surreal sense of humor. He was like an Andy Kauffman-type performance artist. Usually his own goofiness was the butt of his jokes. Although at times there was an edge to it that kept you guessing.

When I was a little kid I used to ride with him in his tractor-trailer truck. The cabs of the trucks are high in the air. When I would go to jump out he would tell me, "Now remember Caeser never trust anyone, not even your father. Now go ahead and jump, I'll catch you."

Everything he said, you had to think twice about it. You always had to stay sharp or he'd suck you into one of his farces.

At a young teenager I used to travel with him as he shuttled overweight loads of steel between Pittsburgh and Philly. Hanging out with the truckers was an experience like no other. Once I went bowling with a bunch of them just outside Philly. These guys were a hurricane of beer-swilling bad behavior. First they got the lightest bowling balls they could find, then they hurled them through the air like baseballs, usually landing on top of the pins from above instead of rolling down the lane. Often the pins would explode with such force that they would land four lanes over and the attendant would have to come and clear the lanes by hand.

Their loud mouths and foul language must have terrorized the other patrons. The truckers seemed completely oblivious to their own behavior. They acted like a bunch of schoolboys run-amuck.

Their practical jokes were over-the-top and borderline dangerous. When they left the bowling alley they quickly began dismantling each other's trucks. Pulling the pins of their trailers so that when they drove away the trailers were left behind, or taking off the tall silver smokestacks and hiding them in a nearby dumpster. It was total bedlam.

That night I sat in the cab as my father slept. The trucks were lined up in a row by a dirty truck terminal. All night long prostitutes with puffy blonde afros, blue foil hot pants, silver halter tops, and high platform shoes prowled among the trucks. As a thirteen year old virgin the sight of them about made me explode they looked so lecherously enticing.

The next morning a small explosive device was thrown in the passenger window and greeted us with a deafening bang. It seemed the truckers also liked to play with fireworks. But no Chinese firecrackers for these boys, they hurled quarter sticks of dynamite at each other.

The fireworks were illegal in Pennsylvania, but the truckers would buy them on trips down south where anything that goes bang is protected by the law. I took this opportunity to start a side business selling the smaller firecrackers to my school chums. The demand was amazing. I had an eighty per cent profit margin and couldn't stay stocked with enough product to meet the customer demand.

At one point nine of my classmates got suspended for the things in one day. Although they ratted me out like a flock of canaries, because my little business transactions commenced outside of school property they couldn't suspend me.

The school principal called my father in hopes of discussing the matter with a concerned parent. When the phone rang, as a joke my father picked it up and answered, "Maggie's Whore House."

When he heard the principal on the phone he hemmed and hawed and explained that he was expecting a call from a friend. He assured the principle that he would curtail my business practices and hung up the phone. My mother laughed and said, "Well, maybe ya learned a lesson, didn't ya?"

"Yes Dad, what if it would have been one of my friend's calling?" my older sister reprimanded.

I think my father was secretly proud of my go-getter entrepreneurial spirit, but at my mother's insistence my fireworks supply soon dried up.

When he got older the truck driving wore him down. He was always in and out of jobs. Sometimes he would be off work for months. During these times he would sleep on the couch for days at a time. Looking back I wonder if he suffered from depression. A subject people didn't talk about much in those days.

By the time I was a teenager he was swallowing handfuls of amphetamine so he could drive all week without sleeping. He would eat twenty or thirty pills at one time. That amount would kill most people. He would go from doctor to doctor asking for 'diet pills,' in order to get the things.

Then after driving all week without sleep he would drink all weekend so he could knock himself out. Sometimes he would go so long without sleep that he would fall asleep in restaurants. More than once my mother had to pull his face out of a plate of food after a crash landing into some mashed potatoes and gravy. The combination of uppers and downers made him a little crazy. He was never physically abusive, but he could sure make a lot of noise. It seemed like he would yell for days on end. Often he said things that were completely ridiculous.

"Goddamit, Louise I haven't eaten in three days! Can't a man get a fuckin' thing to eat around here?"

My poor mother would reply, "I just made you breakfast an hour ago."

His bellowing was enough to make life miserable. As a teen I swore I would never be like him when I grew up. After he died my sister told me a story that my mother told her. Apparently my grandfather (whom I never met) was very mean and physically violent. When my oldest sister was born my father was afraid to hold the baby because he feared that he would be like his father and hurt the child. Finally my mother placed the baby in his arms to force him to face his fears. Because of my grandfather's violence my father swore he would never hit his own children, and he never did.

I look at this as a project of decreasing generational violence. My father never said much to me about his own father, but he did mention that one day on a hunting trip he shot his and his brother's dogs, just for fun. He also once told me that his father took the family cat and hurled it against the wall.

When I was small one of my first memories is of my father telling me that one of the worst things you could do was hurt an animal. I never put the pieces together until after he died.

After years of taking pills ('Bennies' as the truckers called them) and not sleeping, it began to get the best of him. For awhile his life got tangled up in the teamster's union and all its craziness. He took part in many of their strikes and protests. One method of protest they employed was to stand on the highway and force trucks to stop who were not supporting the strike. It was a nutty business. The one thing that was illegal was to stop a U.S. Mail truck. Of course, dear ole' dad had to be the hotshot to walk out onto the middle of the road on a dark night and stop a mail truck. An act that landed him in the pokey for a night.

Later, after endless strikes he found himself on the other side, by driving during a strike. On one occasion he came home with his front windshield broken. It turned out that a striker had dropped a cement block off an overpass onto his truck.

Around the time that Hoffa disappeared things got increasingly dangerous. The terminal of the trucking company he worked for was blown to the ground when someone placed a bomb inside.

At another time he told me that the same company had a side business selling 'wacky-weed,' as he called it. It seems they were growing their own pot in a field outside of Pittsburgh. They got word that they were going to be busted the next morning so they got their people to plow up all the pot fields before morning came. When the feds arrived there was nothing to be found.

Near the end of his trucking days he came down with a bad case of pneumonia, but kept driving without sleep until he became delirious and began hallucinating. Between the unions involved with organized crimes, the companies involved with criminal activities, and the Feds trying to bring them down, rumors of undercover agents were rampant. In his delirium he became so paranoid that he began to hallucinate people looking in the windows of our house. In this state he was ready to go out on another road trip until my mother finally put her foot down and took him to the hospital.

Eventually he got completely entangled in the web of confusion created by the unions, organized crime, the government, and the trucking companies. When his trucking company wanted to fire some longtime employees they gave him two separate places he had to be at the same time. When he was only at one they fired him. The union took the case to court, but the judge refused to let his lawyer provide any evidence in his defense and the case was lost. He claimed the judge had been paid off. That pretty much ended his trucking career.

After he quit trucking he was still addicted to the amphetamines. Later the drugs brought on a new obsession. He became convinced that there were splinters or pieces of metal in his hands. He would stay up all night picking at his hands with a needle until they were raw and bloody when the morning light came. When he finally got his hands X-rayed it turned out there were calcium deposits in his hands, but there was nothing the doctors could do about it. After that, he seemed to forget the whole thing.

Years later he and my mother were having severe financial problems and they had to move in with my girlfriend Leilani and I in our house in the woods. It must have been horrible for them. I am sure they didn't feel at home there. My father must have felt like a failure for not being able to stand on his own.

My father was an alcoholic most of his life. Usually his drink of choice was Iron City Beer. On the rare occasions when he drank hard liquor he completely lost it. One autumn day during that period a couple of his younger trucking buddies took him out and got him drunk on whiskey. Then they gave him a double barrel shotgun and tried to get him to shoot the owner of a trucking company they had it in for. Luckily he didn't follow through on that plan.

When he didn't return home for hours I went looking for him. I found him sitting in the woods with the end of the shotgun in his mouth. I begged him not to do it and he collapsed into the leaves sobbing, "I don't want to live anymore, I don't want to live anymore." After that he finally stopped taking the pills and mellowed out a bit.

Despite all the negative stories I relate, when he died none of his children held any anger towards him. Whatever demons he wrestled with, you could see the struggle was a war he was waging within himself.

Both of my parent's were depression era children and seemed unprepared to deal with the changing world we live in. They did the best they could in a world they didn't understand. Both gave everything they had to their kids. We had a strong sense of family, we always knew we had their support and had a home to go to. We always felt loved.

When it was all said and done it was his childlike and playful side everyone remembered. He knew everyone in town and always had a joke on his tongue. He was outgoing to embarrassing extents. In a restaurant he could always be heard teasing the waitresses and yelling across the room to people he knew.

One of his favorite gags was to choose a bad joke and tell it again and again for years on end. Often two or three times a day to the same person. He wore you down until you laughed at the absurdity of his behavior.

A favorite prank was to wait until my mother was doing the dishes and then yell at her, "Louise, I told you to do those dishes! Now get out here and do them right now."

She would respond, "Are you blind? I'm standing right here doing them."

Then he would turn to me with a surprised look on his face as if to say, "Can you believe she fell for that?"

If I ate with him in a restaurant with a group of people he liked to offer his used tea bag to me and say, "Caeser do you want this? You still collect these don't you?"

I got news that my father had cancer on one of the most important days of my life career-wise. He tried a few chemo sessions, but it didn't seem to help so he decided to just accept his fate. He lasted about four months. He didn't want to die in the hospital. Luckily my sister and aunt are both nurses and stayed with him during his final weeks.

My sister related that the cancer caused gastric problems for him. In the last days he went into a mild coma. She said he came out of the coma long enough to utter his last words after smelling his own flatulence. "Who shit?" he asked incredulously, then fell back into the coma.

In the moments before he died he sat up and held his arms out towards the ceiling and moved his hands as if reaching for something.

He had prepared everything for his funeral and burial. A few years before he had purchased life insurance from a television ad aimed at elderly people. Unfortunately when it came time to pay out the benefits it turned out to be a rip-off. This meant there was no money for the funeral expenses and he had to be cremated instead of buried. It seemed an all-too-fitting postscript on a working class life....

When I finally reached California I crossed the border on a highway that seemed to be suspended high in the air. To my right was a steep cliff from which tall pine trees shot into the air. The highway seemed to float among the tops of the trees. The scenery was majestic. Deep green covered the landscape and the sun was warm and bright.

Ten or twenty miles into the state I got off the highway to have lunch in a little college town whose name I have forgotten. It was very clean and immaculately groomed as rich college campuses are apt to be. Lots of walkways lined with green hedges and tall shade trees. I walked around the town looking for a friendly place to eat. The houses had an old fashioned quality about them. Potted plants hung from wooden porch trellises and country-charm decorations adorned the railings and doorways.

I settled on a bohemian looking café with outdoor tables. It had been quite awhile since I had any human contact and was feeling rather lonely, hungry for some stimulating conversation. The students came and went enveloped in their own worlds. This clearly wasn't a place for a stranger to make new friends. After forcing down half of a bland sandwich I got back on the highway.

Driving with one hand I scrolled through the phone book in my cell phone, searching for someone to call. Thanks to long lonely highways and the magic of cell phones I found myself reconnecting with friends I hadn't spoke to years. This time I chose my old buddy Spig.

"Hallow?" he answered the phone as if asking a question.

"Spig, what's happening?" I asked.

"Caeser? Aaahhhll, not too much. Are you in town?"

Spig spoke with a bemused drawl. Most people took it for the sound of a depressed man, but I recognized it as carrying a tinge of sarcastic humor. He way a guy who always perceived life's absurdities even as he labored under them.

"Oh, I've been getting some overtime in. One day they say they might be closin' down the plant, the next we have to work weekends to catch up," he explained when asked about his days.

Spig worked at the old steel mill that my hometown was founded upon. The town grew from a bunch of row houses the factory built in order to entice workers to the area. Spig had a wife and a kid or two, and built a house in a lot beside his parent's home.

"What do you do for fun these days?" I inquired.

"I really don't get out too much," he explained a bit woefully, "ahh, Y'know with the babysitters and all. I go fishin' every now and then, and went huntin' a few times."

I was searching for away to pierce the façade of his humdrum existence and tap into the more rebellious spirit that I knew was hidden there, but all my jousts failed to connect.

"When I came through town I noticed that they are trying to reopen the old Embassy Theater," I put forth, "Remember that time we snuck all those Malt Ducks into that horror movie and caused a ruckus?"

"Oh yeah, I remember that," he repeated with a little more energy. "You stood up and yelled 'what the fuck is wrong with you people watchin' this shit! You disgust me,' then we ran out the fire exit," he laughed.

"I won't admit to anything," I countered with a laugh.

His tone again sinking, he asked with a sigh, "What was wrong with us, doing that stuff? Do you know?"

"I think we were just alive," I offer.

This seems to hit a little too close to the bone. "Ah yeaaaah," he responded with a long drawn out sigh.

Spig and I became friends in high school when we sat near each other in a history class. Just after I met him he got suspended for making a bomb threat to the school. Soon afterwards he smoked some pot that was laced with something nasty and had a nervous breakdown and refused to come to school for many months. He later told me he was walking down the hall in school and began to hallucinate. He said felt it like he was walking on the moon and each step seemed like a giant bounce. After that he was stricken with debilitating anxiety attacks.

In time we became cohorts in bad classroom behavior. I don't think anyone was doing much learning in that place anyway, but we sure didn't make it any easier. And if you're going to be a class clown it's always good to have someone to play off of.

After high school we became drinking buddies. We would hang out in front of a beer joint and wait for someone over twenty-one who would buy us a few six packs of Genesee beer. Then we would spend the evening driving around getting drunk and blaring the tape deck at maximum volume. We would cruise the dark streets of our nowhere town looking for excitement, wishing we knew how to meet girls.

Spig had a penchant for getting his hands slapped by the authorities. Once while we were driving drunk a cop pulled us over on a dark country road. Spig threw a can of beer out the passenger window in hopes of avoiding an underage drinking charge. When the cop came to my window, even though I was driving and obviously wasted, Spig got a $300 fine for littering and I got off scot-free.

On another occasion we were drunk and walking down the street when we passed a 'no parking' sign that some other vandal had bent into a U shape. For no apparent reason Spig decided to straighten the sign. It was a rare good deed on his part. But as soon as he put his hands on the sign we heard sirens.

"Mr. Spigelmeyer, why do you feel the need to destroy public property?" the officer asked.

He protested that he was fixing the sign, not destroying it, but they weren't buying his story. The more he talked the deeper he got into it with them. I couldn't stop laughing the whole thing was so ironic.

When my punk band Friction formed, Spig became our court jester. He would follow the group and entertain us with his antics. These were the days when Quaaludes were the drug of choice and Spig would eat a couple of them and then invent crazy new dances. While the band played he would be found at the edge of the stage doing spastic jerks and jumps with a comically blitzed look in his eyes.

During those days Spig and I worked at a government run tree nursery hidden high in the mountains up in Amish country. On any given morning we would start the day by grinding a couple horse-pill sized Quaaludes into a chunky powder and then shoot it up our noses with a cocaine bullet. (A pocket-sized contraption that blasts powder into your nose.)

The shit made you an instant moron. If you could stay on your feet it was a minor miracle. Of course the brain trusts that we were, in this state we would arrive at work and climb tall rickety old ladders to paint the government buildings and garages. That we survived is a mystery that defies logic.

Except for one gay party-boy named Joe Slemons, and a violent drug addict named Randy Himes, our co-workers at the nursery were mountain Mennonites and hillbilly rednecks. Spig and I had a habit of saying surreal things to freak out the crew. The first day that we worked with Randy Himes I casually remarked, "Man, I shouldn't have eaten those last three hits of acid. I'm gettin' the heeby-jeebies."

It was total nonsense, I hadn't eaten any acid, and the implied four hits seemed like suicide to me. To my surprise Himes replied, "Do you have some? I ate three hits, but I could do another!" And he wasn't joking.

It's hard to imagine that a guy would do acid on his first day on the job, but three hits really *was* crazy. But Himes was a crazy guy all around. He was way-too into violent action films and often came to work with a tall tale of the previous night's adventures.

"Ooh man, last night I was walking along route 522 and these four big guys pulled over and came after me. I pulled a reflector post out of the ground and took them all on fuckin' ninja style. I split this one guy's head wide open."

Himes was usually good-natured with us, but on one occasion he took off his shirt to impress us with his manly physique. Spig responded by plucking one his chest hairs. Suddenly Himes got a look in his eyes that spoke of murder. He made it clear the affront was no laughing matter. It was a Jekyll and Hyde switch that left me warning friends that one day he would actually kill someone.

One morning he told us that the night before he had went to a gas station with a ski mask and a hunting knife. His story was hilariously absurd and I assumed it was just one of his tall-tales. It sounded like something from "The World's Stupidest Criminals."

"I took the gas-station guy into the office," he said with his head tilted in frustration. "Then I showed him the knife and told him to open the safe. He was dickin' around with the safe and a fuckin' car pulls up at the pump! Damn, I'm standing there with a knife and a ski mask... I told him to go pump the gas and not say a word or I would kill him. So he pumps the gas and comes back and starts fuckin' around with the safe again and another fuckin' car pulls up! I tell him again, 'go pump the gas but don't say a word or I'll stab ya.' So he pumps the gas and come back and starts messin' with the safe and another fuckin' car pulls up! I finally just left without the money, fuck it, what a bunch of fuckin' shit," his voice trailed off with disgust.

It was such a nutty story that I didn't think anything more about it, but about a week later the cops came and took him away. They should have locked him up for good because a few years later my murder prophecy came true. First he threatened his parents with an axe, then set the house on fire. When the firemen came he shot and killed one of the firemen and wounded another. When the police came he shot and wounded one of them. The last time I saw him he was in shackles being led from the courthouse to the county lock-up. He now resides in the state pen and should be there for a long time to come.

The boss of the tree nursery was a crusty old Marine that carried himself like a peg-legged pirate. One day he came into the room, stopped in his tracks, and took a long look at Joe Slemons the gay party-boy. Spying his earring he came up and placed his rugged face a few inches from Slemon's doughy cheeks and yelled, "You fuckin' faggot! You see that? You fuckin' queer."

He pointed to a shredded ear that looked like a piece of chewed-up beef jerky. "I used to have one of those and it got torn out of my ear by some motherfucker."

Turning away he said with a cold laugh, "I got you pegged you fuckin' queer."

The workers were a ratty collection of hicks if ever I saw one. There was a big bloated Mennonite kid who used to brag about harassing his Amish kin. His favorite hobby was to drive up behind their buggies and push his car bumper against the buggy wheel. It must have been a frightening form of harassment for the Amish folks. At least once a year some hot-rod white-boy plowed down one of their buggies on a dark country road.

Spig and I used to egg the bastards on, just to see what kind of racist rednecks our co-workers really were. We'd usually start by making a racist statement then waiting until they felt comfortable enough that they were among likeminded-company to show their true colors. Then once we got them riled up and revealing what a band of bigots they really were, we would take it further and further until our statements were so mind bogglingly idiotic that it began to dawn on the dimwits that either we were completely out of our skulls, or were playing them for fools the whole time. Needless to say we weren't making a lot of friends among our country cousins.

Among our co-workers was a crippled Mennonite named Rob. I'm not sure what happened to him, but his spine was bent up and his feet pointed in such cockeyed directions it was a wonder that he could walk at all. When he spoke, his speech was a jumbled slur.

He didn't say much anyways, but he worked harder than anyone. No laughing or joking around, down to business all the way. I think he was the only honest one of out of the entire bunch, bosses and workers alike, present company included. I always respected the guy because no matter how absurd the situation became he tried to keep his faith in an honest day's work. And I'm sure that wasn't easy given that the entire job was a bit of a farce.

The state gave us the jobs to "provide a positive work experience." The problem with the thing was that the nursery no longer planted trees, and therefore there was no actual work to be done. Our bosses would scrounge up any menial tasks they could dream up, then come up with the most ass-backwards way to do it, so that it took as long as possible and kept us busy. Because of this no one took the job seriously. Except Rob, who refused to admit that the whole thing was a farce and no one really cared about a job well done.

Finally, near the end of it all, after a weekend of rain a large mud puddle formed in the lower side of one of the fields. Our task for the day was to remove the water from the field. To achieve this goal they gave us a couple of shallow shovels and a handful of garden rakes. Now in the unlikely event you've ever tried to move water with a garden rake, you would quickly learn that it just ain't gonna happen. It don't work!

The group spent the day in the hot sun half-heartedly shoveling and raking the water. Through it all we bitched and moaned while Rob went about his work as earnestly as ever. Then about two in the afternoon something seemed to snap. Rob's belief in truth, justice, and the American way seemed to crumble. He threw down his rake and ran into the middle of the mud puddle and began to jump up and down, splashing in the muddy water while flapping his arms like a trained seal and braying "Fuaaackkkk, fuuuaaackkk!"

At first the rest of us stood shocked and a bit stupefied, but soon we broke into applause and cheers. After a few moments he picked up his rake and quietly returned to his Sisyphean task as if nothing had happened.

It was funny as hell to see him finally admit that he saw the absurdity of it all, even if it was just for a few sweet moments. Afterwards he never spoke of his moment of doubt again, but from then on we always felt he secretly understood our cynical point of view. He also warmed up to us just a little bit. I think he knew that although Spig and I were a different breed, even while we harassed the others, we accorded him a little bit of unspoken respect.

The tree nursery job was seasonal and not long after Spig married a local girl named Debbie who had pretensions of becoming a rich sophisticate, and Spig and I soon began to drift apart. Quite a few years later he went home one day to find that his wife had unexpectedly left and taken the furniture with her. She left a few words on a scrap of paper and left to start a new life. It appears she felt that even though Spig always held down a steady job, that he wasn't motivated to strive for great wealth. I've heard she is now an alcoholic call-girl living in a run down apartment in Harrisburg.

By chance, at the same time I was ending my long relationship with Leilani. It seemed such an odd turn of fate that the women who came between our friendship would both disappear at the same time. It seemed destiny had paved the way for two old friends to re-unite. For a few short weeks Spig and I spent our weekend nights as bachelors prowling the local dives, looking for girls and having bizarre adventures with the oddball yokels we would meet.

Debbie had been the purpose of Spig's entire existence and the breakup had wrecked his confidence. He decided that the cure for his depression was to pick up a couple of local sluts for a night of meaningless sex.

To this end we found ourselves at a local dive we called "The stab and shoot" because of all the violence that took place there. It was going on 2AM, which is closing time for bars in Pennsylvania. It was the time I called the desperation hour. And Spig, like all the others singles who were hoping to avoid spending the night alone were desperately seeking a willing accomplice. I was sitting on a bar stool trying to keep my vision singular after all the vodka I had swilled down over the course of the evening. Spig stood beside me with his back leaning against the bar allowing him to survey the room looking for a likely prospect.

Eyeing a pretty girl across the way he asked, "Do you know Moose?" with a tone of lecherous despair as he drew on his Marlborough.

"Yeah, we were close friends when we were kids," I responded.

"Man, look at her. I'd love to bang that!"

Before I knew it he had taken off in the direction she was walking and soon returned with her by his side. To my surprise he returned to his place against the bar and Karen, as I knew her, wedged herself between my legs and kissed me in a manner that was at minimum more than friendly.

"Spig said you wanted to talk to me," she whispered in my ear.

I was feeling a bit disoriented by the drink, and the desperation was now so thick you could smell it in the air. The alcohol soaked scene cracked with frantic energy as normal reserve and social etiquette was thrown to the wind as the sad and lonely searched for any offer of intimacy that might stave off another night of loneliness. Loneliness made worse by the emotional feelings brought to the surface by a night's worth of drinking.

"I just came from my high school reunion. Do you like my dress?" She twirled in a circle causing the thin lavender material at the hem of her dress to float high above her lovely white thighs causing me to reconsider my disinterest in a one-night stand.

With the sharp wit of a drunk I responded by moaning, "Wow…wow."

Again sliding between my knees and grabbing my hands with a gentle touch she looked into my eyes and purred, "I still love you."

"I think about the past a lot Karen," I said, referring to our childhood friendship.

"How's Lani," she asked

"Oh, we split up. She's in Hawaii with her parents."

"She's so beautiful, you'll work it out," she assured me.

After another deep kiss she held her face an inch from mine and asked, "Caeser do you know where I can get any white?"

She did look beautiful, but now with a moment to inspect her face I could see the signs of the fast life she had lived.

"Y'know Caeser I've been fucking judge Searer for three years now and he protects me. We could both make some money."

I tried to stare into her eyes and ignore the dark lines her makeup couldn't quite conceal.

Running her hand up the inside thigh of my jeans she held her cheek against mine and got to the point, "Listen you can get something I want, and I think I have something you want."

Candy the bartender began flashing the lights on and off to signal last call.

"I don't know Karen, I'm not involved in that stuff anymore," I explained

"Can I at least call you," she asked.

"Yeah…yeah, you can call," I stammered.

Suddenly she turned and signaled a man who was sitting at a nearby table.

"Do you know my boyfriend Eric?"

He walked towards us with his face aimed at the ground as if used to such humiliations.

"Eric, this is Caeser, when we were kids he was my sidekick."

He shook my hand begrudgingly. Then looking to her he said, "I'm going home. You can come if you want."

"I've got the keys," she called to home sweetly. Turning to me she squeezed my hand one last time, "I'll call you, OK buddy."

As she walked off Spig leaned over and said, "Man she looks hot. Why didn't you get her to stay?"

Before I could reply another drunk and boisterous old friend joined us. Ron Boi had recently taken on the lifestyle of a biker gang member, which included no bathing, no working, and wearing a leather jacket, chaps, and long stringy hair.

The bar was now officially closed and only a few stragglers remained.

"What's the story with them?" Spig directed Ron's attention towards a trio of young women who sat at a table nearby.

"Aaah those bitches! You wanna party with them, man?"

With audacity that I found a bit embarrassing Ron walked toward the girls.

"Hey girls, ya wanna party?" he shouted with way too much enthusiasm for past two in the morning.

"Yeah Ron, where is it? Got any beer?" one of the girls replied.

"Yeah, at his house," he said pointing toward Spig. "Ya gonna come?"

"I gotta go to church tomorrow," the prettiest of the three responded.

"Awe, c'mon c'mon," Ron coaxed.

Although they argued against the idea, Ron soon convinced the other two to join the party. Since there were now only two girls for three guys I decided to drop them off at Spig's pickup truck and end my evening of fun.

Just as I was about to drop them off one of the girls, a blonde with high cheekbones and slender hips fitted into tight jeans, leaned over the seat from behind me.

"Aren't you going to come? Please come, please!" she pleaded.

Before I really knew what had happened the plans were changed and I was driving the five of us to the same girl's house which was in a farming village about fifteen miles away. Ron was in the back with the two girls and Spig was in the passenger's seat. As I attempted to drive a straight line I listened to the conversation from the back seat.

"I've gone six months now. If I can go another six without a job I'll be cool, hey cats?" Ron bragged.

"Cats? We're not cats!" the girls laughed uproariously.

"I believe we shouldn't have to work. I'm a bum by profession now," Ron continued undeterred by the girl's laughter.

But the girls were in their own merry little world and the laughter continued. "Cats? Do we look like cats to you?" they roared.

Once the hilarity had died down the blonde girl leaned over my seat again. "Don't mind my house. It's a mess. I wasn't home all day to clean. Just don't even look at it," she insisted.

As we drove I began to dread what might lie ahead. Although the girls were attractive and nicely dressed, from their hick accents and inane conversations I began to suspect we might be heading for one the broken down shanties that littered the edges of this village of subsistence farmers and Amish homesteads.

As we drove she directed me past the main street of the town and up a desolate mountain road. Near the top we turned onto a dirt road that wound back down the mountain for about half a mile. When we reached the end we stopped beside a large swimming pool lit by blue floodlights. To my surprise her home was actually a small mansion hidden back in the forest.

Once inside, the house was immaculate. It was filled with a pool table, pinball machines, oak furniture, lush carpets, big screen TV, and high-end stereo equipment. The 2nd girl lay down on a leather couch while the rest of us sat on the floor. I was still trying to make sense of it all as our hostess poured white wine into tall thin crystal glasses.

The pieces just didn't fit together. How was it that this white-trash girl we picked up at last call in the seediest bar in town lived in such opulence? To some degree the girl's personalities simmered down to match the more sophisticated surroundings. As we sat and chatted it turned out the hostess was married to a wealthy man who was always away on business, leaving her alone and lonely in her luxurious mountain hideaway.

"I love my husband," she said, "But I am young and I'm stuck out here in the woods by myself all the time," she explained with an air of melancholy.

As she told her story an air of sadness overtook the group. For Spig and I, who were both ending long-term relationships, these emotions were right below the surface to begin with. Our hostess seemed resigned to her lot, but hungry for a little innocent companionship. Her friend lay on the couch saying very little. To me it began to seem apparent that this night was not going to end the way Spig hoped it would.

As the wine glasses waxed and waned our hostess became more melancholy and Spig became more desperate. He wanted her. He wanted her to give him back the dignity that his wife had taken with her sudden departure. To give him back a bit of his self-esteem and confidence. But all she was searching for was a little human contact to dispel the loneliness of her life.

The two of them stepped out onto the deck and stood looking out over the swimming pool and the dark forest. I watched them through the glass panes of the sliding doors. Without hearing their conversation, their body gestures told the whole story. The hostess gazed out over her empty property, and Spig aimed his face and body towards her. Offering, wanting, waiting.

I walked out on the deck with them and stood a few feet away. Their voices were a murmur. The hostess was certainly the smarter and deeper of the two women, and I felt absolutely no connection with the second. She was like a pretty decoration that was there, but without purpose.

Through it all Ron sat on the floor drunk and happily oblivious to the melancholy ambience. He chatted and joked non-stop, uncaring that no one was listening. Finally he wandered off and collapsed into an unconscious stupor in another room.

With the energy drained out of the little group, and no prospects for a night of debauchery, Spig and I took our leave. Ron stayed behind happily sleeping in the lush surroundings. As we drove home the sun was beginning to rise over the Amish farmhouses. He seemed deeply discouraged by the whole affair.

To me the boy's night out and getting into trouble aspect of the adventure was what made it all a good game. I thought the bachelor's life was great fun, but Spig found it too empty. It seemed he couldn't wait to return to the security of domestic life. Before long he had remarried and lived happily ever after.

I'm not sure why after a certain age people seem to panic if they are not married. With each year more and more friends join the breeder ranks. Men who were once full of fire quickly dissolve into contented homebodies, working their days to support their broods then collapsing each evening in front of the idiot box. The qualities that made them unique characters seem to evaporate into the numbness of conjugal bliss.

For some, even mentioning their bachelor days is taboo, like alcoholics who fear that a nip of the sauce will knock them off the wagon. One of my friends refuses to come see The Imperial Orgy perform because he fears that if he steps inside a barroom he will revert to his bad boy ways.

People seem to think that to be a single adult is a disaster. Once I ran into an old female friend in line to buy popcorn at a movie theater.

"Are you married," she asked.

"No, not yet," I smiled back.

"Ooh, you couldn't find anyone," she intoned with a sympathetic frown.

I nodded my head and smiled like a friendly dolt, but was secretly thinking, "Couldn't find anyone? Christ, what does that mean?"

Contentment is a dangerous thing in life. While contentment may feel nice, it is also a form of surrender. Happily ever after means the battle is won, one can rest on their laurels, grow lazy and fat.

For me, even just being in a long-term relationship seems to steal away my very will to live. I grow numb way too quickly. For me there is nothing like a long lonely night to fill me with the urge to fight, to take on the world, to work harder, reach further, strive for loftier heights.

It was once believed that male animals fought each other for the best females. After some study it was learned that most male animals fight over real estate or dominance in the social hierarchy. Then the guy with the best piece of land, or who is the top dog in the pack, gets the best females based on his achievements.

The world of human interactions is far more complex, but essentially the same. I must admit that when I find myself as a single male in a public gathering with a beautiful woman in the room that I can't have, a subtle taste of rage seeps unto my tongue. A primitive instinct beckons from within. This little fire makes my spine grow stiff and my eyes acquire a steely gaze. There's no time for merriment. I would rather work, struggle, fight, be smarter, more creative, more aggressive, more wiley, more cunning, more vicious.

This feeling in public has often led to no good. I can often become a trouble starter at a party. Pushing people to misbehave, seducing and antagonizing them into losing their cool composures and behaving with uncouth manners. I can't stand to just be a face in the crowd. I would rather instigate a riot that causes the whole scene to self-destruct, than just be a member of the herd.

Anthropologist Margaret Mead expressed a theory that it took eons of social conditioning to make men devote themselves to a family unit and help care for offspring. It is a modification that benefits the species, but goes against a male's more primordial instinct to spread his DNA far and wide.

As I write these words, I can testify that this tug-of-war between the two instincts still goes on within me. There are times when I see cute little black, Asian, or Indian children and I feel the pangs of desire for fatherhood.

There is also a constant social pressure, a herd instinct to conform, to settle down and breed. It's funny that often when people tell a man to grow up, what they really mean is to settle down with a family. It seems that people think you can't be a mature adult unless you are married with children.

It seems a single adult male makes married people a little uneasy. To them it is a dangerous social aberration. The universe will always be off-balance until he finds a nice girl and moves into a house with a white picket fence.

Meanwhile each year I see my male friends fade into the woodwork. Often when they marry they cease to exist. They permanently retire from the roaming pack of wild dogs that they once inhabited.

I am left feeling like the last man standing, making this strange left hand path I have chosen a little more lonely. My married male friends can't quite decide whether I am a tragic figure or their secret hero. While they might live vicariously through my tales of adventure and sexual exploits, I suppose they also secretly resent it. And if their wives were to learn that I was sowing the seeds of discontent with the monogamous lifestyle, I would surely be banned from the realm of acceptable house guests.

Guilt has always been a factor in my relationships with women. I could never quite be what women wanted me to be, and they could never quite accept me for what I am. Usually my sense of failure was associated with money. I grew up in a traditional household and have always felt a failure because I couldn't support a wife and children, even though few men can these days.

But as an adult my financial troubles are all connected with being a musician and artist. I would likely be a millionaire if I weren't an artist. As an artist one has a separate goal that defies the demands of family, and often logic. And again the pressure arises to get serious, grow up, and drop all this artist nonsense.

There is a quote from psychologist Carl Jung that always rang true for me: "A person must pay dearly for the gift of artistic fire. Can the life of an artist be otherwise than full of conflict, for two forces are at war within him: on one hand the justified longing of the ordinary man for happiness, satisfaction, and security, on the other a ruthless passion for creation which may override every other personal desire."

It does seem to me that to be an artist is to be cursed. Although the life of an artist is idealized by pretentious young art school hipsters who haven't faced the reality of what it really means to be possessed by the need for creativity, my experience is that it is a curse that as often as not ruins life and steals away happiness. I can't see why anyone would subject himself to this blight unless they had no choice in the matter. Unless the artistic impulse was so strong that they couldn't escape it, like a demon that possesses them, or like a calling from God that cannot be ignored.

Every day I see how this impulse hurts those around me and fills my life with anger and frustration. I feel the guilt of not being able to settle into the role that society demands of an adult male. If I could I would walk away from the artist's life in a heartbeat, but I know I would soon die. The mind and the soul have a way of demanding we follow our destiny. If we disobey, the consequences can be horrifying.

This leaves one with a dilemma. For a man who loves art must surely also love women, more than that he must surely love Woman. Woman as the great Goddess of human beauty, the greatest work of art and possessing the greatest beauty of all artistic creations, and created by the greatest of all artists, whoever or whatever that artist may be.

It's odd how we grow up with these traditional ideas about life and love. People assume love automatically leads to a lifetime commitment. Possession is inherent in most people's understanding of love.

I don't believe that in-itself love has anything to do with possession, or marriage, or even sex. Love is something more pure and simple, something that is born and dies in each moment. All the baggage we hang on love limits our ability to love, and limits the amount of love in the world.

I have been lucky enough to experience a few rare occasions when the limits we place on love have been abandoned, and the results have been beautiful, amazing, having taken me to spiritual and physical highs that few people ever know.

People tend to see a difference between the love one feels for family and friends, and the love one feels for a lover. I really don't see that distinction. To me it all springs from the same source. The fact that you have a sexual relationship with someone, or make some kind of commitment to them, are separate practical issues. Love is not practical. It is inspired and purely spiritual.

I might see a withered old man sitting on a stoop watching the traffic go by with a bored look in his eyes, and be filled with love. As I write these words I sit at a table at a small café. A young woman is at the counter. It is a gray, gloomy, wet day. Everything feels like it is moving in slow motion.

Although it is fairly warm out the girl at the counter wears a long heavy winter coat. Her brown hair is tucked underneath a knit cap. From the tangled strands that have fallen out from underneath it, it appears the cap was meant to hide the fact that she didn't bother to brush her hair before she ran out for the morning coffee. She looks tired and her hands look so small as she reaches for her cup. Although I will likely never know her name, and might not even wish to make love to her if the opportunity were to arise, still in this moment I feel awash with love for her. I feel inspired by her ragged beauty. I feel a paternal sympathy for her weary expression on this dark day.

Tantrists believe that the material world is the body of God, and to love another is to worship God. Our ability to love is boundless, but too much love threatens the social order, so love is bound and shackled by religious edicts, social taboos, and legal sanctions. Love, like truth, can destroy the old order and threatens to bring revolutions both in societies and in the hearts of men and women.

Love is a dangerous thing, more threatening to the status quo than a terrorist's bomb. If it is not carefully kept in check the walls might tumble down, and God only knows what might be left after the fall.

#12 – This Strange Troubled Girl

By the time I reached San Francisco night had fallen. San Francisco was supposed to be the goal point of the trip, so when I arrived I was surprised to realize that I felt at somewhat of a loss as to what to do now that I was here. Perhaps I just spent too much time hanging out with East Coast Dead-Heads who talk about San Francisco like it's some kind of shining Shangri-La. Heaven itself couldn't live up to the picture they painted of the place.

I drove around the downtown area and didn't see anything that looked any different than any other city in America. The streets were cluttered with traffic as I attempted to take in the surroundings; Bank Of America, Barnes & Nobles, Kinkos, Starbucks…the same old shit, no sign of Shangri-La, no trace of peace and love.

After circling the city a few times without finding anything to catch my attention, I found myself in the park overlooking the bay. I walked along the dirty beach, looking out over the water. It was a dark night, barely a star in the sky. Looking out over the ocean, the dark waters and the dark sky merged into a single black void.

There was a chill in the air, the first sign of the coming winter. The thought of winter seemed too horrible to face. Just give me an endless summer with no responsibilities, just freedom to travel without direction or destination.

Here I was, the goal achieved, it seemed I should be popping a Champaign bottle and celebrating, but the reality was that I was walking alone on a dark beach and it's hard to celebrate with a party of one. I tried calling Jodi, then Jeanie, then Samantha. Nobody home, nobody home, nobody home.

It was a bitter loneliness, a mixture of yearning and despair that was heightened by the emptiness of the ocean and black horizon.

Ever since 9/11 a disheartening feeling had taken me, a quiet collapsing from within, a spiritual deflation. This dark cloud had been partially staved off by the excitement of the journey, but now faced with this empty climax, I was left with too little to buoy my sinking spirits.

This lonely moment was the pinnacle of the journey, from here it was just backtracking towards home. And then what? The life I was returning to was beginning to stagnate. I hated my day job, yet was frightened by the fact that given that my office was right at ground zero, I might not even have a job to return to. My work as a musician and an artist was stuck in the mud. It went on, but showed no signs of rising up so that we might reach a wider audience.

Pulling my jacket lapels together over my chest I sat down on a rock near the water's edge. I tried calling a few more friends who I might share my moment of triumph with, but just couldn't seem to connect with anyone.

After giving up on the phone I began to think about Her, now only a short distance away. I could easily call her up and ask to see her, or simply show up on her doorstep. But I wouldn't dare do the latter. She has too much fear. Her friends and mother have demonized me, persuading her impressionable mind the way one scares a child with stories of a bogeymen in the closet.

But in her secret heart she knows what the truth is. She knows the secrets we share. But that truth could only be recalled if she has the courage to look inside herself, and it is that honest introspection that frightens her most. Her fear was always fear of her own reflection. The hate she felt for me was always self-loathing. A hate born of seeing her own reflection in the mirror of my eyes.

Near the end she articulated it herself, "I hear everything I say and see everything I do through your eyes. You're like a mirror that's always with me."

I scrolled down through the numbers in the phonebook in my cell phone and stopped on her name. After a pause I closed the phone, not quite ready to hear her voice, or to face the rejection I would likely find.

I walked over to the parking lot and began to urinate against a wire fence. As I stood there I noticed something moving in the darkness. On closer inspection I realized that right in front of me were not one, but two skunks. While still urinating I tried to take a couple steps sideways to move away from them. As I moved to the left I heard a rustle further to my left. Squinting my eyes in the direction of the sound I saw three more skunks coming down an embankment towards me. Further to the right two more skunks were coming in my direction, and all of them moving with some sense of misplaced urgency. It was a virtual stampede of skunks! I don't know what they wanted with me, but I didn't want to stick around and find out.

I zipped my pants and tried to move slowly towards the car so as not to get them too excited. As I moved I was like a magnet and my herd of stinky friends adjusted their course to follow in my direction. Finally I just threw caution to the wind and broke out into a full speed run until I jumped into the safety of the Blazer.

After my close call with the skunks I drove around the city looking for the Haight-Ashbury district. Once I found it I drove up and down the street a few times. It looked a little bohemian, but didn't seem like anything special. The hour was getting late and many of the stores were starting to close down. Here and there scruffy looking people haunted the street.

I parked and as I prepared to get out of the car I noticed a knife that I had found beside the highway in Alabama was laying in the glove box. I looked at it briefly then slipped it into the pocket of my jacket. It gave me a strange sense of confidence to have it nearby. Noting the irony that on a street known for promoting peace and love I would choose to carry a weapon.

I walked down Haight trying to get a sense of the place. The air had a slight chill that made my body tight. As I walked it seemed every worn-out hippie either had his hand out for a free meal or was running some con to get a buck out of a stranger. I stopped to chat with some street musicians, but their only interest was in pressuring me to buy some acid from them.

My sense of loneliness was deepening as the night went on, soon reaching almost desperate proportions. As I walked I tried to make eye contact with passers-by, the response I met with was as cold as New York City at rush hour.

A young woman walking in the other direction said something to me I didn't quite catch. I stopped in my tracks hoping for a little conversation.

"Are you buying?" she said again.

My expression must have registered that I was still a little confused as to what she was talking about.

"Weed, are you buying?" she insisted.

Realizing she was just another salesman I shook my head and began to walk away.

"Wait, what are you looking for?" she asked.

Then assuming I wanted a prostitute she said, "Oh you want sex, sorry."

Feeling wrongly accused I mumbled, "No, just looking for someone to talk to."

She seemed disarmed by this, but didn't gave it a second thought as she immediately turned and headed up the street looking for her next potential customer.

"Christ, how did we get to a place where if a man speaks to a woman she assumes he is looking for a prostitute?" I thought to myself. Something was clearly lost here. The ideals of the past had decayed into something truly ugly.

I walked into a brightly lit café that had a sign on the sidewalk that read "open mic night." I sat down at a side table as a young man finished a song with an acoustic guitar. I must have landed on the last note of the last song of the night, because as soon as I sat down the whole crowd seemed to stand up and walk out of the place. You would have thought the skunks had actually sprayed me the way I seemed to clear the place.

I drank a warm cup of tea in the now empty café and wondered what to do in this place. Surely in San Francisco there must be creative artists performing every night. I thumbed through an entertainment newspaper looking at ads for local bands. Unfortunately all you had to do was look at the photos to know what they sounded like. It was the same generic formulas and the same boring shit as the rest of America. It doesn't even occur to most artists anymore that creativity is a good thing. Originality is not even a goal these days.

As I walked back out onto the street a hairy guy sitting on a fire hydrant reached out his hand towards me.

"Hey man, could you share a dollar with a brother?"

"Sorry man," I replied.

Most of the street people in San Francisco appear to be brain damaged from years of drug abuse. I suppose that before my eyes I am seeing the proof that the excesses of the 60's lead to social decadence. But the truth is that most of the 60's radicals are now locked snugly away inside the middle class homes that surround the area. They lead productive nine to five lives. If they ever were really against the system, they have embraced it now.

I suppose we are all trying to find our place within the system, on our own terms. I'm not sure what "outside the system" really means. Does such a thing even exist?

I know in my heart I feel I am against the system, but in practical terms it just doesn't mean much. And to condemn the society one lives in, ultimately seems like an act of flagellation, a sign of self-hate. One thing I am sure of is that seeing yourself as "against the system" is a spiritual state that leaves you feeling isolated and alienated. And as a friend who grew up in San Francisco once told me, people who saw themselves as against the system once came to Haight Street to be among a community of like-minded people so they didn't feel isolated.

If that's what I was searching for on this trip I had surely struck out. Walking the dark sidewalks of Haight Street that isolation was weighing heavily on me. Back east the Dead-Heads look at San Francisco as some kind of distant paradise, a last refuge of the 60's ideals. Walking these streets it was clear that this idea was a sad joke.

As midnight encroached it was now too late to call her. The streets were filled with nothing but ghouls and zombies. The chill was beginning to bite so I crawled into the back of the Blazer and pulled the blankets up to my chin. Through the tinted car windows I could see the nice row of houses I was parked in front of. Some of the windows were lit by a warm yellow glow. Their blinds pulled down to separate those inside from those outside. I felt tired and discouraged.

But sleep didn't come. I tossed and turned, trying to get my pillow into a comfortable position between the spare tire and the orange Goodwill suitcase that held my clothes and barely-used shaving kit.

Perhaps it was delirium from the exhaustion of the weeks of travel that compelled me. Digging through some papers scattered in the car I found her address. Without a map to guide me I began driving randomly through the city trying to find her street. The fates, be they kind or cruel, must have been with me because within a few minutes I stumbled onto it.

I drove up the steep hill at a slow speed so I could try to make out the house numbers through the darkness. Near the top of the ascent I found her house. I pulled off into an empty parking space on the opposite side of the street and looked up at the unfamiliar house that is now her home. It looked conventional in every way. I knew that she lived with three other women. It seemed every window in the two-story house was lit up brightly. The house glowed with energy.

I rolled down the car window a few inches so I could get a better look. The open gap sent a rush of cool air across my face. My eyes peered above the glass of the tinted window like a teenage boy overlooking a backyard fence as he dreams of the girl next door. I thought of Gatsby reaching his arms out across the abyss of the bay towards the unattainable Daisy.

A form moved past one of the windows on the second floor. It was just a quick flash. A shadow really. It could have been her, but it also could have been the queen of England for all I could really make out.

Turning my face away from the house, a wave of self-consciousness washed over me. Here I am ten years later still acting like a fool. It was pathetic. And why was I here? I didn't feel any trace of the love I once felt for her. I suppose if I dug deep enough I could connect with the anger I once felt as our relationship dissolved.

There was something else that I couldn't quite articulate that brought me here. Some sense of unfinished business. It could be as easy as turning the last page of a paperback novel, a page that simply reads "The end." Yet even as years and distance separated us it seems I could never quite take that final step and turn that last page and place the book on the shelf. Judging from the short phone conversation we had a few weeks before, the same was true for her as well.

I think of the last time we spoke before the years intervened. She was still in rehabilitation from the auto accident that spelled the real end of our relationship. At the time of that conversation it had been six month since our split. Although only twenty-two years old, during those months she had managed to have an affair with the aging rock star Robert Plant while he was on his "No Quarter" nostalgia tour with Jimmy Page.

I had sent her a tape of some new songs I had recorded. Six weeks after sending the tape I called her. As soon as she said "Hello" I could tell she was crying.

"Sasha, what's wrong," I asked somewhat alarmed.

"You," she responded tearfully.

"Me? What do you mean?" I asked in confusion. Given that it had been months since we spoke it seemed impossible that I could be the cause of her tears.

"I don't know how you do it. I got this package and I let it set there for months. I didn't even want to open it. Fifteen minutes ago I opened it and listened to the tape and now you call. How do you do it? How did you know?"

Sasha always believed in the occult and she sometimes felt afraid of me, due to a belief that I had powers and could read her mind or watch over her from afar.

For the next three hours we talked late into the night. The first two hours were filled with anger and bitterness. I tried to persuade her that we should at least try to end things as friends, but she insisted that she wanted nothing to do with me. Finally as I gave up and began to say goodbye her tone changed and we spoke for another hour in which she reminisced sweetly of her fond memories of our time together.

Throughout those three hours she said, "I have never hated anyone as much as I've hated you. I've never felt such anger at anyone like I felt for you." And, "I never want to see or talk to you again."

Although she seemed completely oblivious to her own contradictions, in the same conversation she also said, "I've never loved anyone as much as I've loved you. I've never felt such tenderness from anyone as I did from you." And as we said our final goodbye she whispered, "I want you to know the door is still open..." and after a prolonged pause, "...for us to be...friends...or whatever."

A few weeks later I heard she had moved to India. She never called to say goodbye. She never wrote a word to ease my mind. By chance it turned out that the same day she left for India I had mailed a letter to her. Her mother returned it with a letter threatening me with legal action if I ever spoke to Sasha again. I called her mother to confront her. Her mother said that any time Sasha spoke to me or heard from me she would become ill and it would take her many days to recover. Given these facts I never tried to contact her again, and so ten years passed.

Over those years it seemed that a shadow has hung over my life. In the first years is was a smothering blanket that stifled my ability to act, to love, to dream new dreams. As years passed that cloud has slowly faded, but now I wanted to wash away the last wisps of that shadow and be free from it forever.

Tonight I long to look at her, talk to her, to try to understand why this woman possessed me so. My life has been filled with beautiful, brilliant women, yet it is the memory of this strange troubled girl that has bound me, and who once inspired a love so entrancing that I was ready to give myself body and soul to the fleeting whims of her chaotic mind.

The despair and exhaustion returning, I lay my head back against the headrest. The emotions and memories of the past arising in my mind like graveyard spirits who have suddenly been freed to haunt their victims. The phantoms take my hands and transport me through time and space. Their smile is friendly and inviting. Seducing me to come and play, to bathe in the sweet memories of days long gone by. "Better days, happier days, days full of hope and wonder," the phantoms promise.

But my seducers are the Goddesses of Lamia. As my will collapses and I succumb to their call, I am doomed to be devoured by these beautiful cannibals whose succor is to taste the flesh of a weary heart.

Out of the left side of my vision I catch of glimpse of her house, but my vision is fading. I am entering that world of the past, twisted by the tricks of memory, filtered through emotions that raged for years before simmering to a cool blue flame, and now this dying ember. The scenery before my eyes dims to grey, then fades to shadow.

Like a dying man giving way to death my mind surrenders to the dark spirits that beckon me. I hear the echo of my own words, written for her, to her, so long ago…

Sasha,

Tonight I dream of you. I dream of love in explosion. Right now I want to be inside you. I want to lick away your lips. Bite off your nipples. Ram your wettest of all cunts into oblivion.

So driving into the cornfield and throwing you over the hood of the Topaz didn't work out so well. We spent too much time laughing as the blanket I placed over the still hot metal began to slowly slide downward, pulling us towards the ground.

You still came violently. Me on my knees on the cool earth. My belly pressed against the grill. Scorpio and Orion shone above our heads. A warm breeze caressed our skin.

Did you know I could still taste the rancid flavor of the lubrication from the Trojan condom every time I inserted my tongue into your brown lips? Your lips are the most abundant I've ever known. Like two tiny elephant ears folded into a welcoming smile. It only took a few minutes of gentle sucking, my index finger inserted slightly into your anus, before your convulsed. With my face furtively buried I couldn't watch your expressions of ecstasy as I am so fond of doing.

Now tonight I am alone and dreaming, but Sasha know this thing - although you may be safely at home under the protective gaze of your mother and father, although you may be in another state hundreds of miles away - I am fucking you. I am fucking you every minute of every day. I am fucking you astrally, spiritually, mentally, symbolically, everything but physically, and I will be fucking you until the cosmos cease to expand and all of creation gravitates in on itself imploding into the lotus belly of the sleeping giant.

What's more Sasha, you know the secret we share. The secret which reduces the word 'fucking' to mere semantics which could never ever communicate what really takes place when our bodies lie together. That secret has enveloped every cell of my being and transformed me in a manner a billion years of evolution could never have accomplished. So hold that secret tightly in your bosom when you lay down to sleep, and know I am fucking you for now, and forever more.

APOLOGIA

On the cross of humanity's sorrow
shall Narcissus reign

July 8, 1994

Zero. It is down to this. God forbid one can exist in the minus. Zero is nothing enough.

I am living in a rundown Mercury Topaz in York, Pennsylvania. I am a stranger here and all I view is strange to me. I came here to be a scab worker during a factory strike at the Caterpillar plant, the company that makes those big yellow steamrollers and dump trucks.

Living in a car makes you feel degraded to the level of an animal. No shower. No way to store or prepare food. Even brushing your teeth or finding a bathroom is a major task. Every day I ask myself, "How did I come to this?"

Only two years ago I had a long-term relationship with a beautiful woman, a home, a rental property, a fifty-percent share in a small business, and was well on the way to a college degree. Now all that is gone. The cruel course of fate took the net of material security I had so laboriously created and revealed it to be a crepe paper illusion.

Ten years ago at this time I was struggling to find money to eat. I vowed I would escape poverty forever. I worked, conned, connived, committed felonies to climb my way into the middle class. But once again I am reduced to the life of a peasant. Worse than this - the life of a vagabond.

The situation is exacerbated by the gnawing irony that for the first time all my hopes and dreams are a realistic possibility. Yet they lay right outside my grasp and I am unable to even enter the arena wherein I can begin the struggle to make those dreams a reality. And if the truth be known, it is not really money and wealth that I truly seek. Money is only a means to an end, and even then, what I desire cannot be bought.

Despite my circumstances I feel clear-sighted. The chaos of my life suddenly makes sense. I see that it was also ten years ago that I began a journey. A journey set sail with a momentary flash of light within my mind, and which is ending only now after a Homeric cycle of creation and destruction. I have nearly come full circle. Only time will tell whether this journey's end will bring a complete end to hope, or a beginning to the life I have always felt would start on some distant tomorrow.

From the beginning I already had a sense of what life had in store for me and what was existent within myself. Although unrealized, I already carried an understanding of the impenetrability of life's underlying mysteries, the goal of my desires, and that my destiny offered the extraordinary.

At the same time I also carried a sickness. An all-pervading bitterness for an evolution's worth of unfulfilled human potential. A bitterness for the unfulfilled potential in my own life which only the most naively idealistic and childlike mind could formulate.

Immediately I held the view that all of life was a game. Yet I played that game more seriously than any of those around me. The doctrine of inaction was apparent to me from the first breath. Yet I acted with more volition than all others. Even now I am often told that people feel uneasy when first meeting me because they can see "something in my eyes."

This bitterness soon grew into a murderous feeling of rage. Rage against God, country, human values, the cruelty of life, and most of all, myself. I became a conundrum of the jive soul in search of perpetual resurrection. I was greedy to savor every drop of life's essence yet I constantly ignored life in hope of finding that day when I could begin living. I reach out, yet am described as unapproachable.

And it is the doctrine of inaction, the ever-present awareness of futility, which fuels my self-hatred. Because this rage, at this very moment, mocks every word I place on paper. I accept that these words are purposeless, pointless, absurd, ridiculous and grossly egotistical. I continue because not to continue would be to lie down and die for all the sorrow and hopelessness that seems apparent in all I perceive.

And 'egotistic?' I am acutely aware that self-hatred is the highest form of egotism. It is this dilemma that is the final barrier for those seeking the zero. For those seeking annihilation of the self.

My first memory of Sasha wafts through my mind like a mirage. It was at one of the first Imperial Orgy gigs at a seedy little hick bar called the Beerhaus. In the middle of a song she suddenly appeared on the stage. She was drawn to the light of celebrity no matter how slight that celebrity might be. Whatever the environment was, she gravitated towards the center of attention, and whether it be male or female, she began to seduce and if possible, dominate that point of gravity.

When I saw her onstage, although uninvited, I simply felt happy to see a pretty girl on stage with me. To me The Imperial Orgy was always a community experience. As soon as I saw her I picked her up and raised her as high into the air as I could lift her, then I let her slowly slide down, her soft body rubbing against mine until she again stood on the floor with our arms wrapped around each other.

After the show, as the band members and I drove home we excitedly went over the events of the night's performance.

"Who was the Indian girl that was onstage," I asked.

The response from those who knew her was full of criticism.

"That stupid bitch!" Michael Mordes our guitar player expelled. "In the middle of a song she starts trying to have a conversation with me. Is she too stupid to see I'm playing guitar here?"

I sat silently, hearing the criticism yet not being swayed by it. This was the beginning of what would soon be a dynamic that surrounded my life. Sasha seemed to bring out the worst in people. Even her friends criticized and mocked her, sometimes viciously. As far as I could see, the behavior they criticized her for all stemmed from deep insecurities that lay just below the surface in this odd girl.

Sasha was Pakistani by nationality, but her family was Hindu and had migrated to India when Pakistan broke away from the mainland. Sasha was a first generation American. Her parents came to the states to take advantage of job opportunities during the early 1970's.

She was lovely and exotic looking. Her complexion was golden. To look at her you would think that her skin might offer the flavor of caramel and honey. Her large oval eyes were dark orbs full of mystery. Her hair was a long luxurious mane that framed her face with silken streams of black shadows that sometimes glowed with hints of purple and blue when the sunlight shone off it in just the right way.

She was a small woman, but her presence was large. She often wore soft flowing clothing with just a hint of her ethnic background reflected in her attire. Her body was adorned with jewelry, silver rings decorated each finger and large necklaces often lay between her breasts.

The thing that seemed to give her a bad reputation was her tendency towards the Dead-Head hippie culture and her belief in outlandish occult practices. She would speak about the flakiest new-age nonsense with complete openness. She seemed to be completely unaware that to most people such things seemed a bit loony. Although I found much of it silly, I felt for her when people mocked her eccentric behavior. I once walked down a similar path and knew what it felt like to be in her position.

I can recall running into her on the street on a sunny winter's day.

"I seem to run in to you everywhere I go," I teased her.

"Some things are just meant to be," she answered without a trace of humor. Then looking up towards the sun, "You should take in the sun," she intoned. "There is a yogi in India and she gets her nourishment from the sun. She doesn't eat or drink, she just meditates in the sunlight and takes in the nourishment through her skin."

I smiled slightly and looked straight ahead as we walked side by side. Allowing the subject to hang in the air without comment.

After the first meeting, the next thing I heard about her was that she was going to start taking photos of The Imperial Orgy for a college photojournalism class project. She started calling on the phone and saying that she wanted to photograph my day-to-day life. "I want to capture you having breakfast," her soft voice suggested on more than one occasion.

Soon she was a regular fixture at Imperial Orgy shows, always with camera in hand and flashbulbs flashing. Although usually by halfway through the show she could be seen doing her hippie dances at the edge of the stage.

In January we played a gig at a backwoods tavern outside of Harrisburg, PA where the audience looked at us like we were the alien freak-squad from Pluto. The night was rough because what few women there were in the audience, all kept a very safe distance from what they saw as the bizarre behavior onstage. This meant that there were no women for me to interact with during our songs of seduction. During one such song I ventured out onto the empty dance floor searching for someone to play with. At one point I looked down and there was Sasha at my feet looking up through the camera lens. I sat down quickly, straddling her between my legs as I

172 Murder Of The Holly King

sang to her while looking straight into her eyes. She was compliant, accepting me as if it were the most natural thing in the world.

After that she was always ready for a bit of exhibitionism. One night at a small club called Stony's Posthouse Tavern I pulled her under a table and gave her a passionate kiss. As we kissed she reached up and grabbed a picture of water off the table and poured it over our heads. The cold water soaked our faces, and streamed down our necks and bodies as the entire audience watched the erotic spectacle.

Soon I began to hear rumors that she was in love with me. I was flattered, but there were so many women around at that time that I didn't think too much about it. A week or so later, before another gig I sat down with her at a table to view some contact sheets from the photos she had taken. As she looked absent-mindedly at the sheets she casually remarked, "I think I'm falling in love with you."

She made this statement as if she was commenting on the weather. There was no sign that she was waiting for a reply or trying to gauge my reaction. I sat quietly, pretending not to have heard her, taking it all in stride, as if women professing their love to me was a normal part of my new life as Caeser Pink.

When March came to an end and her class project was complete she invited me to her apartment to check out the photos. I entered her apartment and we went into her bedroom. It was permeated with a sweet smell of incense and had an exotic feminine look to it. Soft tapestries with Middle Eastern patterns were draped from the ceiling providing the seductive aura of a harem girl's tent.

We sat on the floor and chatted while we looked at the photos. She would occasionally burst into rambling lectures on feminism or new age spirituality. These explosions of verbosity seemed to come from nowhere and lacked any connection with the conversation that preceded it. During one exceptionally intense soliloquy that seemed to come right out of Women's Studies 101, I sat staring at her thinking, "Why the hell is she telling me this?"

Suddenly she went silent for a moment, her face aimed down at the floor. Then peering up at me she confessed, "I'm sorry, I talk when I'm nervous...and you make me nervous."

It was the first warm day of spring so we went for a walk to enjoy the mild air and bright sunlight. As we walked, out of the blue she began to recite a poem she had written as if she was gracing me with a gift from the heavens. I thought, "This girl is a wacky character. She'll be fun to hang out with and give me something to write about."

When we got to her backyard she decided she wanted to lay down in a small parking lot behind her house. Although most of the ground was still spotted with piles of dirty snow, we sat down on the cold cement. She laid her head on my lap as if we were long time lovers. I tried to be cool about it all, but felt a bit awkward about the situation.

As we lay there I examined her face, considering whether I should want her. At the time I had made a resolution not to get involved with another woman that down the road I wouldn't be committed to. I studied her face, noting her pointed nose and the fuzzy outline of a mustache, and rashly decided that she was not for me.

But still there was something about her that was magnetic. Her head resting gently in my lap inspired warm feelings that made my mind swim. Trying to regain control of my emotions I said a silent prayer, pleading to the skies, "This is not my girl, please don't let me fall in love with this woman."

7/13/1994

I sit fifteen feet in the air overlooking the maze of conveyor belts that fill the factory floor. It reminds one of a child's train set multiplied to the realm of nightmare. The sound is deafening.

Amid this I try to be a poet. I try to be a poet, but all I feel is violence. I have just hung up the phone after speaking to you on my lunch break. Sasha this violence is for you! Sweet as ever, the near perfect mate. Why do I wish to reach through the phone line and strangle you?

I see you doing dishes in the kitchen while your mother cleans the counter. Your father watches television and your brother plays basketball in the driveway. Just a typical scene in a typical middle class American family, yet it fills me with rage.

If I could find a way to express the emotions you inspire in me it would split the most complex of atoms and sear the fiber of the material world. Your windows would shatter. The trees would bend. Sirens would wail from coast to coast. Your beautiful long black hair would melt into your flesh and the flesh would melt away from the bones, which would disintegrate into dust.

Burn the sky. Smother all of humanity in atomic ash if that is what it takes to shake you out of your complacency. I want to live now! I want to bite the most exotic fruit, see foreign lands, explore depravity, converse with the most outlandish bohemians and the simplest peasants. And reach new heights that can only be done in union.

I am the most selfish man who has ever walked the firmament and what I want is you. And when you speak I want every word to be straight from the lips of God. I want your every breath to be a sigh of desperation. I want to look into your eyes and see the universe in creation at every moment. Shine for me. Radiate life itself. Do it now because each time I think of you every electron in every atom of my body jumps an orbit, emitting a particle, becoming a wave, lacquered in the sperm which seeds the void and beckons all of existence into bloom.

It may look to you like I'm driving a car, reading Kant, walking on my hands as I jump through a hoop to prove my devotion to you, but you are sorely mistaken. Clear the static and you will plainly see that I am trying to conquer the world. And I plan not just to rule the earth, but to displace the godhead with my own personal consciousness and hold dominion over all space and time.

I can see the future and it is coming quickly. You and I both have gray in our hair. You plan a year with your parents before you break out. So be it. Know that every day of that year I will be bored with life.

Let the prostitutes grab at my cock as their torsos hang from the window of my moving car. Let the trannies smash out my car windshield on Eighth Ave. Let the con-men drug dealers put a knife to my neck in the New Orleans projects. Let Nicole change into something more comfortable that is even more revealing than the mini dress she wore as she holds my arm on Monica's couch. Let Robin, Angie, and Krista proclaim that they were always ready. Give me every object of desire on a silver platter and with no strings attached. Give me it all with streamers and fireworks and I will still be that river turned unto itself which you so eloquently warned of, and don't ask me to be otherwise because I am a man in love.

I will wait for the possibility of that union of souls that will breathe life with fire and serenity co-existent and ever enlarging. But for me waiting means anger, laughter, insanity, vanity, insecurities, broken mirrors, swollen phone bills, your mother's vacillations, factories, New York squatting, jealousy, lies, sneaking, masturbation, doubt, fidelity, asceticism, dreams of cannibalism, chanting in my car under the full moon to ease my pain, bodies piled on couches at 522 College Avenue, and struggles which take the most subtle and deceptive forms.

I love your strength. And every day I yearn to destroy it. To run from you. To hurt you. To tell you it's over. I demand to see a crack in your composure. Until you hand me the scepter of your unconditional love, I will be at war. Until you submit to our eternal love I will be filled with violence. The violence of the most selfish man who ever lived. The man who wants it all. The man who wants you by his side.

With the first hints of spring in the air I lay in my bed with Samantha sleeping beside me, I felt an emptiness, an all too familiar yearning. I whispered to Samantha that I wanted to drive around and think. I drove in circles through the silent streets, hungry, not for anything specifically, but for something more, for life itself. Finally I stopped at a phone booth and called Sasha.

"I'm just driving around…feeling restless," I told her.

"If you want to talk or something you can come by my place," she offered, both of our voices soft with expectant tension. Then out of the blue she added, "I've never been in love before."

When I arrived she was dressed in worn looking long-john underwear and a loose fitting button-up blouse. She read me another one of her poems. This one was an invitation to a 'secret lover' to come and take her and fulfill her yearnings. It seemed clear that the poem was written for me.

It was one of those nights that were soft with emotion, when two strangers began to bare their secrets to each other.

I suppose that in my unconscious mind I knew that I was moving towards something with Sasha and I wanted to make my circumstances clear to her. I began to lay out my situation.

For five years, my life had been full of chaos. Full of lover's tears and broken promises, full of jealousy and betrayals, full of violence and destruction, full of tragedies as friends and lovers had mental breakdowns, emotional collapses, and drug overdoses which some survived and some did not. I had been chased from my home and hometown by a police conspiracy. I had showdowns with barroom bullies and truck-stop lotharios. In search of self-destruction I wandered the most dangerous streets in strange cities, walking alone through the sordid surroundings, daring, challenging the creatures of the night to take me.

In search of solace I had paid for the most pathetic form of human contact provided by whorehouse hostesses and dark alley streetwalkers. I had watched all those I love suffer pain and sorrows too heavy for the human heart to bear, and I imagined that most of those pains and sorrows were inflicted on them by my own actions, my own self-centeredness, my own boundless egotism. I sometimes felt that the only moral thing I could do for those around me was to blow my own brains out.

I had survived so many dramas and traumas that I felt as if I carried ten lifetimes worth of karma within me and I didn't have the slightest clue how to face and let go of the past. The past was a burden that weighed heavily on my mind at every moment.

Only two years earlier I had ended a very long relationship with Leilani, and that ending took the form of a year of drawn out violence, guilt, gut-wrenching emotional dramas, and eventually her mental breakdown. It was a horrible thing to live through. And just that week I had received news that Leilani had been put in jail on attempted murder charges for stabbing her new man. He was a violent alcoholic ex-con who was kicking the shit out of her at the time of the stabbing. I felt terrible guilt about this news because somehow I felt responsible for how her life had turned out.

At the time I was living in a house in a little town called Lemont with three of the Imperial Orgy band members: Dave Surreal our keyboard player, Michael Mordes our guitar player, and Samantha our background singer, who I was also in a romantic relationship with. Although I loved Samantha, I told Sasha that I felt the relationship was coming apart. I also told her that Samantha had asked me not to end the relationship until the Autumn after the band members all moved to New York, and that I intended to honor that request.

I also explained that my financial situation would soon be disastrous. I was in the process of losing my house, I had recently lost my business, I had been laid off from my job at the film production company, and my unemployment benefits were about to run out. The future looked bleak.

Most important to me, I explained to Sasha that I had been through so much pain in relationships that I didn't want to get involved with anything that anyone would get hurt by. I didn't want to be involved in anything too serious. Plus there was too much added chaos brought on by The Imperial Orgy's local success and all the sexual experimentation that the band seemed to inspire among our fans. Even Sasha was exploring her lesbian desires and talking of group sex parties. It was all getting very complicated.

After my declaration I fell silent. She said, "I'm not the jealous type. I just wanna hang out with you. I don't want to shake up your life."

"I don't wanna shake up your life." I placed a lot of trust on those words. I ended the evening feeling assured that she understood that if we were to have any kind of intimate relationship, that it would not be a traditional monogamous coupling. When I left I gave her a long warm kiss at the door.

A few days later I returned to Sasha's apartment to pick up some photo prints. She seemed full of energy. I sat on the floor looking at the prints as she moved about the room lighting incense and choosing music for the CD player. She chattered non-stop as she went about her business of making everything just right.

"Sneha and Joan and I were thinking of having an Orgy... maybe up on the top of Nitanny Mountain...just girls and one guy...we were thinking you might be the one."

She said these words nonchalantly, as if it was commonplace as an invitation to lunch. Although excited by the idea I made no reply. In my arrogant state of mind this seemed like another part of the bounty that was my just due, and if it came to pass it would be wonderful. If not, other opportunities were sure to be on the horizon.

Letting the subject drop she joined me on the floor as we reviewed the photos and chatted. Suddenly the lights went out. She sat quietly as if nothing unusual had happened.

"What happened to the lights?" I asked.

"They're on their own wavelength," she replied cryptically, but made no effort to fix the problem.

After a period of sitting quietly in the dark without speaking, I reached out and gently touched her hand. At this slight provocation she stood up and crawled on top of me and straddled her legs around my waist.

We kissed and held each other close. She put her nose to me and said, "I just want to breathe you in."

I carried her to her bed, which was a small mattress that lay on the floor covered in a black sheet and black pillowcases. She pulled off her shirt and then mine, "I want to feel my skin against yours," she whispered.

I looked deep into her eyes and a chill went through me. My stomach fluttered as I was pulled into the depth of those mysterious black pools. In that darkness I felt as if I was seeing something eternal, that I was peering into a deep secret of my own soul that had been long forgotten, but which was pregnant with meaning and waiting to be born. What she inspired was like a fruit so swollen with seed that the slightest touch might make it burst forth, spilling its fertile bounty to he who has the vision to see what lies in wait.

My eyes took in the form of her face in amazement. "I didn't realize you were so beautiful," I gasped with a voice raspy with desperation.

Still half clothed we fell into the throes of sexual fervor, grinding against each other like two creatures starved for passion. As it became increasingly hot and heavy I tried to cool things down, "I don't want this to go too far so fast," I moaned.

When I left I walked home. It was a gray day and the landscape was covered in dirty half-melted snow. I walked along the edge of the highway at a leisurely pace. Cars whizzed past me as I reflected on what had just taken place and wondered where this new adventure would lead me. I felt excited, but also an unfamiliar sense of peace. Although if I really understood the path I was heading down I might have run in the opposite direction.

July 18, 1994

It's hard to continue sleeping once the sun begins to spill through the car windshield. Last night I parked in Samantha's driveway. At least there I have less chance of being arrested for vagrancy or having the police find out that I am driving without a license.

Samantha's parents are on vacation for a week leaving their luxurious house at her disposal. I don't feel comfortable spending time with her or accepting her assistance because she is constantly tormenting me with the deceptively cutting comments that roll off of her angry tongue. She is a master at floating remarks that sound innocent enough at first, but lay in unconscious wait, with razor sharp fangs and saber claws, to prey on moments of doubt and devour confidence with stealth precision.

Her half Thai lineage is seen on her face, which sits unexpectedly on a tall thin frame. It is morning and I sit on the opposite end of the kitchen table watching as she eats bagels and drinks orange juice. I went to sleep hungry and the aroma of the bagel re-awakens that hunger. My eyes are hypnotized by the richly inviting color of the juice. She drinks it out of a crystal wine glass as she chatters with a gay, childlike air. Underneath she is a woman scorned, and every bite of that sustaining bagel, and every generous draught of that juice is a calculated act of vengeance.

Usually her attacks are hidden beneath a veil of civility. On occasion the veil is lifted and she simply taunts me with names like "asshole" and "loser," or she chides Sasha – "Why does she dance like her wrists are broken?" "How can you love someone with a honker like that?"

I always try to feel compassion for her situation even while she pummels my self-esteem. I tell myself, "I'm strong. I can take it." So I smile through the pain in my guts as she smears blue jam over the bottom half of the bagel, thankful to be sitting here out of the hot sun for awhile.

It was through Samantha that I got the factory job. Her father is the head of the janitorial staff and she is also scab working. Being the only person I know in this town, I am forced to depend on her at times for matters of survival. The price I pay for this is placing myself within the domain of her manipulations.

After her breakfast we sit on the deck overlooking the community of small mansions from our position on top of a hill. The neighborhood is sterile. No signs of life. No trees. No children. On the next ridge seven tiny golf carts move to and fro, saving their passengers the burden of walking from tee to tee.

From the portable CD player the soundtrack to the film 'The Commitments' plays. Samantha is a background singer and dancer in The Imperial Orgy. As such she idealizes the romanticized vision of her role that the film portrayed. Considering it was only a year ago that I convinced her to have confidence in herself and attempt the role of musician and performer, I suppose such naiveté is understandable.

The music plays and she dances around the deck singing. As I gaze outward over the ridge I try not to notice the way her ass sticks out of her bikini-bottom, which she has pulled up between her cheeks like a G-string. She turns away from me and wiggles her bottom a few feet from the left of my vision.

"Do you think anyone would notice my boobies from the next house?" she asks as she pulls off her top and plops down on a lawn-chair. Since I struck out on breakfast I escape the situation by moving on to my second basic need.

"Could I get a shower?" I ask blandly.

"Can you make it quick?" she examines the tan line on her abdomen with a sensual stroke of her forefinger.

The guest shower is in the basement. After I undress she opens the door without knocking.

Handing me a bar of soap she says sarcastically, "Don't wash your dick with my washcloth. I don't want to get any Indian germs."

The shower doesn't have much pressure. The water is warm and washes away the dirt in noticeable streams of brown on the tub's bottom. It's been two days since my last shower. My body is showing the signs of wear from my unsanitary habits. My face has broken out and my legs have begun to rash behind the joints where I sweat.

It is the dirtiness that makes me feel sub-human. I would like to find a quiet stream where I could bathe daily. The area is a sprawl of concrete and geometric forms. Order: the hallmark of civilization. There are too many people to expect to find a private spot in nature. Nature has been reduced to the green patches between the shopping malls. And even if I could find a stream it would never be private enough to avoid the social shock of the nudity required for bathing.

Only a half hour left before it's time to go to the factory. The streams of water heading towards the drain are no longer brown. The water bounces off my face like a massage of warm needles. Sasha comes to my mind as she does every other moment. I wish I could call her, but I can't afford the call. Plus I don't want to annoy her by my lack of frugality. Our relationship has evolved into an almost childlike position for me. This may be a natural role for her based on what I see with her parents. She often scolds me quietly for the irresponsible way I handle my botched financial affairs. After years of hopelessness I am having a hard time returning to long term planning.

Somehow our positions have changed and I have become her suitor. It is I who holds demands for future commitments, and she who remains logical. In order to prove my love I have prostrated myself before her and what is more boring than love handed over so easily.

On top of this the degradation of my financial mess and the humiliation of my living conditions has broken my pride, which makes it impossible for me to relate to her with my usual confidence. My mind is a pendulum swinging between turmoil and resolve. The insanity of my dark moments must surely be apparent in these writings.

It was not always this way with us. In the beginning I was at my height of surety. The Imperial Orgy was showing the first small bloom of success. At this time she came to me unheeded. Writing me poetry, sometimes nervous below my gaze. When I cried she called me a king. When I was weak she saw my openness as strength. She urged me to let go when I hesitated to feel deep emotions.

But it's been five months of chaos and struggle. In her writing she called me her "Scorpion knight who laid down his armor." To exist in this world one needs protection. When I placed my armor back on it was tarnished in her eyes.

We are both fraught by our personal situations and our relationship show signs of wear. Before I can hope to rebalance the relationship I must first achieve some success in my own life.

With this thought I am brought back to reality by a piercing buzzer on the factory floor. The screech warns me that a conveyor belt is clogged and I scurry to climb the yellow ladder to clear it. I have no sense of what our labors here lead to nor do I care. Just give me my paltry paycheck and the meager hope that comes with it. This hope is the hope of a man clutching at straw.

For weeks my relationship with Sasha went on like a dream. Being with her was like hiding out from life. On warm spring afternoons I would sneak into her basement lair and suddenly my worries and responsibilities seemed a million miles away. She offered her love to me for free, and I enjoyed taking it as such.

Besides Sasha there was another woman named Joan who I was beginning to court. I moved slowly. I would call her occasionally and we would talk about eventually getting together for lunch. Joan and Sasha were friends and both were supposed to be part of Sasha's proposed orgy.

The promise of free love was in the air. It seemed to be on the tip of everyone's tongue, yet no one could muster the courage to quite say the words. Free love was implied in the message of The Imperial Orgy lyrics and called like a siren song to the women who frolicked in mock petting orgies on the dance floor during each concert. Free love hung in the echoes of the 60's that the Dead-Head scene that followed us attempted to recreate. Free love was a beacon that seduced these girls into their hesitating explorations of lesbianism and talk of orgies. They seemed to be just waiting for someone to show them the way. Waiting for a Pan, a Dionysus with a steady hand and a reassuring voice to free them of their fears and inhibitions and lead them into a life of pleasure.

Looking back I see this all with perfect clarity, but at the time it was a vague notion obscured by the noise of day-to-day life. An unconscious ideal that we could never quite articulate into a clear thought. The ideal was repressed by fear, and lost amid emotional confusion. Although we longed to break through the social binds that held such freedoms in check, instead we danced around the periphery of the sacred fire, unable to jump in to die and be reborn.

It seemed that those who were drawn to this flame of free love were also looking for community, family, and acceptance. The desire for free love is always complicated by the need for personal, possessive love. The way of traditional monogamous love is a well-worn path that is easy to fall into, and once one possesses it, the call of free love can appear to be frightfully threatening to that security. Free love is often a destructive as well as a creative force. Rebirth always requires destruction, and free love is a passage to a new spiritual state, a journey fraught with perils that most fail to survive.

As for myself, somehow I felt this orgy and these women represented a divine right I was destined to fulfill. I believed it was understood that I belonged to no one and that the situation was fair and open to all involved. But I too was caught in that tug-of-war between the desire to experience free love and the desire for personal possessive love. And as is often the case, what is offered for free later comes with a price tag.

One gray morning I called Sasha from a phone booth and in a serious tone she said, "I need to talk to you."

I knew there was trouble. "I don't want to lose what we have," I responded sincerely.

We met up on a deserted side street and sat in my car. She said, "I want to reconsider this. I don't think I can put myself through this again."

After beating around the bush for a while I finally got the real story out of her. On the previous night, after an Imperial Orgy show, she and Joan were in Sasha's apartment. They began to kiss and caress each other. They were opening their hearts as well as their bodies to each other. In the middle of their lesbian exploration Joan confided to Sasha that she believed that she and I were moving towards a serious relationship. Although this serious relationship was only in her own mind, it caused a rift between the two, their lesbian affair came to an abrupt halt, and now Sasha was angry at me.

I was completely surprised by this because I had no idea that Sasha saw us as having any kind of monogamous relationship. In fact, I thought it was understood that there were no commitments. After I told Sasha that there was really nothing between Joan and I, she held me and caressed my face.

I told Sasha I didn't see how we could have a serious relationship when she would be graduating soon and returning to her home in New Jersey. She countered that she would be near New York City where the band was planning to move, and she wanted to stay near both me and The Imperial Orgy. She said she planned to move to New York after living with her parents for a year. Despite this, in my heart I assumed the relationship would fizzle out once she moved back to New Jersey.

With each day that followed I found myself spending more time with Sasha. We would spend magical afternoons in her bedroom, listening to Indian classical music, lying in each other's arms, talking and making love. I cared about her, but I really didn't lose control of my emotions and fall in love with her. Then one day she said, "This is really special for me. Is it for you too?"

I thought, "Oh no, what am I going to tell this girl?" I mumbled some nonsense while weaseling my way out of really answering. On another day as I left her apartment she said again, "This is really special for me. Is it for you?"

Without thinking I said, "Well this is the first time everything lines up, there's nothing missing."

She seemed satisfied with my answer and I went on my way. On the drive home I began to reflect on the words I had so casually spoken. "For the first time everything lines up."

I found her utterly beautiful. Although her body type was not usually what I would look for, I now craved the sensuality of her small form. She was creative and strong. She was intelligent and introspective and fascinating to talk to. Something that is extremely important in a long-term relationship. She was very feminine in a way you don't find in American women that often. She was soft and pliant, yet had a forceful will of her own. Best of all, she embraced life with passion and had a free and adventurous spirit, a quality I longed for in a woman.

And there was a secret desire of mine that has quietly controlled my destiny: for my whole life I have been searching for someone I could share my spiritual life with. Someone who had an inherent sense of spiritual wisdom, but also a desire to learn and build on that knowledge.

I wanted my spirituality to be present in my day-to-day life, and if you can't share that with your partner, not only does it impede your own spiritual growth, it steals away life's richness.

It made me think of a night early in my relationship with Samantha when I attempted to explain my spiritual beliefs and experiences to her in one passionate outburst. She looked at me as if I had just told her the moon was made of green cheese. After that, such things were never spoken of again and I continued to live a lie, keeping my deepest beliefs a quiet secret and feeling the isolation that came with living in such a way.

Soon after these events with Sasha, Michael Mordes, Dave Surreal and I went to a house party where a bunch of hippies were hanging out. It was a brisk spring night when the moonlight painted the landscape with lavender highlights. Although there was a nip in the air that reminded one more of autumn than spring, one could feel that the warmth and fertility of spring's bounty was ready to burst forth. The air was sweet with fecundity that seemed hidden just below the surface of every living thing, plant and animal alike.

Sasha was in the basement dancing alone in the middle of the room to a drum-circle jam while a crowd of wallflowers passed around joints and stared at her movements with a stoned-eyed gaze. As soon as she saw me she left her spot at the center of attention and we snuck outside and held each other in a dark corner beside the house. "My moon came today," she whispered.

She had eaten a hit of LSD and asked me to follow her home for safety's sake. Once we arrived she begged me to come inside for a while. Picturing Samantha at home waiting for me, with a guilty heart I told her I could only stay for a minute. Inside we kissed for a few minutes then I stood up to leave. As I went to walk out the door she whispered, "Caeser, I love you."

I felt a weakness overtake me. I went and lay my head against her breasts. My eyes were wet and I was speechless.

The next day I gave Sasha the lyrics to a song I had just written called "To Whom It May Concern."

I don't want your happiness
Please just give me pain
I don't want your happiness
Pain is what I deserve

My heart gives birth to rage
My soul breathes violence

And this is fair warning
I'm gonna devour your life
And this is fair warning

You'd better save yourself

Did I tell you I love you?
No! And I never will
Did I tell you I need you?
Those words will never be spoken

I don't want the beauty of love
Please just give me hate
I don't want that paradise
You can't hate me more than I hate myself

Your love falls by the way
Cause when I feel pain - at least I know I'm alive

I've always been ruled by savage instincts
I've been corrupted
Now should I drag you down too?

Could I rule the world?
Yes! If you get on your knees
Would I like to kiss you?
Or maybe tear you to pieces?

Haven't you figured it out yet?
I don't care about anyone but myself
And if it feels right
I know there must be something wrong
And if you see me smile

My panic is rising inside

But you won't believe I'm serious
Until you see me lying dead
Why should I tell you what the voices say?
You won't believe until it's too late

Pain is like an old friend returned
Pain is a sweet fix
For a cruel addiction
And when I hurt you is when I need you most
And when I need a savior
Is when you'll give up trying
And when I need a savior
Is when you'll say goodbye
But I don't want a savior so just go your way

The Lyrics felt potent to me, as if it summed up everything that was rotten in all my relationships with women, and revealed the ugly secrets of my sense of self.

Despite this I was falling in love with her. A few days later we were sitting in her room and as I looked into her eyes I warned her, "If I let go I'm going to overwhelm you."

She looked directly back into my eyes and replied, "Overwhelm me."

July 26, 1994

Eight days ago Sasha returned to State College to attend the annual arts festival. One of the peculiarities of my situation is that on a moment's notice I will go from living like a cretin to living it up. One day my stomach aches for food, the next it is filled with fine food and drink. Her visit was two nights of lavish partying.

The visit starts off on a bad note when Sasha is late for our meeting on a street corner in the center of town. Throughout the early part of the night she seems distant. She seems starved for attention, but not from me. After a month trapped at home under parental restriction her ego is in a rage. Although she would deny it, or might even be unaware of it, her manner of communicating is flirtatious. Every man thinks she is coming on to him. At a bar she leaves me with her friend Ornelia and goes towards the bathroom and does not return. When I go to look for her she is sitting on the lap of a large man who sits on the stairway by the Ladies room.

When I give her a threatening look she follows and apologizes, "Sitting on his leg like that, I didn't even think about it because I was never in a relationship. He's just an old friend, it doesn't mean anything."

Later she, Ornelia, and I end up at a rambunctious college aged party where a band plays in the basement. I am ten years older then everyone else and feeling a bit alienated from the youthful exuberance. The band is a lame Pearl Jam imitation and I feel frustrated because The Imperial Orgy hasn't performed in months.

I leave the basement and wander around upstairs where there are only a few stragglers milling about. Soon the girls join me. Somehow the three of us end up lying on the couch with a strange fellow who seems to be confused by the entire situation. Our bodies are piled on top of each other and I gently caress Ornelia's upper thigh, just below the hem of her short skirt.

After the strange night with Sasha I am feeling a bit insecure and angry. Lying with both Sasha and Ornelia's bodies on top of mine it is a moment of erotic possibility, but again I feel that tug-of-war between the desire for sexual freedom and the need for the security of personal love. I can smell the sweet odor of Ornelia's perfume mixing with the familiar scent of Sasha's shampoo. Their bodies are warm and soft, but no one moves too much. No one has the courage to take things too far.

When the failed orgy breaks up we find ourselves walking through the back yard where a line is formed in front of a keg of beer. Sasha wants to hold my hand and in my sour mood I refuse. When we leave Sasha is distressed.

"Why didn't you want to hold my hand?" she asks in a hurt voice.

"I don't know about all this.." I mutter.

Suddenly her own insecurities burst through. "I can change," she exclaims as if about to breakdown in tears. Although to anyone with a little perception it is clear she is fraught by insecurities, she has willed a hard outer surface into existence that makes her appear strong and confident. For just a moment her vulnerability was revealed. Then just as quickly the moment is gone. She has a solid veneer and the whole subject is dropped.

When we get back to my apartment she is eager to please. I say I have never seen her drunk and she takes a long swill of a bottle of Vodka that is stored in the kitchen. Soon her stomach is understandably upset. Despite this we make love and go to sleep feeling close.

On the second day of the arts festival I run into my old film professor Deirdre Pribram. She is a devout feminist and has always viewed me as a Neanderthal who manipulates those around him to get his own way. Our relationship has always been one where she feels free to tear me to pieces at her slightest whim. I always accepted this laughingly because I felt I could use her criticism as a form of tough self-analysis. When we meet I quickly update her on my life's course.

"Caeser you always keep it exciting" she says disparagingly.

Shaking my head I respond, "I've had enough excitement now. I'm ready to stop this insanity."

"You couldn't take it. You'd get too bored," is her reply.

"Just wait and see," I prophesize.

This is a vision many of my friends have developed of me over the last five years. The persona of the searching, suffering artist has become my image, and even more dangerous, my self image. This persona is definitely a part of my character, but during these five years this enfant terrible has been in control of my life. And the battle with him gives birth to many of these pages.

The enfant terrible is a trick mirror. Look at the mirror from a distance and you see an ego standing on a platform in all glory and splendor. There are marching bands, uniformed security guards, bullhorns, whips and batons. But look at the mirror a little closer and you see a black hole of apprehension in emaciated human form quivering in the corner of a self built chamber of desolation.

Sunday evening Sasha leaves for home. She doesn't want to leave and is running late by the time she gets on the road. A few hours later her mother calls me concerned that her daughter is late. To ease her mind I tell her that she got a late start and she should be arriving soon. Later that night Sasha calls and is angry and emotional. When she arrived home she told her mother that she was late because of traffic and didn't leave late. Only then does the mother admit that she spoke to me. This might seem like a minor infraction, but within the twisted dynamics of her Indian family traditions it becomes a major issue. In her emotional state Sasha blames me for telling her mother the truth about her late departure. In the middle of the night she calls back to apologize but it is too late.

Her anger awoke the insecurities of the enfant. He leaps from behind the bed and runs madly through the streets like a primal beast. Furry, feral, and with curved spine. Ready to devour. He wanders the streets, from bar to bar, seeking solace, self-pitying, gushing pathos, pathetic and insipid. Tonight no words of assurance will ease the beast.

Sasha,

In the morning it was he who called you. I swear to you it wasn't me! When you told him you thought you might be pregnant. That you were emotionally distraught and obsessed with fear. He did not listen. Instead he attacked you. In your weak moment he tormented you and then ask you to comfort him when it was you who needed understanding and support.

In the end he hung up the phone saying he didn't know if our love was worth it. Although you told him not to give up, he did not listen. By the time I called back to apologize you had been through enough.

He had awakened when I read your old poetry. The ones written for all the men in the past who had hurt you. He said that you would never react that way if I left you and he said he would prove it. The irony is your tears finally fell when you told me it was over between us. I want to kiss away those tears. I wanted to taste the salt of your emotions. You sobbed and I was not there to hold you.

I believed I could walk away from you without looking back. Only then did I really understand how unbearable separation was. I was shaken to the core. I am still shaking.

Although you gave us another chance we dance on a razor's edge. The ties that bind are pulled taught with stress that could break at any moment.

I hold an image in my mind. I dig down deep. Relics reveal. The dust falls by the way. Carbon begets coal. Coal begets diamond. Diamond begets a crystal more perfect than any the mind can comprehend. I hold an image in mind.

Can you hear me calling you? I am far away but listen with your heart. Listen with your soul. Listen with the memory below. Can you hear me calling?

I awake with the full moon hanging in the tree branches outside the car window. The sky is purple and the clouds roll by hurriedly. In the back seat of my car Jim Morrison is dying. So is Jimi Hendrix, Janis Joplin, Lenny Bruce, Sid Vicious and an endless pantheon of self-destructive heroes. The image is an American archetype that can be unconsciously imitated by every school kid in the western world who dares to pick up an electric guitar or step in front of a microphone on a rock and roll stage. Drugs, power, sexual abandon, fast driving and howling at night. He is dying in the back seat of my car. I chant for an hour straight. Pain soars through my body. Poison runs through my veins. My eyes rolled up in my head, I beg the unknowable void for redemption.

Each morning I awake with the sunrise and a voice moves through my mind; "just kill yourself". Not once but repeatedly. On bad days the voice comes at night or in the afternoon. The voice does not mean that I am ready to run a hose from the exhaust pipe to the window crack of the Topaz. Even amidst this suffering I love life.

In my diffracted ego, beside the voice urging my self-destruction are other voices. One proclaims my genius. Reminding me that I am capable of anything if I just get off my ass and do it. These two voices are the extremes of a cacophony of naysayers, cheering squads, wagging fingers, purveyors of ancient wisdom, tempters to childish impulses, and I am floating in the stratosphere the grand mediator of this treasure of psychic babble. I give the voices free reign to be as creatively insane as they like and I attempt to listen like an attentive father and pick and choose what I have most use for.

But at night when I lay my dreams down to the play of the unconscious it is the two extreme voices that speak the loudest. "Just kill yourself. Nobody cares." "You're a genius. You know what destiny holds for you." "Just kill yourself." "You're a genius." "Kill yourself." "You're a genius…"

Soon we were engulfed in love. The kind of love that takes you completely: body, mind, and soul. The kind of love that takes you to the heights of ecstasy that feels like a mixture of drug-induced inebria and mystical euphoria. I felt a deep happiness inside even though my world was falling apart around me.

But once you surrender to love it becomes a madness. Some say it a shared delusion. An addiction supreme. One must possess the beloved. And sometimes it can ever be enough. Your values can be turned on their head. Nothing else matters except to feed the flames of that sweet desire.

The situation with Samantha was worsening. I was staying away as often as possible and she knew we were moving apart. An issue that really put a wedge between us was that she insisted that I hold back my seduction of audience members during Imperial Orgy performances to a minimum. I felt this was an infringement on sacred territory. That this demand stood in the way of both my work as an artist, and of fulfilling my destiny as individual.

The next performance that followed this demand was lackluster at best. I felt that my wings had been clipped. I was trying to do what I do with my hands tied behind my back. Caeser Pink had been castrated.

On top of this The Imperial Orgy was deteriorating. Each gig it seemed we became worse instead of better. When we started I swore we would never play the same town too often. But we were being offered money and soon we were playing the same clubs over and over on almost a weekly basis. The musicians seemed bored and their attitudes became lousy.

Ron Boi, our bass player was an alcoholic and his drinking was becoming a major problem. By halfway through each show he was so wasted that his playing was almost non-existent. We had many talks with him and finally told him he couldn't drink at all during performances. After that he was angry and belligerent.

My financial situation was going from bad to worse. The bank foreclosed on the house I once shared with Leilani. I was without income and was not having any luck finding work so that I could raise money to move to New York City. The rest of the band members were preparing to move. Michael was leaving in a few days and Samantha, Dave and I planned to join him at the end of the summer.

Although I couldn't imagine it would be too much of an issue, one day I casually asked Sasha how her parents would feel about her going out with a white guy.

"That's all I've ever went out with so they'll just have to deal with it," she said nonchalantly.

That was enough for me. I figured it was all cool. No big deal at all. But she was deceiving me, and all too soon I would learn the truth. It turned out her parents were quite wealthy, owning nearly a million dollars in real estate. Plus she was a first generation Indian woman and an interracial marriage would be a disgrace to the family. I did not know it at the time, but this situation was Sasha's greatest fear in life, and she was not mentally equipped to deal with the pressure.

As spring came to an end Sasha was graduating from college and was scheduled to move back in with her parents in New Jersey for the summer, during which she planned to find a job in New York City. When I arrived in New York City in the fall we would be reunited.

One night while I was at her place Sasha's mother called. Sasha had been writing a fictionalized short story based on her relationship with her mother for her creative writing class. She began to ask her mother questions about marriage under the guise of research for the story. She said, "What would you do if I said I wanted to marry a white man?"

Finally her mother asked outright whether she was seeing someone. Sasha told her the truth about me, at least part of the truth.

After the conversation ended I felt relieved. She had told her mother and there were no fireworks. Sasha was not feeling so confident. The rest of the evening she was obsessed. She kept bowing her head down in anxiety and crying, "My mother, my fucking mother! I bet she's telling my father right now. I know she won't sleep tonight. I'm sure she'll call back in the morning."

The next morning the call came. Her father wanted to know what was going on. He was concerned that after paying her way through college she was betraying the family by marrying a white man. He told her, "It wouldn't be so bad if he was a doctor or a lawyer."

That day we went to a local outdoor music festival. There was dread hanging over us and her state of mind was very distraught. She drove like a wild woman screaming the lyrics to an Indigo Girls song on the tape deck at the top of her lungs. She couldn't think of anything except the situation with her parents. Depression and anxiety permeated everything she said to everyone we met. I still didn't really understand what the big deal was, but the drama of her mood carried me with her.

The next week marked the beginning of a nightmare that would not soon end. When Sasha and I first began seeing each other she told me she did not believe in marriage and did not see herself ever marrying, but from the moment her mother found out about us, marriage was constantly on her mind. She was concerned about what the conditions would be if we married. She said, "When I marry it's forever, there's no divorce."

Myself, I felt like I was floating down a peaceful river that flowed through a land of confusion and chaos. I had never wanted to be married, but the thought of marriage now seemed just great. It seemed like a perfect way to celebrate my chaotic past coming to an end. I seemed to go with the flow of these events and felt helpless to stop the tide of change. I was in love and despite all the proof to the contrary I believed that with a little faith everything would work out fine.

With all this talk about marriage my view of my own future began to be altered. I felt a heavy pressure from Sasha to break my promise to Samantha not to break up with her before we got to New York and to end things with her immediately. Things with Samantha had already deteriorated. She was coming home drunk at night and I was never around. She knew there were problems, but believed I would be faithful to her.

Finally I was spending an evening with Sasha in her comforting lair. I was lying on top of her kissing her. I told her the previous evening that Samantha asked if there was another woman and I said, "No."

Sasha froze. She felt that after the sacrifice she made telling her mother about me, that I should be willing to make an equal sacrifice for her.

I decided I would have to tell Samantha that night. I was torn between guilt for both women and I cursed myself for getting into this situation. My decision was that I was planning a future with Sasha and I had to be strong and be honest with Samantha and face the consequences.

When I got home that night Samantha was not there. She came home late that night drunk and incoherent. The next morning when she woke up I told her, "There is someone else."

"Who?" she asked.

When I replied, "Sasha," she went insane. In our circle of friends everyone disliked Sasha and she was the butt of many cruel jokes. This made it a great insult to Samantha that I would leave her for Sasha. She collapsed in tears. She curled up in a fetal position sobbing and repeating, "Love me, love me..."

Seeing her in pain sent my sense of self-loathing into the stratosphere. Samantha had a shy innocence about her and I always felt protective of her, yet now I was the one betraying her. She grabbed a bottle of codeine tablets and began gulping them down. I grabbed them from her and tried to make her spit them out. I flushed them down the toilet, but I didn't know how many she had eaten.

I carried her to the car and drove her to the hospital emergency room. When we arrived she begged me not to make her go in and promised me that she had only swallowed three of the pills. To reassure her I told her she could still live with us in New York and I still wanted her in the band.

From then on I was crippled by guilt. Much of my self-destructive behavior was rooted in guilt. In a dark corner of my mind I hated myself for the people I had hurt, and unconsciously I acted to punish myself for my behavior.

Samantha was a master at using guilt against me. As things crumbled I was trying to hold the band together. Samantha now wanted to torment me for my betrayal and this became her means of doing so. This dynamic: my guilt, her desire to punish me, and my desire to hold the band together became a nightmare that ate away at me, keeping me mentally imbalanced.

But within a few days everything changed. Sasha moved back to New Jersey and Samantha moved back to live in her parent's house in York, PA so that she could save up money to move to New York City with the rest of the band. Ron Boi had been kicked out of the band because of his drinking, and Michael Mordes was already in New York.

After all of the chaos and stress, I suddenly found myself alone, and my life empty. All my thoughts focused on the move to New York. Everything I desired lay there; the band, my future as an artist, and my future with Sasha.

The problem was that this move would be extremely expensive and not only did I not have any money, I could not find a job. I began desperately trying to find any job I could. Each day I went to the unemployment office, scoured the help wanted section of the papers, and randomly went into local businesses asking if they had any jobs. The constant rejection day after day was depressing. It made me feel worthless. Finally I swallowed my pride and went to McDonalds.

When I left college and began working at the film production company I thought, "I'll never have to wear a polyester suit, name tag, and paper hat again." But here I was sitting in a booth at McDonalds with a pudgy, pimply-faced assistant manager who was about ten years my junior sitting across from me looking over my resume.

He seemed nervous in my presence. "So you've had fast food experience?" he asked, even though it was all spelled out on the resume.

"Yes, I worked for years at Kentucky Fried Chicken, both in the kitchen and at the cash register," I announced, trying to muster some sense of pride at this accomplishment.

"We don't have anything right now, but we'll keep your resume on file," he said. We shook hands and I walked out, noting the relief on his face as I left.

When I was turned down for a job at McDonalds I knew I was in trouble. To make matters worse, during an argument with Samantha about New York I told her to live with Dave Surreal without me. The three of us planned to be roommates in NYC, but Samantha didn't want to live with me after the break-up. Now I was on my own. Making the expense of getting an apartment far beyond my means. Despair took me. Getting to New York began to seem impossible. I began to feel like only radical actions could save me.

July 31, 1994

Sunday night I find myself in Giants Stadium. Sasha and I sit in the "interview room" backstage. It has been a weekend spent with her friend Mark. He is the lighting director for a company doing stage production for a joint concert with Billy Joel and Elton John. We are at the concert as his guests.

The weekend was spent hanging out with Mark in Manhattan. For years he has been asking Sasha to marry him. He is Indian via the U.K, wealthy, and living the kind of rock and roll lifestyle she dreams of. Except for occasional bragging he seems like a very nice guy.

Throughout the weekend I have almost no money in my pockets. He is eager to spend his on everyone. He is outgoing. I am quiet and brooding. If you have money it is no big deal to have someone spend theirs on you. If you don't have money it is degrading. Especially given these circumstances with Sasha.

Sasha and I sit in the interview room reading and discussing the author Anais Nin whom she has become infatuated with. Now and then a band member wanders in to meet with their parents. The fathers wear polyester pants and golf shirts and the mothers wear bad wigs, with a tendency towards fire engine red as a color choice for those exalted hairpieces. It is five in the afternoon and we haven't eaten yet. Mark has said he would return to take us to the cafeteria, but seems to have forgotten.

I have told Sasha about these writings that you are reading now, and she urges me to share it with her. Her state of mind has been somewhat fragile and I hesitate to let her read it. Finally deciding that I will read it to her, we retire to a separate room where it is more private. When I pick up the pages to begin reading I am overtaken by a sick feeling inside. I waver. I take a breath to gather courage.

Right as I open my mouth to begin reading Mark suddenly bursts into the room full of energy and good cheer. He whisks Sasha away into a nearby game-room and I am left with a dumbfounded look on my face and my sheets of writing still in my hand as if I am about to begin a great oration and the curtain suddenly and unceremoniously closes in front of me.

In the next room Mark and Sasha are playing a video game where cars race around a winding track. When I finally tag along into the room I find Sasha playing the game while he cheers her on with his overwrought British accent. His never-ending enthusiasm irritates me. His bright disposition against my dark depression makes me feel invisible. Every dollar he spends on her makes me feel like a loser. Every moment with him makes me feel smaller as a man.

As Sasha plays the game she spins the steering wheel and her car turns a corner rapidly.

"Whoa, Sash that's the way to do it buddy! You got it now!" Mark cheers her on.

She is doing terrible and crashes her car with a loud explosion.

"Try again. Try again. You just got to ease the petrol on the turns then floor et on the stretch!" he tells her excitedly.

After a while he urges me, "Whot, aren't you going to try it Caes?"

I take the wheel of the video game. I already feel agitated by the thwarted reading attempt, and all this good cheer has soured my mood considerably. I have always been lousy at playing these car driving video games and suddenly I feel like I am on a high school proving ground and about to be humiliated on the athletic field by some jock while the girl of my dreams looks on.

I take the wheel more apathetic than eager. My apathy is forced, born of pride: inside I am fighting my own childish framing of the situation. I drive, I spin the steering wheel back and forth with reckless abandon, but I am not there. My mind is on page thirty-four of the book 'Zen And The Art Of Archery.'

"What a bunch of bullshit that book is," I think to myself. "Anyone who believes that crap must be insane. Suckers. Suckers the whole world over. Corporate America has its eyes on America's spiritual suckers. And they create more suckers in an never-ending cycle."

I come back realizing I have won all three of the driving matches. Suddenly Mark has lost all interest in the video game and remembers he has some business he must attend to immediately.

It is a pathetic victory. He is still the boss of an operation working on a multimillion-dollar concert tour, and I can't even get a job wearing a paper hat. But my little victory provides a seed of hope. A tiny flame of belief that there is something inside me that can pull me through in the end.

'Zen And The Art Of Archery.' I am a liar. I lie to myself and laugh at my own jokes. I know and not know.

In the end the concert turns out to be a great time. Neither Sasha or I are fans of the performers. None-the-less it is a good show. After the concert Mark takes us up on the stage to check it out. The band's equipment is being covered in clear plastic. As Sasha walks around the stage with Mark I stand on the edge looking out over the seventy five thousand empty seats. I am filled with a confidence I haven't known in months. I believe in my heart I will be back here. I speak the words in my mind. 'I swear to God I will return'.

My vow is not really what has meaning for me. It is that I understand what ease and comfort I would feel on that stage. The knowledge that I could control that stage and move the people in those filled seats better than the rock stars who just left and are now driving back in their limousines. They are not hungry. I am.

Back in State College my financial situation remained desperate and my inability to find a job continued to wear me down. A friend of mind offered me some part time work cleaning parking lots. At midnight I arrived at an empty parking lot behind a large supermarket. The pay was low and the work was dirty and boring. After four years of college I found myself sweeping parking lots on the graveyard shift for a little more than minimum wage.

After a few hours working in the parking lot I went to a bar and had a drink or two. I had also taken some cold pills. For months I had been driving without a license. As luck would have it when I left the bar to go home I was pulled over by the police. Depressed and sedated I was forced to walk a straight line and stand on one leg and touch my nose at the edge of the highway. I felt like a trained monkey performing circus tricks for the amusement of men in uniforms. Even though I was driving without a license the police allowed me to drive my car home. With no money to my name I was given another large fine for driving without a license, but at least I didn't get a driving under the influence charge and end up in jail.

The next morning Samantha called. She was living with her parents in York, PA and was working as a scab worker during a strike at a Cat plant that her father worked at. She said that I could get work there. It only paid seven dollars an hour, but she said I could work overtime and work seven days a week in order to raise money to get to New York.

I decided to take the job and sleep in my car to save money. It all sounded good in theory, but from the first day it was a fool's errand. My job at the factory was to make sure a system of conveyor belts didn't get clogged up as they carried along boxes of equipment parts. It was a mechanical maze of filth and roaring noise. When a conveyor belt got clogged a buzzer went off and the entire factory came to a screeching halt. Then to the rescue, I would run up a ladder and clear the path with a long metal pole.

Most of the time I spent sitting on the filthy concrete floor waiting for the buzzer to ring. Some days it might go off every two minutes, other nights it might be once an hour. The noise of the factory was deafening. The entire scene was depressing.

In order to get the job I had to take a short test that required that I do simple math problems such as adding five and eight. From speaking to some of my co-workers I am guessing that such math problems might have been something of a challenge for them.

After the first week overtime was not permitted. It seems the factory was actually making a killing off the strike and was in no hurry for it to end because they were paying the scab workers a fraction of what the regular employees earned.

Even worse than the depressing conditions in the factory was the experience of living in a car. I thought I was being heroic by doing whatever it took to reach my goals. Yet living like a vagabond made me feel even more of a loser. I was always filthy since there was nowhere to shower. It was the middle of a hot summer and within a short period the combination of dirt and sweat caused me to break out in irritating rashes on my legs and chests. Finding a bathroom to use was a never-ending problem. Plus having no way to store or prepare food meant always having to eat out. I tried to conserve money by only eating one meal a day at the factory cafeteria. Soon the lack of food began to make me weak and ill.

Another source of stress was that having no driver's license I was always in fear that the police would stop and ask why I was sleeping in the car and then arrest me for vagrancy. Throughout this time I was still paying rent back in State College. The situation was crazy. My state of mind was deteriorating so much that I couldn't deal with the stress any longer.

The truth is that it was not my living conditions that bothered me in itself, but that my friends and band members suddenly judged me so harshly. According to Samantha, Michael Mordes, who had lived with me for free for many months now referred to me as a bum. Dave, Michael, and Samantha, all who grew up in middle class homes where they never had to struggle, now all looked down on me because of my predicament.

And the situation with Sasha's parents made my poverty more humiliating. My entire existence had to be lied about for her parent's benefit. Sasha carried guilt about my situation, which put her in a double bind that she was not mentally equipped to deal with. I felt completely isolated and incredibly lonely. The hot summer afternoons left me with nowhere to go and nothing to do. My main goal was to try to stay out of the sun and out of the way of the police. The boredom left my exhausted mind free to obsess on the hopelessness of my situation.

The only person I knew in York was Samantha and when I was with her, she would unleash her anger on me because of the breakup. Seeing that I was living in my car, Samantha's father suggested I stay with them. This caused even more confusion. It lasted about three days before I was back on the streets.

Aug. 3, 1994

It is 11AM and I am running late for work as I drive back from New Jersey where I spent the weekend with Sasha. If I show up late there is no doubt I will be fired. To try to save time I take

what I hope is a shortcut through Lancaster. The speedometer
reads 75 and the heat gauge is in the red. To my dismay I find
myself in a seven-mile strip of road construction. After an hour of
15 mile per hour driving I emerge to find myself thoroughly lost.
Checking the road atlas I find I am miles off my path. I pound the
steering wheel angrily. This is the last straw. I have definitely lost the
job now. I have completely fucked myself.

I arrive at the factory hours late. As I am about to drive in
through the factory gates I notice there is a melee of some sort
occurring. Within a few seconds chaos breaks-out. The strikers
begin rioting. They throw down their protest signs and begin
attacking the cars of the scab workers as they drive through the
factory gate. Car windows are smashed out and fists our thrown.

I turn and continue driving down the road, leaving the
factory and the riot to recede into my rearview mirror. I never felt
good about going against the unions in the first place. The whole
thing was getting me nowhere financially, so I was glad it was done
with.

In this moment it seems that everything in my life is
wrapped so tight that the slightest incident is elevated to a major
disaster. A few hours lost on the highway has put me in a situation
that could leave me living on the streets.

I have one more paycheck that should have been delivered
to Samantha's house over the weekend so I stay around town to get
it from her after she leaves the factory. At 10:30 in the evening I call
her from the phone booth in front of the Burger King. She is cold
on the phone. She says the check did not arrive.

I am feeling so isolated and destitute that I ask her to meet
me so we can talk. Despite her cruel moments I still think of her as
a friend and wish to ask her advice and perhaps receive some
comforting words. Much of the time she is caring and kind, and in
some ways she has really helped me through these troubled times.
We meet in a small playground behind a church near her house. We
sit on a bench beneath a tree. In her usual way she chatters
cheerfully.

"I can't wait to get out of here. It's a really cool apartment. I have to study the subway maps. It takes ten minutes to get to the ferry then I'll ride that across to Manhattan."

She turns to me as if she just noticed my sullen presence, "I'm sorry I keep taking about this, but if you're not going to say anything I'll just keep talking."

I sit quietly. It seems all I have to say has been said before. Even I am tired of hearing my own complaints. She continues willfully.

"Michael said he'd be my friend up there. His chick-babe Denise too. Boy I sure was walkin' around with my booty swingin' down in the village. My parents sure would be mad if they found out what a bad neighborhood Michael lives in."

Suddenly she pauses, "Are you gonna talk or not?"

We sit in silence. The crickets call out. A green maple leaf floats down suddenly unhinged from its limb. I reach out my hand and it lands directly within. In the close stillness of the night heat I crumble it absentmindedly. The crackle of the crisp foliage reverberates in my ears with a violence amplified beyond reality.

"I just want to thank you for all you've done and I'm sorry for everything that's happened."

She is not impressed by my worn out apology.

"I just don't know what to do. I fucked up everything. People try to help me and I let them all down." My voice has begun rising in pitch and passion as I sink into self-pity.

She speaks calmly, "If I had a million dollars..."

"I don't want a million dollars," I exude.

"I wouldn't give you a million dollars, but I might help you," she asserts, now clearly irritated.

I stand up and pace around the bench. "If I had just a little hope. My entire future depends on getting to New York and I don't stand a chance."

"Well you should've thought ahead", she retorts.

"I did think ahead! I thought I was going to be living with you and Dave. It's so expensive to get an apartment on your own."

She responds defensively, "You dumped me. What do you expect?"

"We're in the band and we're friends. I thought we'd look out for each other. And why am I the one that gets shut out?" my voice betrays anger.

"Probably Dave knows I'll clean up after him. I don't know. Maybe he is in love with me."

My mind sinks into childish depths of self-pity while my mouth attacks, "You guys wouldn't even be friends if it wasn't for the band I started, and now you get together and turn your backs on me!"

"Well Dave sees you've been outta work, he probably doesn't trust you!"

I shout with venom, "Trust me? I've worked my whole goddamned life, against struggles none of you have ever known, and you all have your rich parents to fall back on. Now I have one bad time and I'm untrustworthy. I hope just one time you guys find out what it's like. Poverty sucks you down in a hole and the further down you go the more the hole constricts so you can never escape. Because when you're down people won't give you a break."

"I'll have to pay more for a fucking flophouse than you'll be paying for your rent," I continue to rave. "And that's all because on my own I can't afford the deposits and fees. When Dave and I moved into that house in State College and I put up all my artwork he was so proud he brought all his friends around to see how he was living. You know how he lived before that, dirt and filth everywhere. I've got a stupid art collection worth thousands of dollars that I can't sell fast, yet I've got no money and no prospects. It just boggles my mind. I just can't understand how this happened and I never thought my friends would judge me like this!"

She begins shouting also, "What do you want? Do you want to live with me? Is that it?"

I pace frantically, running my hands through my hair, "No! It just hurts. You people were supposed to be my friends. Michael lived with me for eight months and never paid a cent. You lived for free for almost a year. Doesn't that mean anything? I just didn't realize the world was so cruel."

"What do you want?" she screams.

"I just want a chance," I stop in front of her.

"You'll never even be able to get past the credit check. You'll never be able to get an apartment there on your own," she glares at me. In childish rage I kick the back of the wooden bench as we shout simultaneously.

"I try to help you..." she pleads

"I might as well..." I interrupt.

"...and you just yell at me!" she completes her sentence in frustration.

"...just fuckin' give up now!" I shout.

Catching hold of myself I freeze in place. Samantha stands and begins walking towards her home hurriedly. I follow behind trying to keep pace. My voice is mild now, "I wasn't yelling at you. I just get frustrated. This stuff is driving me nuts."

She enters her living room and shuts the door quickly. Worried that I will wake her parents I knock quietly. She peaks through the curtain on the glass door. I must look pathetic because she tries to suppress her laughter when she looks at my face. Opening the door I whisper, "Could I sleep on your floor tonight? I'll be gone tomorrow."

On the basement floor I feel gratified to be able to stretch my legs instead of being cramped in the back seat of the car. In the morning I will face despair. Tonight I am too exhausted to care and I sleep deeply. No dreaming. Refreshing nullity.

In the middle of the night I am awakened by a warm feeling on my back. I lie on my stomach and I feel a hand gently sliding between my buttocks outside the biker shorts I am wearing. I am too groggy to comprehend the situation as Samantha's fingers squeeze my balls through the elastic material. Coming to, I reprimand her, "Samantha...No!"

She stops and I return to unconsciousness. Soon she begins again. She attempts to reach between my legs and grab my penis from under my belly. Still only half aware I press my body against the floor making it impossible for her to touch me. She runs her fingertips softly against my inner thighs giving me an erection against my will. I lie still for a moment, forcing my will. For the first time in years I am practicing fidelity and I don't want that to change. She makes a second futile attempt to grab my erection from underneath my weight.

"Samantha, please? I'm trying to do the right thing for once," I plead.

"Just one time. It's not the right thing to have sex with me?" she coos with a girlish voice.

"No. I don't think it is," I try to respond firmly.

She rolls unto her back and spreads her legs, rolling her hips slightly as she fingers her vagina and rubs her breasts. "C'mon don't you want to?" she moans.

I sit up. Staring at her half-asleep and wondering if I am dreaming or awake. Her thin lips sparkle as she spreads them slightly, revealing deepening shades of pink. Animal lust battles love's resolve. She reaches for my cock with both hands. With my left hand I pin both of her arms brutally against her waist. Her hips still writhe and she places her foot on my stomach and moves her toes down to my crotch.

I lay down on my back rubbing my eyes with my fingers trying to gain some clarity of mind. She mounts me, slipping my penis inside her and writhing her hips in a circle as she sits atop me.

At this point I surrender. The last thing I want to do is be unfaithful to Sasha, but I suppose I have done so just by taking this job in York and sleeping in Samantha's house. It is futile to fight it now.

Samantha lays down flat on my chest and begins to kiss me. Somehow the kiss angers me. I roll her over so I am on top of her and fuck her angrily. It feels more like a rape than lovemaking, but I am not sure who has been raped. She seems to take my anger calmly. When I come, not just my body, but my entire spirit collapses. Samantha holds me in her arms with a faraway look in her eyes. Her face reads that although this is some sort of victory for her, it is a hollow one. Her body feels warm and familiar to me. We both know this might be the last time we ever lay like this together. After a few minutes she walks through the dark basement to the bed where she sleeps, and I am left alone on the floor.

I lay in darkness. One of the greatest things about my relationship with Sasha is our total honesty. We have shared everything from our darkest secrets to our most private journals. But I am ashamed of this night. My weakness created this event.

The rest of the night gives little relief from my troubled thoughts. I am still awake to hear the first bird songs and see the emerging morning light. It glows through the tiny basement window. First gray. Then blue. Now blazing white. My breathing is a measured, questioning sigh. A new day.

In the morning last night's events are thankfully not spoken of. Neither can I forget them. By mid morning the sky has turned appropriately gray and gloomy. Samantha and I sit on the deck while I make calls trying to locate my missing paycheck. It seems to have vanished and neither the post office nor the temp service who hired me will take responsibility. The immediate cash seems vital for survival.

The phone rings and it is Dave Surreal, the Orgy's keyboard player. He wants to speak to me. One of the major complications of my financial situation has been that I have a lease for an apartment I share with Dave. I don't live there but I still pay $400 a month in rent. The lease is over in two weeks and I owe him almost $800 in back rent. All my earnings from the factory go to repaying him. When I speak to him on the phone he is extremely understanding. We agree he will hold my Salvador Dali lithograph until I take care of the debt. He says to make sure I have money to move to New York before I pay him.

When I hang up the phone Samantha is in an unexplainable rage. "I want you to get your stuff and get out of here for good!" she hisses.

I am completely perplexed. "What's wrong? What'd I do now?"

"The way I see it you dumped me when I needed you. Why should I, or anyone do anything for you? All you want is a free ride. Remember last week when I told you that you were the most talented man I ever met? It was all a lie. You're a joke!"

"Samantha. Why..." I don't have the will to match her steaming energy.

Her eyes glare and she gestures dramatically. "If you want somebody to go to, go to your little Indian bitch. But you can't because she doesn't want to hear it and neither do I! She doesn't give a fuck about you and nobody else does either. Why should they? If she loved you, you could go to her. Everyone's sick of you. Why don't you just kill yourself and it will be a relief to everyone?"

I am stupefied. "Samantha..." I plead

"Just go ahead and do it," she challenges me.

"Samantha I'm ..." I whine.

"Just kill yourself! You don't have the nerve. Do you? Kill yourself! Kill yourself!" she screams.

For an instant there is a total logic to her diatribe. It would be the most dignified thing I could do. It would be as simple as making the decision.

In panic I run off the deck, through the yard, and jump into my car. I drive off. As I move down the highway I suddenly feel serene even while her words echo among my thoughts.

I drive with no direction. All around me cars, trucks, and buses charge towards their destinations. Construction workers build. Factories shoot steam into the sky as they create their wares. Each human works to fulfill their desires. Their goals lead them through their days. The swarm passes me, but I have become unhinged. For this moment I am not a part of this world. I am on a mountaintop looking down as the insectiles blindly create a frenzied, delirious maelstrom. The Protestant work ethic clasps hands with greed. Corporate kings hire ad execs to condition the statistical consumers into delusions of need for products that lend nothing to life. Darwin's theories are proven by the whirling activities of the free market.

But I am moving slower. The cars pass by as indecipherable blurs. The people race by like a kinescope in hyper drive. I can no longer distinguish man or object for it all moves too fast. All colors fade into white. All sound congeals into a thunderous Aum. The galaxy is a ripple in space moving outwards from the sun. The stars paint a bed of ecstatic white heat. Einstein's theory moves in reverse. Maya bows her head. Heaven exhibits itself with a tightrope walk on the cusp of two worlds revealed as one. The world has not changed, only my perspective on it. Inside I am still.

Hours later I pull into the driveway of my apartment in State College. I have this place for two more weeks. I feel sadness when sitting on the bed. It is a storehouse of memories. Years of lovemaking took place on its broken coils.

My thoughts return to my predicament. I have one last desperate plan. I will call each of my oldest friends and borrow twenty-five dollars from each of them. With this money I will get a flophouse in New York for a week and pray that in that time I will find a job. Only after I am settled in will I tell anyone where I am and what my status is. I have always hated borrowing even small amounts of money so the prospects of this desperate plan are embarrassing beyond belief.

I begin with Bob Pacini. He was my boss at a fast food restaurant and now works at an upscale hotel.

"Hi Bob, how are ya doing?" I ask trying to sound casual.

He seems to realize I have an ulterior motive already. "Good Caeser. How about you?"

"Well actually that's what I'm calling you about."

I try not to reveal my embarrassment, "Y'know I've been going through some really rough times and I need a little help. You know I would never ask this if it wasn't a serious situation. But...I was wondering if I could borrow a little cash?"

There is a thoughtful silence. "How much did you have in mind?"

"Twenty-five would help, but fifty would be great." I assert hopefully.

He begins slowly and mournfully as if he is embarrassed for me. "I'd really like to help but I just refinanced my house. Susan and I divorced last year and..."

His voice continues, but in my mind I have already hung up the receiver. My first and wealthiest potential patron and I come up empty. The outlook is bleak. I feel sick all over knowing that I will be repeating this ignominious performance all night. Swallowing what little remains of my pride I dial the phone again.

By evening's end I have scrounged up a measly hundred and fifty bucks. Hardly enough to take the big apple by storm. With no other options I accept the facts and go with it. In the morning I will collect and make the best of my circumstance. Once I'm in the city and walking the streets at least I will feel alive.

Overall my begging spree was a failure, but I am still touched by the kindness of those who were eager to help. I lie down in my bed of ghosts. The shame of soliciting handouts has been humbling beyond belief. If tomorrow I walk with my back straight and my head up, if I summon the courage to look another person in the eye, I hereby confess that my demeanor is a lie. An actor's attempt to feign self-esteem.

While trying to survive the trials of my financial problems the drama between Sasha and her parents began to unfold. Sasha convinced her parents to let me come to visit for a weekend. Early in the morning I pulled up to a large white house in a sterile looking neighborhood full of such houses. It was one of those planned communities. The houses were all large, but without porches where neighbors might sit and socialize. The yards were green but treeless. All adequately groomed, but none with interesting gardens or showing care and creativity of any kind.

Sasha answered the door still half asleep. Once inside, the house was large and modern. I took off my shoes by the door, as is the Indian custom, and followed her to her room. Falling into her bed and looking into each other's eyes, broad smiles covered our faces at the joy of being together again. We began to make love, but she stopped me for fear that her mother might come home unexpectedly.

That evening I met her parents and younger brother. I sat for a long period alone in the study with her mother. I always hated meeting parents, but this was the worst. I felt bound and gagged by Sasha's fears of her parents. Sasha had told them so many lies about me, and about our relationship, that I had to consider every word I spoke lest something might trip me up in this tangled web of deception.

Her mother delivered a long despairing monologue about the troubles at her job and of her desire to return to India. I suppose she was trying to make comforting small talk, but I was never very good at small talk.

There were so many issues hanging over us that needed to be spoken of, and I would have rather cut through the veil of civility and face those issues head on. I felt that not to do so was hypocrisy. But figuring that once they got to know me that my sparkling personality would win them over and everything would be just dandy, I played along with the situation.

Throughout the visit the situation at her house continued to be a charade of just barely concealed prejudice. At times it was not really concealed at all. On one afternoon Sasha and I sat on the swing in her back yard with her mother.

"I think we're going to send Rishi to India when he's of age so he won't marry a white woman," her mother said of Sasha's younger brother.

"Why aren't you going to try to send me to India?" Sasha asked.

"I've already failed with you, otherwise Caeser wouldn't be here," was her mother's dry response.

I sat mute. Allowing myself to be insulted without a word of complaint. The racism inherent in her statement went against all the values I believed in, and by not speaking up for what I believed in, I was not only allowing myself to be degraded on a personal level, I was betraying the ideals which I tried to live by. It was the beginning of a compromise in the name of love that would further destroy my already war-torn self-esteem.

The reason for my extended visit was so I could attend Sasha's graduation party. The conditions under which I was permitted to attend the party were another insult. The main condition was that no one could know that I was Sasha's boyfriend. For this to be found out would cause a scandal and an embarrassment to the entire family. This alone made me lose all respect for her parents. If they believed in their daughter they should have stood up for her choices regardless of the opinions of their friends and family. This lying and deceit showed a complete lack of character and was done for the sake of race and class prejudices that I found immoral from beginning to end.

This lie added a set of logistical problems that required another web of lies. The first problem was explaining why I was the first guest at the party. The cover-up lie was that I had arrived with some of Sasha's Indian friends, but they had gone to run an errand and had left me behind. When these friends, Sneha and Monica arrived hours late, Sasha was frantic that the lie would be discovered. She drove herself mad with worry that the party guests would see through the deception.

The absurdity of it all was that all that the guests had to do was look in my eyes when I spoke to Sasha to see how much I loved her.

But before the party even got started we gave ourselves away. As I sat with the extended family in the living room Sasha was trying to figure out which sari to wear for the event. She walked into the living room wearing the second option that was a white satin sari with black embroidery. After discussing it with her mother she turned to me and asked which one she should wear. The manner in which she deferred to my opinion, and the authority with which I answered her made it clear to all present that we were more than just friends. Sasha was unaware that we gave ourselves away at the time, although she later found out that everyone knew I was her boyfriend, but did not let on because they didn't want to embarrass her parents about having told the lie.

So this tragic comedy of errors played itself out and no one, including myself, had the courage to stand up and admit the emperor wore no clothes so that the entire farce might come to an end. I would have done so gladly. It would have been the greatest relief. I did not do so because Sasha feared the truth so deeply.

The party was mostly Indian and everyone spoke Hindi. I stayed with the young people and minded my own business. While most of the young people were Indian, there were a few whites mixed with the crowd. One of these people was a plump neighbor who had been Sasha's childhood friend. Throughout the night Sasha made a point of introducing her to everyone in a manner that revealed something of her character.

With a cheerful voice she would announce, "This is my neighbor Debra, when we were in second grade I called her and asked if I could come to her birthday party and she said wait I'll take a vote, then she told me everyone voted that I couldn't come."

Sasha told this story as if it were a quaint tale that everyone should laugh, but one could only guess how much this story of childhood cruelty accounted for her adult insecurities. And every time she introduced her supposed friend and retold the tale it was an act of revenge for the never forgotten insult. After repeating it many times Debra finally spoke up and asked her not to tell the story anymore.

For the climax of the party everyone circled around Sasha while she ate cake, opened gifts, and received congratulations. As this symbolic moment took place I stood banished to the upper balcony level of the luxurious living room, looking down at her from afar. Knowing I should be beside her. Feeling humiliated.

That night I slept on the floor of Sash's living room. Her two female Indian friends, Sneha and Monica slept on the floor beside me. In the morning I awoke and stirred a bit. Sneha whined, "I'm cold."

Trying to be a gentleman I slid closer to her and covered her up with half of my blanket. We were all fully clothed and not really that close to each other. When Sasha's mother awoke and saw us lying together she was aghast. She said that was the last straw that she could not tolerate the values of American culture. She said Sneha should have known better and that in India an woman would have been stoned to death for such behavior. From her attitude one might have suspected that she would have approved of such a punishment.

7/29/94

In the morning I am possessed by a feeling of solitude. I feel completely alone. I pack what I can fit of my belongings into my car and head off to begin collecting the loot I've been promised by the benefactors accumulated during my begging spree.

I feel as if I'm on a mission full of potential drama. I am fully aware that I stand little chance of making my desperate plan work, but with no other options open to me, I resolve to continue.

My first stop is to see Tom Keiter, my old boss at the film production company I once worked at. He owes me seventy-five dollars for a job I did for him months ago. I climb the steps to the office area self-conscious of my disheveled appearance. Tom sits in front of a group of desks in the center of the room.

"Caesenator how'r you doing?" he says, mimicking an annoying character from a Saturday Night Live sketch in a failed attempt to sound young and hip.

"Oh it's been pretty exciting," but the shake of my head reveals my true feelings.

"Caeserrrr," he drawls, "So you're working at the Cat plant? I didn't quite get the story."

Laughing slightly I try to avoid rehashing my tale, "Let's just say I'm not working there anymore."

"Well what are your plans now?" he asks, "Are you gonna...well what I'm trying to get at is, y'see we've got a ton of jobs due right now and we just can't keep up. We were thinking you might be the one to edit this big one we're way behind on. It would be about a month's work, pays about two grand."

After our conversation I leave the office in a smiling stupor. After months of fate throwing hurdles in my path, when I am finally at the end of my rope, I am granted a reprieve. Considering the past few months, hell the past few years, my mind is boggled by

this sudden good luck. I feel like laughing. To celebrate I walk to the
Cafe 210 and lounge on the patio drinking red wine. The wine's
blend of bitter and sweet lends an appropriate flavor to my mood.

8/4/94

I sit in a coffee shop on Beaver Avenue in State College.
The town is filled with thousands of middle class college kids living
off their parent's money as they are educated to become part of the
economic machine. The coffee shop is where the ones come who
want to play the part of sophisticated bohemians. The pretensions
glow from their line-less faces as they sip cappuccinos and nibble
strawberry scones.

The boys to my right are discussing Nabakov with a serious
air, a copy of Sartre's Cuba lies conspicuously on the table. The
young woman to my left is declaring that she can never allow her
creativity to be stifled by entering the work force. The man with her
scratches his goatee in agreement, occasionally suggesting they go
back to his place to listen to his new Washington Squares CD.

Matt has just designed a "new international symbol for
peace." He moves from table to table trying to sell the hand-
painted T-shirts that bear the design. Tomorrow he is leaving for
the 25th anniversary Woodstock concert where he hopes to strike it
rich with his creation. He asks me, "Do you think I should go to
MTV with this or not? I just don't know if I want to corrupt
myself with the MTV generation."

The anal computer lab attendant from the university stops
by my table to ask of my ancestry. He's sure I look "particularly
European" and says I remind him of an underground film actor.
The girl from the comic book shop is telling me I shouldn't eat
beef. Taking a drag from her Marlboro she says coyly, "Besides
cows are beautiful people."

"They sure taste good," I reply in agreement.

Gopha the skinny Indian boy feels inclined to sing me a
verse of "It Ain't Me Babe" when I ask him if he's a friend of
Monica's. Jason is trying to talk Gopha into a dollar bet on a game

of chess. Between games Jason will chew your ears off with his plans to conquer the music industry while studying entertainment law, but when it comes to his never ending dollar chess matches he's quiet as a church mouse.

I sit among them. To all surface appearances one and the same. If they could only see that I am hate incarnate. That I would rather reach into their flesh and tear out their shallow little hearts than listen to another second of their prattle.

Since my return to State College I have been leading the writer's quiet cafe life. Spending my free time outdoors drinking iced tea and cheap wines. With a friendly facade I chat amiably with whatever stalwart geniuses are inclined to squander away their hours in my vicinity.

But behind my eyes is an unspoken challenge to any and every one of these social elites to just say one thing that would inspire me. Just one little idea that is new and meaningful. Any emotion that would incite my animal passions to seek enlightenment. Unfortunately original thoughts are nil here. Even a crude spark would enliven me, but they only deliver the failure of dull mediocrity.

In my secret mind I wish to run like a madman banging gongs and speaking in tongues. Or maybe jump on a table and shove a baklava stick up my ass as I sing the Star Spangled Banner in the forgotten language of the Hottentots.

I know these thoughts only reveal me as a foolhardy simpleton because the spark I search for cannot be shocked into existence by Dadaistic acts of obscene performance art. Where it truly comes from is one of the mysteries that will always trouble me.

But alas, the woman to my left has acceded to the temptation of the Washington Squares, and Matt has made a T-shirt sale to the scruffy girl in the tie-die frock. Jason moves his rook to check, and for my wrath all I receive is a bitter taste in my mouth that all the Chablis in America won't wash away.

8/7/94

The film project I have been hired to edit at Filmspace has suddenly fallen behind schedule, leaving me with nothing to do and extra free time to spend writing and sharing hours of leisure with my priceless stable of peers. On returning I have felt completely disinterested in my friends here. When spending time with them I am restless and irritable. Neither can I stay inside, so I wander the two main streets that make this metropolis a town and put myself at the mercy of whatever experiences take me.

I feel unmoored, afloat on a lucid sea that tosses me ceaselessly on the troubled waters of the personalities that cross my path. The events of recent months have left me raw. I am unable to remain detached from the parade of lost souls that move in and out of my life.

When returning to State College after losing the job at the factory I found myself strangely compelled towards an acquaintance of mine named Ornelia. She is a tall white woman with fiery red hair, of Irish/Polish descent I believe. Ornelia distinguishes herself with a smart feminine fashion sense that leaves an impression of strong character. Chaotic streams of hair bathe her oval face, and her long flowing layers of dressing evoke sepia-tone photographs, subtle aromas of dried rose petals, and horseless carriages on dirty town squares.

Besides a natural propensity that drew me to her, I felt she would be a safe friend because she is a close comrade of Sasha's. As our friendship grew my surface perception of her soon gave way to a living breathing human being who could not be experienced with indifference or ignored when convenient.

I first began to see beyond her hale composure as we drank at Zino's, a basement pub that Sasha and her cohorts call home. The small room was packed to capacity. The roar of the conversation swallowed her voice as she began to speak with a softly nostalgic manner.

"There was this man I was seeing, his name was Randal, your writings to Sasha reminded me of the way he used to write to me. He went to England and a lot of stupid this and that... y'know.. began to get in the way. It was such a great relationship...when we broke up I said 'how can you let go of this?' We still talk a lot. He's in Alaska now. I know someday I'll settle for someone else, but he'll always be the... I was never one to use terms like soulmate or whatever, but he'll always be the one I feel I was meant to be with."

Her openness seems out of place in this raucous environment. There are tears in her hazel eyes and I am burning inside. Her story is one I've heard often of late. Stories of the true love let go. I fear the feeling Ornelia speaks of. The feeling of settling.

Thanks to the barroom clamor I have lost the thread of Ornelia's story. A Dos Equis bottle at the next table is knocked to the floor with a momentous crash. But through the noise one phrase catches my attention; "About two years ago I was raped."

The strange circumstance in which she reveals this secret tugs at my insides. We lean in to each other so that I can hear her voice amid the drunken bellows of our fellow patrons and the too-loud classic rock that blares throughout the joint. Her face is a few inches from mine and her eyes are soft. Her beauty is as elegant as our surroundings are dingy and dirty. I feel honored that she feels safe to share such intimacies with me.

At evening's end I walk Ornelia to her apartment. She invites me up to her room to get a blank cassette so that I can introduce her to the music of Billie Holiday. Once upstairs she plays Robert Johnson softly, lights candles, and brews herbal tea. We sit on the floor of her tiny room. I am at a loss for words and to create conversation I ask absentmindedly, "Do you read poetry?"

"Some," she replies guardedly.

Feeling the question to be awkward I retract, "I don't know why I ask that, I rarely read poetry."

"It was pretty rude of you to ask then, wasn't it," she states seriously.

I am taken back by her rebuke. To my further surprise she pulls out three books and begins reciting, more from memory than the pages, various poems with a new, deliberate tone of voice.

After the reading she insists that I borrow several books. The warmth of the ambiance of her room and the intensity of her emotional swings has made me soft inside. She stands up to pull down the window blinds. As she reaches into the air I notice for the first time that she is wearing a sort of mini-dress that turns into a thin veil of gauze just below the hips and down to her ankles. As she reaches up for the blind the lower half of her white bottom is clearly revealed beneath the black gauze. I assure myself that she is not aware of her exhibition. But I also recall Sasha's comment that Ornelia can be very competitive. Although I act as a gentleman, I am overcome by a mix of lust, and an urge to escape.

For years the only sexuality that has interested me was the exploration of decadence. Twenty-dollar prostitutes, spontaneous blowjobs from chance encounters in moving cars, and frantic gropings with nymphomaniacs thinking that this might be the way to melt my heart.

With Sasha I began to feel again. Perhaps for the first time I knew the pleasure of animal abandon equaled by emotional connection. Afterwards nothing less would do.

At the same time my sexuality has been re-awakened with a forceful vengeance. For days I have carried a perpetual erection. For the first time since adolescence my mind is filled with spontaneous fantasies. My desire is a dull, ever-present ache.

Sasha, I am overflowing. It has been almost a month since I've battered your succulent wings. Images of your body flash through my mind and my semen drips without request. I can no longer imagine just making love to you. In my dreams I am attacking you, humiliating you, debasing you, destroying you, so that you are reborn even more of a woman than you are now.

I hold your virtue sacred. In my mind you are purity. I feel no one is good enough to defile you, even myself. Although you are well experienced, the two years of celibacy you claim to have undertaken before we met makes you virginal to me.

If I could I would place you on a pedestal, but I know doing so would eventually create an uncontrollable compulsion in me to knock you down.

Sasha, to me you are the essential, the universal form of forms. But you are also the personal, and that is why I call your name. Because women exist everywhere, but none are you. And it seems the scourge of my life is that there is only one for me, and she is you.

So now what Sasha? The truth is out. My hand is played. Perhaps you could put a leash on me and kick me if I make too much noise. Shout out 'sit! heel!, roll over and play dead!' Toss me a bone, pat me on the head, muzzle me or I may maul you.

I am at your mercy. What will you do now?

8/9/94

Thursday night finds me drinking with Ornelia and her Indian roommate Mita. We are on the patio of Cafe 210 sharing a carafe of red wine. An unanticipated rainstorm erupts and we move under the awning to avoid the downpour. I sit beside Mita, a small woman with beautiful sharp features who seems to have an impenetrable wall around her insides. As the wine disappears and the night goes on we are joined by Walter, a dubious suitor of Ornelia's who is accompanied by his girlfriend.

In my mind something about the atmosphere seems off kilter. Walter's girlfriend is shooting loathsome darts from her dark eyes. First at Ornelia, then Mita, then glaring at me as if a question mark is sitting atop her crown. Walter chatters to the wind, his attention obviously agitated by Ornelia's presence. Mita and I have gotten into an animated discussion on the trials of being a first generation Indian woman.

In the midst of the conversation I catch a glimpse of Ornelia. She sits quietly, as if taken by a deep sadness. In that moment I feel like I can see through her. Simultaneously she appears like a lonely child, a tearful red-faced clown, and a worn old woman grasping at the beauty and gayety of youth.

But these are merely fleeting thoughts and the discussion on India continues. Walter has lapsed into a private conversation with his girlfriend. Again I notice Ornelia, only now her countenance is that of the cruel bitch.

Throughout the evening she has been making a gesture of keeping the smoke from her Marlboro cigarettes from wafting into the breathing space of the non-smoking Mita. Now, with a cool, empty expression on her face she blows a long, slow cloud directly into Mita's profile.

My thoughts disturb me. I can't decide whether I'm suffering from overactive imaginings, or I am in heightened perception, discerning the ulterior motives of all present.

The next hour finds us at Zino's. Again there is a roaring crowd. Ornelia has become rambunctious. Her vocabulary has taken a vulgar tone. She, Mita, and I are crammed onto a small bench. Ornelia and I share a glass of wine as she speaks in disconnected spurts.

"There he is again," she points to a large, longhaired man who she shared a mostly sexual relationship with. "He always sees us together. I'm sure his filthy little mind thinks I'm gonna be fucking you tonight. Good! Let him. He lost his chance."

Mita is whispering to me hints of a lost love who broke her heart. I tell her she is intelligent and beautiful and could get lots of guys. To my surprise, and perhaps for the first time since I have met her, Mita's shield seems to come down.

"You think so?" she asks. She looks happy and grateful for the compliment. Her face seems to beam like that of a little girl.

The alcohol is kicking in now and I try to conceal the stagger in my step as I weave my way through the crowd towards the men's room. Everything appears increasingly cockeyed. Mita is craving pancakes-immediately! So we move on to a nearby diner.

Walter had long ago departed. On the way to the diner we find he has dumped his girlfriend and is eager to accompany us on our way. Once inside the diner Walter has ceased to exist. His words fill the air as he desperately interjects himself into the conversation, but I do not hear him.

Ornelia appears to me like a rampage of shattered crystal. I can't quite comprehend what anyone speaks about. The reticent Mita is giving me the thumbs up over the pancakes and there is an argument about the water smelling like worms and Clorox. The fey waiter is delivering Broadway soliloquies. Ornelia is debating breaking her eight months of celibacy for the ex-beau at Zinos. Walter is mocking the women, and Mita can't remember the name of the Hindu god with the long angry tongue, a mask of which haunted her childhood home.

It is a simple carefree evening out with friends. Why then does it seem filled with double meanings? This happy moment seems undercut with sadness and longing.

That night I lay down to sleep feeling as if taken by madness. I see too much, and what I perceive behind the eyes and actions of my friends breaks my heart and makes socializing almost unbearable at times.

As I sleep I am at a table writing poetry when a hideous looking old woman walks up and begins reading it over my shoulder. Without welcome she sits down beside me. I am so repulsed by her appearance that I jump to my feet. I gaze at her face in disgust, hypnotized by her revolting features. Moving to the left of the table I see that her right leg, from the knee down, is actually the hind leg of a horse with the flesh stripped away from the dried bone. In horror I scream, "Leave me alone!"

I awake from the dream sure that I am too neurotic for social contact. I pledge to stay in my room where it is safe. I feel so absorbed in every expression of those around me that my mind is hopelessly cluttered with psychic noise.

A thought enters my head that Ornelia is insane. I feel afraid of her and I know the old woman in the dream was she. I tell Sasha of my feelings on the phone. When she asks me to explain I cannot find a reason. It is just intuition.

In the evening I call Mita. Ornelia is out of town for the weekend. Mita's feelings about the previous evening were the same as mine with the exception that she noticed nothing odd about Ornelia.

"That's just how she gets", she says unconcerned.

Agreeing that we both just think about things too much I forget my negative feelings about Ornelia.

Mita and I spend the evening sitting on the floor in her bedroom. I am pulled by a curious impulse to see behind the protective wall that this odd girl hides behind.

During the course of the evening casual discourse soon gives way to confession. I find that instead of penetrating her barriers I am spilling my guts in a verbal rampage. In three hours I have told her my life story. I do not wish to rehash these things, but the words just pour out. When I've finished an awkward moment settles between us. Without request I have laid myself open before this woman who I barely know.

In our short acquaintance she has never spoken to me of her personal life. Finally by way of subtle confirmation of trust, she tells me a strange story that I cannot quite understand. She speaks of "devastating people." Two young men who she barely knows yet feels compelled to reach out to. A hairline fracture appears in her composure. Her eyes are wet and she says, "Every time I'm around these people they devastate me. I just feel like I have something I have to tell them. I know this sounds weird, it is weird, I just can't explain it."

Suddenly she announced she is tired and is ready to go to bed, and I am ushered out of the house. As I walk to my car I reflect on this odd new woman that had entered my life. Although her words are more mysterious than revealing, she has opened herself up to me as much as she seems able. I feel close to her as a kindred spirit.

I return home at midnight. In a few days I must move out of the apartment and with nowhere else to live, I have been stashing my belongings wherever I can. What I don't absolutely need, I throw out in the trash. Even my bed has gone with the garbage truck. My room is empty except for the few belongings I will keep with me; a bag of clothes, three books, notebooks and letters, a beat up short-wave radio, and a couple of candles.

I sleep on a foam rubber egg-crate mat on the floor. The room seems peaceful and uncluttered. My life's confusion has brought a desire for simplicity. Over the last two years my material possessions have been disappearing at an alarming rate. It now feels like they are all gone forever.

Although sad, I feel as if a burden has been lifted. I have always romanticized the idea of the materialist who throws it all away in order to find spiritual awakening. But unlike the Buddha Guatama I did not simply turn away from my possessions. It is more like they were pried from my clenched fingers one by one.

But on another level I wonder what really is the truth in this matter. I recall a conversation from three years ago with Mhina, the drummer for The Imperial Orgy. I was then still doing well financially, but my relationship with Leilani had been deteriorating for some time. I had just told Mhina of my first sexual encounter with Samantha and he was warning me that I was looking for trouble.

"I know," I responded laughingly, "Y'know the situation could end with me losing everything. I mean, there's not a chance in hell that's likely to happen, but in the very worst circumstance it really is possible."

When I think of this I realize I had foreseen the course my life would take and did nothing to stop the actions that were bringing about my self-prophesied fate. My past seems like a game of hide and seek with my own unconscious mind, where it sets the wheels into motion then I fight against the destiny I have created for myself.

In many ways these words I am placing on paper have empowered me against my own bad karma. Once these truths are put out in the open I am no longer able to pretend that I am a total victim of circumstance, and I am forced to accept responsibility for my disastrous condition.

These words I place on paper reveal my self to myself. It is a grand thing to read Nietche and proclaim bravely, "Yes! I will take responsibility for my actions." Unfortunately if the proclivities of the psyche are unable to be recognized, such proclamations amount to little more than empty bombast.

My own unconscious is a master at contriving complex scenarios for my own self-destruction. So under the guise of 'artistic creation' these pages are a cathartic explosion revealing secrets to outsiders I am not even aware of myself. A game of hide-

and-seek with my own unconscious as a last-ditch attempt to save myself from the dark forces of my own nature.

8/12/94

Tuesday Ornelia returns from Pittsburgh where she has been visiting her parents. She calls when she arrives. "Caeser, can you come out and play," her pretend little girl voice rings through the receiver.

We agree to meet at 10:00. Come evening, she, Mita, and I are drinking at our now usual haunt, the Cafe 210. The women are having a passionate conversation about the joys of dance. Ornelia loves ballet while Mita prefers modern.

It is a mild evening and the wine has slowed my mind. Earlier this evening I had a feeling that I would like to create excitement. Instead I am overcome by a mild lack of confidence.

The atmosphere is calm and cheerful. The women look beautiful in the soft light. I look at Ornelia as she speaks in a cool collected manner and wonder how only recently, I suspected her of being secretly insane. At midnight Mita takes her leave and Ornelia and I move down the street to Zino's.

Tonight Ornelia has a different style to her dress. She wears a pleated black skirt with thigh high stockings and a maroon low cut sweater. The deep color of the sweater seems to bring her face to life. Her long red hair streams over her shoulders, and the deep color of the sweater brings out her full lips that have been painted with a matching shade of lipstick.

We reside at a corner table. Ornelia always likes to have her back to the wall in order to have the ability to view the entire room. She is bored and wants to be entertained. After spending a weekend with her parents she is in a salacious mood.

"I almost walked out of church Sunday. I couldn't believe he would give a sermon on abortion when I'm working on this play."

She is interning as a research assistant for a university theater production dealing with abortion. Rubbing out her second cigarette and lighting a third she continues. "And then I had this big fight with my mother because I wanted to go over to the Northside to see the Warhol museum. I saw two more of his films: 'Blowjob' and 'Haircut.' Only two of us sat through the whole thing. That's how it is though, a man doesn't come in fifteen minutes. A blow job takes forty-five."

A young man that looks like some kind of surfer dude walks past smiling at her. "Hey you." She waves with dutiful enthusiasm. Turning back to me she goes on, "I am proud to say I had five orgasms masturbating in my parent's house. I've never understood frigid women. I always have multiple orgasms. The second and third come thirty seconds after the first."

A husky young Korean man sits down and chats her up with a swagger like a Bronx Italian from the disco era. Morrisey blares from the sound system, keeping me outside their conversation. There are no signs of anger or argument, but the smiling Ornelia has began pinching and punching her friend. He slaps her hands away and grimaces in pain.

To my surprise she turns to me and pinches my neck. She squeezes the soft flesh between her fingers and looks at me questioningly. I sit nonchalant. The pain is a curiosity that I have no urge to escape.

"Doesn't that hurt?" she asks.

"Yeah," I answer.

She manages to squeeze a bit harder. "Why doesn't it look like it then?"

"I'm just going with the pain."

Disappointed she releases her grip and resumes the conversation with her Korean friend. When we take our leave she is feeling the alcohol.

"I haven't drank in four days and already my tolerance is down." After a moment she adds, "I feel pretty obnoxious."

As we walk down College Avenue she begins hitting and pinching me. She walks ahead and charges back, stopping a few inches from my face to see if I flinch.

I laugh at the spectacle, curious to see what will be revealed of her character. Without warning she grabs my neck and twists, inflicting a swell of agony. I grab her and try to tickle her. She immediately turns barbarous.

In seconds pushing and pulling give way to true brutality. I try to grab her arms as she scratches, bites, and kicks. She tears my shirt open with buttons flying in all directions. She claws my bare chest and blood meanders over my nipple.

As I try to subdue her we tumble off the sidewalk and land on the curb's edge. My weight presses her against the concrete as I lie on top of her in the missionary position. She bites my neck, clenching the skin between her teeth. Her lips are an inviting bouquet painted deep red, but they hide a vice-like grip able to deliver torturous pain.

I laugh and moan in pain at the same time. Her breasts are soft below my bleeding chest, but the affliction of her bite is a maddening punishment for any pleasure I might derive from this intimacy.

"Let go or I'll bite harder," her muffled lips warn.

Although, I am not the one in control of the situation I rasp, "I'm letting go."

She releases me and I stagger to my feet. I am dazed. She sings happily as I limp along to a nearby house where a mutual friend lives. She runs up the stairs and into the bedroom where Gavin lies reading in his bed. She jumps on the bed and begins pounding on his back and head.

"You fuckin' bitch, I'll sock you!" he yells.

"Oh Gavin, aren't you happy to see me?" she mocks.

"Yes, Ornelia." Sarcasm is Gavin's natural tone of voice. "Why don't you just go watch one of your Warhol movies? Which ones did you see? Bad? Trash? What high works of art!"

We go down to the living room. It is littered with film canisters, videotapes, and coffee cans for use as ashtrays. I sit in a chair on the opposite side of the room from them. Ornelia glows with licentious strength. She has transformed into every man's fantasy of the proper young lady given way to wanton abandon. She sits on the back of the couch with her feet on the cushion. Her skirt is up to her hips and her legs spread benevolently. I can't look in her direction without savoring her long legs, soft thighs, and the pink print on her white panties.

Soon she can't get the CD player to work so she can hear the Nine Inch Nails song she absolutely must hear immediately, so she storms out of the house and walks hurriedly down the street. I catch up to her and we walk side by side without speaking.

"Have you had enough excitement for one night?" I ask.

"Yes. I'm calm now," she replies.

"Well, I'm not," I whisper and grab her by the shoulders.

She immediately attacks with violent scratching and biting. I push her into the loading dock of an auto parts store and pin her against the brick wall. Her eyes look savage and her head moves back and forth mechanically like Linda Blair in the Exorcist. I grab her left leg and pull it into the air. She wraps her legs around me and my pelvis is pressed tight against her crotch. I am acutely aware that only the thin fabric of her white panties protects her from me.

She shakes her head from side to side vigorously, banging her skull against the hard brick. I place my forehead against hers and moan, "No matter what happens, I don't want to hurt you."

We stand still, gripping each other. I am unsure whether I am trying to subdue her or control myself. She seems restrained but waiting to explode. Letting her go, I step out of the way. Immediately she begins making false lunges at me.

"A little jumpy aren't we Caeser?" she chides.

She sits on the steps of a storefront and fixes her shoe. I lay down my notebook and computer discs that have somehow made it through the evening without being lost. When I look away she grabs the notebook and discs and runs into an alley. I chase her and grab the notebook from her hands, but she holds onto the computer discs.

This brings a new wave of fury. She bites my shoulders like a madwoman. My every limb is in excruciating pain with wounds bleeding from my knees, arms, and nose. She again clenches her teeth into my neck delivering an intense wave of pain. My mind is inebriated with the pain. The smell of my own blood coalesced with her saliva peels away civilized restraints. A rupture of animal instincts transforms me backwards through evolution; Neanderthal...Cro-magnum...Homo erectus...Australopithecus...

My mind flashes red. For the first time I understand the pleasure of misogynistic brutality. I think 'O.K. bitch, you wanna see how easy it could be for me?'

I encircle her with my arms and raise her into the air, believing she will be incapacitated, but her thrashing legs, armored with a brand new pair of platform shoes, still make a perilous weapon.

I throw her down on the gravel-covered macadam of the alleyway. Leaping on top of her I pin her arms above her head and sit on her legs. To add insult to her subjugation I run the flattest part of my wet tongue up her neck and across her face.

Catching myself before I follow an uninhibited path to the point of no return, I halt. I am dazed and struggling to control myself. Minutes pass as we both breathe heavily. A young man walks past gawking at our spectacle as we lay in the alleyway.

After we regain our sanity I allow her to rise from the ground. Still not beaten she runs towards her apartment building shouting, "I've still got your discs and you'll regret it!"

I follow her at a walking pace. When I turn to start down her walkway I see that she is entering her front door. I walk to the door, which is always kept tightly locked. I turn the knob and freely enter. I begin ascending the stairs that lead to her room. All is quiet inside.

I know that if I enter her room all inhibitions will be torn asunder. As I climb the stairs I visualize her legs in those black stockings and her white panties that I imagine must be wet with her own juices. Testosterone shoots through my body and my erection swells with expectation.

As I march up the dark stairs it almost seems too easy. I stop momentarily as a smile crosses my face. Turning I descend the stairs and run out the door and up the street. I am laughing aloud as I picture her bruised body lying on the black sheets of her bed. Perhaps she is wondering if I am lurking in her apartment somewhere. I wish I could hear her thoughts when she realizes I have declined her temptations.

When I return home there is a message on my machine. It is Ornelia. With a petulant sneer in her voice she hisses, "I've still got your computer disks. I didn't think you'd give up so easily. Have a good night, Caeser!"

"Have a good night." I lie on the floor of my empty room. It seems a fitting symbol for the emptiness that has taken my once full life. I close my eyes and wait for sleep. Sasha seems a million miles away, and the abyss between us grows wider each day. I hate to sleep alone. I think of Ornelia, so near and sleeping alone in her room. I hear her words again, "Have a good night, Caeser."

8/15/94

Friday morning I am awakened by a phone call. An authoritarian voice asks, "Is Caeser Pink there?"

Thinking quickly I reply, "He doesn't live here anymore. The last I heard he was living in his car in York."

"Is that right?" he says incredulously, "If you see him this is the sheriff's office and there's a warrant for his arrest stemming from a traffic citation in Altoona."

I hang up the phone and jump out of bed in a panic. If they find me I may never get out of jail. I decide to take a quick shower and avoid the premises for a few days. While in the shower there is a loud knock at the door. With my heart in my throat I wrap a towel around my waist and peak out the peephole on the door. To my relief it is only Ron Boi, the ex-bass player for The Imperial Orgy. His sight is a relief, but still an awkward situation considering that this is the first time I've seen him since I kicked him out of the band for drinking too much onstage.

Ron was the only band member whose working class roots, like my own, hailed from Lewistown. He is known in the area as a legendary wild man and a consummate beer-swiller, but at heart a good and generous fellow. He was the band clown and added an element of insanity to the Imperial Orgy. He was a master at

inventing outrageously creative costumes. Sometimes taking the
stage in wedding dresses, six-inch pink platform-shoes, glitter
coated drum major uniforms, or a pink nylon G-string.

Ron's curse was that when he drank, which was every day,
he became another man altogether. In the backstage dressing rooms
he terrorized the rest of the band with his drunken humor.

While changing costumes he might strip naked and hide his
penis between his squeezed together legs.

"Hey guys! Am I a pussy or what?" he would bellow,
demanding the attention of all.

He was fond of bringing his Budwieser-laden breath close
to one's face and gurgling sloppy intimacies, "Y'know I love you
guys. I might be a drunken asshole, but I'm a wild man!"

A second later he might have a familiar story he must tell
the entire room. "Hey guys, hey guys, this asshole came to my place
and pinched clothes pins on his nipples. I challenged him. I stood in
the cold for twenty minutes with jumper cables clamped on my
nipples. That fucker gave up! Did that hurt though! Shit! Hey,
Mhina imagine what that would feel like clamped on your balls.
Samantha, can you imagine what that would feel like clamped on
your balls?"

Our first approach to Ron was to walk out of rehearsal
when he drank too much to play his instrument. By the third set of
every performance his abilities deteriorated relative to how many
pitchers of cheap beer he gulped down. When it became clear he
was holding back the quality of the music we told him he had to
stop drinking onstage if he wanted to stay in the band. From then
on he was filled with resentment and refused to put his heart into
the music. At his last gig he would not wear a costume. He
complained, "I don't get paid enough to change clothes." During
the next to the last song he tore the strings off his bass and
stormed offstage.

Since his expulsion I heard rumors of his wrath with me.
Referring to me as Caeser Stink and calling us "back stabbers." With
this in mind I open the door. He has come to collect a few odd
belongings and his attitude is friendly. We talk briefly and I update
him on the chaos of my life, including my fear that his knock was

the sheriff at my door. He gathers his assortment of cords and containers and we walk towards the door. As he places his hand on the knob I see the sheriff's car pull into the driveway.

"Shit!" I yell, "there he is."

Ron is calm, "Don't worry man, I'll get rid of him."

Still in my towel I hide in the basement hallway. The sheriff knocks and inquires about my whereabouts.

"I haven't seen that guy for weeks," Ron lies coolly, "I'd like to see him myself. I have a few things to settle with him too."

After what seems an eternity he leaves. It is ironic that after I boot him out of the band it is Ron who saves my ass. Ron and I both know what it is like to be in a desperate situation and this knowledge gives us a bond that cuts through the superficial bullshit when the chips are down.

I leave the house still in a panic. My first urge is to get the hell out of town. I have created such a financial mess here it seems I can never dig my way out. With unpaid fines and a ridiculously scarred driving record, just being here is a risk. On the way out of town I stop at a phone booth to try to figure out how much the fine is for. I call the local D.A.'s office and am put on hold for an extended period. There are a steady series of electronic beeps as I hold the receiver. My paranoid mind begins to race, "What if they are tracing my call? Maybe they're keeping me on hold because the sheriff's on the way here right now."

I hang up the receiver and drive off in a rush. Catching hold of myself I stop at another phone booth and re-dial the number. The D.A. has no information about the fine and it takes five more calls to find anything out. My panic is assuaged to learn that it is only a small fine rather than the one thousand dollars plus I feared. I make arraignments for the fine and return home still shaken.

The next day Sasha comes to State College to help me move. Actually "move" is not quite the right word for it. Perhaps vacate is more accurate as I have no place to move to. My belongings are stashed haphazardly with friends and family. Dave and Samantha have my couch, Papasan chair, and TV. Sasha will be taking my CDs and art collection.

It is a strange feeling to know I will be homeless. I am sure I will be able to find someplace to sleep and shower, but I am not one who feels comfortable as a guest and need a space to call my own. I feel as if I'm stuck in a floating purgatory. From morning to night I wander the streets or work at the university computer labs. This writing fills my time and gives me a vague sense of purpose that helps keep me from sinking into deeper depression.

It is the first time I have seen Sasha since the incident with Ornelia and I have to try to explain why there are bite marks all over my body. I explain the situation to her and am surprised to see how understanding she is about it. Although I have learned with Sasha that things are likely to come out in unexpected ways.

It sometimes seems like we are in a contest to make each other jealous. And all that we really achieve is making the other more insecure and uncertain about the relationship. It is complicated by the fact that both Sasha and I see ourselves as writers collecting life experiences to use in our work. This often becomes an excuse for debauchery in the name of art.

That evening we are planning to meet Ornelia and Mita to go to dinner at the Café 210. We arrive at Ornelia's house where Sasha decides to change clothes. As I sit on a bench in the hallway the three women are trying on outfits and debating with each other about what to wear. Sasha emerges from Ornelia's room wearing a short tight dress. It is a style of dress that is unusual for her, and she looks just a tiny bit slutty. A fact that I am happy to embrace.

As we walk out the door Sasha nonchalantly asks Ornelia, "So why were you biting my boyfriend?"

Ornelia does not reply and the issue is dropped.

Soon the four of us are sitting at the outdoor café. The early evening sun lights the sky and the air is warm and pleasant. Everyone is cheerful and engaged in small talk. Everyone accept me.

On one level it is a perfect moment. Lovely weather, nice surroundings, and three beautiful women as my companions. Yet my mind gravitates towards the hypocrisy of the situation. The sexual tension that lies just below the surface is not spoken of. The women are masters at putting the carnal truths out of mind. Everything is civilized. Everything is as nice as peaches and cream.

I look at each of them. My emotions are confused and confounded by these three sirens. Sasha is animated and seems happy, but I know her well enough to see there is a touch of anger simmering beneath her facade. She looks beautiful as ever. Her golden skin and sharp features glow as she holds her head high. Her energy seems condensed into her small form and gives her a presence that is too large to be ignored.

In contrast Ornelia is a tall strong looking woman. Her fiery mane surrounds her face like the flames that surround the heads of the gods on Tibetan religious paintings. I must admit that Ornelia's attack was one of the most erotic things I have ever experienced. It has inflamed my mind.

Ornelia shares the same Polish/Irish blood as that which courses through my veins. We are the same. Sometime when we are alone and not speaking, I know her. I know her through and through. I can imagine her as my wife and leading a long life with her by my side. A life much as our ancestors must have lived throughout countless ages.

Mita seems the most unsure about the situation, but she is also the least ensnared. Her appearance is similar to Sasha's except her skin is a bit lighter, and her features are a little softer, but her presence is not as bold.

Over recent weeks Mita and I have become close friends. As Sasha and I struggle through the complex problems in our relationship I have turned to Mita in hope that another Indian woman could help me understand the cultural issues I am dealing with. But sharing such intimacies has led us to have a close emotional tie. I feel happy when I am with Mita. One characteristic that she has that Sasha lacks is a playful sense of humor. Mita is one of the few women I have ever met who can make me laugh, and humor and fun are an important thing to me.

As I watch the three of them chatting I have an urge to tear through the veil of civility and force the underlying reality into the open. I would rather have anger, tears, lust, pain, desire, all of it expressed and released rather than carry on with this charade.

But the feminine power of mendacity holds sway. This trinity of witches, these three graces, are more powerful than I. Although I may be the source of the tensions, I am weak, almost insignificant in their combined presence. And each moment of forced civility is their way of making that fact clear to me. In all directions men turn their heads to gaze at them. Their unity, their sophistication, is a reminder both to me and to themselves, that their feminine power trumps that of one lowly rogue. Regardless of what romantic webs he may have weaved around these three pure and virginal edifices of divine womanhood.

Throughout the evening a competition seems to arise as to just how much attention they can draw to themselves. Sasha and Ornelia both know everyone in the scene and as we move from bar to bar there is an endless parade of over-exuberant greetings from the half-drunken men that prowl these locales looking for easy prey for one-night stands. Mita seems outside this competition and soon tires and leaves.

By midnight Sasha appears to be weary of the game. There is a tired look in her eyes, and as she tires she retreats from the barroom Lotharios and gravitates towards me. As for myself, I am bored with the whole thing and couldn't care less anymore. With the smoke, loud music, and endless babbling of college-aged drunks, I just want to escape the entire scene.

When the evening comes to an end we say goodbye to Ornelia who walks home alone. Sasha and I walk back to my car that is in a parking lot on the edge of town. As we near the car we walk across a small field with a few scattered trees. As we walk under one of the trees Sasha's high-heeled shoe gets stuck in the mud. When I go to help her she pulls me close and kisses me. It has been a long exhausting evening and I can taste the alcohol on her breath.

"Throw me down. I want you to take me in the mud," she instructs.

I lay her down on the ground. It is covered in thick brown mud. Her new dress is immediately ruined. I pull down the top of the dress exposing her breasts. The more passion with which I grasp her body, the more she becomes covered with mud. Her face, her neck, shoulders, and breasts become streaked with wet clay.

I pull off her underwear and drop them to be abandoned in the dirt. With my pants pulled down to my knees I enter her. I pin her arms above her head as I thrust with slow deep jabs. Her face, now caked with a mixture of dried and wet mud, reveals an expression of heavenly resignation. Her eyes are serene yet desperate. As if this degradation is the perfect release from all the emotions she felt throughout the evening. Her insecurities, her feelings of inadequacy and self-reproach, are both proven and released by allowing herself to be debased in this filthy form of sexual ecstasy.

I flip her over and pull her to her knees with her back against my chest. Her hair is matted and heavy. I run my hands down the curves of her neck and between her breasts as her head falls back in submission against my shoulder. Then pushing her down on her hands and knees I lift the mud-caked material of her dress up onto her back so that her ass is fully exposed. I begin to pummel her from behind. The smacking sound magnified by the wet mud that coats her ass. Soon her moans give way to shaking. Her arms and legs quiver until she collapses with her face and breast in the thick wet earth. With orgasm I collapse atop her. Both of us weak and depleted, we lie still without speaking.

Finally we pull ourselves up and get into the car without concern for the mess we make of the seats. We ride home in silence. As we enter the house, Dave my roommate is walking into his bedroom. Although his eyes widen at the spectacle we present, he asks no questions and enters his room and closes the door tightly.

Still in silence we peel off our mud covered cloths and step into the shower. The warm water slowly melts away the layers of clay. We wash each other's bodies with care. Her skin begins to emerge from behind the dirt and appears fresh and vital. Now clean we hold each other as the water rains down upon us. Still no words are spoken. Nothing needs to be said. We lay down to sleep feeling the first tastes of trust and unity that most couples begin to experience only after years of life together.

On Sunday afternoon Sasha and I are doing the last of the moving chores. At 3PM she must leave for home and I am due to leave on a ten-day film shoot, giving me time to think of someplace to stay when I return. The house is nearly empty. I am forced to abandon my clothes dryer and an oriental carpet for lack of anywhere to store them. We clean the house as much as time will allow and leave the rest for Dave.

It is a gray, gloomy day and as I load my art collection into Sasha's car a burst of rain pours down. We say an extended good-bye and go our separate ways. Driving away from the house is loaded with meaning for me because I know I am driving away for the last time and moving forward into a future full of doubt and uncertainty.

"Homeless." It is hard to associate the word with myself. When life is secure it seems like an unimaginable possibility. But here I am. Reduced to zero.

Zero. "How did I come to this?" I wonder to myself as the plane lifts off the runway as we began our journey for the film shoot. Far below on the ground I view the rows of tiny houses and the toy-like cars and trucks. Human life appears like a game that I am no longer apart of. I am floating, propelled through space without a sense of belonging to anyplace or anyone. In the three decades of my life what do I have to show for myself? We pass through the clouds and the human world disappears through the soft blankets of white haze.

8/8/94

I am at the world's largest shopping mall: The Mall Of America in, I'm not sure, either St. Paul or Minneapolis. This place, let alone my situation, is positively surreal. The section of the mall where I sit is a grand hive of bare gray girders rising up to the geometric rectangles of glass that make up the ceiling. On the floor below is a combination garden and amusement park. A two-story high Snoopy dog balloon leers at me from the opposite wall. A roller coaster whizzes past where I sit on the third story. Colorful carousels, swings, and merry mixers whirl amid the gray and green.

There are literally hundreds of stores, restaurants and theaters. I walk through noticing the clothes I would like to wear, the gifts I would like to buy. I am in the world's largest shopping mall and I do not have a penny to my name. I have been working for three weeks, but little does this mean. I may be on a two-week film shoot, my employer might put me up in good hotels and pay for fine dining and drink, but still my pockets are empty. The entire situation leaves me even more disconnected than I felt before.

At 8PM I'll meet the rest of the film crew for a feast at the California Cafe, yet I cannot buy a twenty-five cent postcard. The contradiction baffles my simple mind. I wander the mall, my expression that of a deer standing in the middle of the road staring blindly into the headlights of an oncoming car.

The swarm of people fills me with a stinging sense of loneliness. I ogle the beautiful young women: White, Black, Asian, Indian, French-Canadian whatever-they-are around here, and I feel threads constricting around my heart. I want so much to speak to someone. I want to call Sasha, but I can't afford to use the phone booth.

Behind me three Latina girls laugh noisily, sending chills of despair through my intestines. They speak in Spanish. For all it does me they could speak Bantu in reverse because I am outside their laughter. Their mysterious words heighten my alienation. Every day I feel more removed from life's events even as I am inundated by experience. I feel nausea. Nausea at the knowledge that this swarm which disgusts me so, is also what I long to be a part of. I desire humanity itself.

I am a voyeur of my own existence, a lodger in each moment. Misery no longer matters because I am only passing through. Whether with friends in State College, or wandering the streets in whatever city I find myself, I am not a part of these places. Not one of the inhabitants. With each phenomenon of life, with each sunrise and set, this feeling grows. I reside more outside the flux of life.

I peer about the mall and a myriad of faces flow past me. A homely white girl carries a tray of tacos. A tall man in a cowboy hat walks with a short woman wearing a Bon Jovi T-shirt. Two college-aged Asian girls dressed in black pass by immersed in their own chatter. An elderly woman guides her husband who struggles with the challenge of walking. Three white kids dressed like homeboys carry skateboards. A man balding on top with long curls falling from the sides reminds me of a new age musician. Two young black men in muscle shirts escort an overweight blonde woman. A Muslim family: the children and father dress in western clothes and the mother is veiled with only her eyes showing. Teens in tie-dyed shirts hold hands smiling like monkeys.

I view every race, every color, every size, shape, religion, culture, and creed. The beautiful, the monstrous, the gurus, geishas, and gays. The rich, the poor, lonely, vain, blind, obscene, deaf, dumb, insane, paraplegic, automatronic; they're all here gathered together to pillage this obscene bounty of the material world.

I stand to get a better look at them. I ask; how many of you will murder, rape or steal? How many hide hate beneath their brow? Who among you will cast the first stone? Who of you knows how to love? Who will change the world? Who will die tomorrow in a fiery car crash? How many of you are wife beaters, child molesters, depressed, compulsive, perverted, obsessive, artists, fakirs, geniuses, scientists, philosophers, vagrants, cancerous, dying of AIDS at this very moment? How many in Samadhi? How many born again through Jesus Christ, Mohammed or the Blessed Virgin Mary?

If I could only know what lies behind your glazed, apathetic, catatonic, sanguine, beautiful, quivering eyes. What desires lurk in your secret hearts? What delusions rule your most private thoughts?

Here we are: the rulers of the world, God's greatest creation. The future of all earthly life resides in our hands. The existence of all future generations hangs precariously on the decisions we make. When I look at you should I be filled with trepidation or hope? If only I could look inside you just once. Do hearts pump? Glands excrete? Souls seek ascension? Can't you see I am here before you naked and shivering, flesh torn open, corpuscles throbbing and nerve endings pulsing with every vibration you emit.

But they walk on by. I am invisible or they are blind. Would you look into my eyes just once and the story will be told? Can you face the dark secrets that are hidden there? Or will you turn away from the harsh realities they harbor?

The music from the mall speaker system whispers sweetly…"Ignorance is bliss." It is a forgotten melody but I know the lyric well. The tune is pleasant to their ears and they turn their heads with a simple thought; "He is an aberration. Best forgotten and put out of mind." There is shopping to be done, movies to see, and children to feed.

Below the carousel spins. I am surrounded by humanity, but I am alone in an isolation more complete than any that solitude could ever deliver. It is an isolation of the spirit. I will take this misery because I am alive with determination. There must be a better life out there somewhere and someday I will find it. As long as blood flows I cannot give up.

I take a single step from the table and am carried away by the swarm. Swallowed by a human torrent. Adrift in the flow of warm bodies I am swept from floor to floor, through boutiques, salons and supermarkets. I do not even try to grab a passing rail. There are so many people that I surrender my will to anonymity. So many people in one city in this huge world full of cities. Six billion people and the population spirals out of control. In this directionless stampede how could two people ever find each other? How in all of geography, time, space, deceptions of consciousness, migrations of souls, perplexities of dimensions, can two people ever dream of finding each other?

8/9/94

It's been three weeks since my return to State College. My editing contract at Filmspace was supposed to last for a month. The job has now been pushed back till early October. It seems they hired me to edit a film that hasn't been shot yet. To keep me busy they sent me on a ten-day location shoot that takes me across the country. I earn $100 a day. So far I haven't seen a cent from the company, even though I was promised an $800.00 advance.

On this shoot I am working as a location sound recorder. We are doing an educational film about pharmacists. The ulterior motive behind this project is that pharmacists want to play a larger role in hospital medical care. We spend our days in hospitals interviewing and filming pharmacists in action. It is not exactly exciting fare. Often while recording interviews my head nods as I fight the urge to fall asleep on my portable mixing unit.

The shoot began in Cooperstown, New York, a small village that thrives on the tourist's money brought in by the Baseball Hall of Fame. After Cooperstown we moved on to the twin cities of St. Paul and Minneapolis, and then on to San Diego. If nothing else I am taking advantage of ten days of free food.

With this in mind at 8PM I am at the California Cafe, an upscale restaurant in the Mall Of America. My companions are Stan, the director of the project, Rich, the cameraman, and Sheryl, a producer from a Philadelphia based advertising agency that is financing the film.

The waiter is proudly anal. Every few minutes he stops by the table to scoop up stray breadcrumbs with a tool that looks like a curved fingernail file. It is the most expensive meal I've ever eaten. The first bite of succulent swordfish in béarnaise sauce sends shivers of ecstasy emanating outward from my gut. Only two weeks ago I was eating one meal a day, and that was from the factory cafeteria.

Rich and Stan have been working together for fifteen years. I have worked with them on and off for two years, but have never gotten to know them well. Sheryl is new to all of us. The warm feeling brought on by the delectable meal and overpriced drinks has loosened the atmosphere among our small group. Sheryl has just returned from Macy's carrying a large shopping bag. She is a light skinned Egyptian woman who speaks, looks and acts like a Jewish princess. Stan, who is beginning to show signs of middle age with his balding head and growing waistline starts to tease Sheryl.

"So Sheryl what did you purchase on your happy excursion into the mall?"

She bounces her head from side to side with exaggerated cutesiness; her nasal accent leaves one guessing as to whether she is being sincere or sarcastic. "Wella..actoolly I baaught braas and un-dar-waare."

"Well well," Stan laughs. "Did you forget to do laundry before you left?"

"Noo, but you haave to buy these things some-tames. Don't you ever shaap for un-mention-aables?"

Rich is an oversized man with gapped front teeth. He speaks with a gruff, but good-natured Bronx accent that reminds one of Ralph Kramden. "He don't. He just has two pairs he rotates every udder day."

Stan reacts with Mock defensiveness. "Hey! Your wife probably buys yours. I bet you don't even know what brand you wear!"

"What brand?" Rich gestures with his large hand by his head. "What brand da you wear?"

Stan's assumed the expression of an exaggerated pout. "I know what brand I wear! Let me see they're not Jockey...I hate Jockey you can't use the flap in front..."

Sheryl interjects, "You use the flap? I'll tell yaa Sta-an, no men use that fla-ap. That much I know."

Stan acts embarrassed and dumbfounded. "What do you mean, don't use the flap?"

Turning to Rich and I he pleads, "You guys use the flap don't you?"

We supply no assurance. "Jeez" he continues, "I feel like even more of a geek. The next thing you'll be telling me my Spiderman boxer shorts aren't manly."

At thirty-six Stan is an avid fan of superhero comic books and attends Star Trek conventions. As the laughter subsides Sheryl turns to me. "So Caes-aaar what about you? What brand do you weaar?"

With my mouth full of swordfish I lean towards her pretending confidentiality. "Actually that's not a problem I have to deal with."

She is momentarily confused. With realization apparent on her face she lays her head on her own shoulder like a confused puppy. "You don't wear un-der-weaar? Evaar?"

More laughter. Stan gestures towards me, "See Caeser is cool. He doesn't even wear underwear."

Sheryl is not impressed by such 'coolness'. "Tell me Caesaar, what are you goang to weaar tonight at the grand," her tongue slips "the Glam Sla-am?"

We have decided to go to the club owned by the rock star Prince. "I was hoping this was my chance to wear leather," I responded with a coy smile.

Stan reacts like an idolizing teen. "See what I mean!" He speaks to Sheryl, then me, than back again. "You brought leather? See Caeser's the coolest. You know this man has women falling all over him."

Sheryl tilts her head towards Stan suspiciously.

"She looks understandably skeptical," I add, somewhat embarrassed by this exaggeration.

"No. Obviously na-at. I was just wanderang Sta-an, if you aren't livang vicariouslay through Caes-aar?"

"Yes I am!" He gestures over-dramatically. He is on his third tall glass of lager and is fairly ranting. "He has a woman I have lusted after from afar, attacking him and he turns her aside because he is practicing fidelity, and I commend him for it. And his girlfriend is a babe-o-rama I might add."

"Oh so she looks like me?" Sheryl puts her chin in the air vainly.

Stan's ongoing flattery towards me is a recent phenomenon that I'm not really comfortable with. Despite knowing each other for some time I never really knew much about him. It was only three days ago when I opened myself to him slightly, talking to him about music, filmmaking, and art. This seemed to be all it took to gain his admiration and confidentiality. It is an odd feeling because in our filmmaking hierarchy, I am the low man in our group and he is the top dog.

This conversation with Stan took place while he, Rich and I were eating dinner at a roadside steakhouse during our recent stop in Cooperstown. Stan had downed two beers when his tongue loosened, unabashedly revealing his feelings. When the waitress comes by he blurts out to her, "This man's a rock star!"

She looks between us confused by his statement.

"No. Really, he has this great band, and he has the babes eating out of his hand, literally." A reference to my apple biting routine.

Surprisingly his outbreak compels her to break the number one rule of waitressing and seat herself at our table and tell me of her plans to begin a career as a model.

When she departs Stan inquires about Ornelia, who he has seen me at the coffee shop with, and who he refers to as "Tori Amos." I give him a brief account of her violent 'attack' that had occurred just a few nights before.

He is aghast with jealousy. He raves to Rich, "Why doesn't this ever happen to me? This girl is hot! I have this thing for redheads. She looks just like that singer Tori Amos, have you seen her on TV? When we get back if you need somewhere to bring her some night you can use my place."

I assure him that I have no plans to do so and brief him on my relationship with Sasha.

"You're really serious about this girl, huh?" He turns to Rich, "I met his girlfriend when we were doing the Uni-Mart shoot. She's this beautiful, exotic looking babe."

Only minutes later Stan's tune has changed as he takes me deeper into his confidence, "You know Caeser I have a disease. I am a diagnosed obsessive-compulsive. I take this medication every day so I won't go crazy or anything."

I don't quite know how to react to this. Should I say, "That's O.K. I'm a little crazy too," or perhaps inquire into exactly what kind of excitement we would experience if he forgot to take his medication some day? Instead I sit there quietly with a stupid smile on my face.

Now the beer has taken its toll and he informs us of his intention to use the head. "I hope there's nobody in there. I can't pee if I think there's somebody watching me."

Back at the California Cafe I am beginning dessert. Like the swordfish, the first taste of the double ginger cake caresses my stomach with unknown pleasures. The wonderful flavor fills me with money greed. I want to live this way. I know that by next week I'll be trying to figure out how to eat at the local Wendy's hamburger joint for under two dollars. I hold the second bite against the roof of my mouth with my tongue until the sweet fragrance has fully dissolved from my palette.

By the meal's end we are all tipsy as we drive without direction in hopes of finding the Glam Slam. When we find the club there is a long line of young MTV types waiting to enter. Once inside I immediately ditch the others and head towards the edge of the dance floor. The place is packed with scantily clad women and athletic young men in muscle shirts. I pass an area with couches in a dark corner where couples lie together. It fills me with an urge for the decadence of opium dens and petting orgies.

As I walk, a small blonde woman punches me in the stomach for no reason and moves on before I can see her face. The place is thick with sexuality. The sound system blares an incessant dance beat and video screens project sensual abstract images. The room is so full of sweating bodies that I cannot take a step in any direction without bumping into someone.

I stand by the edge of the dance floor peering hungrily at the writhing mob. A woman in front of me bends over pushing her buttocks against my crotch and grinds her hips from side to side. After a minute of this I wait to see if she speaks to me. Her friends smile at me naughtily, but she moves away from me without any hint of recognition.

From an unseen source, a burst of strawberry flavored fog covers the dance floor. Nearby, four short, plump, black kids are doing a bouncing dance on hands and knees. They hump each other rhythmically and switch positions on the fourth measures. The

women get behind the men and spank their fat bottoms in double
time. I am part of a crowd that circles them as they carry out their
blatantly suggestive display.

Another burst of fog obscures my vision and a new groove
blasts from the sound system. I turn and lose myself in the throng
at the head of the dance floor. The music is familiar to the crowd
and they chant the refrain in unison. I dance among them with
aloof, understated movements. I close my eyes and am aware only
of my connection with the music. My skin is vibrating in the heat.
Even in my internal darkness I am pulled towards the anonymous
smorgasbord of flesh. I place my left hand on my stomach as I
move. The warmth of my own touch brings moisture from my
sweating pores. The bass drum is a primal summons to procreation.
The beam of my consciousness explores my own flesh from within.
Each limbs glows with sensitivity. Under its focus the warm light of
consciousness touches my lips and moves down my neck, chest and
abdomen. My sex is not erect but lies heavily against my jeans. It
throbs off time against the music.

I open my eyes to see two small black women and a
beautiful Asian woman have taken the space in front of me. They
seem to be preparing for an exhibition of some kind. All three wear
extra short cut off jeans. The two black women take a stance facing
each other. In sync they break into dance with spastic motions, at
times rolling their hips and caressing their own breasts and bellies.
Their faces hold a cold hard expression. The taller of the two wears
a loose white vest that reveals the curves of her medium sized
breasts. She gets on her knees and leans her forehead against the
abdomen of the other, who grinds slowly, heaving the kneeling
women's head back and forth. The smaller woman has a darker,
near black skin tone and wears white fishnet tights. She has begun
sinking to the floor with her legs spread wide. Her hips thrust in
frenetic jabs at a pace that seems in-humanly possible, while she
arches her back in and out focusing attention on her jutting breasts.

The motion of her hips calls forth a burst of testosterone.
It is the most erotic display of dancing I have ever witnessed. The
women pull a thin black man from the crowd and rub their bodies
against him lasciviously. I want to be him. I am consumed with lust
as I move backwards against the four-foot high stage upon which

the sound system sets. I arch my back over the stage and lay my head flat against the huge speaker cabinets. I am immediately deafened. The electronic drums and bass swallow my mind with rhythms that hearken the jungle. I can feel the low frequencies of the bass drum vibrating through my chest. Before my eyes a thousand bodies move in pointless motion. Motion for pleasure itself.

I want contact. No names, no talk, no responsibility, just pure anonymous flesh. On the dance floor the shorter woman places her finger into the dark lips of the other. She sucks her finger while staring straight into her eyes. She moves to her, releasing her finger as she bring her lips close as they lock into a gentle kiss.

Above the firm blows of the bass drum a dirty guitar screams frantically. I want to lose myself in pure fuck. Fuck which emanates from every living cell in the natural world. Fuck which echoes back through the annals of history, reaching back to the original thought in the mind of the omnipotent Godhead.

In West Africa in times long past, the tribal village would meet each spring for orgies in the plowed fields to ensure fertility for the coming year's harvest. In ancient India a dark princess sucked the gigantic cock of a donkey until its brute jism covered her naked body to bring about the prolific reign of the maharaja. In the Baltic States the rites of spring were celebrated by viciously slaughtering a virgin to keep the cycles of nature in motion. The Kama Sutra organizes the ancient pleasures of India with analytical precision. When Eskimo societies were gripped by tensions each man switched wives with his neighbor to confuse the evil spirits. From the homosexuality of Greek gymnasiums to Roman orgies, French postcards and English whores, even the Native American women were described as being "generous to manhood." It is rumored that Chairman Mao packed his swimming pool with naked teenage girls and rolled his fat body over the mattress of wet young flesh.

This libidinous horde on the dance floor was willed into existence by the creator when the first spark shimmered in the primordial ooze, when the first cell split, when the first fish spawned. The whole of evolution led to this spectacle. As surely as nature bursts into green with the fertilizing rains of spring this moment in time had to be.

My prurient mind surveys the luscious crowd. I want them all stripped bare, skin and hair gleaming in the colored lights, bodies piled on each other, fucking, sucking, licking anonymous limbs, penetrating faceless cunts, assholes, mouths and armpits. The monstrous mound of flesh lubricated with a coat of glistening cum.

The Asian woman who accompanied the two black girls dances a few feet in front of me. Her unseeing eyes peer past me as if in a daze. I am hypnotized by the bottomless black pools. In them I seek every sexual encounter of my life. Every fuck, every blowjob, every jerking hand. The lost encounters of my teen years. The hundreds of forgotten orgasms in Leilani's all too familiar snatch. The sideways position she preferred for orgasm, her face pulled taut in one single wave of ecstasy. Samantha's shrieks that would send the neighbor's dog howling for hours. Inserting the tiny vibrator into her anus as I plunged her tight vagina. Chrisanne's conically shaped breasts and clinging behind. The nameless encounters in parked cars on city streets, in hidden corners in hometown parks, in front of friends in cheap hotels. And most of all Sasha's ever-moist abundance. Her endless, earth shattering convulsions; in my lap on the freeway as tractor trailers pass, on golf courses, in hot tubs, beds, hotels, and in her parent's house.

Inspired by this eternal dance of creation I want to rule the world. I am possessed by the insatiable will to power. I long to be crowned the ever-reigning God of fuck. To have cunt served on pristine trays to my bedside. Beautiful sleek bodies lining my chambers. Like the mad monk of Russia I want my cock cut off by a jealous wench and hurled across the room magnificently. Like Napoleon I want it auctioned at Sotheby's a hundred years hence when it is but a dried shriveled sea horse.

In this dark world there can be no equality of the sexes because I see women only with desire. Every beautiful face I seek to possess. Every short skirt urges me to rape. My friendship is a deceit and this is your only warning. Ornelia I want to return your affliction by tearing your pussy into bloody shreds, pulling out your red locks from behind as I pound your white bottom dog style. Robin, object of desire for so long, why did I turn you down when

I want to take my place among the multitudes that have released themselves in your ravaged hole. Heather your thin black frame beguiles me. I still recall the taste of your thick dark lips, the odor of your sweating body as I lie beside you in New Orleans. Mita I'll tear down your wall and wash away the sexual curse you complain of. Your small body will be putty in my grip. I will lift you into the air and pummel you while suspended in my embrace. Sneha and Joan, I long for those sensual moments on the dance floor. The stolen kisses as the music blared. Let me fuck you in unison, on jungle gyms, on swinging trapezes.

The nameless bodies I touched while singing. Who are you? I want to make your bellies swell with my seed. To my sweet friend Jill, drop the kid sister act long enough so I may fill your mouth with my cum. Angie those drunken kisses in my car after the Stoney's gig are haunting me now. Krista, Pocihontes, Wendy, how I loved those touches in the Beirhaus. The girl in the teddy on the floor of Cafe 210. "Thanks for the fuck," she said. I have forgotten your face but I remember your breasts as I lay atop you. Brenda, after a year of seduction why did I turn you aside when you finally acceded. I want you all before me naked, mute and craving my explosions, lapping at my loins. I feel incapable of love. Except for the love of hedonistic decadence. I am alive and I want it all.

8/17/1994

In the afternoon I find myself invading the privacy of a psychiatrist's office in a V.A. hospital in San Diego, California. As the psychiatrist questions the patient about his medication I cling to the wall of the tiny office in a vain attempt to be unobtrusive. I record the conversation while the doctor's questions become increasingly personal.

Dr: Have you had any feelings that you want to hurt yourself or others?

Patient: No. Not lately. (He seems unsure) Not that much.

Dr: No suicidal thoughts?

Patient: No. But I don't see any point in going on.

Dr: Have you had any flashbacks?

Patient: Not really. Maybe one or two a week. And lately my nightmares haven't been the blood n' guts kind. I realize I've been taking scenes from the field and putting people and places from my daily life into...(He looks confused)...it's like I feel the emotions from the war, but they're in a situation from my life now.

Dr: So you do feel hopeless at times?

Patient: When I feel hopeless I really feel hopeless. So I would have to say 'no.' But I just have my normal day to day feelings that there's no point in going on.

This man's words shock me. It is amazing that twenty years after the Vietnam War he still suffers it's traumas. As a young child I recall the body counts at the end of the news reports. I was too young to understand what it all meant, but the strife that tore this country apart over Vietnam was in the air and in the media. The entire aura of that era played a huge part in my psychic make-up.

Even at that young age I was affected by the sense of revolution and the feeling that people could be part of something that would change the world. Although a lot of what the hippies said now seems naive, I have always felt nostalgia for that era, and that something was missing in the decades that followed. It seems now that there is little worth believing in, and there is a disheartening apathy among all segments of society.

Some have argued that this created a bad seed in my generation. That this nostalgia for social action and community spirit created a generation of despair-filled nihilists who ground out their frustrations and emptiness with drug use, promiscuity, and self-destructiveness.

After I graduated from high school one of my teachers referred to our class as "the Vietnam generation," and claimed that we were the worst students to ever pass through the doors of the Chief Logan High School.

I believe it's true that this nihilism was reflected in some of the youth of that time. Although I can tell you firsthand that my classmates didn't have a clue why they acted the way they did. Most of them knew nothing about Vietnam or the social revolution. The nihilism was a quiet spirit that snuck in through the unconscious and struck out at society with the giant proclamation of our generation: "So What!"

Punk became the voice of the counterculture. A voice of anger threatening society by portraying the youth of America as the idiot sons and daughters that the elder generation had created with their hypocritical morals and materialist values. Punk was a warning that there was a poison brewing among the youth that could burst open and destroy our society from within.

Although many believed that punk rock would create a social political movement equal to the sixties, the music business stubbornly ignored punk, and it all quickly faded away in a country caught in the tide of Ronald Reagan's Moral Majority.

During my high school years I first began to experiment with drugs. A change in my life was triggered by a modest philosophical thought. I was daydreaming in my problems of democracy class, and as the teacher droned on I found myself thinking about death. I thought, "I know I'm going to die so I might as well get out and enjoy life while I can."

Afterwards I began to party with a vengeance. Each day I entered school with my eyes glowing red from the dope I had smoked while cruising around the school parking lot. In homeroom the potheads spied each other knowingly, as if we were members of a secret fraternity. Being a drug user gave one a sense of community and a feeling of being against the system and the status quo.

Drugs were everywhere in those days. In our school the drug users became the dominant forces during my senior year. Kids were smoking hash in science class and dropping acid during lunch. The users formed an unspoken alliance that eventually succeeded in total disruption of the already ailing school system.

One of the defining factors in this drama was the faculty's decision at the beginning of my senior year to reestablish order and respect for authority among the students. To achieve this they hired a new principal, ex-marine sergeant Clyde Colwell, and an ex-football player who was a member of the New York Jets when they won the Super Bowl: Vice-Principal Ralph Baker.

On the first day of classes I knew I was in trouble when walking down the hall I heard a deep voice calling out, "Hey fuzzhead. Hey fuzzhead!" (At the time I wore my hair in a long afro.) I was used to such mockery form the backwoods cretins that were bused in from the outer regions of the county. This time I was oh-so-pleased to find that these sophisticated insults were coming from the new Vice-Principal Baker. From that day he had his eye on me and we were bound to clash.

Among the faculty's plans to reestablish order were rules such as one-way halls, limited locker stops, and arranged seating in the cafeteria. These new rules did little more than create more confusion, but that fact was secondary to the prime objective; instilling respect for school authority.

In response to the new authoritarianism the drug users began carrying out ridiculously disruptive acts that served no purpose other than forcing a confrontation with the faculty. Although I was not familiar with performance art at that time, the irrational nature of some of these actions would certainly have passed as such.

Some of my favorite examples were a straight-A student who would fill his mouth with water before class started, hold it for as long as he could, then fake convulsive vomiting as he spewed the liquid across the classroom. My friend Spig had the adolescent genius to wait until the English teacher would finish her lecture, then when she asked with finality, "Does anyone have any questions?" he would raise his hand and innocently ask, "What's the meaning of life?" Another fellow in my class was fond of bellowing "Quaaludes" in response to every question the teacher asked.

In time this rebellious spirit penetrated the entire student body. Random noise became an effective means of disrupting classroom activities. At least every hour a student would release a spine tingling primal scream that would be echoed by other students until the entire school was pierced by the chilling howls.

There were other more violent actions also taking place. Early in the year a cheerleader was expelled for throwing a brick through the principal's living room window. By mid-year commodes were regularly being exploded by small sticks of dynamite, and during the graduation rehearsals the vice-principal's tires were slashed on his brand new BMW.

My own troubles with the administration seriously began when a car battery exploded and my mother was taken to the hospital in the morning before school. Despite this I was only a few minutes late. As I entered the school I heard the opening of the National Anthem that signaled I was officially late. When the Anthem began all in the hallways had to freeze in place as if we were playing a bizarre game of Red Light, Green Light.

While I stood frozen in place like a statue honoring dope crazed youth, inside the glass doors of the administrator's offices I could see secretaries and students going about their business. The office was the one place where the freeze in place rule did not apply, making it clear that it wasn't really important for adults to respect the Anthem, but that it was something merely intended to teach students to honor authority. The absurdity irritated my sense of dignity. My teenage mind raged against the hypocrisies of the system.

In my previous five years attending the school a few late days were overlooked as a fact of life. But with the new discipline, my tardiness created a snowball effect that gave me my first true taste of authoritarian mentalities. As punishment for my tardiness I was given detention the following evening. Because I had to be at work at a fast food restaurant at that hour I did not go to the detention.

The next morning Vice-Principal Baker paid me a visit in my first period art class. He said that my punishment for missing detention was T.A.P. I'm not sure what the acronym stands for, but it meant that I had to spend two days in solitary confinement. In the stone dead silence of the art class, Baker and I had a stand off when I refused to go to the isolation room. For this bit of insubordination I was expelled for three days.

I argued my case fervently before the administrators, stating that the circumstances of my tardiness were legally considered an act of God, and that the reason why I did not attend the detention was because real world financial considerations take precedence over symbolic disciplinary acts. Finally frustrated with the arguments Baker took me into his office and shut the door.

"Listen Caeser," he said as if clearing away the slates. "It doesn't matter if I'm wrong in this matter. I have the authority here, and if you check the law books you'll find that students have no legal rights. What I say goes and you're just going to have to accept that!"

But I couldn't accept that. I clung stubbornly to the naive idea that justice existed inherently in the world and one just needed to fight a little to set things right. To this end I fought their actions with any means possible within the system. First I tried speaking to the superintendent of the school district. I told him my story, including that to drive the point home, after the three days suspension, upon returning I would still have to spend the two days in the isolation room and attend the day of detention.

At first the superintendent was encouraging, "You're right, I think they've taken this a little too far. I'll see to it that the T.A.P. and detention are cancelled." The following day and thereafter he refused my calls and nothing changed.

I wrote a letter to the local newspaper, and although they refused to print it, the newspaper's editor called to say that it was a well written letter and he supported my "spunk," but it would not be appropriate for the paper to question the school administrators. This fear of questioning authority among the local newspapers would come back to haunt me later in life when the stakes were much higher.

Finally I acceded and took my punishment. Really I only gave in to the fact that you can't beat the system by working within it, because those in authority look out for their own. They reason that if people are allowed to question authority at all, then it is a threat to all in authority. Instead I embraced the disruptive actions of the subculture full force. I figured I couldn't beat them, but I could certainly make their lives unpleasant.

When I was placed in T.A.P. the room chosen for my isolation was the tiny cubicle that housed the school P.A. system. For no particular reason I stole the tape that contained the National Anthem and the pledge to the flag. My thievery did succeed in relieving the students of these early morning forced shows of patriotism for a while. After about two months a new tape was bought and all returned to normal.

Near the year's end I was again given T.A.P, giving me an opportunity to carry out my most fulfilling act of rebellion. My trouble this time was caused by a series of obscene essays I had written in English class. Under the influence of Saturday Night Live, and the music of Frank Zappa and the Tubes, I began writing in a style of social satire based on the blackest of humor I could fathom. I began this after our class read Gulliver's Travels.

I found the scene of Gulliver exploring the cancer holes in the giant bodies of the Brobdingnag queen to be disgusting, and the book's symbolism was so obscure that it was rendered meaningless without the correct historical background and knowledge of the social/political circumstances of the era. By way of protest I began filling my essays with absurd satires of our society's consumer values, and the perverse sexual appetite of the national media.

After about a month of this Ms. Frankhouser, a young overweight woman who wore skin tight pants that revealed every bulge and crevice of her cellulite laden form, came to me with my latest essay.

"Caeser I've tried finding something of value in these. I even brought them before the entire English department, and they all agreed that this is simply rubbish. Until you're ready to stop this, report to the office instead of coming to class."

In the office I was taken to the guidance counselor. The counselor joked with me briefly, obviously trying to show me what a regular guy he was, then he began uneasily, "As you know we're concerned about these essays you've been writing. We were wondering if these might represent...we were wondering if they might be a cry out for help. If you would like we could arrange for a psychiatrist to speak with you."

This stunned me, "A cry out for help? Let's see; I am in a school system where the teachers don't have a drop of passion for the subjects they teach. My career prospects are nil. I live in a society whose values I find hypocritical, and sometimes downright obscene. There is nothing to believe in either spiritually or politically. And the threat of nuclear annihilation hangs over our heads in the balance of the cold war. Do you think you could help that?"

I did not have the slightest inclination to debate philosophy with this man so I assured him it was all in naughty fun, we discussed English humor for awhile, and I was transferred to the Principal's office.

"What's wrong with you?" Baker gestured at the white pages filled with my scribbled handwriting. "Some of these things deal with necrophilia!"

At the time I wasn't sure what necrophilia was, but I did my best to look very, very ashamed of myself. As he rambled on I noticed a small crucifix on his desk beside a photo of his family, and suddenly I was overcome by an uncontrollable urge to sneeze.

"Aaachooo!" I expelled loudly. The unguarded spray speckled the crucifix, family photo, and his hands, which still held one of my essays. He stopped mid-sentence and we stared at each other, both somewhat shocked by the magnitude of my nasal explosion.

My eyes widened with fear as steam began to seep out of his ears and his flat top bristles stood on end. Finally he growled through his teeth, "Just get out of here. You're on T.A.P. for the next three days."

The first two days locked in the isolation room passed uneventfully. At the end of the third day I stole the new tape with the National Anthem and pledge to the flag and replaced it with the old one that I had re-recorded with a special message for Vice-Principal Baker.

The next morning in homeroom the class rose as usual and faced the small flag at the front of the room as the Anthem crackled through the aged speaker above the chalkboard. Then the pledge began. A few students mumbled along, "I pledge allegiance to the flag of The United States Of....."

"Fuck you Baker!" my voice blared through the speaker. Instantly the song School's Out by Alice Cooper shrieked into the air. Not only my homeroom, but the entire school roared with laughter.

I thought for sure I could kiss my diploma good-bye after this stunt, but I was never even questioned about the incident. For the rest of the year neither anthem nor pledge was heard again, and

I felt at least somewhat vindicated. And more importantly, I was having the time of my life.

By this point the situation had deteriorated to such a degree that the faculty seemed to give up. On one of the final days of school a fight broke out in the cafeteria between two girls. Vice-Principal Baker, who was one of the cafeteria monitors, rushed over to stop the melee. When he did the entire lunchroom, which had previously been hooting and making catcalls at the fighting girls, began to chant "Kill Baker, Kill Baker..."

He stopped in place, quickly forgetting the fight and peering about the chanting crowd of students. He looked towards another teacher and tried to laugh, but his face registered an obvious expression of fear. He turned and left the cafeteria never to return.

On the last day of classes it was revealed that both Principal Colwell and Vice-Principal Baker had resigned their positions. It seems that although you can't beat the system by working within it, acts of civil disobedience carried out by a group of civilians can ultimately win the day.

During graduation practice Vice-Principal Baker was standing near the soundboard when someone threw a quarter stick of dynamite behind him. The sound tech, who was the brother of a friend, ask him why they didn't just flunk all these people. He responded that they just wanted to get them out of the school.

Next the students were told to walk back to the end of the field and practice entering and taking our seats. As we walked to the back of the field we began to pick up speed. Soon most of the class was running full speed. We ran off the field and into our cars never to return until the graduation ceremony.

At the graduation ceremony Principal Colwell made his final appearance to congratulate the graduating seniors. When he finished, as we tossed our square caps into the air he was greeted with a unified bellow from the students; "FUCK YOU!!"

At the graduation party a friend ask me, "What are you gonna do now that you've graduated?"

"Get drunk," I replied.

8/21/94

The film shoot is over. We eat our last meal on the company tab in San Diego. The restaurant sits on the beach overlooking the Pacific Ocean. This trip has been my first time on the West Coast. As I watch the sun slowly set over the gray waves I am taken by a mixture of melancholy and serenity. Children frolic on the beach and two lovers pass arm in arm. The rest of the film crew is immersed in conversation, but I quietly eat my fried bass, finish my second glass of wine, and gaze at the horizon.

Streaks of pink glow among the clouds as a voice from within whispers, "*No one dreams, no one hears.*" Tomorrow we will return to State College. The voice whispers "*Dream, dream, forever more.*" I don't want to return, because to return is to face the harsh realities that await me there.

The sun has disappeared behind a large curtain of gray clouds that hang near the horizon. When I get back to State College I will be facing my first night as a homeless man. Sheryl offers me a piece of her calamari that I chew without tasting.

The sun emerges from below the clouds spotting the gray waves with orange crescents. The others try to draw me into their conversation, but I can't turn my head away from the sand, water, and waves. My mind is empty. Tomorrow's trials and tribulations can't be won tonight. For now the future must be left to faith.

The bottom of the sun has disappeared below the sea. "*I hold an image in my mind. Dig down deep. Carbon begets coal. Coal begets diamond…*" The wine glasses are being refilled.

The sun is eclipsed by a third and the gulls cross its center while skimming across the waves. The conversation continues but I have nothing to offer. "*Dig down deep. Relics reveal.*"

Only half the glowing disc holds darkness at bay. One lone figure walks along the waters edge with his head hung low. "*Diamond begets a crystal more perfect than the mind can comprehend.*"

Eclipsed by two-thirds the sky surrenders. Shades of pink and blue dim to gray. The voices of the past months echo as a soft din in my ears, but it is all far away. Words of love, words of pain, words of longing and fear and confusion, all just a distant hiss that merges with the wash of the incoming tide.

The sun ceases to exist. I hold an image in my mind as darkness overtakes us.

8/27/94

The flight back from California is a hellish experience. The last leg of the journey, we rode on a small commuter plane that bounced and swayed with every air pocket. By the time we arrive in State College I am still swaying back and forth as I walk down the street.

As soon as I arrive I go directly to Ornelia and Mita's house. As I stand in Mita's room telling her about my adventures in California, I am suddenly overcome by dizziness and begin to sink to the floor. Mita runs to get me a cup of water that revives me enough so that Ornelia and I make our way down to Café 210 for a bite of dinner.

That night, having nowhere else to go, I sleep on the floor beside Ornelia's bed. With the light's out we speak with soft hushed tones. Ornelia speaks of her love for the book Alice In Wonderland. Before turning in to sleep she parts the curtains and looks out the window to announce it is a full moon. From my vantage point the moon makes her red hair glow with a greenish hue. She is dressed in a soft white slip and looks lovelier than ever bathed in the moonlight. As we settle down for sleep she offers her hand to me. I take it and hold it in mine. Given that the sexual tension between us previously took the form of violence, it seems a soft and gentle gesture. Her hand feels warm and I hold it as long as I can without it seeming too awkward. As we become quiet I recall a past conversation where we both admitted that we hate sleeping alone. I want more than anything to crawl into the bed and lay beside her. Nothing sexual, I just wanted to hold her and feel the warmth of her body next to mine. It seems the most natural thing in the world to do so, but instead I stay in my place on the floor, quietly longing for her.

8/28/94

It is my second day back in State College after the California trip. Filmspace has paid me $200 of the $2,900 they owe me. My original contract was for a maximum of five weeks of editing to begin on August first.

Since that time the project has been pushed back for over a month and I am stuck here waiting. Hanging out, killing time, just waiting to begin the job. I begin the day by heading for The Daily Grind. To save money I try to eat my meals for under two dollars, so I buy a cup of tea and two bananas for breakfast. I take a table outside on the sidewalk. It is a quiet morning and the place is empty. As I sip my tea a scrawny man walks up the street and stops at my table and stares as at me.

"How'r yer doin?" he says. His lips seem to slide uncontrollably over his mouth.

"Fine," I reply blandly.

He stands waiting for me to inquire about his state of affairs. I smile without enthusiasm, trying not to encourage the conversation. I am in an introspective mood and not interested in outside intrusion. Despite this he flops down on a chair beside me.

"I'm not doin' to good and I'll tell you why," his voice takes on the tone that demands pity. "Ever since last night I been trying to get somebody to help me, but nobody'll help," he says as if truly perplexed by the situation. "I don't have a cent to my name and I'm trying to get to Phillipsburg."

"I know how it feels," I reply, trying to maintain a friendly smile.

He leans back on the chair. "I need to get twenty dollars for a bus ticket, and if somebody would help me I wouldn't drink or nothin.' I'd go right to the bus station and get on," he promises with the tone of a child who has been caught lying too many times.

I nod my head in his direction. With each passing second my smile becomes more of a charade.

"It's my mother's birthday…and mine too!" he throws in for an added bonus. "I gotta get to Phillipsburg and have dinner with her and my sister. If I don't she'll get mad and throw things at me. Last time she just missed me by this much," he spreads his fingers a quarter of an inch to impress upon me the peril he is in. "And I was only jokin' with her that time, I was."

I have surrendered my smile, but still gaze in his direction in an attempt to maintain some semblance of politeness. He falls into a lull, but soon resumes his tale of woe.

"If I just had a little help I'd be OK. My mother isn't in too good of health and I'm tryin' everything not to upset her, so I do."

By now I can't take it anymore and begin peeling my banana. He leans up in his chair bringing his face close to mine. As he speaks I slowly chew the banana while staring at him like a contented chimp.

"I'll tell you I have to get to Phillipsburg or I'm gonna do one of two things and they're both stupid, and they both involve a knife."

I have finished the banana and a low burp squeaks out like an insulting punctuation to his plea, or to his threat as the case may be. He again leans back on his chair.

"No lie, I gotta get to Phillipsburg today or I'll die, that's the way I look at it," he says, now raising the stakes even higher.

This pathetic human being has been reduced to pleading to a complete stranger and I find my only reaction is apathy. Not that I am in any position to help him, but one may think that given my own struggles I would feel at least a little sympathy for him.

On the opposite side of the street four women walk by pushing four baby carriages. Each carriage carries two toddlers. They are a smattering of races: black, white, and Asian. Their innocent faces gawk at my new friend and I with an expression of eternal wonder. Their expression reveals that the world they view is a complete and total mystery.

I feel close to the children. Increasingly the world appears to me much the same as it does to them, and only minutes ago I was staring at this tragic figure beside me with a similar expression. I am vaguely aware that my friend is still talking even though I have long ago quit looking at him or listening.

"Nobody cares about me so why should I go on living? If I had the help I need…but nobody cares enough to help me so I should just leave this damned world, that's true too," and he stands up and leaves, perhaps not the world, but at least me and my indifference.

Although I often seem to be echoing those same expressions of self-pity, he at least nailed that one right on the head. I don't care. I don't care about anything. Except of course, myself. My selfishness is a theme that both Leilani and Samantha constantly threw in my face.

At this moment it is more than not caring, I am succumbing to a numbness brought on by the purgatory that being in State College represents to me. My entire future awaits me in New York, but fate has trapped me here as I wait for the Filmspace job to begin.

The boredom is debilitating. I spend my days writing and re-writing. I am sleeping on the floor of Stan's second apartment. There is no TV or telephone, and no kitchen to speak of. I feel more comfortable staying out during the day. The place reeks of cat piss even though there are no pets on the premises.

8/29/94

Night falls and I am restless and lonely. My frustration is a poison that floods my veins and annihilates all sentimental emotion. Yet if I look to the past I fear I will turn into a pillar of salt. To combat this I have made myself hard inside, using my mental focus to believe in a future that logic tells me is hopeless. I have to believe otherwise I'll die where I stand.

At midnight I walk the streets without direction, sneering at all who laugh loudly or who are publicly displaying good humor. It feels as if I am possessed. It is possible this is the next step downward from the disconnected, voyeuristic feelings that have overtaken me in recent months.

I end up at a Café with a glass of cheap red wine in my hand. Under the dim lights I read my own writings and see the seeds of my self-destructive behavior. The pages are a mirror. In that mirror I see the reflection of my personal Mephistopheles, the enfant terrible. I see he is struggling for control of my will, creating games, manipulating me and those around me even while I plead innocence.

The diversions that were supposed to pull me through this empty period in purgatory have now become the danger. I seek out beautiful women as friends, then act as innocently as possible, all the while I try to become the object of their desires. Once I succeed in gaining the opportunity to become intimate with them, at the last minute I turn tail and run. For Sasha's sake I decline these pleasures. Yet my ego proceeds with this sport of inflating itself through these psychological deceptions. The result is that there is drama all around me. Tension and jealousy pervade my social circle here in 'Happy Valley,' as State College is called by the marketing people and local radio DJs.

Thursday night I find myself in Lewistown speaking with Robin, an old friend who invites me out for a drink on her birthday. I tell myself, "It's just a drink with an old friend." But in my self-critical mode I realize my ruse. Robin is a beautiful woman who is openly promiscuous, she has already expressed her desire for us to be together sexually, it is her birthday and we will be drinking. It is simply asking for a sexual encounter.

It reminds me of a statement Mita made a few days earlier in an unrelated conversation. "I would never invite a man back to my room at the end of the evening because he would assume I would do something with him. If I didn't I would feel like I was tricking him. Don't you think?" she asked cocking her head to the side like a cute puppy-dog.

After considering briefly I reply, "Yes, I might think that."

Immediately I recall an incident when Sasha invited a blues musician back to her room after a late night bar gig he was performing at. With childlike naiveté she told me of his disappointment when she wouldn't kiss him. She claimed it was an innocent act, but after Mita's words I wonder if Sasha might play similar games with people to stroke her own ego. Being a woman it is even more dangerous because in that circumstance she could have easily been raped and it would be hard to claim that she wasn't leading him on.

After recalling this, my own actions seem all the more offensive. Writing about my own self-deceptions is embarrassing. I would rather burn these pages, smash the mirror so I don't have to see the truth of myself, let alone for it be seen by others. But I swallow my pride and let them exist because part of the agreement I have made with myself is that I must face the facts of the revelations they produce. Each embarrassment, each moment of shame, is another pinhole puncturing my ego, deconstructing it and myself, battering it down and moving toward the goal of self-annihilation.

It has always been my way that when I feel hurt or insecure with a woman, I compensate by being with other women. Now with the distance between Sasha and I, and the hurdles that lay before us, it seems more tempting than ever to turn towards easier and more immediate prey. At night the songs of sirens fill my head. My male friends urge me toward debauchery.

Many of my male friends seem to idolize the enfant terrible. Some of my friends feel a bit disappointed that I would turn away from my previously mischievous existence for the sake of Sasha. It seems to fracture the image they hold of me.

For some of my male friends I was the first one to introduce them to the forbidden delectations that haunt young men's fantasies. To two of my closest friends, Mhina and Donn, my relationship with them began as acting as a bad-boy role model for their emerging sense of their own masculinity. Our society is lacking in initiation rites to manhood that many tribal societies provided. In America, the lost boys in search of guidance fall into the clutches of the modern equivalent of witchdoctors and voodoo priests such as myself to fulfill this function.

I met both of these fellows when we were all enrolled in the Penn State University film department, and each separately approached me and asked me to work with them on film projects. They seemed to see my chaotic life and personal suffering as the flip side of my work as an artist. My suffering was seen as a symbol of tragedies that man is condemned to endure in this world, and my cruelty was seen as a strength that man must selfishly possess in order to partake of life's pleasures with vitality. If I told them of an erotic encounter in a ghetto alleyway, or of the emotional pains that Leilani and I endured at each other's hands, all this was perceived as the process of spiritual growth that a male must pass through in order to pass from adolescence into that lofty mythic image known as Man. 1

Also the spontaneity of some of my adventures tugged at the archaic fetishes of their unconscious minds and propelled the process of self-realization by bringing them face-to-face with the instincts that lie within their unexplored libidos.

In one instance, on the spur of the moment I whisk Mhina off on a trip to Manhattan. At 10PM I called Donn at his home in Philadelphia and convinced him to meet us at the Newark Airport at 2AM. Once inside the city I took them on a tour of the luscious whores that strolled along the West Side of the 10th Avenue area. Their testosterone was ignited as I pulled them into conversations with amazingly beautiful woman of all races, colors, and flavors, many wearing teddies, spiked heels, garter belts, and stockings.

They were further charged with adrenaline when a sudden police raid sent men and women running frantically for cover in all directions. Although good judgment warned us to leave the area, I purposely stayed in order to heighten the danger of the titillation.

Finally, after hours of driving around and window-shopping for living dolls selling sex, I found three gorgeous ladies and invited them into the car. Donn tried to stammer that he didn't really feel up to anything, but I quickly motioned for a long-legged blonde who called herself Babydoll to jump into the backseat of the car with him, slipping her a couple twenties with a knowing smile as I nodded in his direction.

The other two, a tall dusky black woman who we dubbed Bootsy, and an oaken complexioned Latina woman who called herself Shorty, squeezed into the front seat with Mhina and I. Pulling beside a small park on 36th Street Mhina and Bootsy headed for the park where homeless men slept on benches and in cardboard boxes. Donn, Babydoll, Shorty and I stayed in the car. Before long our new friends were delivering oral pleasures with well-rehearsed expertise. Outside the car homeless men watched with disinterest as Shorty's head bobbed up and down behind the dashboard. In the rearview mirror I could see Donn's perplexed expressions of pleasure as Babydoll lay in his lap.

Soon I leaned my head back against the headrest and moaned as I came into Shorty's mouth. My breath shot geysers of steam into the December air as two homeless men shared a cigarette a few feet from the bumper of my car. I opened the car door and Donn and I dropped our spent condoms onto the heavily traveled roadway. Just a little something to catch the tourist's eyes as they pass through in the morning light.

Shorty took out a tissue and tenderly dried my cock then fixed her lipstick in the review mirror. The women seemed to immerse themselves in casual conversation in order to avoid making too much personal contact with us. While they talked about the cost of getting new heels put on their thigh-high boots, I marveled that although they were completely comfortable with physical contact, they seemed to protect themselves from thinking of us as real human beings who could be related to as brothers, friends, or husbands.

When Bootsy and Mhina returned we joked about the possibility of Donn taking her home to meet his mother for Sunday dinner. After laughing at the prospect, Bootsy, who seemed more mature and comfortable than the others, began to speak poetically of motherhood and her fond memories of the Sunday feasts her own mother always prepared. "Mothers," she said nostalgically. "They always have Sunday dinner waiting for you...no matter what."

"No matter what," her finals words hung in the air with sad poignancy. I drove them to a bus stop so they could end their evening of work. The sadness of her statement was shared by all in a warm silence that almost seemed reverent. Suddenly our little group was united by the encounter we shared and the knowledge that to most of the world, it would be condemned as sin.

A week later Donn gushed over how the experience had effected him. His voice resonated over the phone line earnestly, "Caeser....I'll tell ya man, the next day I went to work, and all these guys with their lunch pails working their lives away putting up ceiling tiles, I just look around and the whole culture looks like a big fucking joke! I just wanna pull out my hammer and bang on their hard hats a few times…wake up assholes! It's a fucking game! They seem like they've never experienced a raw moment in their entire miserable existences. I know I can't live like that. If I give in…man, fucking just blow my brains out! I'll die without creativity, man."

After such experiences, some of my comrades felt left down that I would betray my amoral religion of sensuality and adventure. While they might not wish to live the lifestyle for themselves, they found it reassuring that the archetype existed.

8/30/94

In the evening I call Sasha to find her happy and excited. She said her mother had a complete change of heart about our relationship, and told her that if we are determined to be together, we should decide on our plans and be together. Sasha was eager to meet so we could discuss our options and begin planning.

After hanging up the phone I felt stunned. Over recent months I had begun to expect that it would be a long hard road to gain acceptance from her parents so we could be together. Because of her mother's conflicted feelings and previous flip-flops on the subject, I was still a bit hesitant to trust that this positive turn was real.

As I lay down to sleep that night a frightening thought snuck into my head. Throughout the summer I had been in the habit of suggesting that Sasha and I take radical steps so we could be together, such as eloping to California. I suppose this was easy to do because I didn't really believe she would ever agree to such a thing. Now that it appeared we could actually be together, I was taken aback.

The situation presented itself to my mind as a question: "If you enter into this relationship that you've been dreaming of, if you get what you want, will you still be alive as an artist?"

It is said by many that artistic insight is born of suffering. Much of my own creative work is born from the emotions brought on by the rise and falls of romantic relationships. Plus my adventures with debauchery bring a vitality that inspires me to create. Could I be happy and contented and still be creative? The dilemma forces me to question whether I am really ready to give up the reign of the enfant terrible.

At a time when my life was stagnate the self-destructive behavior of the enfant acted as a conductor connecting me with the true spirit of life, giving me the power to break with my mundane existence and to explore myself as a man and find myself as an artist. Faced with his death, I am forced to admit that in some circumstances the enfant has acted as a positive force in my life that I fear losing touch with. I doze off to sleep with the question lingering.

3:30AM

I am standing at a table in a dark wooded area. Three young men of native-American or African descent stand beside me. An elderly man with a crude double-bladed knife comes and circumcises each of the young men. Each expels a muffled grunt as he tries to suppress the expression of pain from the bloody wound. The elderly man moves towards me. He stands in front of me and takes my limp penis in his hand and brings the knife close. At the last minute he stops and places a larger knife in my hand and points me in the direction of a patch of thick green bushes. When I walk near I notice a small infant sitting within. I walk up to the child with the knife in my hand. I think of Abraham, but find no lamb or goat to spare the child. I think, "I guess it is a matter of faith." As I place my hand on the child's head he raises his eyes and peers knowingly into my own. I awake.

9/2/94

It is a lonely night in State College and I call Sasha from a pay phone. I have a small roll of quarters in my pocket. Money that could be used to procure a good meal. For weeks I have been eating junk food. For lunch each day I go to the local mini-market. For two dollars I can get one hotdog, a twenty-five cent bag of potato chips, a cookie, and a can of Tom's-brand grape soda. On Tuesday nights, Café 210 has hot wings for eleven cents each. A buck-ten gets you ten wings and some celery to boot. On other nights, there are other low budget bargains at other places, and you can bet I am there. The food might not be healthy, it might not even taste so good, but it keeps the belly full and gives one the energy to get through the day.

As soon as Sasha answers the phone she says, "I need to talk to you."

Immediately I sense trouble. "Is it negative?" I ask.

"Things got really crazy here. My Mom denied saying the things she did, and she got so upset she started having these pains and having trouble breathing. My father said that if I even think of moving in with you without being married, I'll be disowned by the family. He said you were a member of the pig-race. I feel like I'm right back where we were at the beginning of the summer."

"Shit!" I moan. "Now what?"

"It doesn't change anything as far as I'm concerned," she reassures me. "I'm not going to stay here."

Although Sasha is trying to stay positive, I am angered by it all. The pig-race comment is especially shocking. I tell Sasha I want to see her that weekend, but she has a family function she must attend. I pressure her to let me attend with her, but given the circumstances there's not a chance it will happen. Soon our conversation dissolves into an argument.

In the middle of it all the recorded voice of an operator breaks in asking for more quarters, but my roll is empty. Without a chance to say goodbye the phone line goes dead, ending the conversation with both of us upset.

When I hang up the phone my insides are twisted. As soon as I allow myself to feel happy I am knocked back down again. I meander down Gill Street in a depressed stupor. Ornelia, Mita, and their third roommate Holly are sitting on the front porch. Mita, who I once viewed as quiet and serious is in a silly mood. She has her hair tied up in a bun and she is wearing mismatched colors. Her baggy clothes appear to be thrown on without thought.

"Should I take this tap-dancing class or not?" she ponders aloud. "If I don't I'll feel guilty, but if I do I'll be so busy I'll be miserable."

Despite her heavy talk the conversation is punctuated with bursts of loud laughter. Her giggles turn my depression on its head. My despair explodes into bitter, deranged laughter. Just looking at this cute little woman with her gaping smile and boyish, gaily colored clothes brings a grin to my face.

In the middle of the conversation two policemen walk up to the porch. My entire body goes stiff at the sight of them. I still have outstanding fines and the last thing I want to do is go to jail in this state of mind.

"We've had a complaint about the noise," the first officer warns sternly.

Holly takes control of the situation with a mature air. "Oh, that was down the street. They were yelling and singing the theme to 'One Day At A Time' at the top of their lungs."

The policemen drag the situation out as if they are enjoying the intimidated expressions on the women's faces. I try to shrink in my chair.

Once they leave Mita breaks into a wide toothy smile, "One Day At A Time?" she laughs. "Can you see them putting the cuffs on you and dragging you into the car for singing 'One Day At A Time?' I'd still be singing as they take me away."

She bursts into song with an off-color melody, her head bouncing form side-to-side as she snaps her fingers. "One day at a time..One day at a time...One day at a time.."

Mita sings and I am laughing. It doesn't matter what I feel inside, I am laughing. I can't imagine how Sasha survives her home life. I should have been more compassionate with her instead of getting angry. I can't imagine what she must be feeling tonight. But she is hundreds of miles away and I have no quarters for the phone booth so there is no way to express my regrets or to try to comfort her.

My own feelings grow darker each day. My view of the world is increasingly clouded by depression. Every minute, every

emotion is colored by hopelessness. But right now Mita is singing
and I am laughing. Laughing loud from my guts. My body shakes
like an epileptic. My laughter shudders like the sobs of a madman.
Even the ever-ladylike Ornelia is covering her mouth and silent
guffaws bounce her head up and down.

It is 10:30PM in State College, Pennsylvania. For the last
two days I dared to care, to give in to happiness, and now I am
laughing from the core of my being. "One day at a time, we're
gonna take it," Mita's voice echoes through the neighborhood,
"One day at a time.

9/9/94

It's a cool evening. The murmur of the small crowd to my
left feels like a soft aural blanket that cushions the weight of my
thoughts. A nearly full glass of wine sits in front of me. It stands on
a white paper napkin, on the edge of which lays a pack of matches.
My swelling manuscript rest in its black folder on the opposite side
of the table. This is no longer a book. It is an explosion of ego. A
gastric fur-ball smothering me with hyper-perception. A neurosis
burst onto page.

I wanted abnegation of the self, but the survival instinct has
me in its grips tonight. I want to grab the matches and burn these
pages before they steal the life out of my lungs. I despise the very
words as I write them. They are a snare for the ego, urging my
libido into the open where I can mortally stab it. My self-loathing
has reached new heights thanks to the revelations of self-knowledge
these words have forced upon me.

I would drink faster if the wine would only quit curdling my
half empty stomach. I have to fight the impulse to get up and leave.
My instinct is to walk hurriedly through the streets with no
direction. To walk blindly in hope that the demons that have taken
me will collapse in exhaustion before my body does.

This writing has become inextricably intertwined with the
course of my life. I have made the foolish, addicting mistake of
allowing my friends to read the pages shortly after they are written.
This mistake has poisoned life itself. Now all in my presence act as

if a spotlight is shining upon them. Every act, every gesture, becomes a performance that my friends know could come back to haunt them by being revealed to all in these pages. No one can take me into their confidence. It has made me untrustworthy. I betray all. I have become a non-entity whose humanness is overshadowed by my artistic creation.

At times I accidentally call my friends by their character names rather then their real names. When Ornelia attacked me Sasha exclaimed, "She just wants to be the next chapter in your book."

I no longer live freely because I am always aware of the need for the next chapter. When things first started going badly with Sasha the writing brought us together. She cried when she read the words. Last night when we argued on the phone she said, "Then you'll go and write something about..."

I never heard how she finished the sentence, but I knew that I must choose between the writing and life itself. I have come to despise these words because they mirror my inner-self, and what I see in that mirror appears unbelievably ugly to me. I am watching myself deteriorate and chronicling it in the process. The suicidal voices whisper their desire. I am a liar in the grandest sense. I imagine all my friends standing together and shouting in unison, "That's not the way it was!"

Ornelia is aware that I have written about her and is concerned about the content. I feel sure that when she reads these pages our friendship will end.

Yesterday as I was standing at a phone booth trying to reach Sasha, Mita walked by and gave me a broad smile. We have become close and I feel a strong attachment to her. She invited me back to her place where we sat on the porch. It was a beautiful sunny day and the large maple tree shades the porch where we sat beside each other on an old couch.

I told her of my concerns with Ornelia. I let her read these sections and she became visibly angry. She tells me sarcastically not to worry that Ornelia will be flattered by the words. With a few words Mita devastates me. She insinuates that I caused Ornelia to attack me and says, "I can't believe that's all it takes to get a man going. I don't even care what you do. I'm just mad at men in general."

Despite the close friendship we had developed over recent weeks, since that day she has not spoken to me. I feel heartbroken by this loss and I curse these words, I curse myself as an artist, I curse myself for losing someone whose friendship I now realize meant more to me than I understood.

Mita's anger hits me like a sledgehammer, impacting me with a final blow of self-awareness about my game playing with these women. When I left her side that day I felt as if a fog had clouded my mind, but I also realize I have been empowered to understand and control my actions. For a moment I feel pure. And perhaps this purity is what I need.

I have plans to visit New York on Friday and spend the day with Sasha. I am thrilled to be getting out of State College, riding the train to Manhattan, and finally having a chance for Sasha and I to discuss our future plans. Unfortunately after weeks of Filmspace having nothing for me to do, suddenly I must work on Friday or I will lose three hundred dollars. Wednesday I call Sasha to see if she can meet me Sunday instead. She can't because she has to attend yet another family function at which I am not welcome.

In my unstable state of mind I vent my frustration on her, yelling like a madman and throwing a tantrum. By the end of the conversation I am apologizing for my behavior, but it is too late, we have both said things that have hurt each other.

Each night I sleep less and less. Although my mind's eye remains lucid, I am sinking. The months of sleeping in cars, eating bad food or not eating at all, and being under massive stress have taken their toll. I swing between deep despair and manic energy. At times my blood is flushed with adrenaline. It feels like poison. It feels like being possessed by an evil spirit. Other strange things are taking a place as well.

There was a time when I felt able to see into people and grasp their inner selves almost immediately. This ability often made me uncomfortable with strangers so I held it in check. Now it returns full force. I find myself playing with people and manipulating their thoughts for no reason other than to entertain myself. The other worldliness of this, and the raw emotions it brings out in others, seizes me with a feeling of being surrounded by irrationality.

The people who cross my path seem to gravitate towards me immediately. Within minutes they are sharing their deepest secrets and laying their burdens upon me. Even though after a few hours they may pass through my life never to be seen again, I feel the weight of their despair. I carry it with me. I take their sins and their sorrows into myself and each day I die just a little bit more for their sake.

With these thoughts in mind I begin to walk. The weekend has brought thousands of people to State College to attend the season's first Penn State football game. The town swells with middle class tourists. I see them lined up waiting to enter a dingy downtown diner.

As I look at them I realize to what extent I am not a part of America. Middle class values and the middle class way of life are a mystery to me, and no matter how hard I have tried and miserably failed, or how much money once filled my now non-existent bank account, I will always be excluded.

America: home of the brave, land of the free. How I love the promise you proclaim: of individuality, of the melting pot, the classless society, the equal opportunity.

But America, how I hate the reality you deliver; of homogeneity, the veil of civility, the moral imperialism, the inability to break through the mundane, the materialism, the conservatism, the media induced apathy, the endless mind numbing diversions that fill life with activity but steal away its meaning, the blind patriotism, the racism, the bigotry, the intolerance, the sexual obsession simmering beneath unspoken oppression, the Protestant work ethic which reduces the population to insectiles, the class barriers which incite prejudice between the middle and lower classes, while the true rich have unimaginable power and wealth and are so far beyond sight that few even know they exist, meanwhile their multinational corporations exploit the workers who are not only blind, but grateful to be pining away their lives for an endless pantheon of worthless, overpriced, consumer products, until old age withers their bodies and suddenly they look back on their lives and wonder what it all amounts to when death sums up the final tally.

America: shooting skyscrapers into the stratosphere, shitting factories onto the countryside, building computer networks that bring new addictions to the young and big brother into our homes. The mechanical human virus devours the land that once belonged to the bison and the red-skinned natives. The concrete covers all that's green then cracks and crumbles in the summer heat and winter cold. The smell of urine pervades every city street. Even in small town State College new hotels and apartment complexes arise daily.

And I long to raise them all with their inhabitants still enclosed. I would feel more at home in the ruins. Give me war, terrorism, revolution without reason. Let it burn like Rome, explode like Dresden, crumble like Pompeii.

I awake from my reverie to find myself sitting outside a yogurt shop wherein a jazz combo plays with a true minimum of passion. A pickup truck drives past and two frat boys in the back yell, "faggot" at me. I flip them the finger and motion for them to come back. I love the feeling they inspire in me. I long to be beaten up. I want to stagger with wounds bleeding. To smell and taste my own blood.

Perhaps I just don't have the courage to kill myself so I want someone else to do it for me. My good buddy Bad Brad used to say, "At least when you're feeling pain you know you're alive."

I go into the men's room of the yogurt shop and piss in the sink out of boredom. For a second it actually seems interesting. It is Sasha's birthday on Thursday and I attempt to write her a letter. The words come out filled with anger instead of love so I throw it on the sidewalk in a crumpled purple ball.

The band is butchering my favorite Miles Davis tune so I stand up and begin walking. My mind is racing at hyper speed: Library. "Sorry we're closed." Tough actin Tinactin. A sexy Asian girl in platform shoes and soft skirt passes by. Smooth well-formed legs. Reminds me of a prostitute in a war movie.

Red light. I walk across the street with the smell of hot dogs coming from somewhere. *Maybe you saw the one you dream about.*

Walking hand and hand with another... There's Renee. A Wiccan. That apple was good. Should eat more like I used to. Little dog. A wonder it doesn't get stepped on. Nowhere to go. Coffee shops. Sound and vision fade as my mind wanders into madness.

The more the more. All will be decided. As I am? Rotting with vanity. Friend of the minus sign. Stagnate. Intoxicated by horrible darkness of mind. Narcotic of boredom. All is saccharin. The world is my emetic. The wrath of God. They walk with square eyes. I want my MTV. Jesus weeps and it's only right. Buddha? Signed off. Goodbye world, hello nirvana. Mohammed. Sends his madmen to clean house. Don't Walk.

I step onto the street and a bus wakes me from my daze as it misses me by a few inches. It seems like a joke. The white mask I carry with me at all times. "Savor these moments," it whispers in my ear. When I think of what I want to be doing, where I want be, the time I waste; it laughs sardonically. *The white mask threatens with the truth.* How I have worshipped you, studied you, danced with you, ate, breathed, and touched you.

On the streets I am a tortoise without its shell. Every waking moment lived out in public. The streets are full of young men and women who have walked off their front porches for the first time. Parties roar everywhere. Music echoes from both sides of the street. The bars are overflowing. It appears the football game was won, so celebrate. Of course if it was lost - celebrate also, because who really does give a fuck? Line up two groups of proud young sons and bash their heads together so we can celebrate! Cause we misdirected, nihilistic, hedonistic, lost motherfuckers need an excuse, something to give meaning to the night's communion. We couldn't dare celebrate the void now could we?

Let's all drink a toast to nothingness itself, shall we? You celebrators have but four years to get drunk, laid, overcome your childhood traumas, and then get down to business. America is waiting. A hungry machine that really doesn't need you at all because there are fifteen million other assholes just like you who are dying to be eaten first.

I walk past Ornelia and Mita's house. On the other side of the street lives my old friend Jill. Beside her Renee. I am too introverted right now to speak so I walk on past. I am so introverted that I am turned inside out. A turtle without its shell turned inside out. A pretty sight mind you.

I walk on. Killing time. Killing mind. Outwalk the demons. Wendy's. Hair Happening. Cafe 210. Tattoo and Body Piercing. Donuts And More.

People walking in the other directions give me disdainful glances. "Hey buddy your fly's open," a beefy jock yells at me, but I am oblivious as my mind races.

Communion. Serpent. Warmth of embrace. "Guy thinks he's in Pearl Jam," another wise-guy says pointing in my direction. Likely mocking my tattered jean jacket.

The stars shine brightly. The star is the god and goal of man. A genius when dreaming. Whereupon the dead were silent. An immeasurable distance. Touch us fool of the church for like the stars we abide in solitude. Love and love's murder, to know it is sickness, to love it is death. Blush. Breathe deep. Wander like cats in heat. Nightwalkers. Drop, chat, blame it on the cat. Nevermind.

As I walk through the crowded streets my pace seems to quicken as my mind whirs chaotically: Stranded, twilight of narcotic daze. Nevermind the afterthought at twilight, days and night, thoughts in phone calls to beloved irrelevant friends invented in bar room stupors for pretense of communion. Bhakti. Chanting climax chant as we search for nothingness in circus of flesh parades of diversionary goals, phantasms of things and things and things all other same as self sink into ground burning with white heat self in 17 in 300 in 1746 in 10,0000 in infinity of eternity as universe takes control of breath as only line to survival when approaching the zero ego dies in self loathing success in failure nihilism, hopeless collapse of faith delivering nirvana circle to ever shrinking circle, ever growing circle in beauty of world nausea until even taste of unsalted bread is too painful to endure and further collapse into place no friend nor enemy of personal acquaintance has traveled in isolation poison of desire delivers final death blows as each of 17 of 300 of 1746 of 10,000 of infinity dissipates in agonizing liberation and all these thoughts are still of mystery of a near future in time and place unknown but greatly foreseen and led towards by mysterious force of self destruction...

Out of breath I stop on the street corner. A heathen. The original man, born of the red clay. Adam resides in my DNA. Let it take possession, claw at my skin to tear away the flesh, to pull out the bone, to dispel my loneliness.

Hold on to the world. Death is unacceptable. "I was in a van and you were driving home for spring break. I was thinking of you and suddenly you appeared," she said. Our meeting seems a thousand years ago. Perhaps it was.

Sasha be positive for I have given up. I am paralyzed because my every action is wrong to you. I am so frustrated my desires can only be expressed in cataclysm. And you are in a tug of war between your two selves. One ruled by guilt. One ruled by love of life. One ruled not only by your parents, but by your ancestral and cultural heritage and which has you in their grips and I am on the outside looking in through the haze of the traffic noise outside the phone booth which is my only way to communicate with you. I try to tell you I love you but all I hear is "please deposit another twenty-five cents for the next sixty seconds." I long to hear your voice but I can no longer stand the fruitless sparring of those accursed phone calls. I sometimes forget that we are on the same side. When we speak of the mundane I am enraged because I seek a validation that words can never deliver. And when we try to speak of what's important it is a nightmare of miscommunication. We are two writers who destroy each other with words. As writers we should know the power of words, but we should also comprehend their futility.

Let us both take a vow of silence. Everything that needs to be said should be spoken with soft caresses and warm smiles. I will burn this book because you can read it in my eyes. I recall my thoughts the first time I held you, "God, I didn't know you were so beautiful."

I paint a picture of you in my mind; long black hair, almond shaped eyes, golden skin, slightly crooked nose, cool soft lips. I want to make love to you at least in my mind.

You love pomegranates? We will walk in that ancient garden of pomegranates of the Pardes Rimmonium. Incarnations of Malcuth and Tifereth and God has revealed himself through our union. God has combined his ever-warring opposites through us. All is good in Heaven and Earth.

I'll sit upright with my legs bent under and you will wrap your legs around me and sit on my lap milk and honey style. I'll look into your eyes as I have a thousand times before and never gotten bored. I'll go to kiss you, but instead I'll lick your lips with a flick of my tongue and pull back before you can make contact. You'll get that funny look on your face like a little girl who doesn't quite understand what just happened.

The next kiss is not a kiss. Just lips resting softly against each other. Then the kiss: slow, eloquent, crooning sweetly like an Ellington melody. I push you back slowly, cradling you in my arms. Unbuttoning your clothes. Perhaps you will laugh if I get confused by the buttons and zippers that keep our skin apart.

Now naked and pure. You lying on your back and I sitting up between your parted legs. I bend down low and bring my lips to your abdomen. The hair there is that funny looking color as if it has been stained by blood. I won't even touch the skin. My tongue will caress the thin hair, only stray molecules of our flesh will mingle, slowly running it up the center of your slightly curved tummy, dipping slightly into your belly button along the way, up across the contours of your ribs, up the full mound of your right breast, stopping on your large brown nipple. It will be slightly hard now. This is my trophy. Do you know that your nipples get erect much less than most women's? No matter, because your sex is ever moist.

On your nipple I finally bring my tongue flush against your skin, applying just a hint of pressure. I lay my head heavily on your bosom, my ear between your breasts so I may hear your heartbeat. It is warm and accelerated. Be alive my dear, because if nothing else, if I have nothing, if I am nothing, I am alive at this moment.

Now love truly begins. The weight of my body is on top of you. I lie still, feeling your presence beneath me. Your breasts touching my chest, your belly against my own, your thighs supporting me, and your breath in my ear. Bring your mouth close to my ear and softly sing me that children's song in Hindi. As softly as possible, and as close to my ear as you can come without touching me. Your warm breath on my ear is a caress worth dying for. Your voice is a bird song dipped in virgin honey. At this moment I am in my personal heaven. I love you. I surrender to you in this moment. Pause and thank God that life is pure pleasure. Linger in the garden and surrender, for now when I lift myself up I am ready to take you.

The new kiss is passion. I steal away your breath. Sucking it out of your lungs into my own, then returning it moist and hot. I bite your lower lip warningly. My tongue enters you deeply, exploring the secrets of your mouth and throat. Again I move down to your breasts, sucking firmly, noisily, hungrily holding as much of you as my greedy mouth can swallow. I move down and nip at your thighs with my teeth, lick your pubic hair, the serpent of your dark dreams emerges as my tongue flickers about your glistening lips. Tickling them just enough to make your back begin to arch into the air.

Inside you. Your taste is my elixir. I drink you as you heave, your face contorted as if overwhelmed with pain. Soon your muscles relax and your eyes are glazed. My cock is hard as I lay atop you. I glide the now pink crown across your dark swollen lips. My wetness mixes with yours. I insert the head ever so slightly, entering slow and firm. Once fully inside we lie still. I am concentrating on what your insides feel like wrapped around me. Your vagina quivers slightly. Without moving my hips I make my penis vibrate inside you. Finally a slow rhythm, picking up speed and pressure at a luxurious, almost imperceptible rate. Holding myself above you I gaze at your face. Mine is flushed already.

Now I pull you up so you are sitting atop me, but only for a moment so that I can study the creature I am about to devour. Satisfied I spin you around and enter you from behind as we both lay on our sides. Now my movements are slow again. I could go on like this forever. It is pleasure with such ease and comfort. Your buttocks press my abdomen with each firm thrust. Next I move close, holding you as tightly as I can. You seem tiny in my arms. I have encircled your body. My left hand holds your right breast and my right holds your head. But you appear to be dreaming so I will make an impression on you. I place you above me and begin to pummel you with violent jabs, as deep as I can penetrate. Our bodies are sweat covered and my breath is heavy. Your crazy hair is everywhere, strands are sweat glued to our limbs and veil your face.

I can still see your expression. It is haggard. Haggard but fully woman. Burdened with a love and violence that can never be separated as long as man is man. Bearing the force of aggression. Strong against the man who loves you, the man who hates you, needs you, devours you, fails you, submits to you, challenges you, pressures you, wants to possess you, to liberate you, to rule you, worship you, fuck, suck, eat, and drink you, to breathe you, grow fat and rich with you, explore with you, hide out with you, fight with you, create new life with you, fight the world with you, support and be supported by you, and most of all grow old with you and leave this world with souls intertwined as one. I scream out as I flood your womb with my semen. My body shakes. I feel the white blood between my penis and the walls of your vagina. I collapse in exhaustion. Let it all drip forever. We'll hold each other into slumber. You curled up inside my arms. Your back against my chest, holding my hand between yours under your chin. I am a happy man.

It is 11AM after a night without sleep. I sit in the Daily Grind coffee shop. Writing this has flushed my face with passion. My insides still quiver with excitement. My sex is fully erect. None of those who sit serenely around me drinking herbal teas and iced coffees know that I just made love to you. It is my secret. But now I am alone again.

Matt walks up to me. He has just returned from his Woodstock trip. "Hey Caeser, good to see you. Are you O.K. man? You look a little..." he makes a shaking motion with his hands and head.

"I'm starting my own peace corps man," he continues. "The peace symbol is now official. Look I got it tattooed on my arm." He shows me a red wound on his arm. "I'm going across the country to promote it. Soon I'll be in High Times, Rolling Stone, and on the cover of Life magazine! My goal is to win the Nobel Peace prize."

Matt rambles and I feign interest. My secret is with me. But I am alone. Inside I tremble with desperation. My organs are poisoned with longing. My sex aches. I am dying of desire. I ask myself, "Is love itself a sin?" I feel the poison flow through my body and I know the end is near. The end of an era. And the end of my self.

10/28/94

I have finished my work at Filmspace and it is my last day in State College. Finally I will be free to begin my new life in New York City.

But everything is wrong. It seems that given two possible outcomes for any situation the negative one is always the one that happens. It has worked out that way so many times it defies the laws of chance. I am starting to wonder what I have done to deserve this run of bad luck. Questions that I thought I came to terms with years ago haunt me anew. The existence of morality? Good and Evil? Fate and determination? Past lives? All of these questions cloud my confused mind.

In recent weeks I have been in a dream state. A walking malaise. I have very little human contact. I work on editing the film on pharmacology during the night when no one is around. I work a few hours then pass out for a nap on the black leather couch in the back of the editing room. On and off, working and sleeping throughout the night, then I vacate before morning comes and the rest of the workers arrive.

I no longer see Ornelia, Mita, or any other friends. My depression has become so dark that I don't want to inflict my presence on anyone else.

For days I have been trying to seek help. Psychological help. Spiritual help. Any kind of help. Finally the darkness becomes too intense. I pick up the phone in the editing room and begin calling desperately, reaching out for anyone. Psychiatrists won't speak to me because I have no money or insurance. I have called priests, preachers, gurus…yet I only reach answering machines or people who think I am crazy for actually asking metaphysical questions, for really thinking about the issues they are supposed to be their domain of knowledge.

Finally, in desperation, I call the suicide hotline. A recorded voice answers the phone, "This is the Pennsylvania suicide hotline. Many people consider suicide for a variety of reasons. If you are considering suicide here are a few things you should consider…"

An answering machine at the suicide hotline? I hang up the phone. It is laughable. Like a scene from a B movie. Gathering my strength I make the final dub of the edited film and lay down to sleep. This moment is the meridian between my new and old life and yet I find myself thinking of suicide.

The following morning I leave State College to begin my new life. I plan to visit Sasha on the way to New York. Our last evening together was both horrible and wonderful. The previous weekend I came to New York to audition for an off-Broadway show called the Blue Man Group. That evening Sasha and I were given free tickets to the show. As part of the audition we were assigned the task of going into the basement of the theater and talking into plastic tubes, the other ends of which emerged under the seats of the theater. We were supposed to ad lib surreal conversations with the audience members who were waiting for the show to begin.

Once the show began we had a great time. We laughed and held each other throughout the performance. Afterward we went to a club where people slow danced to Latin music.

After our evening, as I drove back to her parent's home, she stripped naked as I drove. She said, "I want you inside of me."

I slid my finger inside of her warm vagina as she masturbated. In the green haze from the dashboard lights I looked down over her lovely body. Her long hair flowing over my legs. The expression of passion on her face. Soon she shook with orgasm. As I watched her I was overcome with feelings of love. A love so deep and so intense that it shook me to the core. After her orgasm she began to cry quietly as her head rested on my lap.

"I'm so confused. Why do I have to be a woman? I feel like such an ugly person," she said.

Her tears soon gave way to sobs, "I just don't wanna lose my mother, I don't wanna lose my mother.." she repeated between sobs. "I pray every night I'll get in a car wreck and end it all."

We pulled up in front of her parent's upper middle class mansion. The neighborhood looked cold and sterile. We sat in front of the house and I held in her in my arms while she pulled herself together. She asked that we don't speak for two weeks so that she has some time to regain her emotional balance.

She begged me to stay the night at her parent's house so they don't think there's anything wrong between us. I refused and began the four hour drive back to State College with the night's events weighing heavily on my mind.

After not speaking to her for a week, yesterday I got a message at Filmspace that her back was broken in a car accident. She is laid up in a brace, but can still move about a bit. When we spoke on the phone I said, "Do me a favor, don't pray for anymore car wrecks."

She was silent for a second. "I didn't say that," she replied indignantly. When I insisted that she did, she became hysterical. "I can't talk to you anymore," she blurted out and the phone line went dead.

On the drive to New York it is a warm and sunny autumn day. The nice weather helps to protect my spirit from the hopelessness I feel inside.

When I arrive at Sasha's house she lies in her bed propped up against the wall. A metal brace holds her from head to hips. Her hair is still matted against her forehead with dried blood. It is a ghastly site. Her beauty trapped in a mechanical metal contraption that looks like some kind of torture device.

She tells me it's over. She needs a break from the pressure of the relationship so she can focus on healing.

I am broken, dead inside, but I feel so exhausted by the months of drama that I simply feel too beaten to protest. I bend down and kiss her hand reverently and say goodbye, never to enter her home again.

As the New York City skyline comes into view I realize it is the first day of my new life and I am homeless, jobless, and for all practical purposes The Imperial Orgy no longer exists. I feel humiliated. I have lost face to all. And most of all, I am taken by deep feelings of hopelessness that I have never known before.

As night falls and the chill of autumn begins to sting my skin, out of desperation I call Samantha. She and Dave Surreal are sharing a large apartment on Staten Island. I explain my desperate situation to her. As she chats cheerfully on the phone a P.J. Harvey song blares in the background. "You're not rid of me, you're not rid of me," Harvey's angry voice warns amid the distorted guitars. Is this a message? I am so confused that I can't tell reality from superstition any longer. Samantha invites me to come and sleep on their basement floor. With nowhere else to turn I accept.

When I arrive at their house all is dark. Samantha greets me at the door wearing a green silk kimono. Inside the dark house she hugs me and I realize she is naked under the now open kimono. With her leading the way we fall into a frenzied fuck on the hard living room floor.

My mind is so confused that this event feels like simply one more drama in a stream that takes me in its current. My body, as well as my soul, have surrendered to the torrent of life. I am a whore to the amoral desires of fate and destiny. I have no will to fight it anymore.

Samantha is eager to please. She takes me in her mouth and rubs her lithe frame over my body. Finally she crawls atop me, my back pinned against the hard wooden floor. It seems she is eager to please, but in fact this is her moment of triumph. After all is said and done, she has vanquished her rival and conquered her prey. As I collapse after ejaculation, her triumph is complete. I dissolve into nothingness, small like a raped widow or an abused child. She feels strong and contented.

As we thrashed about on the floor the one thing I couldn't do is kiss her on the mouth. That is the one thing that would be too much of a lie for my soul to bear. It is my one oasis of purity that I won't defile. I just can't pretend anymore. It is impossible.

It is too late to fix a bed for me in the basement, so we fall asleep in her bed. I lay on my side looking out into the darkness of the unfamiliar room. Samantha lies behind me, her arm and leg draped over me. I feel a sense of smothered security. I feel like an errant child who went out into the world to find his dream and came back to mother with his tail between his legs. I feel grateful for her help in this hour of need, but I also feel disgraced. I resent the price I will pay for accepting this help. Little do I know how this night will color my entire future for years to come.

The days that follow pass as if in a bad dream. For months I have barely eaten or slept. Stress flows through me like a poison. I am physically ill. During the preceding months I have remained healthy through sheer force of will. I knew that if I got sick in my situation I would die.

Now my body and mind collapse in exhaustion. I spend my days walking the streets looking for jobs that never come. I manage to get many interviews, but my mental state betrays me, and no employer will hire me.

When not out hunting for work, I lie on my blanket on the basement floor and feel the poison rushing through me. It is like a chemical ocean storm that tosses both my body and mind in any direction it likes. Four or five times a day the poison washes over my body. I go numb, my speech slurs, and my limbs become heavy as lead. My mind goes into a deep darkness. It races with manic thoughts on the inside, but when it tries to direct my body it moves like sludge.

I can understand why tribal people often believed they were possessed by evil spirits. That is what it feels like when the poison takes control of me.

Two weeks later I return to my hometown to retrieve a few of my possessions that were hastily stored with friends when I first went homeless. It is a cool gray November day. Once back in Lewistown the poison takes me. I am haunted by memories I can't bear. The town is a tomb of my dying life. As I begin to drive out of town I look into the back seat of my car at my meager belongings.

My plan is to return to my basement abode in New York and try to set up some kind of home so I might feel some sense of normalcy. I am reminded of a Roman Caesar who after the fall of the empire finds a broken bust of Venus and places it in a cave-dwelling in hopes that it will make him feel like he still retains some of his former greatness. But in the end it would only be a mockery that reminds him of how low he has sank.

My possessions are a bunch of wooden crates filled with tattered books and nick-knacks. Worthless items with no practical value. Looking at them makes me fill ridiculous.

Feeling a despair that is darker than I have ever known I turn the car around and drive to a little shack on the edge of town that houses a gun shop for hunters. I use the last of my money and buy a 20-gauge shotgun and a small box of bullets.

I have lost the desire to live. Each passing moment is misery. I see no reason to continue.

I have always thought that suicide was a coward's way out, but when you have reached a point when you simply don't want to live anymore, when enduring each moment is more pain than one can bear, it suddenly seems that the most logical thing in the world is just to end it all.

I head out of Lewistown and it is dark and cold outside. I am on a narrow stretch of highway. On one side is a high rocky cliff, and on the other the Juniata river. As I drive the gun rests in my lap and I caress the steel barrel with my right hand. Touching the cold metal makes it all seem real...

....I began seeking detachment. Abnegation of the self. But what have I really achieved? My spirit seems dead. I have managed to lose all sense of who I am. As an artist I am dead. Caeser Pink is dead. I no longer believe. My faith in humanity is dead. My faith in myself is dead.

The world is a vulgarity to my eyes. The one lesson I have learned is that human life is treated as valueless by most of humanity. People want to believe in their own altruism, but when it comes to getting their hands dirty, to taking the desperate measures required to actually help someone in trouble, no one really cares all that much. In the darkest hour, in the moment of greatest need, we find we are alone.

It is amazing to me that only six months ago I was full of confidence, full of hope. I see my own descent. Allowing myself to be battered by racism, prejudice, and self-criticism taken to brutal depths.

I was seeking abnegation of the self. Now my ego has been split into pieces that lie underneath the bright lights of the operating table. In the beginning I felt a schism arising. I had conceptualized my "real self" and "Caeser Pink" as two separate entities that I refused to see as one. I now see that my self is a host of entities.

The people of my past have known me as many completely different people. To my college friends I am the troubled adventurer. In Lewistown I am the responsible homebody and a one-woman man. To Sasha I am a weak and desperate lover who is crippled by passion. To some of my oldest friends, I am still the crazy adolescent who would always take things to the most extreme for a good laugh. To others there are still more personas by which I am seen. And to myself the list is an endless cast of demons and angels.

In retrospect I see that I have always had control over which of these personas I presented to people, although the choice was almost always made unconsciously. I imagined that these personas were controlling me. As if these too were spirits that were possessing me. And this holds especially true for Caeser Pink, who is ironically my most conscious creation.

Throughout these months I have meticulously deconstructed my own behavior and motivations. I have questioned every action. Now even breathing or a simple gesture has become a conscious act. The light of consciousness may be illuminating, but it can also be paralyzing. Because of this illumination every action truly reveals its futility and its arrogance of ego.

I have pealed back layers of the unconscious and left a gaping wound. I have removed myself so far from human society that I feel as if I view life from behind a pane of glass. Desire itself, the prime motivation underlying actions, has become poison to me. It is the poison that has flooded my body and contaminated my soul.

I have lived in desperation for so long. I craved the essence of a sensual life. Ironically, in the end the love Shasha and I shared became only a further addiction to desire itself. It was not the loved one I truly wanted, it was the agony of desire as an end in itself. Now even the taste of desire, of this beautiful poison, sends me in flight, gagging and nauseous. In flight from passion, beauty, human emotion, love, and life itself.

I do not believe in myself in any way. I have come so precariously close to total abnegation of the self that death seems as if it is already here.

Abnegation of the self, the zero, towards this goal I have come so far. The journey has stolen hope. The sacrifice has been my self and all I hold sacred. I feel that after having come so far towards this goal that I should continue on and complete what I have started. The mere idea of suicide is comforting. When I lay down to sleep, it is the thought of suicide that provides me with the peace of mind that allows me to float off into sleep.

The thought which is most alluring, most seductive, is this; I know that the decision to take my own life cannot really be made until the gun is loaded, aimed at my own head, and my finger is on the trigger and I begin to squeeze.

But from the moment I make that final decision and begin to squeeze the trigger, until the moment when the bullet shatters my brain, I will have reached my goal. For a brief moment I will have let go of everything. For that brief moment I will feel pure. For that moment I will know perfection.

Purity, perfection, Nietzsche would argue that these things are just ideals that devalue life. This thought is echoed by John Lennon, "God is a concept by which we measure our pain."

In this moment with the gun in my hand I recall the Gita. In Arjuna's moment of doubt Krishna convinces him to carry on, even if his duty is to be a killer. "Each person has a duty and must fulfill it." A beautiful ideal, but politically this ideal has paved the way for eons of social oppression. It is not surprising that such philosophies are often supported by rulers.

In my case, logic tells me that in the long run I could turn things around, with more struggle. The problem is I don't want it anymore. My former goals seem empty. Even obscene. My stars are hidden in dust. I long for nothing except nothingness.

I drive on, my right hand still stroking the gun that rests in my lap. My mind is exhausted. The job may soon be taken care of if I nod behind the wheel and veer over the cliff on this winding mountain road.

As my mind whirs, all the people and places of the past are with me now. Linear time has ceased to exist. All the emotions I have ever felt are with me now. Time has not passed. Leilani is here with me, still in my heart. Twelve years of life, all here with me now: loving, living, eating, drinking, lovemaking, breakdowns, changes…

The death of my friend Rick Barker. Three days in his apartment before he was found. The words he said to me the last time we spoke, "I looked into the abyss. I know I have to pull back if I want to survive. I'm glad we became friends," he said, "I feel like you're the only one I can talk to."

Samantha's halfhearted suicide attempt. "Love me, love me…" she repeated laying in the bed we had shared for the previous year.

Those amazing moments of heartbreak and inspiration over Heather Simmons. Those amazing moments walking and talking with her in the gray spring afternoon when we met. Random smells, notes of music, ambiences of light and temperature and textures all are here with me.

These are so many others and all here with me now. I loved every moment and I loved everyone who touched me. None of it has ever left me. They are all here and they are me. The memories pour out freely. A kaleidoscope of experiences pours outward hallucingenically to converge in an ever-present moment beyond time.

The emotions tied to those memories carry no value judgments. Happiness and sadness are one. From this distance they are all one. As life itself is one. As I am one with it all.

It is this…this which I love too much. I have traveled where few dare to tread. I have dared to care. To love life, the body, the mind, the race, the world…and I have overdosed. We live in a world where life is not to be loved. Love is too real. Don't look into the light. That is the human credo. Don't look into my eyes. Don't tell the truth. Don't truly love for it is a sign of weakness.

To give, to hold another above oneself is a sign of weakness. To truly love makes you an outcast, an unbearable presence, a reflection of reality too intense for the spirit in this heartless age. It is written that even Moses shielded his eyes from the sight of God.

But what is the price of this compromise against life? To love less? The new age values that are becoming the dominant philosophy in our culture are a philosophy of mediocrity. Of passionless existence. Perhaps it is civilizing. So was Christianity in earlier times. But Christianity also became a philosophy that is anti-life. Like the new age philosophies it is a medication for the weak heart and soul. It says "life is too hard to bear, so devalue what is valued most." Love is reduced to nothing. Love of a special individual is devalued. Whereas love of the herd, abstract universal love of humanity is the highest ideal. It is an intellectual love without heart. They portray an air of caring for all they meet, but fail to truly love those closest in their lives.

In this philosophy death is not a loss, but a celebration. If love between a single man and woman is lost, then so be it. Just love the next person available. If something bad happens, then God wanted it that way. Or determinism: "All things happen for a reason." If things don't go right when reaching for a goal, simply give up. "It wasn't meant to be," they say. Weakness, submissiveness, mediocrity, are all accepted and elevated.

I hold their world in contempt. I hold their values in contempt. The values of a society that pours unimaginable amounts of money into building beautiful skyscrapers as symbols of man's power and glory, while the streets below are filthy. And it is this picture that best portrays humanity. Down on the streets where men and women live there is filth and pollution. The quality of day-to-day life does not seem to matter. It is a place of drudgery without joy so why take pride in your surroundings?

We work in buildings that are at best, drab. In the cities noise and stench are accepted without complaint. The backs of the drones have been nicely broken. I often peer into the apartment windows from the raised expressway and even the homes show no sign of pride and caring. Even those few who do take pride in their personal environment will take no responsibility for anything public. Anything social is left for a mythical "somebody else" to care for.

Each thing must either grow or decay. As a society it is clear we have accepted decadence. If we are to be judged by our actions, then nihilism is the gospel of our age. Regardless of what deities we pray to, or what high-minded philosophies we pay lip service to. And I would find the nihilism more bearable if it weren't for the hypocrisy and mendacity with which we deceive ourselves into having a clear conscious. The word "humanity" is itself the greatest of hypocrisies.

Children starve while I waste. The American poor are left to their fate. I watch men dig in garbage cans in search of a scrap of food and I walk past without stopping to help. And yet I call myself human?

I have looked to the animal world and therein seen the truth. Although we dress our actions up in the most bewildering array of rituals and diversions, look behind the surface and our motivations are the same as any other animal. Food, sex, territory and most of all, power.

I can recall over the last five years how my friends and I would raise our glasses in the air and make a toast to "men who want to rule the world." It was spoken in irony, but an irony designed to temper a grain of truth.

I try to clarify the power I was seeking. The power to create the work I want to do artistically. But then the artistic creation itself may be seen as just another means to gain glory, money, and more power. Money to free oneself from the burden of labor. Power to win women. Power to win love.

I look back one last time at what I had in moments past. My home, eight rooms and two baths. It was a great source of pride. Filled with Eastern and African artwork. My rental property, six rooms and a bath and a half. My business, a small recording studio. The bank note had just been paid off. Again, pure profit. Leilani and I were twelve years together. She was sexy, intelligent. A life with friends and security. A good life. All thrown into the trash because I was seeking something else. Something more.

Then there was the band, just before the final fall. Again a beautiful woman who supported me. A group of musicians who were willing to follow my vision. And the reaction to The Imperial Orgy was amazing. People thought we were a surefire ticket to stardom. We seemed unstoppable.

But I turned away from it all, and for what? And did I throw it away or was it taken from me piece by piece as I imagine. Was I a victim of the world, or the unconscious architect of my own self-destruction? Was I my own whipping boy. Both sadist and masochist in a masturbatory game of guilt and self-hate?

I have come full circle and time has shown me the absurdity of my efforts. Because in the end a circle returns to its starting point. In this moment I wish to take full responsibility for my actions. Responsibility for my destiny. Responsibility for my self.

As I drive a soft rain begins to fall. The highway is dark except for the small swath of light cut out by my headlights. My mind is so tired it is beginning to fade. My eyes are hypnotized by the broken white lines that disappear underneath my car in a blur.

It no longer matters one way or another whether I pull the trigger or not for I am already dead. My spirit is dead. My mind, my faith, my soul, my values, my belief, my will, and my ego are all dead. The phone is off the hook with the dial tone intact, but there is nobody home. What once was I, is now just an empty void.

#13 – A Moment To Savor

My sleep was deep and I uncharacteristically slept in till 9AM. I awoke confused, but upon getting my bearings I am embarrassed to discover that I spent the night across from Sasha's home. I slid into the driver's seat and pulled out before there was any chance of anyone finding me there.

San Francisco looked different in the morning light. The air still had an unfriendly chill as I meandered down Haight Street looking in the shops and taking in the sights. It was a city of contradictions. On one hand you have an abundance of neighborhood help centers and outreach programs that suggested a kind and caring community. On the other hand the people I met seemed rather snotty. Snotty in the way the rich-kid wanna-be artists are in New York's hipster scenes. As I attempted to make friendly conversation with people I was met with suspicion and indifference.

When afternoon rolled around I ate lunch at a yuppie café. As I waited for my food I finally picked up the phone and called Sasha. The phone rang a dozen times before going to the answering machine. Speaking as casually as I could I said, "Hi Sasha, it's Caeser Pink, I'm on a trip and find myself in San Francisco and thought I'd say hello."

I could have guessed she might be at work on a weekday afternoon, but I left my cell number and said she could call me if she wished to see me. For the rest of the day I wandered about the city killing time, bored and eager to blow out of town, but wanting to wait until the work day was over so I might have a chance to see her.

As the day progressed the air grew colder and the skies grayer. As the skies darkened so did my spirits. My will began to wane. I stopped in a coffee shop on Haight Street and ordered some tea. The place was decorated with hand drawn signs with slogans and little sayings about the value of love, and community, and peaceful living. I made one last call to Sasha at 5:30 and got her answering machine.

Although I had placed a lot of weight on trying to see her, it began to dawn on me that after all these years I really didn't give a fuck. If I were to see her it might be a good thing, but if not, so what? Sometimes things that seem important pass without notice. And sometimes accepting failure is the only way to succeed. Before I left I went into the unisex bathroom. It looked as if someone has pissed over the toilet, sink, and walls. So much for peace, love, and community...

The last thing I did before leaving San Francisco was go into a CD shop and buy Bob Dylan's "Love & Theft." A CD that had the misfortune of being released on September 11.

The bitter humor born of lost love and aged cynicism that filled the disc, fit my spirit perfectly as I left behind the city of the summer of love. The cool chill in the air provided the first warnings of the harsh winter to come. Given the changes that were taking place in America, that warning held a deeper significance than any winter I had previously experienced. Summer was over, no doubt about it. And these were certainly not days for love.

The US of A was constricting its muscles, tightening itself in reaction to a body blow. The sleeping giant was awakening, but it was blind with sorrow, propelled by fear, and preparing to strike out in anger.

Although it is often said that in the days after 9/11 Americans were united as never before, the rift that would soon split the country in two could already be seen making its first signs of fissure.

On the highways outside of San Francisco people stood holding cardboard signs with anti-war slogans hastily written in black felt marker. Earlier that morning I showered in some kind of spa for a fee of $6. The young woman behind the counter told me that she believed the terrorists should be treated like criminals and law enforcement should be used to bring them to justice. It was an idea that was often repeated by liberals in the days after 9/11. To me it seemed like an idea that was high on idealism, but completely lacking in practicality. Given that we were dealing with governments such as the Taliban's, it seemed realistic only in some kind of fairyland view of the world.

In response to her suggestion I responded, "I think the people we're dealing with don't respect anything but power."

"It seems so barbaric to be dropping bombs on people," she countered.

"It is," I replied stoically.

Both sides of the argument were quickly becoming entrenched and radicalized. The left wanted to sit on their hands and do nothing. The right wanted to kill everyone who followed the teachings of Mohammed.

Looking back it seems like a bad dream. No one was thinking clearly. It was impossible to think clearly given the sorrow and fear that gripped the country. To that extent the terrorists had already succeeded.

As I searched for an exit to take me out of San Francisco night began to fall. My cynicism towards the place was reinforced by the sudden appearance of the pimps, streetwalkers, con men, and homeless people who seemed to appear from nowhere.

"This place makes New York City look like the Garden of Eden," I thought to myself.

As I found the highway and headed out of town, I was glad to be rid of the place.

Early the next morning I got onto the Pacific Coast Highway that stretches along California's shoreline and is known for its scenic ocean view. Unfortunately it was a foggy morning and my view was limited to a few hundred feet, and often less than that.

By this time my cash situation was becoming somewhat precarious. My plan was that when payday came my paycheck would be deposited into my account and I would withdraw funds as needed to complete the trip. Thanks to the terrorist attack my bank, sitting right beside the Trade Center as it was, was no longer open for business, leaving me stuck on the other side of the continent without funds to get home.

Gas was expensive in California so I kept putting off filling up the tank in hopes of finding a better price at some fictional gas station further down the road. As I entered the area known as Big Sur the vegetation began to change. All the plants looked giant-sized, as if I had entered some kind of prehistoric landscape. I pulled up to a fancy café and gas station and stopped beside the pump. The price on the pump read three dollars a gallon for regular. A full dollar above the national average. Disgusted, I spat on the face of the gas pump and drove off.

Down the road a bit I stopped at the Henry Miller museum and library. It was a quaint little shack sitting back off the highway. I wanted to go check it out, but it didn't open till noon and since it was still only 7AM I decided I couldn't wait around. In addition to being low on cash I was far behind schedule time-wise and was beginning to realize that I could no longer travel at my leisurely pace. As it was I would be getting back to New York a week later than I expected.

The highway took me over great cliffs where my tires hugged the edge of frighteningly high drop-offs. Most of the road was natural scenery, although occasionally punctuated with small villages. The fog made the driving a bit dangerous. As the road twisted and turned, often I couldn't see what was coming towards me in the narrow highway.

At about 9AM the cliffs gave way to a small sandy inlet that allowed easy access to the ocean. I pulled off the highway and walked towards the water's edge. The fog hung over the inlet like a ball of white static. The seagulls floated in the gray skies, their cries providing an eerie soundtrack to the scenery.

Standing on the ocean's edge, it should have been the moment to savor, but I couldn't enjoy the view because of the thick haze that obscured my vision. It seemed a fitting analogy for the entire journey. I thought of my murdered neighbors in New York City. They were with me at every moment. My limbs felt heavy. My mind weary.

Standing in the haze I thought of Sasha. I imagined that when I called she might easily have been there listening to my voice but not picking up the phone. After all these years still angry, still bitter, still frightened, still rejecting.

Sometimes a journey has no climax. It just comes and goes. I have seen it often in my own life. We strive for goals, but some of us just keep travelin' on without any real beginning or end. We can either surrender and find contentment in whatever meager happy endings life has offered us, or we can keep searching, keep moving, perhaps never finding anything except more open highways that beckon to be explored.

#14 – Gone Hollywood!

I rolled into Los Angeles in the early afternoon hours. The sun and warmth had thankfully returned. Having no plans as to where to go or what to do there, I parked on the Sunset Strip and began to walk the surprisingly empty streets. Most of the shops were closed. The storefronts included lots of sex shops and clothing stores for trannies and strippers.

The scene was certainly less glamorous than I imagined. Less exciting and electric than I expected. In California even the decadence has less energy than in New York City.

As I walked the streets I was feeling a bit grimy and road weary. I stopped in a dingy little pizza shop and ordered a slice and a paper cup full of coke. As I sat down in the booth the president came onto the screen of a small TV that was sitting on top of the soda machine in the corner of the pizza shop.

It was his first address to the nation since 9/11, so it carried a lot of weight. In the days to come people would rave about what a moment of leadership it was. Myself, I didn't see it. I think people were just so starved for leadership that the slightest hint of it was clung to without question by those who were desperate for something to pin their hopes on.

While President Bush didn't stumble over his words as he was apt to do, the speech was hardly impressive. He mouthed the predictable; "America is great, we'll get through this, we'll get the bad guys, we must stay united and strong." Beyond that there was nothing insightful or inspiring, nothing to change my opinion of him as a dimwitted daddy's boy.

But then nothing seemed impressive in that moment, not the greasy pizza or the dingy décor, not the worn-out glamour of Sunset Boulevard, and certainly not the words of this spoiled frat boy that somehow found himself the most powerful statesmen in the world. It was all mediocrity, all superficial, all a joke so bad it brought tears to your eyes.

In Plato's monolithic work The Republic he argues that the ideal leader is he who doesn't want to be in charge, yet takes the responsibility out of a sense of duty. In America our leaders routinely lie, cheat, and steal to grasp the reigns of power. The countless millions they spend in order to buy our votes are all tainted money, blood money, all the wages of our own bondage.

For the sake of those millions, by the time one of the criminals is actually elected they've already sold their souls. Democracy goes to the highest bidders. Gandhi himself would have been corrupted by such a system.

Now to protect our democracy, to protect our right to cast a vote for the best looking corporate stooge, our commander in chief would soon send young men and women to fight and die in far off places where we neither understand their language or their customs. A time of war was inevitable. 9/11 was our generation's Pearl Harbor, but in this war there would be no V-day. It just wasn't in the cards. That sad fact was apparent from the word 'go.'

That evening as night began to fall I prepared for an adventure into the LA nightlife. After perusing the options in a local entertainment newspaper I decided to visit the legendary Whiskey-A-Go-Go club. As I dressed I felt a surge of testosterone flow through me. I dressed all in black; black jeans, a black dress shirt, and a black leather jacket, topped with a silver bolo tie I bought from some Indians in Arizona.

Looking back I realize that in LA this is a costume sure to make you look out of place, but it was my first night in town and didn't know any better. It felt right, and that was what was important in that moment.

Before locking up the car I slipped the knife into my jacket pocket and massaged it with my right hand as I walked. Like some sort of talisman, the blade again inspired a strange sense of confidence in me that enhanced the cocksure spirit that had taken me. A spirit that was the exact opposite of the low feelings that had engulfed me on my drive along the coast.

Walking the streets of Los Angeles I felt life flowing through my veins. I felt hungry. I felt the aggression that drives man to take on the world. My walk changed, my posture changed, it was completely transforming.

The strange smell of the warm California air filled me with the urge to breathe deep and fill up my lungs. The alien sights and sounds that greeted my eager senses were invigorating. Here I had no past, I had no connections, I was a newborn seeing the world around me through fresh eyes.

I thought I might have problems getting past the doorman at the Whiskey with the knife in my pocket, but it was no trouble at all. Once inside I slid up to the bar and ordered a vodka and seven. The room was a large cavern with a balcony that looked down on a stage that sat in the opposite corner. The place was full but hardly crowded.

The creatures of the night were a cast of colorful characters. Beautiful women could be seen in all directions. I meandered about the club taking in the scene. The first to catch my eye was a black woman in a white dress and a white fur coat with a pimped out dude on each side of her. Her sexuality verged on vulgarity. Just the sight of her made my pulse quicken.

I lurked about the place, cool and detached on the surface, but underneath seething with lust and violence. I don't know if it was the man-in-black costume, or something in my demeanor that made everyone look at me. Everyone I passed made eye contact or gave a little nod of the head as if they recognized me from somewhere. Even the musicians in the band came over and said hello when their set ended, perhaps thinking I was some kind of music biz exec that musicians are always hoping will show up at their gigs to tell them how brilliant they are.

Up on the balcony long limbed girls dressed in high-fashion sat at tables emptying their drinks. Everyone seemed to be waiting for something to happen. No one seemed content with where they were or what they were doing. Everyone was looking for some excitement that wasn't there, some change of pace to come and steal them away from their boredom.

The next band to take the stage was a generic grunge/punk band. Their music sent all the boys onto the dancefloor for a session of slam-dancing. While the boys beat each other up, the girls watched from the sidelines with boredom written all over their faces. They seemed to be wondering why the boys were more interested in beating each other senseless than paying attention to them.

I leaned against a cement pillar to the right of the stage, trying to feign interest in the music, when all I really wanted was to check out the girls. My attention was taken by a tall blonde girl who was leaning against another pillar and watching the proceedings with a look of annoyance on her pretty face. She had a simple, wholesome beauty. Not overly hip, definitely not slutty, but fashionable enough to turn heads.

I came up behind her and whispered in her ear, "Why is the most beautiful women in the room standing alone?"

I thought I was being shot down when she gasped, "Get out of here," but she turned towards me with a warm smile and explained, "This really isn't my favorite kind of music."

Her back leaning against the pillar she looked up at me coyly, but confidently. With her blues eyes and soft white skin she looked as fresh-faced as a summer's day. It only took a few minutes of conversation to see that she was likely more mature and intelligent than whatever guy had abandoned her in order to roughhouse on the dancefloor. It always strikes me as comical how often men are busy showing off for a woman while another man is giving her the simple attention she really desires.

As we chatted about the mundane details of our lives, I thought, "sometimes just being in the presence of a beautiful woman revitalizes a man's will to live. Ahh yes, ..now I remember, this is I why I get out of bed each morning. This is why I fight for my place in the world."

Looking back, I don't remember her name, but I certainly remember her face. I certainly recall how her knee bent just below the edge of her dress as she leaned against that pillar. In that place she seemed like a daisy in a dustbin. Not to say that she seemed frail. She seemed strong in character. Here was a woman you could take home to meet the parents. A good woman who you could trust to share your life with and pin your hopes and dreams on.

As the band began their last song and her date would soon be returning to claim her, I prepared to take my leave.

"Why aren't you married? ...or are you?" she asked.

"No, never been," I assured her. Without asking myself what the truth really was, I tried to deflect her question with humor, "I don't like contentment."

To that she crinkled her nose slightly and an odd look came into her eyes.

Perhaps I wasn't so different from the boys bashing it up on the dancefloor while the girls watched from the sidelines with disinterest.

I often joke that young musicians pick up guitars in order to get girls. But what was I doing at this point in life? At this stage of the game it wasn't about conquests or one night stands. Somewhere in the back of my mind I believed I was trying to make my mark on the world so I might be worthy enough to win a woman like the one standing before me. Yet it was all a farce. After all, here was a dream of a woman standing here ready to be taken. And there have been a hundred more who have passed through my life. Yet I am off fighting a battle of career and money while I turn away from the prize time and time again.

I took her hand in mine and said goodbye before setting my half empty glass on the bar and heading out the door. The hour was late and the streets were empty. Still it didn't feel dangerous. Even the prostitutes and small time drug dealers that haunted the shadows had a lazy, laid-back air about them.

I meandered through the streets with a hunger that was now tinged with desperation. After weeks on the highways I felt as if I didn't want to sleep alone tonight. Yet to suggest female companionship seemed laughable when everything is about sex: scoring sex, preserving sex, selling sex. A man can't say a word to a woman without sex hanging in the air.

I walked past dark store fronts whose metal grates masked their faces. I walked past convenience stores, donut shops, and late night motels. Now and again a car would pass by me at a slow pace, likely another late night prowler searching for something he can't find.

I came upon a beat cop at a red light and tried to make small talk with him. "Just move along," he said, obviously not liking the looks of me.

Demoralized, I began to head for the Blazer that was parked on a side street off of the main drag. A few blocks from the car I came upon two black women who were standing in a shadow along the road underneath some scaffolding. One was in her early thirties, tall and thin. She had a short dress on, but she didn't look sleazy. She could have been heading to church in it. The other was a young girl who I later found out had just turned 19. She was dressed in homegirl clothes: baggy jeans and an oversized sweatshirt. She had nappy hair and a little gap in her front teeth, but her face was quite pretty.

As I passed, the older of the two ask me if I wanted a date. I said "No," but we struck up a conversation. I was glad to share a bit of friendly banter even though I realized that they had a service they were trying to sell and since I wasn't buying I was standing in the way of their ability to find customers who were. Although money was tight, as a gesture I gave them ten dollars for their time. I told them I was a writer and traveling across the country looking for inspiration.

By this time a slight chill had come into the air and the older woman asked if they could go sit in my car so they could get warm. We drove around the city a bit with the car heater running. With two ladies of the night in tow, we took a scenic tour past the Hollywood sign and the famous Capital Records building.

I soon found out that the younger girl was thinking of becoming a prostitute and the older woman was showing her the ropes. The younger girl sat in the back smiling nervously. The older one was very excited about the prospect of being a mentor. "This is so sweet, I remember my first night," she recalled fondly.

Suddenly the older woman turned to me and said, "So are you going to write a book about me?" Then as a means of showing off, she began to tell the younger woman the ropes of the business. "Don't date drunks. They never cum. Always use a condom. It's not your job to make them cum. You're just paid to make them feel good."

The younger woman sat in the back nodding like a self-conscious schoolgirl. The older woman was really beginning to enjoy the teacher role and seemed to take great pride in her work and knowledge of the business.

To cap off the girl's lesson the older woman offered to give me a free blowjob to demonstrate her skills to her pupil. Before long she was down on me in the front seat as we sat parked along the boulevard. As she slid her warm lips up and down the length of my penis, I peaked into the back seat to see how the apprentice was taking to her lesson.

When I looked at her she smiled at me sheepishly. She looked embarrassed and her face had a deep sadness written on it. Without thinking I reached into the back seat and took her hand in mine.

I suppose it is the blowjob I should have been focused on, but all that I remember is how wonderful, warm, and soft the girl's hand felt in mine. Soon I began to go limp because my attention was drawn towards the warmth of her hand instead of the front-seat fellatio.

I looked back again and the girl had my hand held close to her face and was staring out the car window with a far away look in her eyes. A wave of emotion washed over me. I tried to pull myself away from the woman in the front to get her to stop, but she became determined to make me cum.

The teacher did not want lose face by failing in front of her pupil so she sucked harder and began moaning, "I love hard cocks, I love it when they cum in my mouth."

Since I hate fake sex talk I became even limper. I could feel the young woman in the back squeezing my hand tightly. I turned to the back seat again and she was looking at me with her eyes moist and a pleading expression on her face.

In an instant I blurted out "stop," letting go of her hand and pushing the woman in the front away from me. All three of us sat there dazed by my outburst. The older woman had no idea what had passed between the girl and I. After we regained our composure I drove them back and dropped them off.

As we drove I felt desperate to say something to the younger woman. Finally as they got out the car I grabbed her hand again and looked into her eyes, but couldn't find any words to say that would express what I felt. I wanted to protect her and save her from her fate, but who was I to save anyone from anything. She smiled and the two walked away into the night.

With my emotions reeling from the night's events, I drove to a quiet side street and parked underneath a palm tree in front of a swanky townhouse in a residential neighborhood. As I crawled into the back of the car and laid my head down on the pillow my mind was too tired to try to make sense out of any of it. Is this what they mean when they say someone's "gone Hollywood" I asked myself as I drifted off to sleep.

#15 – The Desert Is Where I Belong

I hit Vegas in the late afternoon hours. The nights had
become increasingly cold for sleeping in the car. There were
advertisements for hotel rooms for $25 a night, so I thought I
might get a room and sleep in a bed and maybe enjoy a hot bath.
Unfortunately once in Vegas these discount hotel rooms turned out
to be a mirage. Some of the motels even offered the cheap rooms
on their marquees, but when you went in to get one they didn't
exist. It was the most brazen form of false advertising, and I was
soon to learn this is the Vegas way.

Giving up on the idea of getting an affordable room I
began to search for a place to shower. Vegas is basically one long
strip of bright lights and casinos, surrounded by a decrepit white-
trash ghetto.

Off the strip it was a nasty place where every dime store
cowboy in a rusted pickup truck has a worn-out stripper with
bulging fake breasts in his passenger seat. These couplings must
have seemed like quite a catch for the local boys, but likely a less-
than-happy ending for the stripper whose youthful dreams of
glamour and fame soon gave way to the realization that giving lap
dances to tourists was never going to lead to bigger and better

things, and that with each passing year the tips grew smaller and the lines on her face grew deeper.

I don't know if it was the heat and the sand or the squalid surroundings, but everyone in the godforsaken place seemed angry. Ready to explode on a moment's notice. Just waiting for someone to give them the slightest reason to go ballistic. In traffic, people screamed at each other through open windows, hurling threats and insults like madmen. Inside the truck stop where I got my shower the cashier scowled through her teeth as she growled a dutiful, "Have a nice day." Face to face people looked like they would rather spit on you than say hello.

After the shower I grabbed a nap in the truck stop parking lot then prepared for a night in Las Vegas. I didn't even dress for the adventure, my heart just wasn't in it.

At first glance the Vegas strip looked like a fun place. Lots of flashing lights, weird architecture, and zany themed facades that looked like pirate ships, Egyptian pyramids, and circus tents. It had the flash and energy of a boardwalk carnival on a summer's night.

The streets were crowded with tourists. It seemed odd to me that the crowd was so middle class, middle-America looking. You couldn't go ten feet without someone handing you an ad for prostitutes on call. Yet there they were, yuppies! Many with children in tow, out for a night in Vegas. I guess the T & A shows have been toned down to even cheesier family fair. And the place certainly did have a Disney look about it. But still, Vegas is known as a city of sin; gambling, cheap booze and cheaper blowjobs, gay lion-tamers and organized crime bosses. The devils playground disguised just enough to make America's moral hypocrites feel safe to flirt with debauchery.

Once inside, behind the glassy façade the casinos were dreary places. No high rollers in flashy suits, no buxom beauties in expensive evening wear, no old-time gangsters or con men, it was all a mirage. All that could be seen were a few tourists who looked as bored as I felt.

The décor looked as if it had seen better days. The undoubtedly once glamorous surroundings now frayed and faded.

I got ten dollars worth of quarters and slipped them one by one into a slot machine until about two dollars had evaporated. I leaned against the machine looking about the place, bored with the whole process already. The entire place looked blasé, nothing to tickle the imagination. Gambling never really was my vice, I suppose.

I walked back out into the street and breathed in the dry desert air. I stood by the dancing fountains made famous in countless Vegas movies and TV shows. The waters danced in an array of colors as the row of fountains changed directions and exploded in rhythmic spurts like a line of chorus girls in a Busby Berkeley musical. The show was stranded in the middle of a shallow lake, set in the center of a courtyard.

"All of this is man made," I thought to myself. A desert oasis dreamed up to suit the tastes of death squad guidos, and later tailored to appeal to mainstream America. Hipsters might decry the cheesy architecture and Mickey Mouse aesthetics, it might be so tacky that even a New York drag queen wouldn't be seen here, but like Graceland at the beginning of my journey, there was a strange melancholy beauty to it all. It was a sordid soul with a bright happy-face painted on its mug. All surface. Its smile was a shallow as a TV sit-com.

Standing back at a distance it looked like a cheap movie set. Like one of those westerns where the building fronts are a half inch thick and there is nothing behind them. An illusion painted on an illusion. Travel a few miles in any direction and the illusion dissolves into the monotony of sand. Nothingness on nothingness.

The illusion itself, maintained only through the will and never ceasing efforts of man. Like the dance of Kali, seducing us into believing in the illusion, into losing ourselves in the dream and to never awake. I walked the strip, searching for something that seemed interesting with which to while away a few minutes of my time. But my appetite for the illusion had faded. The lights flashed, the echoes of bells and bleeps from the slot machines beckoned like sirens, but they failed to ignite my passions. My ability to lose myself in the dream was gone. My taste buds had soured, leaving only the flavor of bitterness on my tongue, now dried by the desert air. In the end I decided the desert was where I belonged.

As I drove away the mirage receded into the darkness of my rear view mirror. The lights continued to flash, but their brightness waned as the circle of darkness surrounding them grew. Somewhere on that speck of light scantily clad women crab-walked with magnificent headdresses balanced atop their skulls. Somewhere on that far away universe Celine Dion sang with all the passion one can muster for the tales of survivors of a long-ago shipwreck. Somewhere Cirque du Solei acrobats twirled like dervishes while new age music soothed the audience into a dream within a dream. Only the French could sell such irony with a straight face, and only Americans would gobble it up whole like a nation starved for any cheap semblance of culture.

Soon the speck of light flickered and went dark. Now it was just darkness in all directions, except for a small patch of light carved out by the beams of the headlights. As I was prone to do on these long stretches of open roads, I made use of the cell phone to stave off the isolation. Tonight's victim was Brian Held.

Brian was part of a group of guys that followed the punk band Friction that I played drums for when I got out of high school. The band was always followed by a gang of lunatics who came to our shows and made trouble. Often they would do something that would cause the band to be banned from the clubs we played at. Random acts of vandalism seemed to be a favorite pastime for these guys.

These people created a circus-like environment for our entertainment. It wasn't unusual for half of the audience to find its way into the dressing room to snort coke and act like idiots.

One of these was Brian, or B.R.ian as he went by as a cartoon artist. When I first met Brian he came to my apartment with a mutual friend. He dressed in tattered jeans, a motorcycle jacket, and carried decorated clubs made of large animal bones with screws protruding from them for extra menace. They looked like something out of a Mad Max movie. Brian soon became a regular with the group. Often riding to shows in the band's van.

Other hanger's-on included Vince Pacini, an Italian kid with a bum eye who was born into a slightly wealthy family. The eye was a little distorted and aimed way off course, and was rumored to have been caused by a bout of childhood cancer.

Vince was a compulsive liar who always had an outrageous tale of some adventure he was soon to undertake. Usually it involved gold mining in Saudi Arabia or the like. He would tell you his yarns in all earnestness, even while you were laughing in his face. There seemed to be a disconnect from reality on this issue.

He was also prone to walk into a McDonalds and set upon an unsuspecting cashier and demand free food for the entire crew because his father owned the place. He would lie with such force that the poor girl would be at a loss as to what to do. If you didn't know he was a lunatic, his lies were just outrageous enough to sound true.

Once, in a moment of brilliance Vince and a friend of his were driving and partying and decided to break into a rural convenience store to steal the money and get cigarettes. They went in and rifled a few bucks from the till and then left. As they drove away, the owners, who lived above the store saw them out the window and called the police.

After driving away Vince and his friend realized they forgot the cigs. And here's where the smarts come in, they went back to steal the cigarettes even after they'd been spotted. Of course when they got there the police were waiting and a high-speed chase ensued. After the chase went on for 20 miles or so they missed a turn and ended up stuck in someone's front yard. For their exploits Vince's friend went to jail, but because of his family's money and connections Vince got off scot-free.

Another of the Friction hanger's on was Barney, who became our lighting man for a period. Barney could always be found with a bottle of Southern Comfort in his hand, which he ceremoniously pushed on everyone else. A brutal form of refreshment to say the least. You could pour a lid full in the bottle's cap and light the stuff on fire to warm your hands on a cold winter's night. The only catch to Barney's forceful generosity was that the next week he'd be whining that everyone should buy him a case of the rotgut because we drank up so much of his stash.

Barney also had the unholy distinction of being known to greet guests in his bathrobe. And for good measure he could always be counted on to accidentally flash you before the visit was over. Eventually someone with his name was arrested for wearing a dress and peeping in people's windows. He denied it was him, but after wards he disappeared from our little scene.

Then there was Steve, a soft-spoken man who hauled our equipment and crew from gig to gig in the back of his old green bread truck. Steve always traveled with a German Shepard dog. He bred the dogs in a mountain cabin and traded them to the local Hari Krishna farm in exchange for magic mushrooms. The Krishna trained them to be seeing-eye dogs and sold them to fund their community.

Steve was also a very successful pot farmer whose seventh generation skunkweed yielded 12-inch glistening buds that would put you halfway into a coma. He always kept a garbage bag full of the stuff above his dashboard and when the group went to gigs out of town, we always arrived brain dead from a non-stop supply of his Cheech and Chong sized spliffs.

Then there was Bad Brad. He was your stereotypical bad boy in black leather and dark good looks. A ladies man to the white-trash sluts who haunted the local dives. Brad seemed to be completely without morals. He would be your best friend to your face and stab you in the back in a moment's notice.

Brad was also a bit of a storyteller who told of his heroic exploits in Vietnam, although it was rumored he never actually left the mainland.

Eventually this crew became known as the "Sick Pies." The name came when Friction played at a huge outdoor party at the Sig Phi fraternity in some forgotten college town. Brad was drinking with some of the frat boys and someone ask him, "Are you a Sig Phi?"

A little wasted and not sure what they had asked him, he answered, "Yeah we're all sick pies."

And the name stuck.

So our regular group of Sick Pies along with an ever-changing cast of extra stragglers would follow the group from town to town. They never served any real practical purpose, such as carrying equipment or paying the cover charge at the door. It was always, "I'm with the band." Sometimes half the audience would be "with the band." Meaning we got paid nothing when working for the door. But mainly the Sick Pies just partied and caused trouble.

Now the aforementioned Brian was something of a genius who had never read a book. He was a walking performance artist who spoke in surreal abstractions. For those that learned to understand his bizarre form of communication, he could make cynical comments on social situations without those being commented on knowing what he was saying.

He was a true working class punk who had contempt for everything and tried to poke a hole in every bit of mendacity. You could always count on him to say the wrong thing at the right time. On one occasion Friction was playing a small yuppie dive in Harrisburg, PA. Right as Craig, the band's singer, was holding a coke spoon up to his girlfriend's nose the club's manager walked into our dressing room. Now you might think that this sort of behavior would be expected from a punk rock band in the 1980s, but the manager was shocked and outraged.

Sitting in the dressing room was the entire band, our manager, the folk singer Jeffrey Gaines, a few groupies, and Brian. The club manger gave us all a stern lecture as if we were naughty schoolboys caught chewing gum in the classroom. As silly as it sounds, we all sat in total silence as he gave his speech and tried to set all right with the world. When he finished, the room was taken by an awkward pause. On cue, Brian opened the door to exit yelling behind him, "OK, see ya later guys, thanks for the horse."

While the fans of most bands yell out their favorite tunes or adoring accolades such as "You guys rock," on old recordings of Friction shows Brian and our other fans can be heard shouting inspirational chants such as "Shoot your breakfast for dinner," "Bleed from the hole," and "Play one we know."

Brian was also known to do some creative dancing while the group played. The 80's were a horrible time for punk bands in most of America. On a usual night the dancefloor at our shows would be filled with preppy couples who would rather be hearing cover versions of the latest Flock Of Seagulls hit than a punk band playing original music. In the middle of a crowd of such people you would find Brian dressed in a spiked collar and black leather, po-going in the middle of the floor by himself. He didn't seem to give a fuck what anyone else thought, he did his own thing.

On the same night as the cocaine incident, Brian was in rare form on the dancefloor and smashed his head against the corner of the PA monitor causing a bloody gash on his forehead. Despite the bleeding wound he kept dancing the rest of the night. By the evening's end the entire dancefloor, the walls, and the clothes of anyone else who was brave enough to venture out on the dancefloor, were covered in patterns of crimson blood spots.

At 3AM as the band was loading our equipment out to the van, Brian was alone with a mop and a bucket cleaning his own blood from the floor and walls. The manager bullied him into it after angry professionals complained that their white party dresses and khaki trousers were ruined by a bleeding lunatic who was "with the band."

When asked why he banged his head he explained, "Most people fall in love, then it goes bad and they suffer pain. I'd rather just skip the love and go straight for the pain."

Brian was the guy who could be counted on to smash a bottle over his own head to liven up a boring party. He once took it into his bean that he wanted his fingers to be longer. To this end he tried to cut the webbing between his fingers. Luckily the plan was abandoned before things got too bloody.

On a personal level Brian was a gentle and giving person. Always the one you could go to when you needed help. His violence was always symbolic, an act of performance art. He once told me he wanted to write a manifesto against society and make copies of it, then strap explosives to his body and climb to the top of the memorial tower in the town square and blow himself up. Not in a manner that anyone else would be hurt, but to scatter the manifesto copies far and wide.

Being punk rockers in the age of hair bands always kept Friction in the underdog status. The local hair bands always made more money than us, and always seemed more favored by the club owners. None of us knew a thing about the music business, including our coke-dealer manager who wouldn't have known a recording contract from a crack-pipe, but succeeded in making money by selling $90 grams of blow to the band members before every gig. Thanks to his side business the band members often walked onto the stage all simultaneously wiping our noses from the last minute lines as if we were doing some kind of choreographed stoner-version of a boy-band dance routine.

Because of our naiveté about the music business we spent our time and energy playing endless gigs in backwoods dives to people who wanted to hear top 40 covers or heavy metal. Nightly we endured catcalls for Sweet Home Alabama, Back In Black, or when dissatisfied audience members wanting to hear Eric Clapton's hit, yelled out, "Do Cocaine," we dutifully responded, "Give us some."

It was years of beating our heads against the wall without any long-term goal in mind. No plan at all. We thought some record label executive would just happen to wander into a bar in some nowhere town in rural Pennsylvania and reward our undiscovered brilliance with a recording contract.

This was the backdrop that fueled our major attitude problems. Within our first year we were banned from most of the venues we performed at across PA.

At Princeton University we played a ritzy frat house where our entire audience was one hippie chick practicing her ballet moves. I was in my political-radical phase and had taped Time Magazine pages with Ronald Reagan's photos all over my drum kit.

During the performance the Sick Pies wrote graffiti on the walls saying "Anarchy For Princeton," which brought weeks of harassing phone calls to my house from the Princeton boys asking for money to cover the damages.

That night the hotel room was like a decadent nightmare from a 1950s drug scare movie. People wasted into oblivion, both males and females were passed out on beds, on the floors, and in the bathtub. Lit cigarettes burned holes in people's clothing as those who passed out were demoted to serve as human ashtrays. The powerful downers that everyone was taking put people in such a comatose state that they were undressed and molested without waking from their stupors. Hotel room lamps and bed frames were set ablaze. Pillows and beds were shredded and tossed about. It was pure bedlam.

In Elizabethtown we were booked to play at an alcohol-free Christian school. We rolled in with cases of Budweiser in tow, causing a panic among the students. Our audience consisted of two geeks in skinny ties trying their luck with the new wave look, and two chubby girls who sat in the corner with a sour look on their faces.

Near the end of the night a guy walked through and yelled "These girls say you suck!"

Joe our guitar player asked the girls, "Why don't you leave then?"

The event got so blown out of proportion that the next day the newspaper claimed that we threatened to rape the women and tear down the building.

In State College, PA a fraternity booked us for an annual salamander eating party. I knew it was going to be trouble when we were setting up our equipment and a muscle bound frat brother came into the room and stood in front of us and crossed his arms.

"So you guys are punks, huh?" he asked.

For the night's festivities the frat boys had created a couple of small ponds in their basement and filled them with hundreds of live salamanders and newts. Within the first hour of the party all the doomed amphibians had been gobbled up by these shining young examples of American manhood, and all for the sake of some cockeyed show of bravado.

The first half of the gig went OK, even though no one had ever heard the strange music we were playing by odd artists with names such as The Clash, the Talking Heads, and the Velvet Underground.

But soon it all went haywire. The frat boys shut off the electricity on us and started playing disco records. Since the only thing they couldn't shut off was the drums, I played an extended drum solo. I was never clear on what happened next, but I recall some furniture was broken and a switchblade was pulled. The last thing I remember is hauling out our equipment while one of our entourage was holed up high in a tree in the frat house's front yard yelling "I hate fucking frat boys!" over and over again.

At the biggest punk club in Philadelphia, as our show ended one of the Sick Pies unrolled a long fire hose and threw it down the stairs. On the way home we realized we were low on gas. We scraped together 20 bucks to fill the bread truck and pulled into an all-night gas station. Craig and I, and a few of the Sick Pies headed for the bathroom. As soon as we entered all hell broke loose. Within 30 seconds the place was demolished. The toilet was smashed, and as I was pissing in the sink, the fluorescent ceiling lights, fixtures and all came crashing down into the sink. The station attendant ran in to see what the commotion was about as we ran back to the van. As the attendant threatened us with arrest Vince kept yelling mindlessly, "Call my lawyer, call my lawyer!"

Finally we gave him our 20 bucks even though we never got any gas and drove off before he could have us arrested. As we pulled out I looked out the truck's back window with my Quaalude-blurred vision to see him fold his forehead into his arm and bow down on top of the gas pump as if he didn't know what kind of black tornado had just hit him.

Now we were back on the road but dangerously low on gas. I had mixed Quaaludes and cocaine and was babbling to the poor sod who was unlucky enough to sit beside me about the fluidity of reggae rhythms as compared to rock beats. Driving on fumes we reached a rest area on the turnpike to refuel. Piling out of the van we swore to the more level-headed members of the entourage, Steve and Jon, the group's bass player, that we would not engage in any illegal activities inside.

As I came out of the bathroom I noticed Craig was at the phone booth stacking torn out pages from the phone book into a crumpled pile and holding a lighter as if he was preparing to start a campfire. Luckily at that moment Jon also spied the action and dragged Craig back to the van before he ended up in prison for burning down the Howard Johnsons.

All in all it seemed a wake of destruction trailed behind us wherever we went. As one club owner said to our manager, "I understand you guys are artists, but we don't want that kind around here."

Often it was just the vast amounts of drugs and alcohol that our fans consumed that scared off club owners. It wasn't unusual to see people passing out on the dancefloor in barbiturate stupors. I used to judge how successful a show was by the amount of vomit on the bathroom floor. The police showed up at our performances so often that we dubbed them, "The Fan Club."

The band's dressing room was always a madhouse where some stupidity was taking place. I would hardly bat an eye when I walked into the room to find Brian huddled in a ball in the middle of the floor with garbage cans, chairs and other debris and furniture piled on top of him like a sculpture that reached towards the ceiling. To add to the merriment Vince the one-eyed Italian was hurling beer bottles at the creation, covering the floor with shards of broken glass.

Trying to work the music business with the Sick Pies around was hopeless, but then again, perhaps they kept us from becoming whores. The biggest club in Harrisburg, PA was the Metron. The club's manager was a local music mogul who wasn't too fond of Friction, but booked us for a series of dates because our manager blackmailed him with threats of exposing some homosexual secrets he held.

We often double billed with other 'up & coming' acts. One such act was a glammy new wave hair band whose name long ago faded from memory. The group's manager was rumored to have label ties and we were hoping to impress him. The dressing room had one large mirror that both bands shared. As might be expected the hair band was hogging the mirror all night long as they primped and sprayed their magnificent quaffs.

The group's portly manager sat on a couch beside our manager. A coffee table with a pitcher of soda sat in front of them. As our manager tried to chat up theirs, Brian stood directly in front of them and began mocking the hair band by pretending to comb his hair in an effeminate manner. He then unzipped his fly and began combing his pubic hair, and then dipping his comb into the pitcher of soda that both mangers were pouring drinks from, before he continued to comb his pubic hair.

Throughout Brian's performance both managers sat looking, theirs dumbfounded, ours exasperated. Looking at the pitcher of soda their manager simply said, "Well, I don't think I want any more of that."

Needless to say he didn't take us under his wing and lead us to fame and fortune.

Bob Dylan has said of his music, "Every song I write is a protest song."

I think we felt that way in Friction as well. Our very existence as a band and a small-scale social phenomenon was a protest. But in the end, the reality we protested against was unmovable. In the end we would always fail. The best you can hope to do is be a thorn in the side of the placid status quo.

But perhaps what is more important is the experience of expressing rebellion. It is a statement of life. A declaration of individuality.

In our later years the group fell prey to our own bad behavior. Band members became consumed with drug and alcohol abuse, which hampered our ability to perform or record music. Once the music was gone there was nothing left. No point in going on. Instead of going out with a bang we just ceased to exist without much notice. By that time the scene surrounding the group had already begun to dissipate. Soon everyone just faded into the woodwork of small town life. It was as if nothing had ever happened. What was left of a local music scene returned to the usual heavy metal, grunge, and top 40 cover bands.

Back in the desert outside Vegas I drove with the phone to my ear. After a few rings Brian answered the phone with a gruff voice, "Hello?" he said as if asking, "What kind of trouble are you going to give me?"

After a few pleasantries he pronounced, "Well those cool guys went and did it this time," referring to Osama Bin Laden. "Yeah they sure fuckin' did it."

True to form Brian always had a way of expressing things that was layered in irony and double meanings.

"Yeeeah, maybe it's good those Republican assholes are in power, they might have a little more load in their guns to go after those muthafuckahs," he continued.

Brian now lived in a house with his wife way out in the rural woodlands. Once the Friction days wound down he began to lead a quiet life without alcohol consumption or any trips to the local beer joints. Most of his leisure time was spent hunting or fishing.

"Everything's a fuckin' lie," he said philosophically. "I just try to keep my shit to myself."

Then after a pause he went on, "Y'know, that stuff that happened on Electric Avenue still carries me through. I think about that all the time."

I was taken aback by his reference. In twenty years "that stuff that happened on Electric Avenue," as he referred to it had never been spoken of by he or I, and I assumed he had washed it under the rug as a bad dream caused by too many drugs and too much youthful exuberance.

"After awhile it became a very private thing for me," I explained. "It seemed like every time I tried to talk about it things became so fucked up."

"I don't talk about it to anyone either," he agreed, "but I still think about it all the time. I just remember you telling me that stuff and it was like a whole world opened up for me."

"Yeah, it was a pretty amazing time," I replied, hesitant to show my enthusiasm, but feeling moved by his thoughts on the subject.

Just then the cell phone bleated and burped and then went dead. It tried to call Brian back, but a recording warned that my bill was over its limit and my service had been terminated. I managed to get through to the Sprint customer service line and I explained my predicament with my bank being destroyed by the terrorists and being left far from home without access to money. The young man on the phone was not interested in my hard luck story.

"This is a time of national crisis," I argued, "Given these highly unusual circumstances can't you give me a few days?"

"Sprint had made a donation to the Red Cross, other than that there's nothing we can do," he responded robotically.

When I pushed a little harder he became surly, "Your bill should have been paid by the due date, beyond that it's not our problem."

Seeing it was going nowhere I thanked him for his help and hung up the line, resigned that for the rest of my journey my lifeline to human contact would not be available. Now it was just the darkness of the desert night and the purr of the engine.

#16 – The Big Country

After leaving Las Vegas I somehow found myself in the northern plains, crawling my way through Wyoming, Nebraska, and Iowa. This was the big country. Empty space as far as the eye can see. That song about the deer and the antelopes playing was no joke. I could see them. They were all over the damned place! The land was so big and so empty, one might wonder why the red-skinned natives and the bison had to be killed off.

The highway was a lonely, narrow path that split the horizon in two. The speed limit began to creep up faster and faster, first 75, then 80, then 85mph. Nowhere was there a curve or a bend to be seen. Just a straight line that in the mornings aimed right into the heart of the sunrise.

This was an America I had never seen before. An America of legend and myth: ranchers, cattle herders, and the children of frontiersmen. Although along that stretch of highway there really weren't many people to be seen. The few people I did meet at run-down truck stops and dilapidated convenience stores, all seemed a joyless lot. There wasn't a smile to be found for three states running.

Even though I was scruffy enough to fit right in with the locals, they usually eyed me with bored disdain. It was something more than just skepticism. It was a weariness with life itself. A surrender to the unpleasant fact that there ain't nothin' goin' on and no'en goin' anywhere fast or doin' nothin' much important.

This weary spirit, now a way of life, was passed on from generation to generation. It was a bitter pill that must have stolen away life's laughter when barely out of the womb.

Perhaps their great, great grandparents were headed for the good life in sunny California, but just got plum too tired of the journey and laid stakes right where they stood. Or perhaps they just settled for what was available and didn't ask no more questions on the matter.

Either way, their decisions cursed their bloodline to a way of life that few ever did have the gumption to escape.

In this big country

with open skies

and nature's awesome majesty

held out before them

one might think it would bring them closer to their God

In this land

celebrated in pioneer folklore

and Hollywood westerns

one might think the inhabitants

might still carry those values and ideals with them

those ideals which we revere

as the best of America's independent spirit

But as far as I could see

written on the brows

of these denizens of the prairies and flatlands

they felt little sense of pride in their lot

If God actually were here
right in front of their eyes
their eyes had grown too dim
to see what was laid out before them

There seemed to be an echo of fear throughout the land
not fear from the land
not inherent in the land
but from the hearts of the people who live there
a fear bred
through the land's long and violent history
a fear gifted by their ancestors
who lived in this emptiness
with no hand to help them
and a fear of what danger
might be brought into their lives
by any stranger
who penetrated their delicate existence
in this harsh land

Like so much of America
when we encounter our own myths
we find they are a shabby
rusted
yellowing
ghost of what we dreamed them to be

Too often
they turn out to be ugly

plastic
cheaply manufactured
and up for sale at a discount price
that is still twice what they are actually worth

Only when we peel back the surface even further
can the true beauty be found
a beauty hidden
in its pathos and fragility
hidden in its eccentricity and its ridiculousness
a beauty hidden
beneath stained sheets and collapsing barns
where the swift axe falls on barnyard creatures
who give their lives
for the sake of an evening's feast

Where the events of birth and death
have no screen between them and the entire family
as they sit down at the dinner table
for prayers before supper

Here the life between birth and death
 is a small arc on a big land
and if one cared
to stand back and look at it from a distance
the course of that arc
could be mapped out from the first breath
and without the use
of palm reader or crystal ball.

And in the end it is that clear vision

that sense of one's own limited destiny

that tempers their spirits

which steals away their hope

which makes a strong man walk with his head bowed down

and which dims their eyes so much

that in time

they can no longer see that vision

yet they are not free from its curse

because its memory lurks like a shadow

over each and every golden sunrise

in this big country

That night I couldn't find anyplace to sleep where I felt safe so I had to settle for a highway pull-off where some old construction equipment sat behind tall piles of gravel and sand. It was deathly dark all around me. I went to sleep, but in the middle of the night awoke to find two flashlight beams shining in through the rear window.

It was two police officers nosing around, just the kind of thing I feared might happen parked in a location like this.

"So what do we have here?" the officer closest to window asked with a condescending tone in his voice.

"Just tryin' to get some sleep," I replied as friendly as possible.

"Hmmm, I don't see any hotels around here, do you?" he asked his partner sarcastically.

I kept my mouth shut. Out alone in an empty area like this a police officer can get away with murder, literally. I wasn't going to give them any excuse to make trouble.

"Do you have any guns or drugs in this vehicle?" he asked, shining the flash light beam around inside the Blazer.

"No, nothing like that," I answered without emotion.

"Have you been drinking?" he asked, now shining the flashlight directly into my eyes.

"Not at all," I smiled as best I could with my eyes squinting.

He leaned back a bit, surveying the situation, seeming to ponder what laws he might be able to accuse me of breaking. The second officer stood further back, overseeing the situation with his right hand resting firmly on the handle of his billy-club.

"We'll I don't think I approve..." he said, then caught himself giving away the fact that he believed authority came from his personal likes or dislikes, "I believe...I know there's an ordinance against sleeping on state land."

"I was just taking a quick nap," I cut him off, "I didn't want to be driving half-asleep. I'm getting back on the road right now."

"You do that," he said with a smirk, revealing his pleasure at having intimidated me.

I started the engine and pulled out onto the highway, relieved to be out of the company of the men in uniform. Too many men turn into monsters as soon as they don a uniform. As I've learned from experience, a couple of bored cops on a dark lonely road can be the worst kind of criminals.

It was many years ago when I got my harsh lesson in small town authority run amuck. At the time, I was in college and working full time delivering Dominos Pizzas. One evening after a day of university classes and an evening of delivering pizzas, when I came home my girlfriend Leilani had prepared a late dinner. She asked me to drive around the block to the soda machine in front of the Laundromat and buy a couple cans of Sprite.

I pulled into the Laundromat parking lot and turned off the car. I walked over and bought the two sodas and was returning to my car when a police car came screeching into the parking lot at a high speed. Just as I was getting behind the wheel of my car two officer's rushed over to me and began shouting questions.

"What are you doing?" the first officer shouted angrily.

"Buying some soda," I answered nonchalantly. For years I had good relations with the local police and had no reason to feel antagonism towards them or from them.

"Why are you driving with your headlights off?" he screamed.

I tried to answer that I didn't know that I was doing so, but before I could reply he continued to bellow more questions into my face.

As he shouted in a manner that seemed irrational it became clear his questions were intended to intimidate me rather than to gain information.

One officer, whose badge read Robert Brackney seemed to be doing all the shouting and the other officer, a William Benson, stood back from the action. My first impression was that the officers were using me as a way to have a little excitement, as police work in a small town can be pretty quiet.

Officer Brackney continued his over-the-top interrogation with an inflated air of machismo as if I were a dangerous criminal and he was a heroic lawman, forced to go above the law to rid the world of evil. Through it all I tried to remain cool and collected and respond with a calm, respectful tone of voice.

I was not drinking, I did not use drugs, I was just a citizen who apparently forgot to turn on his headlights so I saw no reason for the abusive behavior. I never once gave him any argument concerning the headlight issue. I sat in the car seat and they looked down on me from the window. As he continued his torrent of abuse I finally became exasperated and whispered under my breath, "Fuuuuck you."

This seemed to be just what he was waiting for.

"What did you say," he shrieked.

"I said fuck you," I replied with an even voice.

"Now you're gonna to get it," Officer Brackney shouted as they pulled me out, threw me against the car, and cuffed my hands behind my back. For good measure they kicked my feet out from under me, knocking me onto the ground with a hard thud. Without the use of my hands to cushion the fall, my chest and face slammed against the parking lot macadam.

Police have very precise procedures that they must follow that are designed to protect the public. Many police also know how to twist those procedures in order to inflict pain on those in their custody. Operating in this manner gives them added protection because they can simply say, "I was just following procedures," when accusations of abuse are made. In short order, I was the recipient of two such abuses of procedure.

First, when they walked me to the car, procedure calls for them to guide me by holding the chain between the two cuffs behind my back. The cruel twist is that if you pull up on those cuffs just a bit you can inflict a great deal of pain, since the arms just don't bend in that direction and the cuffs easily cut into the soft flesh of the wrists.

When the individual in custody is placed in the police car, procedure dictates that the officer should place his hand on the head of the accused so he will not bump it on the roof of the police vehicle. This procedure also provides a wonderful opportunity to push the head of the accused downward, twisting the neck at odd and painful angles. I can attest that the officers had these procedural twists down pat and applied them with sadistic precision.

As they had completely bypassed reading me my Miranda Rights, once in the car I protested, "This is the United States, I have rights."

"You just lost your rights," Brackney snickered.

The arrest happened to be taking place during the trial of the police officers who savagely beat Rodney King in California. When I reminded them that there were laws governing police actions Brackney sneered, "Rodney King got what he deserved!"

As we drove towards the police station I began to glean the dynamic between the two officers that likely lead to my unfortunate situation. It seems officer Benson was a rookie, and officer Brackney was in charge of showing him the ropes. To that end, he was engaged in a bit of showing off for his underling, leading to his abusive behavior.

Like most schoolyard bullies, Officer Brackney appeared to be a man who felt small and insecure inside and to compensate he puffed himself up, physically by bulking up his body with weight lifting, and psychologically by using his uniform to find people he could degrade and abuse.

There is little that is more dangerous then a weak ego in a uniform. When we look back over the history of mankind, we can only guess at how many of humanity's greatest cruelties were perpetuated by such weak men in uniforms.

When we arrived at the police station the place was dark and empty. They sat me in a chair in the middle of the room with my hands still cuffed behind my back. It looked like a torture scene from a second rate spy movie. Quickly it began to dawn on me that I could be in real trouble here. They could essentially do whatever they wanted to me and easily cover their tracks.

I was trapped and bound like a criminal and in the hands of a couple small-time sadists whose authority had been challenged. They crept around the outskirts of the room looking at paperwork and whispering to each other. Occasionally hurling insults at me for good measure.

"You're scum, you're the same as any rapist or murderer," Brackney snarled.

A chill came over me as I craned my neck to look around the room in hopes of seeing another witness who might stand in the way of whatever the officers might have planned. I contorted my neck like Linda Blair only to find that each hallway, every window, and every doorway was dark and empty.

"You're garbage! You have no rights," Brackney continued.

Until one experiences it firsthand, it is hard to understand how losing your free will degrades your self-esteem. I was essentially kidnapped by a couple of small-town jokers with limited intelligence and questionable morals, yet because they wore a uniform they were unleashed on society.

As I sat in my bondage Brackney's words echoed in my ears, "Rodney King got what he deserved."

The situation was completely surreal and I was helpless to defend myself. I began to truly fear what might come next. To be treated like an animal, to be held in bondage by another person, especially when sanctioned by the state, has a profoundly devastating psychological effect. One's spirit shrivels and your confidence evaporates.

As my mind raced in fear, cataloging the possibilities of what my fate might be, I began to understand that the horrible feelings I was experiencing inside were worse than any physical abuse they might inflict. In fact, physical abuse seemed preferable to the spiritual degradation their terror was causing. With this in mind I decided to respond to their verbal abuse with the only weapon I had – my own voice.

"You guys give the police force a bad name," I blurted out.

They looked at me surprised and annoyed, but went about their business. Realizing how good it felt to stand up for myself I began to lecture them on their duties as police officers, on the U.S. Constitution, and on morality. I noticed that the more I pushed them, the more uncomfortable they seemed to get.

"You guys might be happier working in Cuba or China," I mocked, "Your behavior would fit right in."

As I went on I became more aggressive. When Brackney left the room I looked Benson in the eye and said, "I bet he's fucking you up the ass, isn't he?"

Benson looked not only shocked, but also frightened. When Brackney returned I continued my tirade. Relishing that the more abusive and foulmouthed I became, the more unnerved they became. Benson whispered to Brackney in a worried voice, "What's wrong with him? Is he crazy?"

Finally Brackney came up behind me and took the cuffs off my wrists. They both took a position on two chairs a few yards in front of me.

"Listen, we're gonna give you a break," Brackney explained. "Call someone for a ride home. You can go. We'll just forget the whole thing."

It seemed clear to me that they had made a mistake and had overstepped their boundaries. Thinking I had them in a bind and wanting them to be accountable for their behavior I demanded, "You started this, now finish it. Arrest me."

The two officers looked at each other with confused expressions. Then stared at me for a long pause. "I just said you can go," Backney repeated.

"Arrest me!" I demanded.

With weary movements they raised themselves from their chairs and completed their paperwork. The judge had to be summoned to come into court after hours to arraign me. At every step of the way I expected someone would put a stop to the nonsense and put the officers on the carpet for their behavior. But oh how naïve I was!

I was transferred from the courthouse to the jail. Inside the jailhouse office I sat in a chair while three guards filled out paperwork. The guards at the county lock-up tended to be a particular type of character. Usually they were holdouts from the 1950's who had pork chop sideburns and drove worn out hot-rods. Most got their start by listening for fire or police reports on their CB radio scanners, even though they held no position of authority, they would put blue bubble lights atop their rusted hot rods and rush to the scene on any incident. A friend of mine on the local police force told me the police hated those guys because they were always getting in the way of the real work.

Usually these guys were too overweight or too dimwitted to get on the police force, but were desperate to feel some sense of authority. A rampant condition in small towns. Luckily for them, to be a guard at the county jail only required a high school diploma, giving this gang of Fonzi wannna-bes a perfect opportunity to be in a position to lord it over some other unlucky fool such as myself.

As a matter of course these three insulted and belittled me as they processed their paperwork. Eventually one of them threw a piece of paper in front of me and told me to sign it. When I began to read it one of the guards ran towards me and bellowed, "I said sign it, not read it!"

By this point the situation had become so surreal and the players so pathetic that I had enough. I leaned back in my chair as if sunning in an easy chair on the beach and flipped my pencil up into the air. It seemed to float slowly towards the ceiling while spinning in circles like the leg bone turned spaceship in the movie 2001. At first the three seemed to be in absolute shock. Once they were able to gather their somewhat limited wits about them, they went ballistic.

The other two rushed towards me, "OK, wise guy, we're gonna make things rough on ya now!!!"

They took me to a tiny room and made me strip naked. One got on his knees and looked underneath my balls. They made me bend over and spread my ass cheeks apart while the inspector bent down low and looked up my ass to make sure I didn't have a crate of dynamite hidden up there.

They seemed to take a perverse glee in all this. They were definitely finding homosexual excitement in degrading me in this way. It reeked of the same mixture of sado-sexual perversion one got a sense of in the photos from Abu Ghraib prison.

When they finally took me to the cell they refused to give me a pillow, blanket, toilet paper, or return my shoes. The cell was a tiny cubicle just large enough to hold a cot and a stainless steel toilet with no seat. There was one small slit of a window that was too high up to look out of.

All night I seethed with anger at being put in a cage. In the morning I could only think of the film shoot I was scheduled to direct at that hour, and that when evening came I would be missing a day of work. And why all this? The police were so bored that they managed to created a criminal where one didn't exist.

One of the worst things about being in jail was trying to keep your mind from racing. Around noon a book cart came past my cell that represented the extent of the jailhouse library. The reading selection ranged from Dick and Jane level reading material to outdated issues of the Reader's Digest magazine. All of it too inane to hold one's attention.

In the afternoon we were allowed out in the yard for an hour. The other convicts ran in circles around the yard to burn off energy. I was not allowed to see a lawyer or have a notebook and pencil. In the evening they brought a cup for of green liquid and told me to go into the shower and rub it over myself from head to toe because they had to 'delouse me.'

That evening I was released on $1,500 bail. An exorbitant amount for a public nuisance charge. As I headed out the door they returned my shoes with the strings tied together in a tangle of 20 tight knots. Just a little goodbye gift from the guards.

Two weeks later I was finally able to see the public defender. His first action was to tell me he hoped I had learned a lesson. When your own lawyer assumes you are guilty before he even meets you, you know justice is not in the game plan. By this time I was so dispirited that I signed anything they wanted and plead guilty to any charges they asked. Anything as long as I could maintain the freedom to live my life.

The truth is, I *had* learned a lesson. I had learned that there is corruption at every level of authority, and that the justice system will protect its own rather than uphold the law. I learned the depth of fear and despair one feels when the liberties that Americans hold so dear are trampled into the ground by those in power. But most important, I learned that if you question the authority of those in power, it shakes them to the core. They react like frightened animals trapped in a corner, and will do anything it takes to restore their sense of unquestioned dominance.

A few days later I was speaking to a friend of mine who was a civics professor at the Penn State University. She urged me to file an official complaint against the authorities. I knew it was the right thing to do. The truth is I was afraid that if I made trouble the corrupt elements would make my life rough for me, and being locked in a cage had made a strong impression on me, now all I wanted was to live in freedom.

A few weeks later I was walking across a bridge that overlooks the Susquahanna River. At the end was a monument to the local men who had died in World War II. As I read the names of those who had given their lives for our country and its ideals, I felt ashamed. In the end I lacked the courage to stand up for those same ideals of liberty and justice that these men had given their lives to protect.

When I got home I wrote a letter of complaint detailing my experience with the police and sent it to the two local newspapers and to the state senator's offices. Both newspapers refused to print the letter. Years later the owner of the smaller weekly newspaper the County Observer came backstage at an Imperial Orgy performance and apologized.

"I felt for you," he intoned. "I wish I could've helped, but there are people around here I can't get on the wrong side of."

The main newspaper, The Lewistown Sentinal, told me they would look into the matter and print a story, but never did. When you have no money, no power, and no voice, the media is the only hope the public has to tell their story in hopes of finding justice. When the media turns its back on the public, and when public officials are above criticism, it is a chilling sign of authoritarian control.

The one man who did stand up was a state senator by the name of Daniel F. Clark. Clark filed a complaint against the police officers and the sheriff's office on my behalf. I didn't realize it at the time, but now the war was on and I was a marked man. I had caused them to be called to account for their behavior by a legitimate source of power, and everyone in the local and state police force, the local politicians, the sheriff's department, and the justice system were on alert and had aligned their defenses. I had crossed the line and must be put back in my place.

At the time I was completely unaware of what was taking place behind the scenes. I lead a quiet life as far as Lewistown was concerned. My days were filled with college classes in another town, and my evenings filled with work at the pizza shop. I didn't drink very often and rarely went out in public. I really had no contact with the police or other local authorities. But soon a turn of events would give the police a perfect foil that would allow them to place me in their grips.

At the time my long relationship with Leilani suddenly began to fall apart. She was half Hawaiian and came from a troubled home. Although her stability was always a tad shaky, except that she couldn't seem to go for more than a few hours without sucking down a joint, she had held herself together pretty well. Now that my time was taken up by college and work, she became lonely and soon began to drink and take harder drugs.

When we split she went straight into the arms of a good-looking thug named Robert Murdoch who had just been released from prison for brutally assaulting a young woman. He looked a bit like a Robert De Niro in the movie Cape Fear.

Whenever possible Lealani tried to find ways to force a confrontation between Murdoch and I. On a May evening Leilani called and demanded that I give her a painting I had of the Hindu God Krishna. She was welcome to take the painting, but I had lent it out to a mutual friend to use as set decoration on a student film shoot. Even though she knew the painting was not there she said she was coming over to get it.

I had friends over that night and didn't want to have them entangled in a scene, so when I heard Lealani and Murdoch pull up I waited for them outside the front door. As soon as Leilani came near she began punching and scratching my face and chest. She tore my T-shirt off my body before I could subdue her. Murdoch stood a few feet away making threats and saying he would, "break me in two."

When they refused to leave I called the police for protection and ask them to force Murdoch off my property. The police refused to come. They said it was a personal dispute and they could not get involved. Although I didn't understand what was going on, this was the first sign that the authorities were aligned against me and were simply waiting for a chance to knock me off my high horse.

After about an hour of drama that took place with the entire neighborhood watching, they finally left, but only after I threatened Murdoch with a baseball bat that a neighbor had handed to me.

Later that evening after my guests had left, I called Leilani to tell her she could have the painting as soon as it was returned from the film shoot. Unfortunately Murdoch answered the phone.

He said, "Watch your back. When you least expect it I'm going to come up behind you and stick a knife in your back."

After I hung up the phone, about twenty minutes later I got a call from the state police. They said that Murdoch had filed a complaint against me and I would be placed under immediate arrest. They said I could expect a summons for a court date to arrive in the mail. Although the behavior of the police seemed astounding, I still hadn't put the pieces together to understand what was really taking place.

Not long after that I received news that Leilani had been arrested and jailed on attempted murder charges. It seems that in a drunken rage Murdoch had beaten her up and during the attack she grabbed a meat cleaver and stuck it into his shoulder.

Knowing she had no one to help her, I called her mother who lived in Hawaii so she could arrange bail. The charges were dropped a few weeks later when Murdoch refused to cooperate.

The summer months passed by without further incident. Late in September Leilani's mother called me to tell me that Leilani was having emotional and drug related problems. She said she was too far away to help and ask if I could try to help her. I told her that I had little contact with her and there wasn't much I could do.

Later that week I went out for a drink with friends. After one vodka and seven I returned home to find a note on my door from Leilani, saying she needed to speak to me about something, and asking if I could come to the diner where she worked as a waitress.

On the way to the diner I noticed her car parked at a convenience store gas station and figured she had gotten off work early. I pulled in to see what she wanted. To my surprise Murdoch was there with her. Immediately an argument ensued. Murdoch said, "I'm going to give you a beating you'll never forget."

Then as Leilani and I spoke for a moment he went to a pay phone and called the police. The police must have absolutely rushed to the scene because they arrived in a moment's notice and immediately arrested me. I couldn't believe what was taking place. Even though Leilani told them I wasn't doing anything wrong, they cuffed me and took me away.

These events seemed so irrational that I was left confused and overwhelmed. I ask what I was being charged with and they said public drunkenness. I explained that I had only one drink and requested a breathalyzer test to prove it, but they refused.

In court the judge wisely explained that with a charge of public drunkenness it doesn't matter how much alcohol you have consumed, if a police officer says you are drunk, then you are. A strange bit of logic, but when you're in a madhouse, you learn not to question such things.

This time there were no insults. No roughing me up for kicks. It was all done by the book. The officers just seemed focused on getting me into the jail as quickly as possible.

I was processed and taken to my cell. This time I was given blankets, pillow, and toilet paper. Everything was done in a professional manner. But the mere fact that I was in jail at all belied that something was out of whack with these proceedings.

The night came and went. After breakfast one of the jail guards pulled me into a silent stairway. He was a large pot bellied man with shaggy hair and a big scruffy mustache named Mark Laub.

"I read that letter you wrote," he said menacingly "So you think us guards aren't educated enough huh? I'll have you know I used to be a substitute teacher at every high school in the county."

I stood smiling slightly. Not uttering a word. Not revealing a single emotion.

"How do you think I did that if I'm not educated?"

He peered at me expectantly. Again I just smiled without response. Realizing I would not react he ordered to me, "Go back to your cell, we'll talk later."

At around noon I was taken down to sheriff Jay Laub's private office and told to sit on a chair against the wall. In a nasty bit of nepotism, a guard who was a relative of the sheriff's stood outside the door like a palace sentry. Rising up slowly from his chair the sheriff glared at me.

"I had to fill out a lot of paperwork because of you."

I sat looking straight into his eyes, betraying no emotion in my face. He spoke with a slow, depressed sounding drawl that is common in that part of the country.

"Have you served in the military?" he barked

"No," I replied.

"Well I have! I don't ever want to hear you talk about what people in the military think or feel. Do you hear me? Those people who fought and died for this country weren't fighting for people like you, I can tell you that for sure." His reference was to a point in my complaint that he clearly misunderstood.

All this was followed by a barrage of insults, threats, bragging, and complaints about how much work I caused for him.

"I could squash a piss ant like you and no one would say a word," he warned. "The next time you have a complaint against me, you be a man and come say it right to my face, cause now I am going to make things rough for you."

He hovered above me as I sat in the chair, his face a few inches above my head.

"You can complain to anyone you want, the governor, the president, it won't effect me," he shouted.

Clearly he felt untouchable in his little castle of power. In his personal Barney fiefdom he was a king among men. The alpha male. A regular John Wayne who all others feared. But outside that door he was a feebleminded coward with a yellow streak up his back so wide you could drive a Mac truck on it.

I was well aware that his goal was to get me to react so that he had an excuse for he and his country cousin to lay a beating on me. I was completely unimpressed by him and his bluster. There was something comical about his manner. If he ever had the courage to walk down the street in broad daylight I believe his cartoonish demeanor would have elicited muffled laughter from all directions.

He was a relic from another era that never really existed. A phantom of the American dream become delusion. In his youth he must have dreamed of General Patton. Dreamed that he too might lead valiant men into great battles for the good of all mankind. He was a man of order and discipline. Now those ideals had decayed into tools of contempt to unleash his bitterness onto those around him.

He clung to a worldview that comes into being when groups of men are isolated from the outside world. A world where men are men and women and sissy-boys don't count. He stood for truth, justice and the American way, and he demanded that all others honor those ideals even as he twisted and perverted them to suit his personal egomania.

As his stale breath rained down on me, his words flowed like dialogue from a clichéd parody of a drill sergeant in a 1980's movie comedy. I sat unmoved and without fear. When reality walks off the map into the nether land where the surreal is accepted as gospel truth, then it is a world where I feel firm on my feet. In some odd way I felt that I had the upper hand. In my head I was already plotting the moment when I would call his bluff, and then his true colors would be revealed.

When POWs are captured they often retain their military structure while imprisoned in order to maintain their spiritual strength. So it seemed with this lot. They were a pack of dinosaurs who growled ferociously in order to convince themselves that the world still trembled at their feet, even while the dust and sediment blotted out the last rays of sunshine, heralding their demise.

When he finally accepted that he couldn't get a rise out of me, he seemed to wilt. With a spent look on his face he wearily wandered back to his desk and ordered the guard to take me back to my cell.

During the evening the inmates were allowed out in the cellblock to watch TV and play board games. The inmates were a rambunctious bunch of white trash hooligans, most of who were incarcerated on drug charges or petty theft. Many of them spent their entire lives in and out of the hoosegow.

Jail is a strange social situation that seems threatening due to endless jailhouse movies. The baddest cat in the cellblock was a guy by the name of Matt Robertson that everyone called Spinner. Spinner was a large lanky fellow who certainly looked as if he'd

Murder Of The Holly King

been in a few scraps in his day. As is always the case with a gang of males, the top dog has a group of minions who stay by his side.

My questionable position in the cellblock was raised when someone recognized me as a member of the punk rock band that many of the inmates had partied with during their younger days.

One of Spinner's minions came up and said to me, "Hey man, what did you do to piss off the sheriff so bad?"

"What do you mean?" I asked.

"Spinner said that Lauby, he's the fat fuck who only has his job because he's the sheriff's cousin, Lauby came into his cell this morning and told him to rough you up."

By that I time already felt confident that I was on good terms with Spinner, so I didn't fear that his order would be carried out, but it was astounding to learn what lengths these people would go to exact revenge on me.

To prove his story he yelled, "Hey Spinner, didn't Lauby come into your cell this morning?"

"Yeah, fuck that asshole," Spinner replied with disdain.

Despite the seriousness of my situation I felt lighthearted. The whole system was mad as a hatter and run by a mafia of dimwits to boot. The ones with the badges, robes, and guns, were no better or no worse than the gang of criminals locked up in cages.

Somehow they had managed to get the power and they were clinging to it for dear life. They sure as hell weren't going to let some smarty-pants street punk take it away from them. I could have been in big trouble by now, if they were anything more than a clan of inept clowns.

As the social hour continued spirits were high, the inmates found ways to have fun even under the worst of circumstances. It was like recess in bedlam. I settled into to a lively game of scrabble with Spinner and a few of his friends. My cellblock popularity rose considerably when I scored points by using the word "tit."

After that we moved on to a game of Life. The whole ass-backwards affair seemed to be capped by the ridiculous spectacle of sitting down to a nice game if Life with a gang of supposedly hardened criminals. Yes, we got married, had children, bought homes, built careers, made and lost fortunes. It was a hilarious good time.

In the middle of the game someone called out my name, "Pink, you're outta here."

I shook hands all around and left, never to return. Although the threats, insults, and antagonism registered as little more than a farce to me at the time, when I had a moment to reflect on the day's events, I finally began to understand how deadly serious these people were, and how far they would go to get me. I had to watch my step. And I still had the court date over Murdoch's charges looming in the future.

Once out of jail I figured that the sheriff's office had undeniably broken the law when they tried to get an inmate to beat me. I decided this was the point I would take them to task for. My hope was that I could find someone in authority to take up my case before the coming court date.

My first order of business was to call out the sheriff for the fraud that he was. I wrote him a letter challenging him to meet me face to face as he suggested, but this time outside of his office and in neutral territory, and with video cameras keeping a record of the event. I reminded him of his threats and insults and dared him to repeat them in public and in front of the cameras.

Sheriff Laub,

Yesterday while you were berating me in your office I felt that I dare not speak my peace or you would use that as an excuse to "make things rough on me." Now that I am no longer in your care I feel that it is my duty to do so. You stated yesterday that if I had something to say to you I should say it in person. I would like to do so, but not within the confines of your office, because I fear that you will find some pretext within my words to have me arrested. Therefore, I would like to invite you to speak with me on this matter in public and while being videotaped for the record. I would also invite you to repeat the statements you made in your office for the record. Although I sincerely doubt that you would have the courage to do so.

I am writing to you for various reasons. One, judging from your statements and threats I believe that you have no respect for the ideals that this country and our justice system were founded on. You stated that nothing that the governor or any elected representatives do would have influence on you. It seems clear that you feel that you are above the rule of our government's laws. You seem to believe that you are a separate entity that has succeeded from the union. If you really respected this country I don't believe that you would have this attitude.

Secondly; I would like to remind you that in the United States a citizen is innocent until proven guilty. What you seem to overlook is that the people brought into your jail for the first time have been accused, but not proven guilty. Regardless of this, you and a few of your employees treat people as if they are less than human. If a person on the street treated another person the way you treated me in your office, they would be arrested for harassment. I ask you to remember the names you called me and the threats you made against me. If you were not protected by your office and uniform would that have been legal conduct? If not, does your office and uniform give you the right to act with illegality?

Among your statements, you admitted that I was forced to sign papers without being allowed to read them, yet you feel this acceptable. I was intimidated, threatened, and verbally abused by certain of your employees during the arrest that I wrote the complaint about. Yet you defend these actions against a citizen who at that time was not convicted of any crime.

If you wish to live in a country where citizens have no rights, and uniformed officers are above the law, why don't you move to China, Iraq, or another totalitarian state. Your means of conduct would fit in perfectly.

Perhaps the most obvious proof that you stand against the values of our country is your statement that because I dared to file a complaint against you, that you would "make things rough for me." Remember what you said to me about having to fill out paperwork due to my complaint. Would you repeat that threat for the record?

Perhaps I should remind you once more that in America there are checks on power. It is the duty of an American citizen to report corrupt activities within the system. It was clear from your threats that you planned to make things hard on me in return for bringing the actions of your employees to your attention. I thought you would have been grateful that I informed you of this situation. Why do you feel that my search for justice is something which you should punish. And I ask you now, which inmate did your relative and jail guard ask to 'rough me up' ? Is this the way things are done in America?

*Once again I invite you to meet me in a public place and repeat your
statements on the record and with camera equipment recording it. I will be glad
to speak to you face to face under those condition where your actions will face
public scrutiny. If you have the integrity and courage to do so then please contact
me. If not, then I guess we both know that your integrity and your supposed
respect for American ideals and justice are a fraud. If you do not have the
courage to face me, then every time you look into the mirror you will see yourself
as I see you; as a coward who cannot stand behind his own words.*

Sincerely,

Caeser Pink

Not surprisingly, he did not accept my challenge, and I
received no response to my letter.

After getting released from jail I began calling everyone I
could think of who might take an interest in my case. I went to see
the township supervisors. One of them said without a trace of
irony, "That's Jay Laub, he's an elected official. He can do whatever
he wants." Then he turned and walked out of the room, leaving me
to scratch my head in wonder at how easily fascism is accepted as
the natural order of things.

I tried a variety of legal aid services and government
agencies whose jobs were to investigate corrupt public officials.
Usually I got the runaround, but a couple of them actually seemed
supportive and said they would help me. But in each case, they
never carried through, and then refused to take or return my calls. I
could only assume that something was happening behind the scenes
to stop them from pursuing the charges.

As this process continued the court date with Murdoch
crept closer. If I didn't have someone on my side by that time I
might be in real trouble. I went to the D.A.'s office, but he refused
to come out of his private office and speak to me. Getting
somewhat desperate I returned the next day. The secretary
disappeared into his office and returned after a long wait, "D.A.

Searer can't help you with this because he says it is out of his jurisdiction," she said somewhat embarrassed.

Around that time a tall man in a black trench coat knocked at my front door. He said he was the internal affairs investigator from the State Police Headquarters, they were finally investigating the charges Senator Clark filed against the original two officers that started this whole mess.

We sat at a large round wooden table in the center of my library. He asked a few standard questions then looked me directly in the eye, "You seem like a pretty level-headed guy. What happened that night?"

The insinuation was that this was all my fault and it was time to explain my actions.

Taking time to reflect I appealed to his sense of reason, "Think about this; did they tell you that I never once questioned the ticket for driving without headlights? You have to ask, if I wasn't contesting the ticket, what was the problem all about?"

"I have to tell you I have investigated your claims and I can't find a bit of evidence to support them," he said evenly.

"Did they admit to saying that I had no rights," I asked with a friendly smile as if we were two sleuths trying to unravel a mystery.

He sat silently, maintaining a perfect poker face.

"Did they admit to telling me that Rodney King got what he deserved," I pushed on.

He remained silent.

"If they denied saying those things, then you have two officers who are willing to lie to you, and I think that would concern you."

He stood up to take his leave. "We'll send you a letter regarding our decision," he said as he walked out the door. I felt sure he was annoyed at having to carry out this charade when everyone involved knew that no actions would be taken against the officers.

A few days later a letter arrived from a Captain Raymond J. Mitarnowski informing me that the investigation concluded that the officers acted properly in their handling of this incident and they were within the rules of regulation of the Pennsylvania State Police Force. If that is "acting properly" I shudder to think what improper actions would be.

I hadn't expected anything else. Unless their hands were tied the authorities will always protect their own.

In the meantime my search for help was going nowhere and the court date was right around the corner. A few days before the court date I received a late night phone call from Murdoch, the man who made the charges against me that the police were exploiting.

I had little contact with Leilani in recent months, but heard that she was trying to get rid of Murdoch. Murdoch had called to try to blackmail me into not seeing her ever again. It was kind of stupid on his part because I had no plan to, or interest in seeing her, and had started a new relationship many months before.

"Listen," he whispered on the phone as if he was about to do me a great favor. "The State Police want to get your ass, bad! They want me in court so they can get you into jail and take care of you. But if you swear not to ever see Leilani again I will not show up in court to testify against you."

As I didn't plan to see her anyway, I had nothing to lose so I agreed to his terms. Even though I didn't really believe he would hold up his end of the bargain. Especially considering he was out on parole and the police had a lot of leverage against him. What was most revealing about the conversation was that it confirmed that the police had teamed up with a violent ex-convict in order to get to me.

In a final attempt to find some support before the court date I called the D.A.'s office in the state capital in Harrisburg. An agent got on the phone and asked me to tell my story. As I spoke I heard a series of beeps over the receiver, as if someone was recording the conversation. I assumed it was the state D.A. office recording the call for their records. As I began to tell him about the Sheriff's office trying to get an inmate to beat me, the phone suddenly went dead. I called the D.A. back and with a tone of concern he asked me, "Did you hear those beeps on the phone?"

"Yes," I answered.

"Do you know why the phone went dead?"

"No," I responded.

"Those beeps were not caused by anything in my office. Someone has tapped your telephone line and was listening to our conversation. You'd better get it checked out right away," he warned me.

When I hung up I called the phone company and asked them to check the line for taps. They informed me they couldn't find a tap, but it didn't really matter because if someone was listening they could pull the tap at a moment's notice and there would be no way to trace it.

Now I was starting to panic. Were these people crazy? Did they really see me as that much of a threat? Their behavior was so irrational that I thought they might be capable of anything. Perhaps they might plant drugs on me to put me in jail for years. Or perhaps I might actually end up dead. The situation seemed totally out of control.

Among the things the state D.A. told me was that the local D.A. had to help me, it was his job. I returned to D.A. Searer's office and told his secretary what the state D.A. had said. In what now was becoming a ritual, she disappeared into the D.A.'s office for a long period of time. When she returned she said that if I put my complaint in writing he would look at it.

I went home and did so and hand delivered it back to the office. From then until the day of the court date I called his office each day, but was always told that Mr. Searer was either out of the office or too busy to speak with me.

As the walls seemed to be closing in on me I decided I had to get out of town for my own survival. Lewistown was my hometown and the only place I had ever lived. Moving meant leaving behind my house which I had invested a lot of time and money into remodeling. It also meant leaving behind friends and family.

My new girlfriend Samantha found me a small apartment in State College about 35 miles away. Since I was living in an eight-room house and was moving into a three-room apartment I had to unload many prized possessions. Among them a brand new Steinenger piano.

I felt like it was the Wild West and the sheriff had told me the town wasn't big enough for the both of us. I always knew I would leave Lewistown, but I never expected to be run out of town by corrupt officials.

The morning before the court date I met with a lawyer that agreed to take my case for $75. He felt the facts were on my side in the case. As I expected Murdoch did not hold up his side of our bargain, and he showed to testify against me.

As the proceedings began the judge made of point of announcing that he had been called in from another district so that there would be no suspicion that the court was prejudiced against me. As if I were foolish enough to think that really made a difference. The fact that he felt compelled to mention it, said it all.

When Murdoch took the stand he immediately got caught in a series of lies.

"Have you ever been at the property owned by Mr. Pink," my lawyer asked.

"No. I haven't," Murdoch lied.

"You're sure you've never been there?" my lawyer asked incredulously.

"No. I haven't" Murdoch repeated.

"Mr. Murdoch," my lawyer continued, "Many residents of the neighborhood witnessed you leaving and entering the property during a period when Mr. Pink was out of town on business. Are you sure you've never been there?"

"I might have been there once," he said. Admitting his first count of perjury.

"Now during your stay were you not sharing a bed with Leilani Collinge?" he asked.

"Yes, I was," Murdoch admitted.

"Were you aware that at that time she was in a relationship with Mr. Pink?"

"Yes. I was," he confessed.

"Now that you've admitted that you have been at the property, on the evening that you made these charges were you not only at the property, but also told Mr. Pink that you would "break him in two?"

Murdoch denied it steadfastly. When he admitted to perjury on the stand it was a Perry Mason moment. In anything other than a kangaroo court it would have resulted in the charges against me being dropped immediately.

When it was all over the judge said, "This is really a case of one man's word against another's. In this case I find Mr. Murdoch to be a more credible witness than Mr. Pink, therefore I find the defendant guilty. To prove I'm not a hanging judge I'm going to let you off with just a fine. But if I hear that your are harassing Mr. Murdoch again it will turn out different."

My lawyer was furious and wanted to appeal the conviction. Understanding what was really at stake I said no, paid the fine, and got the hell out of there. Within a few days I left behind my house and my past.

Life in Lewistown always meant dealing with pressure to conform. There was always an element of society that hated anyone who stood out. Once when I was eighteen, a middle aged man chased me down and attacked me because he had seen me wearing one black and one white shoe on a previous occasion. Such behavior was obviously a danger to society and a personal insult to him.

It was the Nietzschian principle at work; the mediocre must destroy those that stand out in order to protect the dominance of the herd. I was often astounded by the violent reaction some people had towards those who don't conform.

Now it seemed I was being run out of town for having the audacity to believe that individuality and individual liberty were important ideals. It was all totally bizarre, although perhaps a fitting end to my life there. As long as no one questions those in authority, everything goes on as always. If anyone dares to question, they may be crushed by an unspoken conspiracy that demands that all in power align against those who question authority in any way. If a crack appears, the entire charade is in danger.

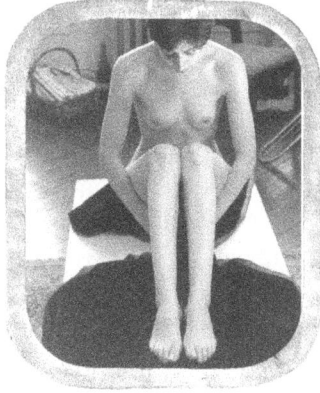

#17 – Hidden Under A Basket

As the flatlands gave way to civilization the weather turned nasty. Cold rain fell for days on end. The skies were gray and the highway was covered with a haze that forced me to lean forward against the steering wheel with my eyes squinting to see what was ahead of me. The nights had become freezing cold and I shivered under piles of blankets, jackets, and dirty clothes as I tried to stay warm.

By the time I rolled into Chicago I was feeling pretty worn out by the treacherous driving conditions. I pulled off a random highway exit and found myself in the sprawl of a modern ghetto. I pulled into the parking lot of a Subway sandwich shop and went inside and ordered a tuna sub. The place was clean enough, but the food had no taste to me.

I sat by the window watching the rain pour down over the bleak surroundings while trying to force down a few bites of the sandwich. I guess this would be all I would see of Chicago. No blues bars or Sears Tower. There was so much of America I wanted to see but couldn't. The Redwood forest, Yellowstone Park, the Colorado Mountains, the list could go on and on. It would take me six months to see America the way I wanted to and still I wouldn't have time to really penetrate it enough to understand this land and its people.

With a sigh of resignation I pushed aside the half eaten sandwich and walked through the cold rain back to the Blazer. Back on the highway I felt weary because the joy had gone out of my journey. It was no longer an adventure of exploration, now just a drive between two points.

I was a week behind schedule to return to my day job. Once I returned it would be the end of freedom. The expansion of spirit I felt out on the open highway would soon dissipate as I marched back into step in my humdrum nine-to-five existence. Plus, now there was the added bonus of living in a post 9/11 New York City. God only knows what that would mean.

Midway through Ohio my eyes were red and bleary from trying to see through the fog and mist from the rain that came down unabated. I flicked on the AM radio and a young woman from some kind of activist organization was being interviewed on NPR. "I believe we just need to make use of the United Nations and the international legal system to bring the terrorists to justice," she said with a slight trace of a valley girl accent in her voice.

In my state of mourning, her words filled me with anger. I have always been for peace. I have always believed war is inherently evil. Turn the other cheek, runaway – live to fight another day, was my motto. But there comes a time when one has to stand and fight. The strong have to protect the innocent. And this was one of those times.

To shut her up I hit the search button on the radio. After a few seconds of static it landed on Rush Limbaugh. "The Libs," he said with an all-knowing voice, "Let me tell you, the Libs, the left-wing radicals, are ready to lay down and admit defeat. Thank your lucky stars my friends that we have George Bush, Donald Rumsfeld, and Richard Cheney in the White House. These men have the physical fortitude to do what needs to be done. They have the courage to go out and get the bad guys, and they aren't going to let the UN or the French or the left-wing hippie radicals stand in their way!"

It made me sick that already the rightwing mouthpieces were exploiting the tragedy for political and economic gain. I hit the search button again.

"It is time for us to come back to the Lord Jesus Christ," a preacher was shouting, obviously pleased that tragedy had befallen the nation. "This is a warning! This is a sign from above. Lust, prom-is-cu-ity, id-ol-atry, hom-o-sex-ual-a-lity! The Lord is watching. Now His voice has been heard…loud and clear. It is not OK to worship your Buddhas and your prophet Mohammed. There is one Lord in heaven and his name is Jesus Christ! Those whom stray will be smitten. Those who fall into Satan's deceptions will burn in hellfire."

It was disgusting. It seemed everyone's reaction was to blame the tragedy on their enemies in order to fan the flames of hate. No one seemed to have any qualms about exploiting the deaths of thousands of Americans for their own profit.

I jumped through the dial, searching for something that wouldn't turn my stomach. "Get the Midas touch," "Oops I did it again," "It's Miller time!' Finally I switched it off in disgust. Sometimes American culture is so saccharine that it makes you gag. Better to be alone with my thoughts.

By nightfall I was beginning to waver. My limbs and face were numb and tingling. Three weeks of sleeping in the car and eating highway food were taking their toll. Although the truth is, I didn't really feel that this is what was at the root of my problem. It was something else. Something spiritual. Something psychological.

I opened the window to get some fresh air and was greeted with a blast of cold. Sleeping in the car would be harsh tonight. I pulled off to the side of the road and assessed my financial situation. After counting my pennies it seemed I might have just enough to get a cheap hotel room for the night. This would be my last night on the road. By tomorrow night I would be back in New York City.

As midnight closed in I pulled off an exit into some dingy Ohio town whose name I never got and soon found a run-down motel with an affordable room. It had tan walls that were so stained it looked like a map of the world's continents were stenciled on it in brown chocolate. The floor was covered in some multicolored industrial carpet that hadn't seen a vacuum in months. By the bed was an end table with a lamp whose paper shade was brown and brittle with age. Although the TV set only had three channels, one of them played ugly 1980's porn movies.

My head was still spinning and my body weak. I decided I better venture out into the rain to find some kind of sustenance. Outside the motel room door I could see a shining holy grail of a convenience store glowing in the distance. It sat magnificently on a large parking lot on the other side of a menacing looking four-lane highway.

After an interminable wait I finally got a break in the traffic and hobbled across the highway and crawled over a three-foot cement barricade at the far side of the road. Inside the convenience store my tired eyes were being burned out of my head by the banks of fluorescent lights that illuminated the place. They glared as bright as laser beams, except for one, that for good measure, flickered at a rapid-fire pace.

With a cringe in my spine and my eyes open but a mere sliver, I copped a 50-cent cinnamon bun and a super sized Slim Jim and got outta there as quick as I could. Back in my little Taj Mahal of a room I scarfed down the goodies and washed them away with a leftover bottle of warm Pespsi that had been laying in the Blazer for a couple of days.

I know it's hard to imagine, but my choice of nourishment didn't seem to make me feel any better. In fact, I felt decidedly worse. In order to escape the motel room and get some fresh air I braved the rain and took a stroll around the hellhole of a town I had landed in. In order to keep the rain off my brain I donned a black leather fedora atop my crown and walked into the cold drizzle that quickly soaked my shoulders and back.

There was nothin' much around. A few closed businesses, some empty row houses, a burned out grocery store, and an unkempt police station with the word "pigs" spray-painted on the front in bright red.

As I walked a strange vision began to appear before my eyes, or perhaps I should say, within my eyes. They were multicolored arrowheads that looked like neon lights that moved in a square pattern around the center of my field of vision. As I walked they became brighter until my vision was almost obscured.

I rubbed my eyes but that seemed to only make it worse. I leaned against a mailbox and closed my eyes. The glowing arrows continued to dance in the darkness of my mind.

Now soaked from head to toe, I headed back towards the motel. The arrows seemed to be pasted over my eyesight. I could still see in the areas of my vision that were not covered by the arrows. It was very disorienting to try to navigate alien streets in this condition.

Back in the hotel room I stripped off the wet clothes and lay in the bed on my side, my body tense with fear of what might be happening to me. I ran the likely options through my head; was it a flashback from some long-ago LSD experience? Or perhaps a brain tumor that was putting pressure on an optic nerve? Or hopefully just the extreme effects of the eye strain from days of driving in the rain.

I laid down and waited for sleep to take me away from it all. I soon fell into a deep sleep that lasted until the morning sunlight began to seep in through the dirt-soaked curtains.

The next morning I awoke with my notebook lying in the bed by my head. In my handwriting were pages of strange poetry. Awaking to find that I had written during the night is not such an odd occurrence. I usually try to write from the unconscious and then afterwards attempt to decipher the meaning of what I have written. I find the unconscious mind is able to create work with more depth, able to intertwine many ideas and themes into a single complex.

Many artists say they believe they are just a vessel and their creative work comes from elsewhere. I don't have a clue about where it comes from. The unconscious mind is a place of mystery. A part of reality that is unknown to us.

As I contemplated the words I wrote I couldn't help thinking about my phone conversation with Brian back in Las Vegas. His reference to "That stuff that happened on Electric Avenue" brought up a whole can of worms that I was not quite sure how to face, and might be directly related to the poetry.

The events Brian spoke of changed my life forever, but also called into question the validity of my life ever since. Because of those events I have always lived with a nagging feeling in the back of my mind that I am living a lie, that my path is the path of a coward, and that perhaps I had been given not only a gift, but also a duty, both of which I shunned.

Even to this day those events on Electric Avenue have rarely been spoken of. In part because words are inadequate to describe what I experienced, and in part because every time I tried to speak of those things it turned out badly. It usually made people look at me as either a freak or a fool. Although on one occasion when I did speak of it to a long forgotten friend, and few minutes later I won ten thousand dollars in a government lottery. So who really knows?

I suppose by this point in the narrative I have related so many strange tales that it is futile to try to maintain any pretension of normalcy, so I will search for the words and memories to try to tell this tale as well.

When I was born my parents lived in a little cement-block house in a rural village called Alfarata. In some ways it was an idyllic setting. There were acres of land and a pine forest whose floor was covered with a bed of soft brown needles. A stream ran though the property and a little wooden bridge led to a pond that we used for ice-skating during the winter months.

I believe my parents took me to church a couple of times during my first years, but religion wasn't spoken of much in the house. I recall being mystified by the strange hymns we sang at the Christian Missionary Alliance Sunday school classes. Soon after I began asking my mother some uncomfortable questions.

"Where is God," I asked.

"He's everywhere," was my mother's unfathomable response.

"Where do we go when we die," I asked.

"To Heaven," she replied.

"Where's Heaven?" I asked.

A straightforward question deserving a straightforward answer it seemed to my child's mind, but my mother was stumped by that one. After that we didn't go back to church for years to come and I soon forgot about those questions that seemed so precarious to the adults.

My father had a philosophical bent that stimulated my thoughts while still a preschooler. I recall being in the back seat of the car and my father talking off the cuff to my mother, "If you think about where this all came from it doesn't make any sense."

My mother sat silent as he went on, "You might think the world all came from a speck of dust, but then where did that speck come from?"

He fell silent for a second before continuing. "If you think about it too much it'll drive ya nuts," he concluded.

With my child's mind I tried to follow the logic through for myself. Life was a mind-boggling mystery. It was clear even to a child. His musing laid the foundation for realizing an inherent truth about life's impenetrable mysteries. At a tender age some very hard facts of reality were made clear to me then and there.

When I was in grade school my folks made a few more halfhearted attempts at going to church. First we tried the Methodist church and then the Baptist. In the Sunday school classes I was completely confused. I had never even heard of this Jesus character everyone was getting so weepy about. It all struck me as a little creepy. My father always left the church services complaining about the hypocrites and soon the churchgoing again faded into the past.

Once in grade school a friend had a picture he had cut out of a newspaper that purported to be Jesus appearing in a cloud formation. (Personally I thought I spotted a pirate ship right next to him) The photo scared the heck out of me. For some time afterwards I thought of Jesus as being in the same pantheon as Dracula, Frankenstein, werewolves, and ghosts. The whole 'Holy Ghost' thing sounded a little scary to begin with.

Despite my lack of knowledge about Christianity as a child, during my teen years I somehow became quite interested in the religion. I took to reading the Bible, and in my 9th grade class photo I have a shiny gold crucifix around me neck. (Not to mention the shiny yellow silk disco shirt with dice on the front that I was also wearing!)

Like many young people I also had a fascination with all-things occult. I read books about witchcraft, possession, poltergeists, hauntings, ectoplasm, you name it. In my senior year of high school I attempted to read the Tibetan Book Of The Dead, but I was totally confused by it. I can recall laying it down and giving up on it while pondering death and heaven and immortality. None if it made sense.

Logically I couldn't see how it would be possible for there to be an afterlife. Christianity only provided fairy tale answers. For someone searching for empirical truth the Bible was a dead end. As far as I could see everything was a dead end. That nagging question I asked my mother as a three year old, "Where is heaven," still eluded me. And everyone who claimed to be authorities on these matters seemed as clueless as I was.

Although these thoughts made me uneasy, I also had a deeply held feeling that answers to these questions would be provided to me at the proper time. With that irrational but comforting thought, I was able to put the subject out of my mind for the time being.

When I got out of high school I began experimenting with LSD. In those days people believed psychedelic drugs were a means to find self-knowledge. And LSD certainly did make one think about the big questions in life. On my first LSD trip it seemed like all the answers were right there on the tip of my tongue. Right there for the taking if I could only put the pieces together.

Afterwards that feeling stuck with me. Soon after I went to the drive-in theater with my new girlfriend Leilani for a double feature of Quest For Fire and Altered States. Quest For Fire was an artsy caveman movie where grunts and moans were the only form of vocalization. We had my little dog Kiesha with us who was quite unnerved by all the grunts and growls, and spent most of the movie growling back at the speaker box that hung in the passenger side window of my old van.

The movie was funny in the way caveman films usually are. In one scene a nude Rae Dawn Chong teaches a member of a less enlightened tribe the joys of felatio and the missionary position.

The second film, Alerted States, concerned evolutionary information stored in the unconscious mind, a theme that somehow struck a chord with me. I had taken a couple yellow cross speeders I had stolen from my father's truck driver stash and the amphetamine buzz was vibrating my mind. As I watched the film I had a feeling that there was an answer to my questions hidden in that vibrating buzz. It was like a long lost memory I couldn't quite recall. My mind kept issuing a question, "What is it? What is it?" But I couldn't quite recall what "it" was.

On another occasion Leilani and I took a hit of acid and shacked up in a cheap motel room to party. The acid was giving me some nasty vibes and I tried to fight off a bad trip. I began to be haunted by an intense feeling of dread. We were watching Saturday Night Live and there was something behind the skits that was making this feeling of dread come on even harder.

Previously on LSD trips I had gone to parties and was troubled when listening to conversations. It seemed that everyone's ulterior motives were exposed. Their egos were laid bare. Every word they said revealed insecurities or the needs of vanity. It was like being a mind reader, yet what I saw was heartbreakingly pathetic. The thin mask we hide behind was gone. Perhaps all those years of reading books about psychiatry and human behavior was taking their toll. It was maddening though. Very hard to bear.

What I felt when watching Saturday Night Live in the motel room was similar, but even darker. It was a realization of an existential gloom that struck me to the core. A still unconscious, but emerging awareness that the premise of every comedy skit, and in fact nearly every word uttered by mankind, was based on animal needs. I was peeking into the nether regions of existence where animal instincts, animal desires, animal passions reigned supreme and ruled every word, every action, every thought.

It was the knowing of a dark vision, foretold by Dante, painted by Hindu monks of frightening masked demons, and used as a whipping stick by Baptist preachers and Catholic priests to scare their flocks into obedience. A dark vision where every living creature burns with never ending hunger, passion, lust, murder, violence, and fear of death.

Inside the vision the pretensions of civilization appeared a sad desperate farce, a top hat and three piece suit forced onto a monkey who puts up with the nonsense only because he knows a tasty banana treat will soon follow. And at the root of this existential dread is the fear that underlies all fears, the inevitable fact of animal existence: mortality.

Although the comedy skits were intended to be, and were seen by nearly all of humanity as lighthearted humor, in my morbid vision each reference emanated from the ego's desire to fulfill its animal needs, and that was a reminder that we are all nothing more than animals, each one fated to die. There is no other destiny. The fight for survival is ultimately a struggle of futility.

Although I can verbalize these things to you now, as they took place I did not understand. At the time these thoughts lay just below the surface of the unconscious.

During this period I would take LSD once every couple of months. During the next two trips I was inflicted with similar feelings of morbid dread. When the dreadful feelings would emerge I would try to push them away and put them out of my mind. But it seemed that they were always there, a shadow lurking in the background and waiting to envelope me.

In those days one didn't hear about eastern religions and new age philosophy in popular culture the way we do now. There were no Barnes & Nobles with shelves lined with new age books. Except for the occasional Hari Krishna member hocking pamphlets at the airport, few people in small town America had any contact with any religious view other than Christianity.

In the town where I grew up Christianity is all-powerful and mightily oppressive. Every street has a church on one corner and a bar room on the other. The wagging finger of Christian disapproval hangs ever overhead. Always there to remind us that we were not good enough, that we were outcasts, sinners, evil, bound for everlasting hellfire.

Once the mantle of Christianity becomes a tool for enforcing conformity, conformity is quickly taken to its most rigid extremes. Church-lady aesthetics soon rule the day. The wrong haircut, the wrong clothes, the wrong music, and you are condemned for eternity. Question any authority, be it political, religious, or local, and you are branded a godless atheist whose only hope is to be redeemed through the blood of the lord Jesus Christ.

The little old lady gossiping in the church basement and the drunken alcoholic who sits atop the barroom stool at 9AM are two sides of the same coin. Two extremes who *will* each other into existence. A pair of doppelgangers who depend on each other for their sense of self, whose self-image is defined by their relationship to the other. But the religious fanatic will never admit that their puritanism creates evil.

At the time I was experiencing a growing acceptance that Christianity wasn't working for me. Not just the Heaven and Hell fairy tale cosmology, but also the values held by the supposedly Christian culture that surrounded me.

The last trigger that I recall for what was to follow was a report on CNN that said a group of scientists made the claim that the Earth was a living organism. I suppose I didn't really think through what that meant, but it felt right to me. Thinking about it gave me a warm, bright feeling, as if better days were coming.

At the time I was living in a little three-room apartment on Electric Avenue in Lewistown, PA. At the time I was feeling very removed from the world. CNN had just debuted in our area and the non-stop images of violence hypnotized me. It overwhelmed me.

I was also smokin' a helluva lotta wacky weed and that enhanced my sense of existential nausea. I felt like a monk sitting atop a high mountain looking down on the chaos of human civilization with a heavy heart. The flurry of human activity appeared like a world of ants always in motion, but ultimately running in circles with no destination.

Even the music I was listening to helped infuse this sense of detachment. Usually the room was filled with the sounds of The Clash's Sandinista opus, Bob Marley's Natty Dread, or the Gang Of Four's Entertainment. It was in this state of spiritual malaise that the events on Electric Avenue occurred.

It was on a cold winter evening and Leilani and I were playing the board game Risk on the living room floor. As was often the case we were imbibing in psychotropic substances. The game

Risk has a board with the map of the world laid out upon it. The players have armies and roll dice to conquer each other's continents in hopes of ruling the world.

As I sat with the die in my hand, looking down on the world map, that feeling of existential dread began to confront me as it had during recent LSD experiences. I tried to force it away and concentrate on the game. It came to me as a wave that emanated from deep inside. This bad thought never quite clarified itself, yet hung over me like a menacing shadow.

Each wave was a little bit stronger than the last and a little bit harder to push away. On the third or fourth of these waves it happened. As simple as pie. It only lasted a fraction of a second, but inside that second was the path to my future, the key to my liberation and well-being, and although not recognized yet, the closest I would come to the answers that I was searching for.

It was like a little bubble had popped in my mind. Immediately the feeling of dread was shattered. What I actually saw in that instant is very hard to explain. Impossible to accurately describe.

The vision was a clear blue sky, and within it was a hazy white form. The form was a sort-of membrane, similar to how sperm or a single celled organism looks under a microscope. The form had a vaguely human shape, but not well defined. It was soft, puffy, and fragile looking. Inside the form its membrane substance twitched with life.

Then suddenly its head region popped open and all its inner membrane substance began to pour out of the open head region and flow into the surrounding blue sky. As this took place my perspective widened. As my vision pulled back and expanded it was revealed that there was a larger form that surrounded the smaller form. The smaller form was actually inside the larger form, and as the membrane substance of the smaller form flowed out it mixed in with the membrane substance of the larger form.

That was all there was to it. It was that simple and it happened in a flash. I didn't really know what to make of it. My first instinct was to just brush it off and ignore it. And I attempted to do just that.

"Three for Irkutsk," I announced.

We both rolled our dice and Leilani jutted out her lower lip in a mock pout as I took two of her game pieces off the board.

We went on like this, playing the game as if nothing had happened. I tried to ignore the strange vision, but in my head things were happening fast. The furniture was being rearranged. The crossbeams and the foundation blocks were being re-organized without my consent. The values and beliefs that my sense of reality was founded on were collapsing, the ground giving way underneath my feet.

Echoes of words from the past replayed themselves in my head. Now infused with new meaning. I recalled my mother's response to my childhood question, "Where is God?"

"God is everywhere." Perhaps her words held more truth than she ever imagined.

A revelation was emerging. Growing in clarity with each passing minute. The problem with religions for me had always been that the answers they provided to the big questions always existed in a spiritual world that bore no relationship with the physical universe we inhabit. Everything was magic. Everything invisible and incomprehensible.

Now thanks to the vision, there was a possible answer. Now the spiritual world had a place within the physical world. It had moved from the realm of myth and fantasy, into the world of theory. There may still be no way to know anything for sure, but at least there was logic to how it could be possible.

Previously the world was a jigsaw puzzle where none of the pieces fit together in a way that made any sense. Now it all fit. The big picture was coming into view. Ideas from every branch of science, human behavior, ancient religious dictums, the words of poets and artists, all were zooming through my head at a rapid fire pace. Each one another piece of the puzzle that now fit right into the big picture.

Suddenly it all made sense, and it was all overwhelmingly beautiful. Every leaf on every tree, every creature, the mystery of the nighttime sky, all the activities of humankind, including the greed, the ignorance, the wars, the violence, it all had its place and made sense. A symphony was playing all around us, and finally I could read the score, hear the melody, get in synch with the rhythm.

The thought occurred to me that perhaps I had gleaned secrets that humankind was forbidden to know, and the laws of nature might destine me to die before I could reveal them to anyone else. As I turned this frightening possibility in my mind the words of poets, lyricists, writers, pundits, and prophets echoed in my memory. They were words that I heard, yet never understood until now. Upon thinking about it, it seemed that actually there were others who knew these secrets and spoke of them in veiled references and mysterious abstractions.

Upon reflection it seemed to me that their words and their ideas had laid the groundwork for my moment of revelation. As if they had covertly seeded my mind with the raw materials and then waited for me to put together the pieces on my own. Suddenly it seemed like a secret conspiracy of the enlightened. Like many people believed during the 1960's, I imagined that the world was on the verge of a grand awakening. That an age of enlightenment was just around the corner, and those of us who were initiated into the mystery, who knew the secret, were duty bound to bring this awakening into fruition.

Stranger still, although Christianity as I knew it was a whole different ballgame, the quotes and teachings of the Bible itself, seemed to reflect the secrets revealed in the vision. "Could it be that Christians don't understand their own religion?" I asked myself.

As all of these mind-blowing thoughts were zooming through my head, Leilani and I continued our game of Risk. She was completely oblivious to the fact that I was becoming a different person right before her eyes.

I think we tend to underestimate how much religious explanations of the nature of reality affect our day-to-day life. These beliefs in life after death, heaven and hell, good and evil, and original sin and redemption, underlie everything we see, think, say, and believe. And now that entire belief system, my entire conception or reality was quickly crumbling. That in itself is a momentous event that few people ever experience, and all this was happening in the space of about twenty minutes.

Luckily the vacuum left by the destruction of my old conception of reality was quickly being replaced by the new vision. With each passing second more pieces fell into place, more evidence convinced me that this wasn't just a drug-induced madness. This unexpected transformation was unbelievable, overwhelming, enthralling. As the picture became clearer my excitement grew.

Finally I felt I needed to try to explain to Leilani what was taking place.

"Leilani, something happened to me, I need to talk to you about."

Still holding the dice in her hand she looked up at me innocently. Then seeing the seriousness in my expression she laid the dice down on the game board and with a trace of fear in her eyes asked, "What's going on? Are you OK?"

I tried to explain to her what had happened and what it all meant. We talked all night, approaching it from different angles, trying to make sense of it. By now I understood that my life was changed forever and I wanted more than anything for her to see the beauty of this new reality through my eyes. As we spoke my excitement infected her as well, helping me to believe that she was experiencing a moment of revelation as I was.

In some instances letting go of the old beliefs was scary and painful. I had grown up with a belief in love between two people as being something prescribed mystically from heaven. That belief provided a sense of security in a relationship in the same way that marriage does. Now that belief too, lay in ruins. In its place were freedom, possibilities, and liberation. But sometimes it takes awhile for the eyes to focus so one can appreciate the new possibilities that replace the security of tradition.

By early morning we managed to get a few hours of sleep. In the morning I awoke to a brand new world. I felt high, a higher high than any drug can give. I was filled with the spirit in the way a born-again Christian might feel.

I looked out the window and everything was raw. Everything was a mystery. I was awake to life as never before. My eyes were stretched wide open. I was in a permanent state of Satori.

I recall looking at the trees and they vibrated with life. Their twisted trunks looked succulent as flesh. The chaotic pattern of their limbs and branches, now bare of leaves in the winter chill, were a sight so exciting that it took my breath away.

When I walked outside the air seemed thick as liquid. I was ever-aware that the Earth's atmosphere was like a fish aquarium in which all of life swam.

We walked down to the McDonalds for lunch. As we stood in line waiting to order I gazed at the people as if they were zoo animals. They looked so solemn and serious. I knew I was living in a different world than they were, in a different reality. I was in their world. They were the majority, but I had checked out and was giddy with freedom.

The high school only had a half-day of classes that day and some of our friends were having a party that afternoon in a nearby house. Usually I loved parties, but now I just felt bored. The old things no longer interested me. It all seemed like diversions, ways to kill time. But I was infused with purpose. Life was filled with meaning and the possibilities were boundless.

I sat on the couch, Leilani beside me, thumbing through a magazine. As I looked around the room at my friends, all were drinking beer, smoking cigarettes, and passing around joints. It began to dawn on me that with this new liberation would come isolation. I was alone. I didn't have a clue who I could talk to about my experience, or who I could share my wonderful new reality with. This made my belief that Leilani could also see this vision as I did, even more important to me.

Over the next few months I kept my secret to myself. It was a strange feeling to have gone through such a profound change and to carry it quietly within myself when I really wanted to shout it out to the world. Although it seems awfully naïve looking back on it, I still imagined that only a few enlightened souls and I knew the secret.

Then one day Leilani presented me with a copy of the Tibetan Book Of The Dead she had shoplifted from the local library. The book had a forward written by Carl Jung. A few pages into the forward I realized he was writing about the secret. More than that, the secret was the basis for Hinduism, Buddhism, and Toaism, meaning that it might be known to billions of people around the globe.

Once I realized this, it began a period of intense study. I devoured ancient religious texts. Hungry for knowledge, elated that there were others who shared my vision of reality. In those days many of the texts were hard to come by. Some impossible to get. I would ask the public library to order books with Indian names I couldn't pronounce, but it was usually a fool's errand.

As I studied, although I was searching for truth, I found myself being pulled into the religious dogmas associated with the religions I was studying. Each religion has its myths and beliefs designed to appease the masses. When I freed myself from Christianity it was this aspect of the religion that I was glad to have discarded. Now I found myself getting tangled in the same aspects of Hinduism and Buddhism. Suddenly I was accepting reincarnation as easily as I might have once accepted heaven and hell.

Since the moment of the vision, the understanding of reality that had been imparted to me by family, friends, teachers, the media, and society had been destroyed. In the interim I was attempting to develop my own understanding of reality based on conscious analysis. To this end I was devouring books on every subject from physics to geology to history to classical literature. It seemed that all information I received now fit into a grand scheme, where once it was just more chaos in a meaningless void.

Now that I realized that the vision was related to eastern religions, my new conception of reality was attached to those religions. Although the books were hard to come by, I began reading the Baghavad Gita and the Vedas.

Unfortunately these ancient texts were intermingled with analysis provided by modern writers associated with organized religions such as the Hari Krishna. Usually there would be a paragraph of the original text followed by a paragraph of explanation from the modern writers. As I delved deeper into the books the amount of original text grew smaller and the amount of modern analysis grew longer.

Over the course of a few books these commentaries had
the effect of brainwashing me into buying their perception of
reality. In my search for truth my perception of reality programmed
during childhood had been destroyed and I was trying to rebuild a
reality based on logic and critical thought, but the brainwashing
from the text analysis was pasting a new fairy tale reality where the
void was unfilled. Soon I had traded a world of heaven and hell for
transmigration of souls and reincarnation. In my enthusiastic state
my critical guard was not as sharp as it should have been and the
search for truth suffered a setback.

What gave the original vision its strength was that it was a
simple and basic concept. It presented a way, it offered possibilities,
but it didn't define details. It didn't overreach. The mystery of life
was still left intact.

If we look at the history of our ancestors, if we imagine
what might have been at the dawn of humanity, it seems a few wise
men had developed a metaphysical conception of reality. But even a
hundred years ago most of the people in the world could not read
or write. Plus at the dawn of humanity people did not have the
basics of science to help them, and to understand metaphysical
concepts was beyond the ability of these tribal peoples.

We must also wonder when the ability to understand
concepts and abstractions became the tenant of every man and
woman. How did primitive people understand the concept of
things they could not see? Could they grasp the concept of a forest,
or a species, a germ vs. a disease? Or loftier ideas such as 'the
environment' or an 'ecosystem?'

I wonder how recently the word religion was invented.
People followed other gods, they might practice other rituals, but
did our primitive ancestors understand the concept of a 'religion?'
I do not believe the word religion appears in the Bible. And I don't
recall running into it in any other ancient texts either. Although
there is certainly references to groups who followed what we would
now refer to as other religions.

In early cultures gods were used to help people grasp
concepts. The Hindus seemed to not only have a deity for every
force of nature, but also deities to represent every imaginable
psychological tendency. Their knowledge of what we would now

call psychology as represented in their deities is astounding. They seemed to have mapped out every complex, every passion, every impulse known to humanity.

Because our ancient ancestors did not have the educational background to grasp the concept behind religious theories, the wise men and religious leaders tried to explain things to them with parables and childlike stories. If they ever did understand the ideas these stories represented, soon the original meanings were forgotten and the stories were believed as literal truth.

Although study of religious texts reveals that all religious systems seem to be originally based on a similar concept of reality, because each culture had different stories and different deities to represent and explain the concepts, they soon looked so differently that their common base was unrecognizable without close study.

Complicating things even more, human history reveals that the issue of power struggles between church and state are as old as human society. While the kings of Egypt were considered Gods on Earth, a Native American or African tribe might have both a chief and a medicine man. Essentially separate bases of power between church and state.

Either way the rulers of old had two forces with which to control the populations that they lorded over. The first was the military and police who controlled with violence. The second was the priests who used religion and religious dictums to control people.

While the stories that fill religious texts may have originated with the purpose of teaching people to understand the religious concepts, soon these stories were recreated with the goal of controlling the behavior of the population.

Perhaps in a sense the two goals have something in common. Human instinct propels people to think only of their own animal needs, or perhaps those of their immediate family units. And even training males to think of the needs of a family unit may not have been that quick in coming. Human development has been based on the process of widening the concepts by which individuals identify themselves.

Societies have bettered themselves as humans learned to work together as tribes, and then races and nations. All of these steps required the individual to forego the self centered instinctual desire for the good of the larger group, and to achieve this the individual has to be able to grasp the concept of this larger group, be it tribe, race or nation. We are still in the process of this struggle to develop past races, nations and religions, and conceive of ourselves as a single humanity, and even as one with the Earth and the universe. This struggle is the root of war and our challenges to save our environment.

Religion has been one of the greatest tools for this transformation from animalistic survival to our great societies. Unfortunately it now seems that religion is the next impediment we must transcend.

But because of the use of religious stories to control human behavior instead of to teach abstract spiritual concepts, the stories we have at our disposal seem even more confusing to those seeking truth.

It was in this quagmire that I found myself as I traded Christian stories and fables for Buddhist and Hindu stories and fables. As a result, I was moving away from the truth instead of closer.

It was during this phase of my journey that the notorious Brian Held entered the picture. At the time I had only known Brian for a few months. One evening Brian was visiting Leilani and I at my Electric Avenue apartment. Many months had passed since the vision, but I had not spoken to anyone about it except Leilani.

Brian sat on a chair at the far end of the living room and I sat on the floor with my back leaning against the couch.

"Do you have any interest in the occult?" I asked him.

His eyes sparked, "Yeah I love that kind of stuff!"

With that simple overture I spilled my guts. I told him the whole story. Not only telling him what happened, but endeavoring to explain the secret of the vision, plus all the bits and pieces of supporting evidence I had patched together from my studies in the months since.

I spoke like a madman visionary, like a deranged street preacher, I was filled with the spirit and all the pent up secrets I held enclosed in my bosom gushed out with an explosion. Throughout it all Brian sat on the edge of his chair, quiet but wide-eyed. Seemingly transfixed by my diatribe. After an hour or two I ran out of words and my sermon came to a close.

After a moment of silence, with a soft voice Brian said, "I want to thank you for everything. And I mean everything because I feel like you've just given me everything in life."

Early the next morning Brian knocked on the door. He explained that the previous night's conversation had changed his life and he couldn't get it out of his mind. It was a beautiful spring day and we stood on the front porch taking in the warmth. Life seemed kind and full of goodness and potential. Leilani joined us and we all just basked in the wonderful feelings we were sharing.

I felt higher than high. I felt that this was the beginning of an amazing journey. To know that I had been able to give something so positive to another person gave me a wonderful feeling.

I think many of us don't realize how good it feels to do something that helps another. We often go through life without ever really having the opportunity presented to us. But when one serves the greater good it gives your life meaning. As Brian thanked me for the gift I had given him, he was unaware of how much he had given me.

In the weeks that followed Brian, Leilani and I were inseparable. We lived in our own beautiful world. Often Brian and I spent time talking about the possibilities of human existence that the vision seemed to present.

On this point our experience has similarities of what people in the 1960's experienced. The 60's were a complex time with lots of ideas being thrown around, but there was an original group of beatnik mystics who started it all, and who had a vision and goal to completely transform society.

The ideal suggested by the vision was of completely letting go of the individual ego. While this ideal is beautiful in theory, (just listen to the words of John Lennon's song Imagine) but in practice it is almost impossible to bring into existence, and requires sacrifices that most of us would never consider possible. "Imagine no possessions, it's easy if you try," Lennon sang.

But imagine trying to get through a single day not thinking of your individual needs, and instead thinking of yourself as one with all of humanity in a literal way. And not just humanity, but literally one with all of life and the universe itself. It goes against all of our basic survival instincts.

In America our entire existence is based on the concept of personal possession of material objects. While letting go of that is easy to imagine, it's very hard to bring into reality. Let us imagine even further that we are asked to let go of our own bodies as a personal possession. What are the moral issues that this leads to?

In fact, just the manner in which we behave in our personal relationships if we were to leave ego behind requires a dramatic change in outlook. The first problem faced by the selfless person living in a society based on ego is that the selfless person is quickly trampled underfoot. When someone gives, people take. And will take and take as if it is their divine right without any thought of giving in return.

America is a land of great egos, of rugged individualism as an iconic ideal. Our economy is based on rampant materialism. On every man for himself in a struggle for survival of the fittest. Our sense of self worth is defined by how many possessions we can accumulate.

In America money is our true God. In a land of unchecked egotism the saint is devoured like a fast food burger. Christ himself would be trampled underfoot.

Throughout history we can find a few instances when cultures or sub-cultures have tried to live in this ideal to a greater or lesser extent. It is said that the highest order of Hindu priests in ancient India attempted to do so. To a lesser degree the modern Hari Kirshna do as well. And perhaps most monks, priests and ascetics do this to some degree, but most of these groups are cut off from the world and do not participate in working class family life.

The communists were working toward such an ideal in an economic sense, and we can see what a twisted mess that became. Then we can't forget the hippie communes, some who tried to share everything. Not just material possessions but also their own bodies with the community. A very complicated business. I am in no position to say all were failures, but at best it is not easy to learn to exist in that fashion. It requires perfection from everyone, and that in itself is an impossible dream.

During those days these thoughts weighed on my mind. I began to search for a utopian ideal that I could base my future life on. After seeming to give Brian a gift of revelation, I was filled with the urge to share our secret with others. Brian began to deliver potential disciples to me so I could sermonize to them. Most of them thought I was a downright crazy, but a few connected at least to some degree with what I was saying.

Increasingly the situation became more cult-like and increasingly our little cult became something of a joke to those who weren't part of it. On one hand I felt a fervent sense of mission to share, but the problems of doing so were becoming distressing. I felt mocked, ostracized, and in over my head as far as building any kind of organization to communicate my message. Each day things got weirder and weirder.

Then one evening Brian, Leilani and I were driving Friction's equipment van to a concert out of town. Somewhere during the conversation Brain referred to me as some kind of Jesus-like teacher. Those words brought a sick feeling to my stomach. I was twenty years old and certainly not qualified to take on that kind of responsibility.

Before the concert a group of Christians came to protest. I went out and argued my vision against their beliefs. I was so taken by the spirit that I didn't notice that most of my closest friends were standing watching the emotional exchange. Any hope I had of concealing my secrets were lost then and there.

The material world is made up of equal parts light and dark. All the good feelings I was experiencing soon began to reveal a dark side. The morning after the battle with the Christians Leilani and I drove into the mountains to relax beside a quiet stream at a state park. As we sat soaking up the sun and enjoying the nature we shared the tail end of a joint left over the previous night. The drugs seemed to trigger something in me. The bright light that had been filling my life since the night of the vision suddenly went dark.

The secret of the vision was empowering. It made one feel anything was possible and that one had the ability to achieve the extraordinary. Now I saw how that power could be used for evil and greed.

Trying to conceal a note of panic in my voice I asked Leilani to take a walk with me. Once again things were happening fast in my head. I experienced having my belief system destroyed on the night of the vision, to having a new one built on the mythologies of the Eastern religions, and now suddenly that new understanding of reality was collapsing before my eyes in a minute's time. In that moment I realized how I had been suckered in by the new dogmas I was encountering. I felt like a fool. I felt confused and deceived. Losing one's understanding of reality once is a dramatic experience, but to do so twice in a year's time was traumatic. My grip on reality was so tenuous that I didn't know what to believe or who to trust. My feeling that the ground was giving way below my feet was made worse by the embarrassment I felt at my pretensions of being a spiritual teacher. Who was I to teach anyone? The arrogance of my pretensions made me feel positively ashamed. I was laughable. A joke.

From that day my confidence was gone and I felt afraid and confused. I grew very quiet and spoke to no one about the vision anymore. Not even Brian and Leilani. I felt sick that I had lost the beautiful ideas from the Eastern mythologies. What was left? Only something dark and hopeless.

But as weeks passed I began to see something else. I began to see that it was good that the bullshit and the brainwashing and the fairy tales had been stripped away from the original vision, and what was left afterwards still seemed as potent and beautiful as ever when I looked right at it. Now I felt like I could pursue truth with a sharper sense of critical thinking. Now I would question everything with an eagle's eye, set on dividing the terrains of faith and fact with a razor sharp precision.

As I continued to ponder the issue of defining a utopian social order to pursue, I began to lean increasingly towards socialism and communism. At the time I so hated the U.S. government that I was ready to take up armed revolution against the power's that be.

Then one day my friend Jon Mertz gave me a copy of Aldeus Huxley's Brave New World. In that book the ideal of a social order based on submerging one's personal ego into the whole, was portrayed with ugly results. It presented the idea that in order for such a social order to exist all people must conform and behave in a prescribed manner, and the only way to achieve that is through the creation of a totalitarian state.

This pretty much knocked the communism right outta me, but still I searched for an ideal to replace it. As I continued to devour the ancient sacred text, as well as books on science, sociology, and history, something new began to come into focus. I couldn't quite grasp it in my mind, but something was coming and I felt frightened by it.

Slowly it began to appear, like a ghost, like the phantom of death itself. Again I was beginning to peer behind the curtain. But this time it was a slow gaze, a mysterious vision behind the vision. One that lay underneath the fabric of the world that was before my eyes.

All of the material world is energy. The ground below our feet, even our own flesh and blood. As strange as it seems, everything material is in fact energy. Stranger still, it is ninety-nine percent empty space. It might seem solid enough that we can bang our heads against a wall, but it is still as empty as the cosmos.

The mystery of our world is how we see it. We grow up thinking that what we see before our eyes, is reality, and that's all there is to it. "Seeing is believing," they say.

Even though radio waves, telephone conversations, wireless internet, and TV signals flow all around us and deliver tangible results in the form of visual images, voices in our ears, and pictures and sounds on our computers. Still people cling to the belief that what we perceive is reality.

In fact, what we perceive is purely based on the tools we are given with which to perceive the world: our eyes, ears, tongue and nerve endings. Many animals see the world in a totally different way.

Dogs see in black and white. Bees see infrared. Yet it's the very same world. If two living creatures can perceive the same world in completely different ways we must ask ourselves what is the true reality. Is there an absolute reality we can hang our hats on?

Our perception of reality is also undermined by the complications of time and space. Video raised to high speeds or slowed down can reveal reality in a different light. A tree over a number of seasons might appear as an exploding creature in constant motion. The movement of the stars and planets become a surreal painting composed of smears and streaks of light. A water drop slowed down becomes a slowly blooming flower. And a nuclear explosion slowed down reveals a beautiful universe in creation.

Why is perception so seemingly haphazard? The energy field that makes up our reality is a continuum. Our senses give us the ability to perceive certain segments of the energy spectrum. We can see some light. Other wavelengths appear as black. But we cannot see infrared light or ultraviolet light, any more than we can hear super high or super low sounds which might be perceived by dogs or whales on each end of the audible scale. Further we cannot pickup the radio or television signal and simply play them in our heads. We don't have the right circuits for it.

The question all this leads to is "what would the world look like if we could perceive the entire energy spectrum?"

There is something called "white noise" that is a sort of chaotic hiss. If you layer any random sounds on top of each other eventually you will always end up with white noise. White noise can be heard as a cacophonous din. But it can also be the sound of ocean waves lapping against the shore, or the oceanic purr that an unborn baby hears in the womb.

Likewise if colored lights are layered upon each other you always end up with white light.

One might ask, what is the purest form of energy we can see? Perhaps lightning? Or maybe the sparks of electricity? Or perhaps the fires of the sun and stars?

It is interesting that we all clearly understand that if we are in a room that is completely dark we will see absolutely nothing.

What we don't usually consider is that if one is in a place bathed in white light without shadow you are just as blind.

This new vision that was emerging in my mind and which gave me a feeling of unease, perhaps even dread, was based around one question; "If we had the ability to perceive the entire spectrum of energy, would we be able to perceive anything at all?" Could we differentiate anything at all, or would it all fade into a singularity?

Would existence simply be a hum of consciousness without thought, without action, without change? Simply a flow without anywhere to go and with no beginning or end, but which basks in the glow of life in its purest form?

This thought seemed frightening and depressing. I felt that I was getting closer to viewing a secret of the nature of reality, but my mental state was frail. After having my entire conception of reality destroyed twice in one year, after the high highs and the low lows, after pushing my intellect as hard and far as I could for many, many months, I was reaching the limits that my mind could handle.

My confidence was laid low as far as speaking about my vision. I felt cynical and mistrustful of all teachers, leaders, gurus, priests, prophets, or politicians. I had overdosed on modern life. It seemed that what I needed was to drop out of the world for awhile.

Leilani found an old house hidden deep in the Appalachian forest. It was nestled in a little valley between two mountain ridges. A stream flowed through the front yard, which was shaded by a large dogwood tree whose pink petals filled the area with color and aroma each spring. On the old wooden gate that guarded the dirt road that led to the house hung an old hand painted sign that read "God's Acres."

In the beginning Leilani and I shared the house with Brian and another member of our little cult. Looking back this could have been the moment when we could have made an attempt to create our own egoless commune, but I couldn't have been further from that place. I didn't even take the first step. I was too turned inward, lost in introspection.

An egoless existence requires letting go, and letting go requires confidence. A man who is as shell-shocked as I was, clings to his possessions, he builds a self-protective wall of security around himself. I was going in the opposite direction of where I needed to be.

With Leilani the only woman in the house I began to be taken by jealousy. As young as we all were, we were not mature enough to create a new and complex living arrangement, and I lacked the wisdom and leadership skills to guide our little commune.

Within months it had fallen apart with angry disagreements. When it was all over it was just Leilani and I alone in the house. We didn't have a cent to our name. We lived without TV, telephone, hot water, and barely enough heat to keep the pipes from freezing during the winter months.

We learned to survive on the bare minimum. We brushed out teeth with baking soda. We had about a dozen chickens so we had fresh eggs to eat each morning. Leilani learned to make food from scratch, and when things got really bad we lived on Kraft macaroni and cheese that went for twenty-five cents a box in those days.

Despite the financial struggles it was a wonderful existence that allowed me to heal and digest all that had happened to me in the past year. In the summer months we bathed in the cool waters of the stream after sunbathing on the softly rolling hills that made up the two acres of the yard.

During the winter pristine snows covered the land. I began each morning by collecting the eggs and feeding the chickens, chopping the day's firewood, and starting the fire in the small stove that only managed to heat a few rooms of the large house. We heated pans of water on the fireplace and took sponge-baths in front of the roaring fire. On winter nights the ice and snow tapped a soothing rhythm on the window whose glass was fogged by the heat inside, while Leilani and I made love on the couch that sat across from the fireplace.

Although I no longer spoke of the vision and the events that followed, it never left my mind. I was still searching for truth, trying to put the pieces together. In the two years that I lived in the forest I devoured great texts: War & Peace, The Golden Bough, The Origin Of Species, The Collected Works Of Plato, Freud, and great tombs on every field of science, history, and religion.

As my mind settled amid these peaceful surroundings, clarity returned to my understanding of the visions. The vision of the perception of energy no longer seemed depressing. Now it seemed perfect, simple, sublime, and full of potential. Like the original vision, its simplicity was its strength. It provided a base for understanding, but did not try to define every detail of existence. It didn't claim to answer every question, but offered a concept that all the evidence in all my studies seemed to confirm.

After all the upheavals, after all the changes and confusion, I was now developing a core of inner peace. On the surface I might be taken by the turmoil of day-to-day life, but at the very center of my being was a place of calm, strength, and serenity.

My study of the perception of energy left me with one word that stuck in my head: "chaos." Chaos as Heaven. Chaos as a spiritual primal bath. Chaos as freedom and potential. Chaos as soothing and calm. Chaos as the primordial source of all creativity and creation. Chaos even provided a bit of an answer to my search for a utopian ideal.

Reading Brave New World helped me to see that the fundamental flaw in socialism and communism is that it requires totalitarianism to force egoless action from the population. But if freedom must be sacrificed it is no ideal that I can believe in.

What social order could provide freedom? It seemed to me in general that the less government the better. Government seemed like a necessary evil at best. The less government the more anarchy, the more chaos, the more freedom.

In the end my search came full circle to free market democracy. While democracy hardly provided values that promoted an egoless existence, it did provide enough freedom that people can choose to live in a wide variety of lifestyles. If one wanted to live on a commune it was possible. If one chose to live a materialistic lifestyle that could certainly be done as well. As much as it might be possible while living under a large government, anything goes in the US. The biggest roadblocks to freedom actually comes from the puritan values of society itself.

And given how impossible it is to live an egoless existence, it seems important to consider the issue in degrees. At the very least the idea could temper the tendency towards unchecked greed and materialism. It is up to each man and woman to make their own choices on these matters. And in the end it would be a battle for the hearts of minds of each individual.

On one side of this battle are the corporations, the government, the retailers, advertising agencies, and the bulk of the entertainment industry, all of who actively promote materialism as the highest good.

On the other side are a few spiritual leaders and a smattering of artists and social critics who struggle to get their voices heard.

Unfortunately with each passing year the promoters of greed have more successfully brainwashed the population until most people cannot imagine that any other way of life could be of any value. Even as the materialistic values lead to social decline, violence, war, poverty, self-destructive drug abuse and sexual practices, nihilism and hedonism.

My time in the forests of God's Acres lasted two years. Although I was constantly studying and learning with the vision ever in my mind, it was now something completely private. The sense of duty I once felt to share the revelation was now hidden. I had turned away from the mission. At my young age I lacked the wisdom and experience, as well as the courage and willpower.

One thing I grew to understand is that a revelation cannot be taught with words or it loses the power of its meaning. It must be experienced from within. Each person must experience their own revelation for it to have visceral meaning for them. A teacher can lead them, can give them hints, but in the end the student must put the pieces together for themselves.

These days there are bookstores full of new age spiritual books that try to teach these things with words as dead and soulless as a high school textbook. In America McBuddhism is a trendy thing to explore in classes lead by enlightened hucksters who try to teach the inexpressible with dry intellectualism. In the end these teachers usually stand in the way of the student's ability to reach enlightenment on their own. In fact they may be stealing the possibility of personal revelation away from them.

The teachers of old in the eastern traditions took a very different approach with their students. A student could expect years of discipline before finding revelation, and it was never handed to them. One school in Japan gave the students the task of answering a riddle that ultimately had no answer. After a dozen years of pondering this conundrum a few might find revelation in their unattainable struggle.

A Chinese teacher would club his student with a large stick every time his back was turned. After many years the student learned to sense when he was about to be struck and avoid the blows. After many more years one blow landed and with it came revelation. Other ancient schools demanded years of deprivation, menial servitude, meditation and quiet contemplation, and then maybe, a lucky few might reach the goal.

Although the revelation has a logical dimension that can be understood scientifically, it cannot be truly understood with the intellect alone. It must be felt within the soul, it must be an electric shock to every cell of one's being. It can only come to those who want it more than anything, who crave it from the depth of their being and will sacrifice all to receive it. This is why even as I tell this story I have held back from trying to share the secrets of the vision. I feel I would do more harm than good in doing so.

One might ask why was this vision was handed to me so easily? It is a question I have asked myself for twenty years and I have no answer. It was a blessing given without asking, handed to me on a silver platter.

Along with the realization that the vision could not be taught with words, came a further sense of isolation. I wanted more than anything to share the beautiful world I inhabited with those closest to me, but as time passed it became clear that even Leilani did not share this world with me. I came to realize that no two people can ever perceive reality in exactly the same way, and we all live isolated in our own little universes.

This was a bitter and chilling fact for me to accept, and it made me turn inward even more. I learned to accept that a gulf existed between my self and all those around me. Living a life where you cannot share those things that are most important to you, makes you cold inside.

Since my outlook on reality differed so much from all those in the society I lived in, I felt as if I had to live a lie. I had to live within their world and keep my own views secret in order to get along.

Years passed. Ten years passed. In those years I had lived life as a regular working man. I had accumulated lots of material possessions; a house, a business, friends, but when it was all said and done I was lost inside. My life was a lie. My tongue was so frozen I didn't have a clue how to speak of my secret world.

Then one day I met a woman. We were friends, we were in love, but we were never lovers. Instantly we shared something deeper than I had ever experienced. She made me believe that it was possible to share those spiritual depths with another and be united within those depths.

After that the life I was living was doomed. I tried to continue but it was hopeless to continue living a lie once I had seen the possibility of living a dream. A dream that I thought impossible.

Within two hellish years from that time I had destroyed everything. Lost all my possession, ended my relationship with Leilani, cut many personal ties, and would eventually end up broken and destitute, but at least I was free.

When I arrived in New York City with The Imperial Orgy I had just ended my affair with Sasha and I was exhausted, financially bankrupt, humiliated, physically and mentally ill, my dignity trampled into the ground. As horrible as it was I had enough clarity to see that I was free. In that moment the vision returned to me. Now was the time, I knew it in my heart. I searched for a way to begin, but felt at a loss. How does a single man imagine he can affect the world? Great men had done so before, but I just didn't seem to possess the wisdom and courage.

Soon I was again lost in the struggles of day-to-day to survival. And in those first years survival was not easy. Again my plan was to find success with The Imperial Orgy as a means to gain access to the media. But for all the artistic achievements we created in the years that passed, we could find no corporate sponsorship, and therefore no access to the media and a wider audience. Soon many years again had passed. And now I find myself here, ending a long trip to try to find direction, and still empty handed and empty headed. A grand failure as usual.

A light hidden under a basket. And with each passing year losing confidence in myself, and in the value of what I once believed I have to offer. Each day admitting defeat and losing hope that it is worth the struggle even to dream and believe.

#18 – The Highway Be Damned

The following day was filled with sunny skies and brisk autumn air. As I entered Pennsylvania I felt at home. Having seen a good bit of the terrain across America I now realized that the northeast is one of the most beautiful places in the country. Deep thick forests lined the highways as far as the eye could see. The land is shaped by rolling waves of mountains and valleys, all covered in green so lush you feel like lying down on it like a bed of clover.

It was still morning and I felt thankfully healthy after the previous night's troubles. By the end of the day I would be reaching the gates of New York City. By tonight I would be sleeping in my own bed. Only the specter of the terrorist attack marred my good feelings.

As I looked back on my journey it was wonderful to feel free and to see sights and sounds that were new to my senses, but I had found no answers, I had done little writing, and I still had no new scheme to redirect the course of my life. Life just went on. Perhaps one day, once I had time to digest it all I could find some worthwhile meaning in my journey. Perhaps I would understand that I learned more about America and its people than I realized.

I drove on route 80, passing by State College and Lewistown, my two homelands. As the afternoon began to fade I passed the Delaware Water Gap on the border of New Jersey, which greeted me with raw mountain cliffs that rose above the highway.

The closer I got to New York City the heavier traffic became. Even 50 miles from the city I could feel the energy level rise. The intensity can be felt in the air. As night began to fall, familiar sites began to appear. First the neon lights of the Marcel toilet paper factory, then the rows of flower shops, furniture stores, and the rows of aged industrial warehouses. Once over the George Washington Bridge I was now back in New York City. As glad as I was to leave, I was happy to be home, wounded or not, it was still home.

Driving down the West Side highway the traffic was frenetic as always. Yankee Stadium sat like a glowing coliseum on the opposite side of the river. I turned off the highway to drive through the heart of the city. The city looked the same as ever.

So far no signs of death and destruction. The restaurant lights beamed in every color, revelers sat at outdoor cafes, fancy store windows on the upper East Side kept their lights on all night so that we might drool and dream over their overpriced wares.

Times Square flashed madly, the streets crammed full, but in my heart it felt like lights on, but nobody home. The Virgin Megastore, The Hollywood Café, The Disney Store, it was all there, all intact, all still in motion.

In the East Village hipsters dressed in black paraded from club to club. Punks in Mohawks carried a look of "I told you so," carved into their faces. NYU chicks held each other's hair back as they vomited on street corners after a night of heavy drinking. The party went on, the city never slept before and it wasn't about to start sleeping now.

As I neared Chinatown a foul smell of smoke began to seep into my nostrils. It wasn't a pleasant aroma of a wood burning stove, but something poisonous that carried the stench of burning chemicals, plastics, and God only knows what else. I turned up Delancy and crossed the Williamsburg Bridge. I was now in

Williamsburg, Brooklyn, just a few miles from my home. Franklin Avenue took me on a path parallel to the East River. On the other side was lower Manhattan. The Brooklyn edge of the river is littered with the ruins of abandoned warehouses. As I drove along the river, in the gaps between the ruined warehouses, I could see the skyscrapers of the financial district. Then as I passed North Seventh Street a large gap allowed me to see the place where the Towers once stood. In that gaping hole a clutter of metal could be seen. It glowed with an eerie white light as the workers tried to haul away the rubble and put out the fires. The search for survivors had ended long ago. White smoke billowed into the sky in spirals that seemed to mock the great Towers that once stood in their place.

Looking at it was like looking at a dream. It still seemed impossible that they were gone. The pit of my stomach was heavy at the site, but I couldn't look away. The heaviness in my blood, brought on by the mourning, came back to me with full force.

After a few quick turns I was on Dupont Street driving down the block towards my apartment. I parked across the street and looked up at the house. Most of the apartments had American flags hung in their windows. The sight filled my chest with sorrow. My neighbors were highly liberal and the last people one would expect to be waving flags. Even the lesbian couple on the top floor had a paper flag taped into their window.

It was all too much. I slouched over the steering wheel and finally shed tears. Tears not just for the dead, but also for the living. For the love of one another, that even amid the toughness of NYC, lay right below the surface. Tears for the world that longed for peace and love, yet was wounded by never ending hate and violence. And tears for the past, because America had changed forever and would never be as innocent as before.

Once I regained my composure I carried my suitcase up the stairs, ignoring the mail that bulged out of the overflowing mailbox, and unlocked the door to my apartment. Except for my two cats Myshkin and Sparky, the place was dark and empty. Myshkin greeted me with purrs, but Sparky hid as if I was a dangerous stranger.

I plopped down on the bed, dropping my notebook from my left hand onto the edge of the bed. Every cell of my body felt tired. My limbs felt heavy. My body relaxed in a way it hadn't in many weeks. My mind put down its shield and began to expand. For tonight there were no thoughts to think. No roads to travel. No need to search for a safe place to sleep or a good place to eat. The open highways be damned, I was home.

I flicked on the tube and turned the volume down low. I didn't watch the screen that was filled with some inane sitcom, but the background noise soothed me. Sleep was coming on fast.

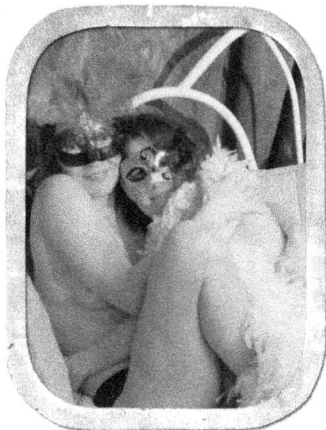

#19 - Caligula Was A Friend Of Mine

I had the weekend to rest before returning to work on Monday. When Monday came I took the L train from Brooklyn to Manhattan. The NR Train that I usually took downtown to City Hall, now only went as far as Chinatown. When I got out at the Canal Street stop everything changed. Suddenly I was in a war zone. The horrible smell of the fires greeted me as soon as I hit the streets. Below Canal Street military men with machine guns were positioned on street corners. The closer I walked towards ground zero the stronger the smell of the smoke became. With each step closer the smell of the poison made my stomach turn sour. Multiple times I was stopped by military personal who checked my driver's license and asked what my business was in the area.

Everyone was cordial, even somewhat gentle, but it was still chilling to see New York transformed into a military zone. As I closed in on City Hall I could see that it was barricaded like a military fortress. The park that I usually cut through in order to get to my job was now closed down. The fountains shut off, the gates locked tight.

The closer I got to ground zero the more surreal things became. A block from where the Towers once stood, the smell was enough to make one gag. Many people walked the streets with gas masks covering their faces. I entered the building where I worked as a web designer for an electronics retailer and made my way to my 4th floor office. I always arrived early and no one was around. When I entered my office I realized that I had left my window open and it faced the Towers. The dust from the destruction covered my office. The gray powder coated the computers and video editing equipment. In some places it was an inch thick.

I sat down at my desk and looked at the dust. This dust was once the Towers. Now the mighty edifices were reduced to mist. Life is fragile. Our existence depends on an amazing amount of trust and goodwill when one realizes that a few individuals can create so much destruction.

To my amazement my computer turned on and seemed to be working fine. Most of the workers in the web group spent the day having a spontaneous group therapy session. One of our co-workers had come out of the Towers just as the jet hit. Glass rained down on her head and bodies fell around her as she ran away. She was so traumatized she couldn't return to work. Another co-worker's wife worked in the Towers. Luckily she spent the day stuck in the subway, but he spent the day believing she was killed in the collapse. The stress caused him to have a breakdown. He didn't leave his house for months after. He was especially troubled by clear sunny days like that on 9/11.

Each worker had their own horror story. Most ran from the dust cloud when the first Tower fell. Most had to make long walks to Brooklyn and Queens like groups of refugees fleeing a war zone. Even the strongest men seemed to have tears just below the surface that threatened to well up at the slightest provocation.

Going out to lunch the first day was a heartbreaking experience. In addition to the Towers, many of the surrounding buildings were burned out facades. Already little old Asian ladies were selling pins with American flags and postcards of the Towers along the streets. At the fence across the street a makeshift memorial grew larger each day: photos of lost loved ones, poetry, children's drawings, prayers, well wishes and encouragement in every language. Even the most hardboiled heart would melt before these outpourings of emotion.

Along the streets hand written signs with photocopied photos were posted on telephone poles and in shop windows by people searching for their missing loved ones. Hoping against all odds that they were alive but couldn't remember their way home. In every direction everything you saw was heart wrenching.

On Broadway down by Wall Street there is a strange hoity-toity McDonalds that has a hostess, a gift shop, and a piano player who serenades customers with soft music during the lunch hours. I sat on the second floor eating food that I couldn't taste. While the piano player played in a black tuxedo on a small platform in the front window, behind him the ruins of a burned out hotel mocked the serene and civilized proceedings.

After eating I walked down Broadway and stopped in the middle of a side street that lead to where the Towers once stood. The vision before me was mind-boggling. The twisted pile of rubble billowed a pillar of smoke that covered the debris with a ghostly haze. Some of the beams of the structure still stood upright, giving the unmistakable appearance of a piece of primitive sculpture left over from some ancient religious site. In the chaos of the ever-moving crowds one could never stand still long enough to really take it in, yet it was always there to catch a glimpse of as one walked the streets.

As I headed back to my office I noticed written in the dust on one of the building's windows were the words, "I love New York more than ever." Although I had made my first excursion into the war zone without losing my composure, these words written by an anonymous finger in the dust that was once the great Towers, was more than I could handle.

The next morning there was a flurry of excitement outside our building. It seems a young woman had bought a copy of the Koran in order to learn more about the people who attacked our city. While in the neighborhood on business she went into a porta-john that was set up for the many workers at ground zero. When she came out of the toilet she found herself surrounded by police and special agents all with guns drawn and pointed at her. It seemed they saw the Koran she was carrying and thought she might be a terrorist plotting to blow herself up....in a porta-potty!

The next afternoon when I returned home from work the small park near my apartment was surrounded by police and fire trucks. The area was blocked off and uniformed men were running in all directions. It turned out there was an old white van that was parked for a couple of days and someone got it into their head that it was an abandoned vehicle that was likely filled with explosives. Of course, it was all nonsense, but the paranoia was running high. Fear was everywhere.

A few days after my return a plane exploded over Queens. Everyone assumed it was more terrorism. It gave one a sinking feeling as if we would be living with irrational violence for evermore. It turned out the plane had a mechanical malfunction, but that information didn't make anyone feel much better. Our hearts, our culture, were now poisoned with fear. The terror had worked its magic.

During the afternoon of my fifth day at work, a week of breathing the poisoned air got to me. In the afternoon my lungs started to burn. I grew dizzy and nauseous. I tried to be a good employee and tough it out, but after a half an hour it got to be too much. I stood up and walked out the door and kept walking uptown until the air began to clear.

Working at ground zero was creepy even on a good day. The knowledge was always with me that thousands of my neighbors had died a few hundred feet away from where I sat. As I was trying to help my bosses hock overpriced VCRs and computer software, we tried to act as if nothing had happened. Meanwhile the weight of the spirits of the dead hung heavily in the air.

The fire burned for many, many months. We breathed in the poisoned air as if it were as natural as a country breeze. One day the news would report that the government agencies said that the air was completely safe. A few days later reports would warn that the air was filled with dangerous toxins, and that the particles we were breathing in included human bone fragments. We never really found out what chemicals were in the air during those days, but all you had to do was take a whiff of it to know it was something bad.

Walking those streets lined with burned out buildings had a psychological affect that undermined one's spirit. Depression set in for all. The country was getting uglier as we prepared for war, uglier as politicians and religious leaders exploited the fear to promote their agendas, uglier as we all bowed down like children wishing for some authority figure to protect us and make it all better.

When the anthrax scare came the fear gripped everyone. Letters were being sent to New Yorkers. Now we even had to fear that our own mail might kill us. Often I would eat lunch at a Burger King in a basement on Broadway. The Burger King had banks of video screens all over the dining area and all were tuned to CNN. I would try to force down the cheap burgers and onion rings while the details of every anthrax attack rung in my ears. It really was terror. You felt like it was all around you. You felt it in your heart.

I can never explain the psychological affect all this had, but it undercut everything. What mattered before, now seemed trifling under our new circumstances.

Every day there would be a color based terror alert. Green was the lowest and red was the highest. You might wake up and hear there was an orange level terror alert that day, but there was really nothing you could do to fight it or even protect yourself. All that it did was cause more fear. Soon every time the president got some bad press there seemed to be a terror alert that would divert the public's attention.

After two months of living like this a deep despair began to take me. Soon I fell ill. As did many New Yorkers. It was a form of flu that no one could seem to shake. I couldn't afford to take off enough work to really get better. I made many trips to the doctors who said there was little that they could do, but mentioned that my lung capacity had been negatively affected by the poisoned air.

By the Christmas holidays I was losing hope that I would ever get well. I spent days on end lying on the couch sedated by NyQuil. I could do little more than watch TV. I watched endless reruns of Law and Order that seemed to be playing on some channel at almost any hour of the day. At one point TBS had a 24-hour Law & Order marathon. The TV must have stayed on for most of those 24 for hours, but I was falling in and out of consciousness. The police dramas merged with my dreams. Death, murder, retribution, sleep and life were merging into a single blur. Often I found myself taken by half conscious fantasies of personally killing Osama Bin Laden.

I had a sense that I was losing the battle for life. The despair, the hopelessness were the real killers, whatever virus had invaded me was just the weapon that the real enemies were using to destroy me.

My hopelessness was deepened by a sense of despair in my personal life. I came to New York full of dreams and had achieved many amazing things, but I was never really able to achieve the level of success I was shooting for. The Imperial Orgy had been performing monthly concerts in New York City but it seemed to be getting us nowhere. If anything it was just wearing us down. I had lost my sense of vision, lost my sense of mission. I felt ordinary and mediocre, and a man who sees himself as mediocre can never achieve the extraordinary.

I had hoped that my trip across America would help me find my sense of purpose, but now I was more confused than ever. My will to fight was lost. As a child, rock and roll was more than just music. It meant freedom, it meant creativity, it stood for equality and social justice. Rock and roll was a philosophy, a lifestyle, a force for social change and an artform that could fight the corrupt powers of authority, deliver spiritual enlightenment, and transform the world.

I viewed my work as a musician within that context. It fueled my drive to succeed. But now it seemed I had lost faith and lost the fire. For nearly ten years I had been bashing my head against the wall and making little headway. We were exhausted and broke from paying dues playing small clubs and bars. Anyone in the right mind would have given up years ago.

Our last gig was a disaster. It was at a little club called Acme Underground. Just before we went on stage the sound-man told us we could only play for 30 minutes. I had to argue in order to do our planned 45-minute set. As we began playing the audience stood 20 feet back from the stage. They looked as if they were at a tea party instead of a rock concert. Their mugs wore an expression of polite apathy. Within that expression was written the fact that music didn't matter. Rock and roll has been reduced to safe entertainment. The culture no longer saw it as vital, revolutionary, transformative. I might as well have been Lawrence Welk blowing soap-bubbles out of my ass.

It was unacceptable. It filled me with rage. I had to do something to stand up for myself as an artist, to stand up for rock and roll as an artform. I stopped the band mid-song. Instead of going into the next song I paced around the stage rubbing my forehead in indecision. Finally, I said "I have to apologize, I'm having an attitude problem tonight. I didn't get my Thorazine, I guess." Then I yelled "I wanna be your dog," which is a cue for our drummer to break into the opening roll of the Iggy Pop cover by the same name.

I jumped off the stage and ran full steam toward the crowd at the back of the room and fell on my back. Pushing myself forward with my legs I slid across the floor grabbing people's legs trying to get them to fall. I got onto my knees and began humping some guy's leg like a dog in heat. He pushed me down and came at me with both fists clenched. I dared him to go further. I yelled "Violence, violence, we've got violence!" and pushed the mic into his face so the audience could hear his reaction.

The exchange went on for so long it became absurd. He shook with anger and seemed barely able to restrain himself. I got up from the floor and he took a fighting stance in front of me. I looked into his eyes and said "Rock and roll, brother." With this, he seemed to finally grasp that I was playing with him for the crowd's entertainment. He broke into a smile then quickly tried to hide it. I yelled, "We've got a smile" giving away the farce.

I jumped on top of the bar and ran the length of it before falling backwards behind it. All the while I cursed and chided the audience. Daring them to react. To hate me. To feel anything. To feel some passion other than apathy.

"Can't you people at least tell me to fuck off?" I screamed. "Here you go, tell me to fuck off….one, two, three," I pointed the mic at the crowd as a few of them shouted "fuck you!" But most just looked confused. Maybe a little scared. They had no understanding that this itself was a punk ritual, that attacking the crowd in order to get them to lose their inhibitions has a long history dating back to Iggy & The Stooges and up through the New York Dolls, the Sex Pistols and on from there.

"What's wrong? Do you need music that is safer?" I mocked. I instructed the band to begin playing traditional Christmas carols over the grinding rock rhythm. As the melody of Jingle Bells filled the room I asked, "Is that better, it that cheesy enough for you? If you want sanitized entertainment the Disney Store is on 43rd Street."

I have to admit that such an experience is exhilarating. The spontaneity of not knowing what I will do next, let alone what the audience will do in reaction, is a blast. And to be on the edge of violence makes one feel alive. It undoes, just a little bit, the soul-death I feel each day chained to the computer screen at my money job.

When I antagonize the audience, it is always funny to me that people don't get it. New York is the birthplace of Punk rock and has a long history of legendary artists that antagonized the audience for the sake of creating a rock and roll experience. Hell, we were playing an Iggy Pop cover - how obvious must we be? And yet, people are confused, shocked and offended.

But I guess I should just be thankful for these perverse thrills. There was a time when men could be hunters, warriors, or conquerors of new lands. I know I would rather be pillaging and plundering than to be one of the eunuchs we have become in modern America. It is so rare to have any experience that makes one feel alive and vital. I feel the violence of men. And I know it is something that can be used as a doorway to a group experience of numinosity. To quote Johnny Rotten, "Anger is an energy!"

Thank God for the resistance of those that don't get it, because without them it wouldn't be impossible. People are numb. They are so brainwashed by sanitized music that they forget rock and roll can really say something. If it doesn't move people then what good is it? We crossed the audience/performer barrier to give them living theater. Rock and roll is the art of the shaman. It's our job to go as far as it takes to reach people, even if it means humiliating or endangering ourselves.

After that night I decided I didn't want to play the New York City club scene anymore. We needed to take it to another level. I needed to go beyond myself so I didn't feel so mediocre. I needed to break the status quo. But what to do? I had no idea. It was all dispiriting, and here I was now lying on the couch after months of being ill, and with nothing to inspire me to want to live.

I knew in my heart if I was going to beat this slow death I must find a sense of purpose. I needed to surpass myself and achieve something that was beyond my means, beyond what seemed possible.

The clubs that we were performing in were not suited to our technical needs. Most clubs had five bands a night and gave the bands ten minutes to plug in their guitars and then forty-five minutes to perform their sets of music. For The Imperial Orgy to set up a ten-piece band with video projection, theatrical props, and lots of high-tech gear in a few minutes was impossible. And to try to present the full range of our music in forty-five minutes did not tell the whole story of what The Imperial Orgy is all about.

Although we were playing a lot of shows it always seemed like we were compromising the original concept. To simplify things we often skipped the video show, I had quit playing keyboards and guitar to save set-up time and stage space, and the short sets meant we had to come out and win the audience and get them on their feet in a few minutes. There was little time to expand into more experimental and darker territory. It seemed like I was losing my way in every direction. We were spinning our wheels and ultimately making no progress.

What I wanted was to play a good room with a large stage. Someplace that would put us on a higher level. Finally an idea started brewing in my mind. All of New York was ailing. Businesses were closing at a record rate. Unemployment was rising and even for skilled professionals it was impossible to find work. The entire country was becoming more conservative. The liberals had grown quiet. New York, always a place to celebrate freedom, individuality, and libertinism, was in no mood to celebrate.

It seemed to me a celebration was exactly what was needed. I got it into my mind to host a big party, a giant party, a gargantuan party! An erotic masquerade ball were all the freaks could come out and play. A party where all the cults and cliques could come together and celebrate as one, and a party where the novice, the curious, and those who were longing to explore could also come and expand the boundaries of their life experiences. It would be a celebration of sensuality! A true Imperial Orgy.

The Imperial Orgy had a gig in our hometown of State College, Pa. in a few weeks. If the show were to go on I would have to regain my health by then. My plan was that the day after the gig I would begin work on the Erotic Masquerade Ball.

The idea seemed to give me hope. I began to slowly recover. The tail end of the illness held on, but by the first band rehearsal for the State College gig it seemed to come to an end. Bless the Lord, I was healed!

The day after the gig I began working on my plan. After a little research I decided I would hold the party at Webster Hall. Webster Hall is a one of the largest clubs in the world. The four-story venue has a long history dating back the early days of the East Village where it was the scene of the first free love parties in the 1920s. Over the years the stage has been graced by everyone from Elvis Presley to Frank Sinatra, and including Prince, Sting, Frank Zappa, Tina Turner, Madonna, your name it, they've likely performed there.

I figured I would need about $30,000 to pay for the party. I had about $17 in my bank account. I knew no one with any money. I had no access to credit. To say the least, the odds were against me. But that was exactly what I wanted. I wanted to achieve something that seemed impossible. I wanted to prove to myself that I could break through the chains of my limitations. I need to believe I could achieve the extraordinary.

I went to my closest friends in New York and told them what I planned to do. Their reaction was all the same; "It's impossible. You'll never pull it off." At first I was devastated by the lack of faith from those I thought believed in me, but then I made myself hard. It made me even more determined to achieve my goal.

I started racking my brain as to where to get the money. I laid out some very idealistic financial forecasts for the profits that could made from the event and posted them on a website.

First I went to a few of my oldest friends who I thought might have a few bucks stashed away. As is often the case in life, the people who really had some money were not willing to part with it. Those who had just a little came through. Although the amount I raised from friends only came to about $4,000.

Next I tried to find sponsors. I went to strip clubs, bondage stores, adult toy stores, and there are many of them in New York City, but I struck out every time. Next I tried to find another band to invest in the project. In this I succeeded in finding a gay artist from DC whose manager put up $5000 for the event.

Next I started on the corporations. It seemed that surely Trojan condoms might have an interest, but no go. Part of the problem was that I was doing it at such a bad time. The economy was in the gutter and the corporations were cutting way back on their sponsorship budgets.

For months I worked from morning to night. I awoke before dawn each morning as if I was on fire. I was sending faxes, sending emails, begging, pleading, and cajoling any potential sponsor I could find. I would work from about 5AM until it was time for me to go to the day job, then when I got I home I was going non-stop until late at night when I was too exhausted to see straight.

The truth is I didn't have a clue what I was doing. I knew nothing about how the business world works. I knew nothing about event planning. In addition to raising the money there were a million details to take care of concerning the production of the event itself.

It took five months of non-stop working at a madman's pace to get the money, but in the end I did it. $5,000 came from an adult DVD company, a few thousand from a lubrication company, it came piecemeal, but eventually I got the money.

I also learned an important lesson, almost a secret of how the business world works. In some way it is similar to how an artist works. You start with nothing and you create something. You tell a lie, you say this thing will be, even though the odds are it will never happen. And if you tell your lie with enough conviction, people will believe in your lie. Once people believe in your lie it becomes reality. The lie magically becomes truth. It's all a matter of faith. I started out like a snake oil salesman and ended up creating a great event.

In the weeks before the event, suddenly the paradigm switched. At the start nobody wanted to hear about this thing, now everyone wanted to be apart of it. It was turning out to be an incredible event. In the lower dancehall we had an array of burlesque performers scheduled including The Fabulous Pontani Sisters, The Princesses Of Porn, The Catfight Girls, Amber Ray, and the Dazzle Dancers. On each floor we had a theme room including a gay/transgender playroom, the lesbian lounge, and the triple-X room that included porn legend Vanessa Del Rio. In the basement we had a full-scale dungeon. On the Balcony we had The Circus Of The Erotic that included sensual message, foot worshipping, the human buffet table, a spanking booth, plus educational booths, rope tying demos, and lots of vendor's booths.

Crammed into the corners were erotic fortune-tellers, safe sex advisors, and performance artists of every type imaginable. The partygoers arrived in elaborate costumes. Everyone was a performer. Everyone was expressing their own creativity. Beautiful freaks filled every room.

There was a warm feeling throughout the hall. Straights, gays, blacks, whites, swingers, stockbrokers and street people all mixed with a smile on their faces. Some explored their fantasies, others displayed their well-rehearsed kinkiness. From burlesque performers to dominatrix', all looked at themselves as artists proudly displaying their skills and talents.

At the human buffet table a beautiful model wearing only a fruit bikini and a gold Roman mask, hand fed people strawberries dipped in rich chocolate. Go-go dancers shook and shimmied in every corner. Boys and girls, boys and boys, girls and girls, shared sensual kisses and soft caresses. Everyone was happy. Everyone felt free. No prejudice. No hate, condemnation, or accusation. Only respect and acceptance for those who are different than you.

9/11 was forgotten. Terrorism was far away. The radical right and their puritan agenda were relics of another age.

At midnight The Imperial Orgy took the main stage. A large video screen behind the stage was filled with a glowing Oz-like face. "Welcome to the Imperial Orgy," the face greeted the large crowd. "Tonight we're going to blow your mind. We're gonna set you free. We're gonna take you to places you've never been. Are you ready to let yourself go and do the things you've never done except in your wildest imaginings? Tonight is your initiation into the secret world of The Imperial Orgy."

Suddenly the band broke into a funky groove. Once the groove took hold I walked onto the stage dressed in a shining black vinyl jacket and pants. I overlooked the crowd that was thousands strong. Up in the balconies faces looked down and heads bobbed with the groove. A young woman ran onto the stage dressed in a black leather bustier, a lollipop rested between her breasts. I took the lollipop out and put in my mouth then rubbed it across her chest, then bent down to lick it off the sticky candy back off her body.

Finally, coming to the mic I began to sing:

Caligula was a friend of mine

The Marquis De Sade used to drink my wine

I was with Krishna when the gopi danced

Now I'm here won't you take your chance?

I'm the author of the Kama Sutra

I'm the singer of Solomon's Song

Embrace the sinner, liberate the saint

Lust for life baby that's the way

When the song was over I looked out over the crowd. They looked hot, sweaty, and bursting with energy. Myself, I felt alive. More alive than I have ever been. With a sultry bass guitar line the band began the next song titled Oak King Blues. I began to sing:

Good evening children

Without horns or fur I rise tonight

Our golden father sleeps in the West and the moon hangs heavy with seed

In the forest deep, the odor of musk rides the warm summer breeze

The fecund fields give birth to green and the peach is swollen with sweet nectar

Here I am

And I've come for you tonight...

Photography Credits:

Page #5 – Caeser Pink

Page #15 – Steven Guyer (Still from Temple Painting #1 video shoot)

Page #25 – Charles X

Page #33 – Still from Backwoods Soulshaker video (Camera by Jonanthan Mertz)

Page #43 – John Fox III

Page #53 – John Fox III

Page #67 – Charlotte Early

Page #89 – John Fox III

Page #97 – Caeser Pink

Page #107 - Still from Backwoods Soulshaker video (Camera by Jon Mertz)

Page #131 – Caeser Pink

Page #157 – Nell Mellon

Page #167 – Unknown

Page #297 - Still from Backwoods Soulshaker video (Camera by Jon Mertz)

Page #303 - Steven Guyer (Still from Temple Painting #1 video shoot)

Page #311 – Still from Easter video shoot (Camera by Louis Terrier)

Page #327 – Still from Imperial Orgy TV Series (Camera by Louis Terrier)

Page #357 – Caeser Pink

Page #391 - Still from Imperial Orgy TV Series (Camera by Louis Terrier)

Page #395 - Steven Guyer (Still from Temple Painting #1 video shoot)

Page #408 – S. Makhijani

Cover art by Miguelangel Ruiz

Back cover photo by Kalina Rumbalski

Special thanks to Jaqueline Gardner and Heather Milburn

Published with support from the Arete Living Arts Foundation
www.aretelivingarts.org

For more information on Caeser Pink:

www.caeserpink.com

www.theimperialorgy.com

www.ingramcontent.com/pod-product-compliance
Lightning Source LLC
Chambersburg PA
CBHW021211090426
42740CB00006B/184